BRIAN FARRELL &
SANDY HUNTER

SIXTY YEARS ON

The Fall
of Singapore
Revisited

EASTERN UNIVERSITIES PRESS

© 2002 Times Media Private Limited

First published 2002 by Times Media Private Limited (Academic Publishing)
under the imprint **Eastern Universities Press**
Times Centre, 1 New Industrial Road, Singapore 536196
Fax: (65) 6 2889 254
E-mail: tap@tpl.com.sg
Online Book Store: http://www.timesacademic.com

All rights reserved. No part of this publication may be reproduced, stored in a retrieval system, or transmitted, in any form or by any means, electronic, mechanical, photocopying, recording or otherwise, without the prior permission of the publishers.

Printed in Singapore

National Library Board (Singapore) Cataloguing in Publication Data
Sixty Years On : The Fall of Singapore Revisited / Brian Farrell & Sandy Hunter (eds.). – Singapore : Eastern Universities Press, 2002.

p cm
ISBN : 981 210 202 7

1. World War, 1939-1945 – Campaigns – Singapore.
2. World War, 1939-1945 – Campaigns – Malay Peninsula.
3. Singapore – History –Siege, 1942.
I. Farrell, Brian, 1960–   II. Hunter, Sandy, 1939–

D767.55   940.5425 — dc21
SLS2002033173

Table of Contents—

Introduction   v
     by Brian P. Farrell

Acknowledgements   xiv
List of Plates and Maps   xv

Part One: Prewar Problems

1 *Reflections on an Enduring Theme: The "Singapore Strategy" at Sixty*   3
     by Malcolm H. Murfett

2 *Australia and the "Singapore Strategy"*   29
     by Peter Dennis

3 *Symbol of Imperial Defence: The Role of Singapore in British and American Far Eastern Strategic Relations, 1933–1941*   42
     by Greg Kennedy

4 *Disaster Foreseen? France and the Fall of Singapore*   68
     by Martin Thomas

5 *Student and Master: The United Kingdom, Japan, Airpower, and the Fall of Singapore, 1920–1941*   94
     by John R. Ferris

6 *The Evacuation of Civilians From Hong Kong and Malaya/Singapore 1939–42*   122
     by Kent Fedorowich

7 *Churchill and Singapore*   156
     by Raymond Callahan

8 *1941: An Overview*   173
     by Brian P. Farrell

Part Two: The Malayan Campaign and the Fall of Singapore

9 General Yamashita Tomoyuki: Commander of the 25th Army 183
   by Akashi Yoji

10 Allied Prisoners of War: The Malayan Campaign 1941–42 208
   by Sibylla Jane Flower

11 The Island Battle: Japanese Soldiers Remember the Conquest 218
   of Singapore
   by Henry P. Frei

12 General Percival and the Fall of Singapore 240
   by Clifford Kinvig

13 The Indian Army and the Fall of Singapore 270
   by Alan Warren

14 "The men who did the fighting are now all busy writing": 290
   Australian Post-Mortems on Defeat in Malaya and Singapore,
   1942–45
   by Peter Stanley

15 The Fall of Singapore Revisited 313
   by Sandy Hunter

Appendix — Sixty Years On: The Fall of Singapore Revisited 321
   Conference Program and Paper Abstracts,
   15–17 February 2002

Index 348

Introduction

by Brian P. Farrell

Great events do not always have great drama, nor great participants. This cannot, however, be said about the fall of Singapore to the Japanese in 1942. In fact, the most famous Briton of the last century, Winston Churchill, did more than anyone else to place a label on that event—over which he presided—that still shapes how it is perceived. The fall of Singapore in February 1942 was, to the hard-pressed Prime Minister, "the greatest disaster in British military history."[1] That perception is one of two enduring things about the fall of Singapore. The other is apparently endless controversy. Controversy over how it happened, why it happened, above all whose "fault" it was. But around those two fixed points, our understanding of this seminal event of the Second World War and the twentieth century has been anything but static.

People from a dozen modern states were directly involved in the fall of Singapore: the United Kingdom, Japan, Australia, India, Pakistan, Nepal, New Zealand, the Netherlands, Indonesia, China, and above all Malaysia and Singapore. Perspectives on the event have been as numerous. From Churchill's "greatest disaster" came the response by some Australians that it was a "great betrayal." To the Japanese it was a great victory, but one certainly overshadowed by all that followed. To Singapore, it remains a defining moment in national memory. The verdict of scholars extended as far as calling it "the battle that changed the world."[2] The passage of 60 years provides perhaps an ideal, certainly a unique, vantage point of retrospect. Enough time has passed for some truly long-term perspective to be available, especially regarding the consequences of the event. But not so much has passed to prevent the gathering of a combination of generations: those who experienced the event in person; those to whom it was both vivid family memory and immediate history; a generation born after the war but grown to adulthood in its shadow; and those now reaching maturity who can engage it only as an event of an ever more distant past—but can still do so by speaking to some who lived through it themselves.

In February 2002, the Department of History at the National University of Singapore hosted an international conference of historians to take advantage of this unique vantage point, to bring together scholars, students and veterans, to reflect on the ongoing controversies surrounding the fall of Singapore and learn from each other. The conference was held from 15 through 17 February, coinciding with the anniversary of the end of the campaign and the Allied surrender of Singapore Island. The venue, the university campus, was itself—appropriately enough—the site of one of the last significant engagements in the campaign. More than 600 people of all ages, from many nationalities, ranging in age from 15 to 85, heard papers presented by historians from Singapore, the United Kingdom, Japan, Australia, Canada and the U.S.A. on various topics related to the central theme: *Sixty Years On: The Fall of Singapore Revisited*, in the largest such gathering of scholars ever devoted to this subject. The theme had a special focus, one influenced by the large literature on the event published after the war—which was itself influenced by what happened during the rest of the war. For most participants, the experience of captivity or occupation under the Japanese lasted a great deal longer than the campaign, and made a deeper impression. While that is understandable, it was time, we thought, to look again at the problem of how and why these people became captives or occupied in the first place. The conference was oriented around these questions: Why and how did war come to Malaya and Singapore? Why did they fall as and when they did?

This book presents a selection of the papers presented at the conference, revised for publication.[3] It is not an attempt to be the last word on all aspects relating to the Malayan campaign and the fall of Singapore. It is, like the conference, an attempt to pull together reassessments of arguments of very long standing about major issues such as the "Singapore strategy," with fresh contributions to our knowledge such as a discussion of how Japanese soldiers experienced the fighting on Singapore Island. Both conference and volume aimed to provide a well-rounded, state-of-the-art discussion of the central issues, and some of the shadows, relating to the fall of Singapore.

The trail followed by scholars inquiring into the fall of Singapore was in fact laid out in full, albeit in secret, by some of those responsible for it. In a secret session of Parliament in April 1942, Prime Minister Churchill intimated that when the dust settled and time was less pressing, an official inquiry would be held regarding the causes of the loss of Singapore. This was never done. Official papers retained for 50 rather than the customary 30 years by the Public Record Office in London reveal why. In January 1946, that wartime speech by Churchill, by now Leader of the Opposition, was published in a collected volume of speeches. This prompted a query by the Australian government, which in turn prodded now Prime Minister Clement Attlee to direct his military advisers, the Chiefs of Staff, to examine whether or not it was in the public interest to hold such an inquiry. They in turn passed the task on to their Joint Planning Staff, who in due course advised against an inquiry. Their argument laid out the broad trails scholars have pursued ever since:

> We consider that the main point which arises from our examination is that it is impossible to discuss our policy in the Far East in isolation. Every theatre was inter-dependent for men and materials which, at the time, were in very short supply. To obtain, therefore, a true picture, it would be necessary to—
>
> a) review the progress of the war against Germany and Italy and to decide whether the strategy pursued was correct and whether more forces could have been spared for the Far East,
> b) review our relations with the Dutch, with the Americans and with the Dominions and India,
> c) review the whole question of the preparations which were carried out in the years between the two world wars.
>
> Such a worldwide review could not be carried out without the evidence of the statesmen and military leaders responsible for our policy both before and during the war. This inquiry could not be confined to purely military matters, and would involve a discussion of controversial and delicate political issues.[4]

When the Chiefs of Staff made one last attempt to narrow the focus to the men on the spot, the planners stood firm:

> It would not be possible to hold an inquiry into the Malayan campaign from the time of the Japanese landing without consideration of wider questions, the discussion of which it has already been agreed would be undesirable.
>
> The implications of an inquiry limited to the events on Singapore Island would be less serious but we consider that such an inquiry would be most undesirable and likely to stimulate public demand for a wider investigation.[5]

Attlee, with relief one suspects, accepted this advice to avoid a public soul-searching into the very system for defending the Empire, and an inquiry was never held. But all that did was deflect the inevitable controversies into other hands, as the challenge was willingly taken up by participants, witnesses, journalists, and historians. A list of good studies saying something worth reading regarding the fall of Singapore would exceed 20 books, one of them published weeks before the conference began.[6] All of them, nevertheless, pursued one or more of the points raised by the Joint Planning Staff: policy for imperial defence; the "Singapore strategy"; strategic relations with imperial partners and potential allies; relations with Japan; preparations for war; grand strategy; the conduct of the campaign itself. The broad outlines of inquiry and argument remain unchanged. What this conference and volume wanted to do was pull them together.

The conference and the volume were divided into two overlapping parts: problems and events related to the prewar period, and the conduct of the campaign itself.[7] As the whole problem began with momentous changes in international relations after the First World War, leading to the British decision to adopt the so-called "Singapore strategy," the conference followed suit. Malcolm H. Murfett summarized the long debate about the strategy, arguing that it was always in the end an unworkable compromise to address an insoluble problem, relying for success on American assistance that might or might not arrive in time. His paper is essay number one in this volume. Peter Dennis explored the Australian debate in the prewar years over whether or not to rely on this strategy for imperial defence, concluding that Australian leaders went along with a shaky premise because they were afraid to ask pointed questions that might lead to blunt answers, and therefore had no case to make for charges of betrayal. His paper is essay number two in this volume. A more positive view of the strategy as a more flexible and reasonable basis for imperial defence was presented in a paper by Chris Bell. His views are laid out more fully in his book *The Royal Navy, Seapower and Strategy Between the Wars*, Stanford, 2000. Rounding off the discussion on the "Singapore strategy" was Greg Kennedy, who also found something positive in it. He saw the strategy as a necessary expression of British determination to defend the Empire in Asia that made a positive prewar impact on the U.S.A., the absolutely vital power in any confrontation with Japan. His paper is essay number three in this volume.

Defining a strategy to defend the Empire against Japan or anyone else was a contingency—until developments in international relations brought war closer. Two papers discussed those developments. Keith Neilson examined relations between the British and the most unpredictable and often overlooked Asian power, the Soviet Union, and concluded that in the tense years just before war broke out each tried to use the other to intimidate and deter Japan. Martin Thomas examined another too-often overlooked dimension of greater direct consequence for the defence of Singapore: French attitudes towards British plans to defend against Japan. He argued that whatever happened in Europe, French colonial authorities in Indochina saw a common interest with the British in upholding the Western presence in the region, but always regarded British defence plans with grave scepticism at best. His paper is essay number four in this volume.

One of the conclusions drawn in recent scholarship is that the long emphasis on the naval dimension of the defence and fall of Singapore has been overemphasized at the expense of the crucial importance of airpower. The conference addressed that in two papers. Henry Probert summarized British and

Allied Air Force preparations to defend Malaya and Singapore and analyzed their fatal failure to retain control of the air. His views are more fully expressed in his standard work *The Forgotten Air Force: The Royal Air Force in the War Against Japan*, London, 1995. John Ferris went back to the earliest interwar years to explain how the British helped the Japanese develop first-class airpower, especially naval airpower, but then lost track of and misread the further progress of their pupil. He argued this was far more than simplistic racism—rather it reflected institutional and reflex ethnocentrism in a complex web of intelligence and appreciations—and explained the consequences. His paper is essay number five in this volume.

Questions of national policy assumed overriding importance as war approached and then broke out, and the next two papers addressed that issue. Kent Fedorowich analyzed the argument over evacuating civilians from Hong Kong on the one hand and Malaya and Singapore on the other, in 1939-42. This most sensitive issue exposed the difficulty of managing a multi-racial empire, raising as it did problems of vulnerability, racial preference, and attitudes in other parts of the Empire regarding providing sanctuary. A study in colonial politics, his paper is essay number six in this volume. Raymond Callahan took up the problem of grand strategy by assessing the role of the most famous person involved in the fall of Singapore, Prime Minister Churchill. Callahan argued that Churchill was probably right to make the choice in grand strategy to concentrate more on pressing dangers elsewhere, but less than candid with his allies about this decision in priorities, and less than fair in his very successful attempt to shape the public memory about how and why Singapore was lost, in his influential postwar memoirs. His paper is essay number seven in this volume.

The first day of the conference sessions, concentrating largely on prewar problems, was concluded by a summary paper presented by this editor. Taking the broadest perspective, it reviewed how the world situation unfolded by the year 1941, then examined the problem of defending Singapore in 1941 by placing it in this widest context: an expanding global total war. It argued that when seen from a global perspective, the most important fact was that the mistakes made by the British that year were far less consequential than those made by their enemies. The very correlation of forces that made Singapore so vulnerable also made it a poisoned chalice for anyone daring to drain it. The purpose of this summary paper was to connect the deliberations of the two parts of the conference in a synthesis analysis. In that spirit, it is presented here as the eighth and concluding essay of Part One of this volume.

The story of the fall of Singapore has always involved at least two "sides," but in English literature the Japanese, the attackers, have too often been underexplored. The conference did not make that mistake. Our study of the conduct of the Malayan campaign and the conquest of Singapore began with three papers addressing controversies surrounding the Japanese. Akashi Yoji presented a biographical analysis of Lieutenant-General Yamashita Tomoyuki, commanding general of the victorious Twenty-Fifth Army. Akashi argued that Yamashita was a dynamic field commander who led more by inspiration than preparation, thoroughly outgeneralled his counterparts and made a decisive contribution. Akashi also raised a dimension hitherto unnoticed in English language studies—the question of Yamashita's personal relations with the Emperor and the influence this had on his generalship. His paper is essay number nine in this volume. Ishizu Tomoyuki studied the conduct of the campaign with reference to the role of Colonel Masanobu Tsuji, controversial planner and Operations Officer of the Twenty-Fifth Army. Ishizu's provocative paper laid more stress on British mistakes than on Japanese fighting power and skill. Finally, Sibylla Jane Flower raised an almost entirely overlooked aspect of the campaign: how the Japanese treated prisoners of war captured on the mainland, before Singapore fell and the whole army went into captivity. She argued that the Japanese reacted inconsistently with these captives, some not being sure what to make of them, but tended more and more towards harshness, especially with officers who might provide useful intelligence. Their disorganized brutality was a harbinger of much worse to come. Her paper is essay number 10 in this volume.

The battle for Singapore Island itself has too often been relegated to an anticlimax. Considering that the Japanese suffered half their battle casualties for the 70-day campaign in the seven days of fighting on the island, and that by February 1942 Allied plans to defend Southeast Asia relied on a prolonged defence of the island,[8] the conference redressed this imbalance. The late Henry P. Frei made available to an English-speaking audience, for the first time, an analysis of how Japanese soldiers themselves experienced and remembered the last battle for the island. Those familiar with the "other side of the hill" will find some surprises here. His paper is essay number 11 in this volume. One of the most popular papers of the conference was presented by three junior college students from Singapore, making their academic debut. Chua Li Shan, Ng Chuin Song and Xie Li Hui discussed "Singaporean participation in the battle for Singapore." Drawing on extensive research in the documents and oral history collections of the National Archives of Singapore (see endnote 3), they argued that Singaporean willingness to fight in their own defence was greater than usually perceived, British reluctance to draw on it was therefore more of an error than sometimes noted, and the burden of carrying on opposition in the occupation years was borne almost entirely by those who did fight.

From the new to the familiar, it was necessary to reassess some central controversies of the Malayan campaign. Two papers did that: Clifford Kinvig studied the generalship of Lieutenant-General A. E. Percival, GOC Malaya Command, the man blamed by many for losing Singapore, and Alan Warren reviewed the role of the Indian Army in the campaign. Kinvig, biographer of

Percival, presented a paper that impressed one conference attendee enough to point out, "You defended Percival more ably than he defended Singapore!" Kinvig's point was that neither Percival nor anyone else could have held Singapore in the situation he was forced to operate in. Percival did make mistakes, and was not ruthless enough on at least two occasions, but of much greater consequence was the impact decisions made by those above and below him in the chain of command had on his own actions. His paper is essay number 12 in this volume. Warren explored the performance of the Indian formations which comprised more than half of Percival's forces and fought many of his battles. He argued that it ranged widely enough, from stubborn at Kota Bahru to feeble at Jitra, to suggest that Indian forces on the whole performed neither better nor worse than the other contingents of Malaya Command. Warren also raised the issues of the rapid expansion of the Indian Army and the recruitment of many by the Japanese into their puppet Indian National Army. His paper is essay number 13 in this volume.

Rounding off the sessions were three studies of different dimensions of the Malayan campaign, to reflect the complexity of such a large military operation that involved so many different nationalities, in such a large area. John Moremon discussed the problem of logistics, always a crucial aspect of any military campaign, noting the avoidable difficulties the defenders had with supply lines, as well as tracing the more familiar story of the risks the Japanese took with theirs. His views can be found in *A Bitter Fate: Australians in Malaya and Singapore, December 1941–February 1942*, Canberra, 2002. Peter Elphick reminded us of the contribution he made in the 1990s to revive interest and controversy about the Malayan campaign and the fall of Singapore by presenting a paper discussing the case of the "Singapore traitor," Captain Patrick Heenan, as part of a study of "cover-ups" of the campaign. His views are expressed in his work *Singapore, The Pregnable Fortress: A Study in Deception, Discord and Desertion*, London, 1995. The final paper of the session was, most appropriately, a study of the first historian and first major post-mortem of the campaign, presented by Peter Stanley. He argued that the wartime collation and composition of a full-length study of the campaign by Colonel C. H. Kappe of the 8th Australian Division, written while in captivity, raised many of the central issues, and key dimensions, pursued by historians ever since. Australian records, including this one, need more attention than they have received from scholars of the campaign. This one hinted right from the start that the men actually involved were less obsessed with national recriminations than many commentators following in their footsteps. His paper is essay number 14 of this volume.

That note of explanation rather than recrimination ably suggested the developing consensus of the conference. The suggestion was expanded by the summary paper that closed the conference and closes this volume, as essay number 15. Sandy Hunter pulled together the strands of the discussions to reflect on whether our vantage point of 60 years on had after all succeeded in shedding new light on the fall of Singapore, reassessing familiar problems, and making the larger connection to how the history of the Second World War is now being understood. It is reproduced here as the conference paper it was presented as, to reflect, while they were fresh, the moods and views of the conference it concluded.

These collected essays are presented as a snap-shot of how an international gathering of scholars, in the company of veterans whose experience they study, and students they teach, saw the multiple dimensions and controversies of the fall of Singapore 60 years after the event. Not every story of the campaign has been told or retold here. This is mainly the study of those who fought for Singapore, not those caught in between, whose stories have been many times told elsewhere. Nor will the last word be found here or anywhere else—albeit this was not only the largest public gathering devoted to the subject but also the first featuring scholars able to draw openly on all surviving British, Australian and Japanese records, something not possible before the release of suppressed British and Australian records in the 1990s. And controversies live on, some within and between the essays of this volume. There was, however, strong agreement on three things, agreement strengthened by this new and revised scholarship. The fall of Singapore was a dramatic and important event in the Second World War, but not decisive to its outcome, not even in Asia. The loss of Singapore was overdetermined, and the main causes lie more in the realm of higher strategy and broader problems before the war than in the campaign itself. Finally, the time is now ripe for studies that focus more on explanation than recrimination, on analysis rather than blame. It is up to the reader to decide whether or not they agree.

Brian P. Farrell is Associate Professor of Military History at the National University of Singapore, where he has been teaching since 1993. He is the author of The Basis and Making of British Grand Strategy 1940–1943: Was There a Plan?, *co-author of* Between Two Oceans: A Military History of Singapore From First Settlement to Final British Withdrawal, *and author of the forthcoming* The Defence and Fall of Singapore 1940–42.

NOTES—

1. W. S. Churchill, *The Second World War IV: The Hinge of Fate*, Boston, 1950, 92.
2. J. Leasor, *Singapore: The Battle that Changed the World*, New York, 1968.
3. With one exception, papers not published in this volume were only omitted due to limitations of space; where more than one paper explored a given topic, usually only that more directly focused on the central theme could be included. The exception was the paper presented by the three Singaporean junior college students. This paper was presented in a format not suitable to adapt for publication, and thus unfortunately cannot be included here. All papers presented at the conference can be retrieved by visiting the National Archives of Singapore, which kindly videotaped the conference and preserved copies of the videotapes in its collection, or consulting the Central Library of the National University of Singapore, where the videotapes are held and are also accessible on its website.
4. Public Record Office (PRO), CAB119/208, JP(46)29(Final), Malayan Campaign—Public Inquiry, Annex, Part I, 5 March 1946.
5. PRO, CAB119/208, Extracts from Chiefs of Staff (COS) minutes, 8 March, JP(46)56(S)(T. of R.), 8 March, JP(46)56(Final), Malayan Campaign—Limitations of a Public Inquiry, 6 May 1946.
6. A. Warren, *Singapore 1942: Britain's Greatest Defeat*, Sydney, 2002.
7. The conference program and paper abstracts are the Appendix of this volume.
8. M. H. Murfett, J. N. Miksic, B. P. Farrell and Chiang M. S., *Between Two Oceans: A Military History of Singapore From First Settlement to Final British Withdrawal*, Singapore, 1999, ch. 8.

Acknowledgements

Publishing papers stemming from an international conference means asking for a lot of assistance, and incurring many debts. The editors wish to acknowledge, with thanks, those without whom the conference and this volume would not have appeared. For their very generous sponsorship:

The Tan Foundation;
The Lee Foundation;
The National University of Singapore;
Singapore History Consultants;
The University Cultural Centre, NUS.

The President and Vice-Chancellor of the National University of Singapore, Professor Shih Choon Fong, lent us his patronage and very graciously opened the conference. The Dean of the Faculty of Arts and Social Sciences, Associate Professor Lily Kong, supported the conference staunchly, and delivered the opening address. The Head of the Department of History, Associate Professor Tan Tai Yong, gave indispensable support from start to finish in many ways. The Department of History threw its collective weight into the conference, and hosted it most graciously. The junior colleges of the Republic of Singapore turned out in strength to support this international event, as did the undergraduate students of the university. To show our appreciation, all royalties from this book will be donated to the Straits Times Pocket Money Fund, a Singapore charity that assists with school expenses. A small army of volunteers actually ran the conference, including assistants from the University Cultural Centre, and students from the Department of History; their contribution was unglamorous but essential. Special thanks must go to Joanna Tan, Erik Holmberg, Chang Yueh Siang, Diana Heron and above all Kelly Lau for assistance far above and beyond any call of duty. From Times International we received important help from Anthony Thomas, Jasminder Kaur, copy editor Eugene Tan and typesetter Pearlie Tan. Last but certainly not least, we must thank our many colleagues, both those who presented and those who attended, for making the conference and this volume such a stimulating experience in scholarship.

Brian P. Farrell and Sandy Hunter
Singapore and Tyneside, October 2002

List of Plates and Maps

	Page

Plates

Construction at the Sembawang Naval Base January 1941 *(Imperial War Museum, K 810)*	10
HMS *Prince of Wales* leaving Sembawang Naval Base, 8 December 1941 *(Imperial War Museum, A 29068)*	19
Fortunate Singaporeans in one of the few air raid shelters, 1941 *(Imperial War Museum, KF101)*	137
The Tiger of Malaya *(Imperial War Museum, NAP 245311)*	185
Japanese victory parade, Fullerton Square, Singapore, 17 February 1942 *(Imperial War Museum, HU 2787)*	235
Condemned by photography: Percival arrives in Singapore, May 1941 *(Imperial War Museum, K 652)*	242
Percival, far right, en route to surrender negotiations, Singapore, 15 February 1942 *(Imperial War Museum, HU 2781)*	317
Students register for the conference, 16 February 2002	326
Prof. Shih Choon Fong, President & Vice-Chancellor, NUS, views Total Defence Day exhibit, 16 February 2002	326
Ms. Kelly Lau, seated left, and volunteers, 17 February 2002	327
The editors and volunteer assistants, 17 February 2002	327

Mr. Lewis Altman, British WWII veteran, raising an issue, 16 February 2002 — 328

Xie Li Hui presenting part of a paper on Singaporeans in the defence of Singapore, 17 February 2002 — 328

Final session, Theatre, University Cultural Centre, 17 February 2002 — 329

Maps

The siting of the naval base, February 1942 — 6

Deployment for the defence of Singapore — 219

The Malay Peninsula, 1938 — 247
(*The Times*, Weekly Edition, Special Singapore Naval Base Number, Thursday March 3 1938)

Part One

Prewar Problems

CHAPTER 1

Reflections on an Enduring Theme: The "Singapore Strategy" at Sixty

by Malcolm H. Murfett

Longer running than even Agatha Christie's "The Mousetrap," which can only claim a hold over theatre audiences in London's West End for 50 years, the "Singapore naval strategy" has fascinated the general public ever since the two capital ships of Force Z, the *Prince of Wales* and the *Repulse*, slid tragically beneath the waves of the South China Sea on 10 December 1941. Explanations for this naval disaster were immediately forthcoming and have surfaced periodically ever since from a legion of professional and amateur sources.[1] While initially the debate focused on the loss of the two great ships, the fall of Malaya and Singapore shortly thereafter ensured that the destruction of Force Z was seen by some at the time as a metaphor for the current diabolical state of British military strategy. Charges of betrayal and indifference to the fate of others, that had already been raised long before the naval task force was assembled, now grew in intensity and passionate denunciation. How could Fortress Singapore have caved in so swiftly and abjectly? Who was to blame for this military disaster? Was it Winston Churchill, Sir Dudley Pound and the Admiralty, the War Office, the Chiefs of Staff, the Committee of Imperial Defence, or the commanding officers ashore and afloat in Singapore?

Despite all the rhetoric and the reams of paper devoted to this subject ever since, the countless explanations that have been forthcoming have not adequately stilled the clamour for more information about this undeniable calamity, particularly from the academic and military communities. This paper will explore this theme by posing a few heretical questions that deserve answering, namely, could the British really afford to build a first-class naval establishment in the Far

East after the conclusion of the First World War? If the money was not going to be forthcoming to construct a first-class base in the region, what was the point of building an inferior one? To what extent was the entire "Singapore strategy" born out of an overwhelming lack of British candour when it came to discussing defence and security matters with their overseas colonies and Dominions? Was it, therefore, yet another case of pride coming before a fall?

Although Viscount Jellicoe, on his grand tour of the east in 1919, accurately predicted a severe deterioration in the security position of British possessions in the Asia-Pacific if the Anglo-Japanese Alliance ever broke apart, his plan to deter or thwart any designs the government in Tokyo might have on these territories—by stationing a large permanent capital ship fleet in the Far East— was too much even for the Admiralty, let alone the cash-strapped Lloyd George administration, to accept with equanimity. Despite robustly rejecting Jellicoe's plan, the British government was unwilling to admit that the defence of its Far Eastern interests might become a future hostage to fortune.[2] One may safely assume that it was all too impolitic to mention. After all, how could any world power worth its salt admit to being uncertain about its ability, under all circumstances, to come to the aid of its own colonies and Dominions— particularly when these were the very same territories that had unstintingly provided men and matériel at considerable cost during the Great War? It was inconceivable for the coalition government in London to have reacted in this way given the diplomatic, economic and political fall-out that would have taken place within the Empire had it admitted any lack of conviction on this crucial question. If the British authorities had hoped to fudge the issue, however, Jellicoe's injudicious revelations at every major port-of-call complicated the process by encouraging his hosts to dream of a renewed *Pax Britannica* in the East. While admitting there was not enough money to fund a permanent battle fleet in the Far East, the Lloyd George administration found itself under pressure to devise some other strategic plan that would offer long-term security to those overseas territories that might be exposed to risk from their external enemies. In this respect, therefore, Jellicoe's tour of inspection had definitely become a catalyst for some kind of naval action east of Suez should circumstances warrant it in the future.[3]

Should the Admiralty be called upon to fight such a Far Eastern war, however, it could hardly be expected to do so with inadequate resources at its disposal. It was a small step from that premise to accepting the idea that if a large battle fleet could not be based permanently in the area, then the Royal Navy would be expected to send a taskforce to the region in an emergency. If that were the case, it was not unreasonable to expect that the fleet to be sent would need a substantial base from which to conduct operations in the region. While various alternative sites were looked at—Hong Kong and Sydney among them—Singapore's advantageous geographical position made it the choice of the newly reconstituted Committee of Imperial Defence and its selection duly received the endorsement of the delegates to the Imperial Conference in June 1921.[4] Thereafter, the die was cast: Singapore would be built up as a major naval base—a fact confirmed by the Washington Conference of 1921–22—and a series of strategic plans would have to be devised by the Admiralty to cater to its use by the Royal Navy in the future.

Two issues need detain us at this point: one is the location of the base and the other the nature of that base and its facilities. Should Sembawang have been chosen as the site for the construction of this key naval base? We know that Selat Sinki, an anchorage lying off the southwestern coast of Singapore, was actively considered and then dismissed on the grounds that its natural deficiencies could only be remedied at considerable cost to the British exchequer and that Keppel Harbour—though less exposed—was too busy as a commercial port to serve as a major naval base as well. This left four other places dotted along the northern and northeastern coast of the island, Senoko, Sembawang, Ponggol, and Tampines, that were identified, examined and mostly found wanting by the experts on the Learmouth–Power Committee. Sembawang was eventually selected not for its stunning virtues but because it posed fewer engineering problems than the other sites on the Straits of Johore.[5] In the opinion of the War Office, however, the defensive vulnerability of the Sembawang base left much to be desired. In fact, such was the position of the base—lying as it did barely two kilometres from the southern shore of the Johore coastline—that the War Office recommended that it would be essential in wartime to impose a 50-kilometre defensive perimeter around the base to protect it from the possibility of artillery fire or infantry attack launched by an enemy, specifically identified as the Japanese, that had made inroads into the most southerly part of the Malayan peninsula. Contrary to the scepticism of the War Office about the alleged merits of the Sembawang site, the Admiralty suffered from no such lack of confidence. In its opinion, as long as the British government could always send the main fleet from home or Mediterranean waters to Singapore upon the outbreak of war, the Japanese would not have sufficient time to mount a credible military threat to the security of the base, let alone the crown colony itself. While the Admiralty assessment was undoubtedly valid in a situation where the lag time between a formal declaration of war and the arrival of the British fleet was between 28–42 days, the prospect of any significant delay in the "period before relief" would, *ceteris paribus*, improve the chances of the Japanese gaining a greater hold over the Johore mainland. If such a situation occurred, the naval base and the entire island would clearly be exposed to great danger from these hostile forces.[6] In these circumstances, therefore, the stronger and more durable

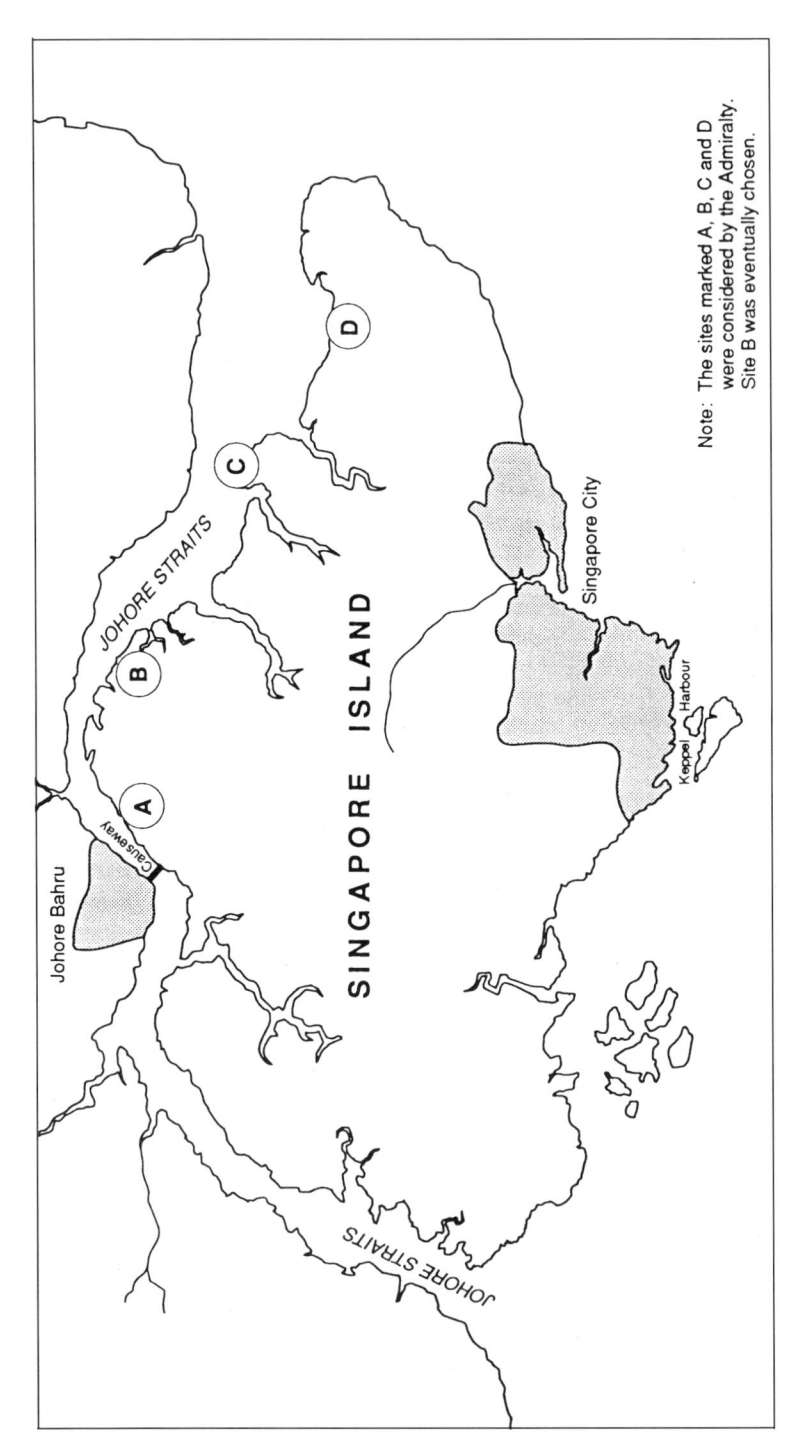

The siting of the naval base

Note: The sites marked A, B, C and D were considered by the Admiralty. Site B was eventually chosen.

the defensive perimeter that the British could erect in Johore, with the Sultan's blessing, the better it would be. Nonetheless, drawing a line on a map was easy in comparison with devoting the large amount of money and resources it would take to erect an effective military barrier along that proposed line in the countryside itself, a fact that Major-General Sir William Dobbie, GOC Malaya Command from 1935–39, discovered to his cost later in the next decade.[7] Without that barrier, however, any of the sites for the naval base in Singapore would be vulnerable should a concerted Japanese thrust take place at some time in the future.

This prompted one of Dobbie's predecessors as GOC Malaya Command, Major-General Sir Dudley Ridout, to wonder aloud in December 1919 whether an agreement could be forged with the Dutch authorities that would enable the British to assume control over some or all of the chain of Riau Islands in the Dutch East Indies. If such an agreement could be arranged, an island—such as Bintan—could become a far better and much safer site for a naval base than anything on the island of Singapore.[8] Sadly, this idea appears not to have been actively canvassed in London or in The Hague on the grounds of its supposedly impractical nature. Issues of sovereignty are always likely to be complex and exasperating, but surely the naval authorities in both capitals ought to have been able to see that mutual assistance was in both of their interests, if not during the 1919–22 period then certainly during the 1930s as the threat posed by the Japanese became more obvious with each passing year. Once this original idea was formally set aside by the members of the Committee of Imperial Defence at their meeting on 12 July 1922, however, it was not revived thereafter.[9] Hindsight notwithstanding, this must rank as a lost opportunity of major proportions. Although the temptation of exploring the counter-factual argument is great, that diversion shall be foregone at this stage. Even so, one is still left wondering "what if?"[10]

Returning to the question of locating the base on the island of Singapore, in January 1923 the Admiralty's leading civil engineer, Leopold Savile, indicated his preference for the Sembawang location over the other possible sites because it had both an extensive waterfront as well as substantial hinterground on which to build a massive dockyard and repair facility. Savile's initial plan, also known as the "Green Scheme," was a grandiose construction project that, if built, would have been theoretically far better able to serve the needs of the main fleet sent out to it than the relatively modest and far cheaper entity, the truncated "Red Scheme," that eventually replaced it.[11] Given the financial constraints that successive British governments were under after the war, however, it is hardly surprising that the Treasury baulked at establishing base facilities for the 19-strong capital ship fleet envisaged in the "Green Scheme." Moreover, in the light of the treaties decided upon during the Washington Conference of 1921–22, the concept of any one naval power having such a massive capital ship fleet in the short to medium term was illusory. Indeed a 19-strong capital ship fleet would only be possible if the two major fleets, the Royal Navy and the United States Navy, were able to join in common cause against a mutual foe, but for much of the interwar period this concept was ruled out either by a lack of trust (the 1920s) or by legal obstacles (the 1930s).[12] Unfortunately, if the "Green Scheme" was too ambitious, the initial "Red Scheme" that replaced it went to the other extreme and was not ambitious enough. As this author noted elsewhere:

> Instead of being sufficient to meet the needs of a full battle fleet and its auxiliary vessels, the "Red Scheme" was supposed to be sufficient to cope with the demands of any peacetime fleet (roughly 20% of the full battle fleet) that might be sent out to Singapore in the aftermath of the Washington treaties. This modified plan retained a floating dock and a single graving dock, but was to dispense with the enclosed basin and most of the other docks that Savile proposed. It also reduced the original wharfage area by 40%, and made sweeping reductions in all other areas of the "Green Scheme."[13]

So one might be tempted to ask why the Admiralty convinced the Treasury to commit itself to the scale of expenditure, £25.45 million, involved in the building of a naval base in Singapore that—even when operational—would still be incapable of performing the essential tasks for which it was intended, namely, looking after the needs of a first-class war fleet? A scaled-down version of the original "Green Scheme" was not thought to be critical at this time, however, because the Admiralty's war plans for use against the Japanese were devised not on the basis that confrontation might take place in the vicinity of Singapore but far from its shores.[14] At this stage one is tempted to ask the rhetorical question, "Which of the theoretical advanced operational bases was of first-class standard?" Answer: none. Did it matter? Answer: yes. If one further asks whether naval action was likely in northern waters, the answer one arrives at is that while it may have been possible in conjunction with the United States Navy, it was never something that truly appealed to the British government on a unilateral basis and with good reason.[15]

But what if the Japanese struck south in fulfilment of their long-anticipated *nanshin-ron*?[16] Should such a scenario have been dismissed with impunity? After all, the Japanese had shown in 1894 and again ten years later that they were the ultimate variable in military and diplomatic terms and capable therefore of eschewing a conventional, gradualist path to war in favour of a sudden pre-emptive attack. Nonetheless, the British blithely chose neither to learn the lessons of history nor to expect the worst military scenario.[17] And that surely would have involved trying to fight a war in Southeast Asian waters without a suitable base from which to do so.[18] One did not need to be a former First Lord of the Admiralty to have realized that the situation was indeed pregnant with possibilities.[19]

Alas, matters did not rest there as the deficient "Red Scheme" was sabotaged still further by the insouciant Churchill in his unlikely guise as Chancellor of the Exchequer in Baldwin's government from 1924–29. By demanding that further cost-cutting economies be made in the construction phase of the base, Churchill managed to eliminate even repair facilities from the limited services on offer to the fleet at Sembawang.[20] It is manifestly clear that he took this decision with few, if any, qualms since he felt, both at the time and later, that Singapore's sheer geographical distance from Tokyo—which he equated as being similar to that from Southampton to New York—made it invulnerable to a surprise attack launched by the Japanese either from the sea or by land. It was precisely this confident and dismissive type of attitude that could be seen underpinning the Chiefs of Staff's interwar assumption that the ships and crews of the Imperial Japanese Navy were approximately 20% less efficient than their Royal Navy equivalents.[21] Although based on little objective evidence, this assessment could not help but breed an inner complacency on the issue of any future British-Japanese naval struggle.

Moving beyond the location of the base and the provision of its limited services, another issue that deserves renewed attention is that of the momentous legacy of the Washington Conference. Although there is little point in replaying the familiar narrative of what took place in the Continental Hall on 12 November 1921, or in the formal and informal sessions held by the various international delegations over the course of the next three months, it is appropriate to reflect on the radical change the various treaties brought to both the diplomatic and naval environments. After all, Washington managed to tear up the strategically important Anglo-Japanese Alliance and substitute it with a four power, non-military treaty on the Pacific designed to be little other than a pale imitation of what it replaced. Every signatory recognized it as such. Regrettably there was worse to follow, because far from solving anything, the abrogation of the Anglo-Japanese Alliance suggested to the impressionable Japanese that the British did not really value their friendship. Professor Ian Nish suggests that the Japanese were not wild about the British either, but even so, the non-renewal of the alliance was grist to the mill of those extremists in Japanese political and military circles who sought a new orientation in foreign and defence policy.[22] Eventually that new orientation would be established at profound cost to the British Empire.[23]

If that were all the damage the delegations at Washington did, it would have been bad enough, but there was far more. As a direct result of the Five Power Naval Limitation Treaty of 6 February 1922, strict proportional limits

Construction at the Sembawang naval base, January 1941

were imposed on the various capital ship fleets. Although numerically inferior to both the United States Navy and the Royal Navy in total fleet size, the modern war fleet that the Imperial Japanese Navy would have at its disposal was able to offset this deficiency to a large extent by maintaining a regional dominance that would be difficult to resist in Far Eastern waters. Apart from the fact that there would be no first-class naval base closer to Japanese waters than Singapore, some 2,888 nautical miles to the south of Tokyo, and Pearl Harbour, a distance of 3,374 nautical miles to the east of the Japanese capital, those bases that did exist within that prescribed arc, such as Hong Kong, Manila, Guam, Truk, and Midway, for example, could neither be fortified nor brought up to first-class standard for the duration of the Washington treaties.[24]

This meant in effect that for as long as the Washington system remained in existence—initially at least 15 years—the major powers with interests on a global scale were going to find it extremely difficult to deploy their limited number of warships in such a way as to defend these very same possessions adequately. Whether or not this problem amounted to a case of "imperial overstretch" would be determined by the ability of the British armed forces to put sufficient ships and men into the breach under all circumstances. This would include the most challenging scenario possible, namely, simultaneous threats being posed to British interests in two or more widely separated theatres of the world by a combination of major powers.[25] Realising this from the outset, the Chiefs of Staff and their planning teams set about establishing a set of priorities to cope with this problem should it arise in the future. Throughout the interwar period, Singapore was always adjudged to lie second in importance behind that of the metropolitan area as far as defence of the Commonwealth was concerned.[26] Did it deserve to be? This is a legitimate question if one remembers that during these years the Sembawang naval base was more of a construction site than a home for any kind of fleet, let alone the main one. It was only relegated to third place behind the Middle East after the fall of France in the summer of 1940.[27] This suggests two things. One, if the assessment was correct and Singapore deserved to be ranked so high for so long in the overall scheme of things, why was it not given sufficient military resources to reflect that position of importance? Two, its lack of real resources demonstrated that the order of priorities was either far more a theoretical tool for planning purposes, or a diplomatic sop to the imperial and colonial authorities who would be up in arms if they thought there was any chance of them being left in the lurch by the mother country. Some revisionist scholars might be tempted to suggest that reliance upon the "Singapore strategy" was not as naïve and feckless as suggested here and that the flexible response its operational plans engendered represented true value for money in a time of great economic privation and one where the outlay of ever-larger fixed costs was bound to receive a cool response from the Treasury. The reply to this argument is simple: Whatever the attraction from an accountant's perspective, it was a risky strategy and the ultimate cost was paid in two bitter instalments on 10 December 1941 and 15 February 1942 respectively.

Although it is easy to concede that the Washington system created an on-going problem for the Admiralty in terms of deploying its limited naval forces around the globe in times of emergency, the tearing up of these treaties would not necessarily be immediately advantageous to the Royal Navy. In the short to medium term, the Japanese might actually benefit from the abandonment of the system and become even more dominant in Far Eastern waters than before. This would have been disturbing enough at the best of times, but within a decade of the Washington Conference a sense of calm could hardly be said to prevail in this region.[28] As the years passed, so did any kind of Japanese restraint. As the period of *Taishô* democracy came to an inglorious end, fizzling out in the face of a growing Japanese militarism, the operational plans of the "Singapore strategy" looked to be resting on a set of assumptions that were increasingly suspect.[29] Whatever the improvisational nature of these plans, the fact that they expected the Royal Navy to take the initiative after war had been declared through the exercise of maximum economic pressure and/or by military confrontation asked more questions than it answered. Would the British be relying upon themselves or would they be cooperating with the Americans? If the former, what would happen if the Americans refused to break off trading with the Japanese? Would the Royal Navy be prepared to intercept all U.S. ships trading with the enemy, remove contraband items and intern those vessels that would resist these measures? Since the U.S. was the most important overseas market for the Japanese and the latter lay third in the American league of trading partners, the reluctance to eliminate the volume of this trade would have been palpable at any time but, during the Great Depression, was it even remotely feasible?[30] Assuming a unilateral response, how could the British expect to throw an impenetrable ring around the Japanese islands and be prepared to meet the full Japanese fleet in its own waters without a massive fleet at their own disposal? If the British sought something other than a unilateral economic and military response, on what grounds could they realistically expect to draw the Americans into joining them in imposing a naval blockade of the Japanese mainland when that initiative was likely to lead to a military confrontation with the Japanese? How could such a possibility be reconciled with the American neutrality legislation?[31] Moreover, could such a plan be even momentarily entertained if the security of Hong Kong was compromised by Japanese penetration into southern China? Without Hong Kong or the use of American naval facilities at Manila, was there any realistic chance of the Royal Navy gaining a viable advance or forward operational base in the region? While few analysts could doubt that concerted economic measures would really hobble the Japanese military-industrial complex if given sufficient time to work, would they ever be implemented during peacetime?[32] And even if they were attempted, what would happen if the Imperial Japanese Navy refused to act as a fleet-in-being and sought to carry out an all-out offensive against its enemies in its home waters? All these are crucial questions that go to the heart of the "Singapore strategy" in any of its various guises.[33]

While many traditionalists scoff at its illusionary nature, it might be going too far to reject all elements of the "Singapore strategy" totally. Even so, for any of the strategic plans to succeed outside a war game scenario, there was so little margin for error that everything was required to fall into place at exactly the right time and if this did not happen, the overall chances of success were remote, to say the least. Obviously the odds against everything working to plan and all theoretical assumptions being upheld in practice were bound to be very long. Sometimes, however, even the longest odds can be overcome, as Foinavon demonstrated so memorably at the British Grand National in 1967.[34] One scheme that looked promising for a time before imploding came from a prominent non-naval source in Whitehall. Anthony Eden, the British Foreign Secretary, may not have known much about the Royal Navy but did not let that bother him. Possessing unlimited self-assurance, Eden sought to pursue an independent line in foreign policy. His proposal in the closing weeks of 1937 for a joint British-American naval demonstration in force in the Far East looks on the face of it to have been wild and reckless, but one senses in it the germ of an idea that might have worked had President Roosevelt been prepared to commit the substantial resources of the United States Navy to this dramatic initiative.[35] By this time, several of the essential pieces of the strategic jigsaw looked to be in place, so in December 1937 the scheme might not have appeared so hare-brained as it may look now from a distance.[36] An explanation is in order.

Apart from plunging into an undeclared war in China with undiminished ferocity in July 1937 and carrying out a series of high profile attacks on Western subjects and commercial investments in the Far East in the weeks thereafter, the unrestrained Japanese military finally went too far and rashly struck at American naval and commercial interests in the Yangtze basin as well. Eden hoped that the bombing and sinking of the USS *Panay* on 12 December would induce a more resolute change in American foreign policy towards the Japanese. If this did prove to be the case, the prospect of a coordinated British-American naval cooperation, joint or parallel, against the errant Japanese would be enhanced. He saw this type of action as a real alternative to the futility of appeasement and one that would demonstrate the democracies were not the supine and inadequate states the dictators were wont to dismiss them as. For his part, Eden was prepared to contemplate sending the bulk of the main fleet—he mentioned eight or nine capital ships and accompanying vessels—to the Far East if Roosevelt would sanction the despatch of an equivalent force to the same region.[37] It is evident that the British Foreign Secretary was prepared for the possibility that such a naval demonstration in force in Far Eastern waters might provoke the proud Japanese nation into committing a rash act of defiant retaliation—an aggressive response that might lead onto a major naval confrontation in which the British-American naval forces could strike a massive blow at the Imperial Japanese Navy and eliminate it from the international strategic equation. It seems, therefore, that his buccaneering spirit did not emerge for the first time at Suez in 1956. But well before the scheme could even be discussed, let alone launched, the Japanese tactfully made a profuse diplomatic apology to the U.S. government and offered to pay an indemnity for the loss and damage sustained by the Americans in the *Panay* incident.[38] This let Roosevelt off the hook. While Eden led the hesitant Chamberlain towards a policy of active engagement with the Americans, Roosevelt now backed away from such an undertaking, preferring instead more modest and less flagrant gestures of support for the British. While content to facilitate the clandestine Ingersoll–Phillips conversations taking place at the Admiralty in the New Year, Roosevelt apparently had no wish to take precipitate action against the Japanese at this stage and would only contemplate doing so after what he described as the "next grave outrage."[39]

Having said that, however, Roosevelt was hardly the most temperate of statesmen as his meeting with Ingersoll revealed before the latter crossed the Atlantic to meet with Eden and the Admiralty team of war planners.[40] One could be excused for believing that as a former Assistant Secretary of the Navy, Roosevelt's knowledge of ships and the sea ought to have placed him in a unique position to assess the feasibility of Eden's proposal. Perhaps it did act as a brake on the President's wilder tendencies, but, as Ingersoll revealed later, it did not eradicate them altogether. Far from dropping the plan for a naval demonstration, Roosevelt urged Ingersoll to raise the proposal of implementing a naval blockade against Japan in which private yachts might be requisitioned and deployed along with an unspecified number of warships to form two lines of vessels that would patrol the Pacific in an effort to cut off all Japanese maritime trade in that ocean.[41] Suffice it to say that deploying private yachts anywhere in a blockade line would have been foolhardy unless it was possible to convert them into a bizarre form of armed raider. Even then such a hybrid vessel could only be expected to survive for more than the minimum length of time in a hostile environment if it could take the element of surprise to a new dimension. Although Ingersoll chose not to pass on the President's cavalier plan to supplement the blockade line with pleasure craft, he admitted that the U.S. Navy was prepared to implement a distant blockade of Japanese trade through the Pacific once war had broken out. He soon came to learn that British plans were well in advance of their would-be American collaborators and that they were prepared to launch their initiative sooner rather than later. It is difficult to escape the conclusion, however, that whatever the detailed nature of the plans devised by the Admiralty—whether calling for a trade embargo/quarantine or a naval demonstration in force—their impact and effectiveness depended to an overwhelming extent on active American naval support on the high seas and not merely expressions of diplomatic approval proffered by members of the Roosevelt administration. Unfortunately, the Ingersoll–Phillips conversations revealed that the Americans were not about to commit a sizeable contingent of their warships to bringing the recalcitrant Japanese military to heel, so the task of the Royal Navy in trying to cope unilaterally with the Imperial Japanese Navy was bound to be, at best, substantially complicated and perhaps, at worst, utterly compromised.[42]

By the time the Eden initiative and the so-called Roosevelt peace plan both came to a tepid conclusion in January 1938, however, few could doubt that the right-wing dictatorships were posing most of the questions in international relations and that the democracies were rather bereft of any constructive answers to the problems they faced.[43] In the following months, one did not need to be paranoid to sense that wherever one looked on the European continent, potential disaster was brewing. Apart from the remorseless progress of the fascists in Spain, the *Anschluss* and the *Sudetenland* issues were only resolved in central Europe in 1938 at the cost of abandoning democratic principles and ethics to Nazi threats and intimidation, so the future looked particularly bleak and ominous. Under these circumstances, therefore, how realistic was it for the British government to imagine withdrawing the majority of its fleet from home and Mediterranean waters and sending it to a far-off destination, for an indeterminate time, to deal with one of the original signatory members of the Anti-Comintern Pact? Could the British really be that sanguine or delusional?

Admiral Sir Roger Backhouse, the British First Sea Lord at the time of the Munich crisis, was neither. A practical man with a wealth of administrative experience, "RB" sensed that the economic and military importance of the Mediterranean and Middle East region was growing and that it should be no longer subordinated to the defence of Singapore in the league of strategic priorities.[44] Anxious to free himself from the fetters of conventional Admiralty thinking on this issue, Backhouse personally enticed the mercurial Vice-Admiral Drax out of retirement in the autumn of 1938 with a mission to "think out of the box" on strategic matters and devise plans that were appropriate for the changing political landscape in the world.[45] Drax did just that. Judging that war could arise on two or more distant fronts simultaneously, he proposed that the British government should concentrate its naval power in the Mediterranean, North African and Middle Eastern theatres at the outset in the hope of knocking Italy—which he identified as the weakest member of that likely hostile coalition—swiftly out of the war. In order to do this, something would have to give—that something was the traditional "main fleet to Singapore" concept. Drax sought to replace it with a "flying squadron" of two capital ships, an aircraft carrier, a cruiser squadron and a destroyer flotilla that could be sent at short notice to Singapore and be, at the very least, an effective fleet-in-being that might dissuade the Japanese from interfering with or overrunning British possessions in the region.[46] Such a heretical scheme was anathema to Admiralty stalwarts, such as Lord Chatfield, who felt that far from being a deterrent to Japanese aggression in the region, sending anything less than the bulk of the main fleet to Singapore might actually encourage the Japanese to attempt to carry out a *coup de main* against the British force.[47] Although Backhouse did not live long enough to promote the Drax war plans or overcome the opposition of his colleagues on the Admiralty Board and within the Chiefs of Staff, the "flying squadron" concept was not lost to posterity as can be seen in late 1941 with the deployment of a truncated Force Z to the base at Sembawang.

While acknowledging that the Backhouse–Drax alternative strategy demonstrated that there was more than a "one size fits all" planning aspect to the "Singapore strategy," it still begs the question of whether or not it represented any real improvement on the original "main fleet to Singapore" idea. By 1939, few policy-makers even in Whitehall doubted that the idea of deploying the main fleet unilaterally in Far Eastern waters was deeply flawed. It stood to reason that without American assistance, the Royal Navy would have its hands full even if it did not seek a pitched battle with the Imperial Japanese Navy in its home waters— not least because the Japanese military might not be overawed by the presence of the Royal Navy in the region and might actually seek to bring the main fleet to action at a time and place of its own choosing. In such a situation, the amount of damage that the British warships might sustain in those fleet actions would be critical. Clearly, the Admiralty could not afford to win a Pyrrhic victory in a Far Eastern battle only to lose the war elsewhere. If the roles were reversed and the IJN decided to sit in port and act as a fleet-in-being, how long would the main British fleet be able to stay east of Suez? What set of circumstances short of a political transformation in Tokyo, or the defeat of the Japanese military, would enable the main fleet to return to Mediterranean and home waters? It was obvious that the bulk of the Royal Navy could not afford to sit more than 8,000 nautical miles away from its home bases for months at a time when there was a real threat to the security of the British Isles posed by Nazi Germany.

So if one can safely dismiss the main fleet concept as being no longer a valid strategic unilateral option by 1939, what about the "flying squadron" principle? Did it offer something better? On its own, the "flying squadron" represented a highly mobile, rapid response force, but even with a carrier present it was hardly sufficient to do anything other than act on the defensive once it reached the Straits of Johore. Would it have served as an effective deterrent to the Japanese military had it been sent to the new base in Singapore in 1939 or 1940? Who knows? Sadly, by the time the limited Eastern Fleet was finally deployed in Southeast Asian waters in November–December 1941, momentous decisions had been made elsewhere and there was no chance of restraining the Japanese any longer.

Whoever was put in command of this fleet, would, therefore, have had a massive challenge on his hands. It is not an exaggeration to suggest that survival itself would have been a major feat in the dire circumstances that greeted its arrival in Singapore. Unfortunately, the officer appointed—acting Admiral Sir Tom Phillips—had been largely desk bound in the Admiralty for years and lacked both recent operational experience and tactical flair. It is difficult not to see in this extraordinary appointment a disaster waiting to happen. Phillips was simply the wrong man in the wrong place at the wrong time.[48] That alone would have been quite desperate enough, but the grievous error was compounded by the fact that he was expected to operate in a potentially hostile environment without a balanced fleet at his disposal.[49] Shorn of airpower by the grounding in the Caribbean of his aircraft carrier HMS *Indomitable*, and without the cruiser squadron that Drax recommended in his original "flying squadron," Phillips inherited a distinctly hybrid fleet that was badly in need of reinforcements. While seeking this type of naval assistance from Admiral Hart, the Commander-in-Chief of the US Asiatic Fleet, and other friendly powers in the region, Phillips learnt on the afternoon of 6 December that 38 Japanese transports supported by strong naval escorts had been spotted off the southern coast of French Indo-China heading in the direction of the Gulf of Siam. Phillips may not have been the archetypal action man but he wasted little time in arriving at a momentous decision; he would take his ships on the offensive and seek to disrupt the invasion force before it could gain landfall and establish a significant bridgehead.[50] Was this a case of heroic resistance or foolhardy endeavour? What chance was there of Phillips being able to bring his ships to the landing areas in time? If time was against him and it clearly was, would Phillips have been better off taking his ships south and east into the myriad islands of the Dutch East Indies archipelago so as to live and fight another day? Although Phillips' decision to take the fight to the enemy may be applauded by those who saw it as reflecting the best traditions of the Royal Navy, surely a commanding officer's duty is to use his fleet wisely and not to endanger it on a whim or flight of fancy?

By the time the old battle cruiser HMS *Repulse* returned to Singapore from her abortive mission to Darwin, and the latest battleship of the King George V class, HMS *Prince of Wales*, had her boilers back in serviceable condition for the sortie northwards, the Japanese had already disclosed their hand in the most dramatic manner possible. As the Americans learnt of the tragedy at Pearl

Harbour, so the peoples of Southeast Asia had to come to terms with a new reality—an aggressive Japanese military presence in their midst. Apart from landing their troops at Singora, Patani and Kota Bahru, the Japanese had also made their intentions known by bombing the city of Singapore and the Allied air bases throughout the Malayan peninsula. Surely, Phillips should have thought about abandoning his offensive operation at this point? After all, what chance was there of Force Z being able either to evade detection on its indirect route northwards or be in time to disrupt the Japanese invasion? Since the monsoon had apparently not conspired to prevent the landing of troops and supplies on the coast of southern Thailand and northeast Malaya, how many transports did he imagine would be left unloading troops and supplies given the hours that would have passed between reports of the first landings and the appearance on the scene of his own ships? These are critical questions and go to the heart of the matter. It must be remembered that Phillips was a former Director of Plans at the Admiralty. He had spent years poring over theoretical logistical situations in the comfortable surroundings of his offices in Whitehall. Now, ironically, when that experience ought to have come into play to dissuade him from proceeding on a risky course with little hope of success, a sense of practical realism appears to have deserted him. Or did it? Phillips was anything but a fool. It seems likely he convinced himself that something had to be done and that a valiant effort against the odds was infinitely better than not trying at all, since to do nothing was to confirm that the game was lost. One might also ask why the Admiralty did not offer him some advice about what to do for the best. Again, one can sense the traditional reluctance of the naval staff to interfere with the decision-making of the Commander-in-Chief on the spot. Moreover, Admiral Sir Dudley Pound, the First Sea Lord, was a personal friend and had infinite faith in his former Vice-Chief of the Naval Staff.

Under these circumstances, therefore, the six ships of Force Z that steamed out of the Strait of Johore in the late afternoon of 8 December bound for the South China Sea looked tragically vulnerable, as indeed they were. Even if one excuses Phillips for his reckless decision to take the fight to the enemy, one should still question his ship-handling skills. For instance, although Force Z was first detected by a Japanese submarine in the early afternoon of 9 December—a fact unbeknown to Phillips—and spotted again by three seaplanes nearly four hours later—a sighting he was aware of—could he have saved his ships and men if he had taken a direct course back to Singapore? Sadly, the suspicion is that the crews of Force Z would have at least seen Sembawang again. Most of them did not because Phillips, working on an unconfirmed report received around midnight from his Chief of Staff in Singapore, Rear-Admiral Palliser, decided to alter course and proceed to Kuantan to check whether the enemy was landing there. Once it was obvious that the report was bogus, he ought to have steamed towards Singapore

*HMS **Prince of Wales** leaving Sembawang naval base, 8 December 1941*

at full speed. He did not. Instead he wasted more than two hours scouring the seas off Kuantan for what was a non-existent invasion fleet. He was still engaged on this fruitless quest when a Japanese reconnaissance plane spotted his ships at 1015 hours on the morning of 10 December.

At this point Phillips had nothing to lose by breaking radio silence and requesting Singapore to send all available aircraft to protect Force Z as the Japanese now knew where it was and were bound to attack it. Amazingly, no such request was ever transmitted from his flagship the *Prince of Wales*. Decades later, the seminal question of why Phillips continued to maintain radio silence at this stage in the operation remains unanswered. Although there has been much conjecture from numerous quarters, no definitive evidence has ever been unearthed to solve this tragic conundrum. In the final analysis, however, it is doubtful whether the limited force of ageing Brewster *Buffaloes* available to the Allies in Singapore would have made any material difference to the eventual outcome, even if they had been covering Force Z over the South China Sea at this time. In the end, despite heroic resistance put up by their crews, the two doomed capital ships, the *Prince of Wales* and the *Repulse*, were simply overwhelmed by hostile forces. It was a sobering lesson for the traditionalists within the Royal Navy to learn, for it graphically demonstrated that the age and supremacy of the battleship and battle cruiser had passed. Tom Phillips had the opportunity to save himself before his ship sank but he chose not to. He was one of 840 officers and men of Force Z who lost their lives as a result of the naval disaster in the South China Sea on that fateful day in December 1941.[51]

It is at this advanced stage in the plot that attention needs to be focused on discordant noises coming from once friendly and trusting governments south and east of Singapore who felt the British had duped them at every turn. Although the destruction of Force Z marked the beginning of the end for the Allied position in Malaya and Singapore, the Australian government of Prime Minister John Curtin was not disposed to accept this *fait accompli* with anything approaching equanimity. On the contrary, the withdrawal, however temporary it was portrayed as being, of the "Singapore strategy" was immediately depicted as "an inexcusable betrayal."[52] Ever since, servicemen, historians and politicians from Australia and New Zealand have often repeated this familiar and emotive refrain as an explanation of the military disaster that overtook the loyal members of the British Empire back in 1941–42.[53] Many critics have pointed to what they see as a litany of intrigue, lies and deception woven by the British so that the Dominions would remain acquiescent throughout the interwar period. It is a serious charge and one that, regrettably, has more than a semblance of validity, but it is also far from being the full story, as this author has noted elsewhere.[54]

Scapegoats are invariably needed when disasters occur. And, alas, the British do fit the bill—not least because many people (and not just those from the

Australasian Dominions) depended upon them for their defence and survival and in the end—no matter which way you cut it—the British let them down. This is not empty populist rhetoric—it sadly happens to be an indisputable fact of life. Why it happened in the way it did is what this book is all about. Whether or not British defence policy in these years deserves to be described as a monstrous deception, a great betrayal, or an exercise in self-delusion will hardly be put to rest by these collected essays. No matter how fluent and erudite these essays are, not every reader will be convinced by their findings. And neither should they since there is no such thing as a definitive history of anything. This is particularly apposite when it comes to reaching any sort of conclusion on the "Singapore strategy."

That said, it is emphatically clear that the "Singapore strategy" did not live up to its prewar billing and, as this author has noted elsewhere, "failed to be the masterstroke of Imperial defence policy that it was designed to be."[55] In the end, overwhelmed by the sheer scale of the logistical exercise involved in the original scheme, the British finally revised the commitment to sending the main fleet to the Far East in mid-1940 once the French had fallen and they were standing alone in Europe in confronting the armed might of Hitler's Germany and Mussolini's Italy.[56] It is remarkable that this defence policy lasted as long as it did, but perhaps the even more surprising fact is that so much faith had been placed in it throughout the interwar period by Australian governments regardless of their political leanings.[57] It is difficult to judge whether it was the result of naiveté, wishful thinking, or, possibly, a combination of the two, but the government ministers in Canberra maintained such a steady reliance upon the "Singapore strategy" that it amounted to an article of faith, whereas those military experts who were not enamoured with this defence policy and warned that it was purely a strategic illusion were consistently ignored.[58] Although telling evidence exists to suggest that the British no longer believed in their own "Singapore strategy" by the time the delegates to the Imperial Conference met in London during the early summer of 1937 and actively began to behave ambivalently, if not disingenuously, on this issue from that time forward, the Australians stoically did not waver and remained staunchly loyal to the concept long after others began to desert it.[59] For the Australians, of course, the Far East was, in Robert Menzies' words, the "near north," so they had a vested interest in supporting and promoting the strategic plan at every opportunity.[60] As we know, when the European war broke out in September 1939, the "Singapore strategy" remained in existence even though the "period before relief" was extended.[61] Staggeringly, not even the loss of Norway in April 1940, followed by that of Denmark and the Low Countries less than a month later, dislodged the "Singapore strategy" from its official place in British defence policy. It was only after the fall of France in mid-June 1940 that the British finally sensed that this aspect of their defence policy—one they and others had relied upon for two decades—had now become a beleaguered monument to another age.[62]

Despite warnings that Churchill's government in London was distancing itself from the "Singapore strategy," seeing it as a distinct naval liability, every Australian government from June 1940 onwards was reluctant to accept the view that the main fleet might not be sent out to the Far East after all. This is hardly surprising given the fact that Australian defence policy had largely rested on this Imperial foundation for 20 years and no viable alternative regional defence option could possibly replace it at short notice.[63] Short of withdrawing all their military forces from Allied control and redeploying them entirely at home in the hope that they could defend Australia against any Japanese invasion in the future—an idea that was supported by some politicians in the Labour Party but never seriously entertained by Curtin after he had become Prime Minister—the Australians had no other option but to involve themselves wholeheartedly in the struggle of the British Empire against the tyranny unleashed upon the European world by the Axis forces.[64] This author has commented previously that while supporting the Allied cause in the Middle East, the Australians "had to trust to luck and the British as far as the defence of Singapore was concerned. Sadly their luck ran out in February 1942."[65]

In conclusion, therefore, despite the very British foundations of the "Singapore strategy," this was a strategic doctrine that came to rest too much on the Americans for its own good. Few doubted that in war the Americans would make a huge difference to its success if the "Singapore strategy" ever had to be implemented and joint or parallel forces deployed in the naval campaign, but the crucial question surely was, "Would that help come in time?" We know the answer. It would not and did not.

Malcolm H. Murfett is Associate Professor of Naval and European History at the National University of Singapore, where he has been teaching since 1980. His publications include Fool-Proof Relations: The Search for Anglo-American Naval Cooperation During the Chamberlain Years, *editor of* The First Sea Lords: From Fisher to Mountbatten, *and co-author of* Between Two Oceans: A Military History of Singapore From First Settlement to Final British Withdrawal. *He is a Fellow of the Royal Society.*

NOTES—

1. Apart from the excellent bibliographical guide offered in the endnotes of Greg Kennedy's essay number three in this volume, the following titles can also be consulted profitably for both the information and the range of sources they reveal: C. M. Bell, *The Royal Navy, Seapower and Strategy Between the Wars*, Stanford, Ca., 2000; D. Day, *The Great Betrayal: Britain, Australia and the Onset of the Pacific War*, New York, 1989; H. P. Frei, *Japan's Southward Advance and Australia*, Melbourne, 1991; I. C. McGibbon, *Blue Water Rationale*, Wellington, 1981; M. H. Murfett, *Fool-proof Relations: The Search for Anglo-American Naval Cooperation During the Chamberlain Years, 1937–1940*, Singapore, 1984; M. H. Murfett, J. N. Miksic, B. P. Farrell and Chiang M. S., *Between Two Oceans: A Military History of Singapore From First Settlement to Final British Withdrawal*, Singapore, 1999.
2. M. H. Murfett, "Living in the Past: A Critical Re-examination of the Singapore Naval Strategy, 1918–1941," *War & Society*, Vol. 11, No. 1, May 1993, 73–103.
3. M. H. Murfett et al., *Between Two Oceans*, 146–48.
4. M. H. Murfett, "Living in the Past," 76; J. L. Neidpath, *The Singapore Naval Base and the Defence of Britain's Eastern Empire, 1919–1941*, Oxford, 1981, 34–54.
5. M. H. Murfett et al., *Between Two Oceans*, 150–52.
6. See the important chapter on the defence of Singapore in Ong C. C., *Operation Matador: Britain's War Plans Against the Japanese 1918–1941*, Singapore, 1997, 19–54.
7. Ibid., 55–87.
8. Ibid., 4, 14.
9. Public Record Office (PRO), CAB2/3, Committee of Imperial Defence (C.I.D.) 159th Meeting (Mtg.), 12 July 1922.
10. In this respect, the author entirely agrees with the following remarks made by Ong in n. 11, p. 14 of his above cited work: "This novel proposal is not mentioned in history books and merits further study. If the proposal had been implemented, it would have had a lasting impact on the geopolitics of Singapore and Southeast Asia."
11. R. Cheong, "The Singapore Naval Base: A Local History," in *The Pointer, Supplement*, August 1991, 11–12; M. H. Murfett et al., *Between Two Oceans*, 153–62.
12. M. H. Murfett, "'Are We Ready?' The Development of American and British Naval Strategy, 1922–1939," in J. B. Hattendorf and R. S. Jordan (eds.), *Maritime Strategy and the Balance of Power: Britain and America in the Twentieth Century*, Basingstoke, 1989, 214–42; R. A. Divine, *The Illusion of Neutrality*, Chicago, 1962; R. Dallek, *Franklin D. Roosevelt and American Foreign Policy, 1932–1945*, Oxford, 1981, 102–08, 110–11, 113–21, 137, 139–40, 156–59, 180–85, 187–92, 200–05, 208, 212, 214, 227, 253, 255, 266, 278, 290–92; D. Reynolds, *The Creation of the Anglo-American Alliance 1937–41: A Study in Competitive Cooperation*, London, 1981; J. E. Wiltz, *From Isolation to War, 1931–1941*, London, 1967, 43–66; M. H. Murfett, *Fool-proof Relations*, 20–21.
13. M. H. Murfett et al., *Between Two Oceans*, 153.
14. See the chapter "Far Eastern War Plans and the Myth of the Singapore Strategy," in C. M. Bell, *The Royal Navy, Seapower and Strategy Between the Wars*, 59–98. As Ong Chit Chung indicates, however, in the early 1920s the War Office's military

appreciations were driven by a number of assumptions totally at variance with Admiralty prognostications about the future. According to these early War Office appreciations, the Japanese were thought capable of attempting an invasion of Johore and thereby posing a landward threat to Singapore. Dr. Ong reveals that the War Office soon changed its tune and came to believe that a large-scale landing on the Malayan coast was unlikely after all and that attempting such an invasion during the monsoon season from October to March would be impossible. Sadly, this revision proved to be wide of the mark in both respects as the events of December 1941 would ultimately reveal. See Ong C. C., *Operation Matador*, 27–36.

15 For an interesting survey of these plans, see C. M. Bell, *The Royal Navy, Seapower and Strategy Between the Wars*, 59–98.

16 S. Hajime, *Southeast Asia in Modern Japanese Thought: Essays on Japanese-Southeast Asian Relationship 1880–1940*, Nagasaki, 1997, 1–73; H. P. Frei, *Japan's Southward Advance and Australia*, 116–28.

17 In the recent past, the Japanese had rejected the traditional diplomatic principle of issuing a declaration of war before opening hostilities with any adversary. They had forsaken this practice in both the Sino-Japanese War of 1894–95 and the Russo-Japanese War of 1904–05 and had shown few diplomatic courtesies in either their seizure of the German Pacific colonies at the outset of the First World War, or their contemptuous attitude towards the Chinese over the issuing of the 21 Demands in January 1915. I. Nish, *The Origins of the Russo-Japanese War*, Harlow, Essex, 1985, 21, 206–20; D. Bergamini, *Japan's Imperial Conspiracy*, London, 1971, 299–300.

18 On 14 February 1938, amidst much ceremonial posturing, Sir Shenton Thomas, the Governor of the Straits Settlements, formally opened the King George VI dry dock at the Sembawang naval base. While an important element, the graving dock did not mean the base was ready for operational duties. According to Paul Haggie, the best thing that could be done with the dry dock for months before the rest of the base was serviceable was to flood it and use it as a swimming pool. P. Haggie, *Britannia at Bay: The Defence of the British Empire Against Japan 1931–1941*, Oxford, 1981, 119–20. According to ADM116/3644, the limited facilities at the Sembawang base would still not be ready until 1941. See J. L. Neidpath, *The Singapore Naval Base and the Defence of Britain's Eastern Empire 1919–1941*, n. 69, 271.

19 Any hopes the British government held that the Japanese would be drawn into a military quagmire in China such that it would restrict their overall ability to pursue any naval operations in Southeast Asia were, of course, found wanting when the Imperial Japanese Navy seized the island of Hainan in February 1939 and Spratly Island on 31 March 1939, besides simultaneously laying claim to 14 coral reefs in the South China Sea. H. P. Willmott, *Empires in the Balance: Japanese and Allied Pacific Strategies to April 1942*, Annapolis, 1982, 58.

20 M. H. Murfett et al., *Between Two Oceans*, 156–57.

21 M. H. Murfett, *Fool-proof Relations*, 76; P. Haggie, *Britannia at Bay*, 165.

22 I. Nish, *Alliance in Decline*, London, 1972; idem., "Echoes of Alliance, 1920–30," in I. Nish and Y. Kibata (eds.), *The History of Anglo-Japanese Relations: Volume I: The Political-Diplomatic Dimension, 1600–1930*, Basingstoke, 2000, 255–78.

23 Despite Professor Nish's belief that the abrogation of the Anglo-Japanese Alliance was not as unwelcome to the Japanese as it has often been described, Professor David Dilks has little doubt that its ending was profound for the British. He sees the conversion of the former alliance partnership into one of hostility and contempt as being perhaps the single most important blow to British foreign policy in the entire interwar period. D. N. Dilks, "Appeasement Revisited," in *The University of Leeds Review*,15, 1972, 28–56.

24 M. H. Murfett, "Look Back in Anger: The Western Powers and the Washington Conference of 1921–22" in B. J. C. McKercher (ed.), *Arms Limitation and Disarmament: Restraints on War, 1899–1939*, Westport, Conn., 1992, 83–103; R. Dingman, *Power in the Pacific: The Origins of Naval Arms Limitation*, Chicago, 1976; E. Goldstein and J. Maurer (eds.), "Special Issue on the Washington Conference, 1921–22: Naval Rivalry, East Asian Stability and the Road to Pearl Harbor," *Diplomacy and Statecraft*, 4, 1993.

25 Assuming that hostilities between the Royal Navy and the Imperial Japanese Navy were likely to take place in northern waters, the Admiralty assessed the advantage to the Japanese as being worth the equivalent of two capital ships. Unfortunately, the waters were muddied further immediately when one recognized that the Sembawang naval base had only limited repair facilities for even a peacetime fleet, let alone the main fleet. This again was calculated as being equivalent to a net loss of two capital ships. Even so, the Admiralty considered that the Japanese High Command would not seek a fleet action if the Royal Navy's numerical disadvantage were only one less than the total capital ship strength of their own fleet, i.e., eight to nine. In the light of the above reasoning and calculations, however, sending eight battleships to the Far East would not be enough and that 12 would have to be sent (a) to have a chance of defeating the IJN or (b) deterring it from engaging in an all-out fleet action. See PRO, CAB16/182, Admiralty Memorandum, "A New Standard of Naval Strength," 26 April 1937, submitted as a paper for the Defence Plans (Policy) Committee, DP(P)3.

26 PRO, CAB4/25, Chiefs of Staff (COS) Review, C.I.D.1305B(Revise), paras.79–81, 22 February 1937.

27 M. H. Murfett, "Living in the Past," 89–95.

28 A. Best, "The Road to Anglo-Japanese Confrontation, 1931–41," in I. Nish and Y. Kibata (eds.), *The History of Anglo-Japanese Relations, 1600–2000: Volume II: The Political-Diplomatic Dimension, 1931–2000*, Basingstoke, 2000, 26–50.

29 P. Haggie, *Britannia at Bay*, 144–52.

30 M. H. Murfett, *Fool-proof Relations*, 55–58.

31 After the *Panay* crisis, it was always possible that a far more active American involvement in the Far East could result from another direct attack launched by the Japanese military on U.S. interests in East Asia. By no means all of the British officials, however, thought this was even remotely likely. Sir Warren Fisher, the Permanent Under Secretary of State at the Treasury, was typical of those who put little or no reliance upon the Americans. "The U.S.A. w[oul]d fail us at the critical moment even in the Far East. Still more w[oul]d she fail us in our consequential danger in

Europe." PRO, T160/693/F15255/01, Note by Sir Warren Fisher on memo by Sir Frederick Leith-Ross, 20 December 1937.

32 American economic pressure on Japan gained ground after the defeat of France in June 1940 and the subsequent Japanese incursion into Indochina. Beginning with banning the export of aviation fuel and high-grade scrap metal to Japan, the trade embargo was extended subsequently to all strategic raw materials, including copper and brass, deemed useful for military purposes. See H. P. Willmott, *Empires in the Balance*, 61–71.

33 J. Sharkey, "Economic Diplomacy in Anglo-Japanese Relations, 1931–41," in I. Nish and Y. Kibata (eds.), *The History of Anglo-Japanese Relations, 1600–2000: Volume II*, 78–111; C. M. Bell, *The Royal Navy, Seapower and Strategy Between the Wars*, 59–98; M. H. Murfett, *Fool-proof Relations*, 43, 55, 57–62, 65–72, 75, 77–79, 82–84, 89, 119–20, 125, 135, 157, 193–97, 207, 263, 265, 277, 279, 297.

34 Foinavon won the British Grand National steeplechase in 1967 at odds of 100-1— the Tote odds were 444-1—when all the leading horses either fell or refused to jump one of the fences on the second circuit at the Aintree course leaving Foinavon clear of the rest of the field.

35 President Roosevelt's "Quarantine Speech" of 5 October 1937 indicated that he at least was in favour of being more assertive with the totalitarian dictatorships. Unfortunately, press and political reaction within the United States to his analogy-laden speech was mixed and led to an almost instant retreat on his part. See M. H. Murfett, *Fool-proof Relations*, 62–65.

36 Ibid., 27–161.

37 PRO, FO371/21021, No.607, F10976/10816/10, Foreign Office to Sir Ronald Lindsay, 15 December 1937.

38 M. H. Murfett, *Fool-proof Relations*, 106, 125.

39 PRO, FO371/20961, F11201/9/10, Minute by Sir Alexander Cadogan, 19 December 1937; M. H. Murfett, *Fool-proof Relations*, 104–27.

40 Roosevelt's clandestine late night meeting with Ambassador Lindsay at the White House on 16 December 1937 prefigured the secret conversation he had with Ingersoll later in the month. See PRO, FO371/22106, F11201/9/10, Lindsay to Foreign Office, 17 December 1937, Nos. 481–3.

41 J. Leutze, *Bargaining for Supremacy*, Chapel Hill, N.C., 1977, 22.

42 M. H. Murfett, *Fool-proof Relations*, 130–38. For another view of this fascinating relationship, see Greg Kennedy's essay number three in this book, and his book *Anglo-American Strategic Relations and the Far East, 1933–1939*, London, 2001.

43 While Roosevelt expressed utter contempt for Germany, Italy and Japan, describing them as the "three bandit nations," the President was held in check by his domestic political concerns and by the strength of congressional isolationism. R. Dallek, *Franklin D. Roosevelt and American Foreign Policy, 1932–1945*, 148.

44 For an excellent summary of the Italian part of the strategic equation, see L. R. Pratt, *East of Malta, West of Suez*, Cambridge, 1975.

45 Backhouse has received poor press in the past for being incapable or unwilling to delegate his powers to others around him. Correlli Barnett dismissively referred to

him as the "arch centraliser." This is more than a little harsh as the Drax appointment demonstrates. C. Barnett, *Engage the Enemy More Closely*, New York, 1991, 50–51, 554.

46 M. H. Murfett (ed.), *The First Sea Lords: From Fisher to Mountbatten*, Westport, Conn., 1995, 173–84; M. H. Murfett, "Backhouse, Sir Roger Roland Charles" in B. Harrison (ed.), *New Dictionary of National Biography*, Oxford, forthcoming 2004.

47 PRO, CAB27/634, F.E.S.37(4), Memo by Chatfield, Reinforcement of British Naval Forces in the Far East, 23 September 1937; see his remarks at CAB2/8, C.I.D. 348th Mtg., 24 February 1939.

48 Responsibility for this appointment rests with both Winston Churchill and Sir Dudley Pound. At one time both men believed that Phillips virtually could do no wrong. He became a popular weekend guest at Chequers, admired for his powers of analysis and sharp acerbic tongue. Given these connections, it is not surprising that he ascended the rungs of the Admiralty hierarchy with remarkable speed and assurance. Churchill's attitude changed towards him, however, after Phillips, as Vice-Chief of Naval Staff, roundly criticized the Prime Minister's policies on retaliatory bombing of German cities in September 1940 and the diversion of troops and supplies from North Africa to Greece in April 1941. Thereafter the two men rarely spoke. M. H. Murfett, "Phillips, Sir Tom Spencer Vaughan," in B. Harrison, *New Dictionary of National Biography*; see also I. Cowman, *Dominion or Decline: Anglo-American Naval Relations in the Pacific, 1937–1941*, Oxford, 1996, 207–96.

49 A. J. Marder, *Old Friends, New Enemies: The Royal Navy and the Imperial Japanese Navy*, Oxford, 1981, 365–88; M. Stephen, *The Fighting Admirals*, Annapolis, 1991, 113–37.

50 M. Middlebrook and P. Mahoney, *Battleship*, London, 1979; A. J. Marder, *Old Friends, New Enemies*, 388–506.

51 Ibid., M. Stephen, *The Fighting Admirals*, 113–37; M. H. Murfett, "Phillips, Sir Tom Spencer Vaughan."

52 *Documents on Australian Foreign Policy 1937–49 Volume V: July 1941–June 1942* (DAFP V), Canberra, 1982, John Curtin to Winston Churchill, 23 January 1942, 463–64.

53 An example of the ill feeling that periodically resurfaces is illustrated in the Rt. Hon. Paul Keating's impassioned speech on this controversial subject in the Australian House of Representatives on 27 February 1992. This elicited a response from *The Times* on 28 February 1992. For an academic perspective on this issue, see D. Day, *The Great Betrayal*; D. M. Horner, *High Command: Australia and Allied Strategy 1939–1945*, Canberra, 1982.

54 M. H. Murfett, "Australia and the Singapore Strategy," in C. Bridge and B. Attard (eds.), *Between Empire and Nation: Australia's External Relations from Federation to the Second World War*, Melbourne, 2000, 230–50.

55 Ibid., 245.

56 Viscount Caldecote first disclosed this fundamental change of policy in a message to Sir Geoffrey Whiskard, the British High Commissioner to Australia, on 19 June 1940: "The collapse of France would provide Japan with the temptation to take action against the French, British or Dutch interests in the Far East. We see no hope

of being able to despatch a fleet to Singapore." Lord Caldecote to Sir Geoffrey Whiskard, 19 June 1940, No. 406, in H. Kenway, H. J. W. Stokes and P. G. Edwards (eds.), *Documents on Australian Foreign Policy 1937–49: Volume III: January–June 1940*, Canberra, 1979, 460.

57   J. McCarthy, *Australia and Imperial Defence 1918–39*, St. Lucia, Qld., 1976.

58   D. M. Horner, *High Command*, 1–8; P. Dennis, "Australia and the Singapore Strategy," essay number two in this volume; P. Hasluck, *The Government and the People 1939–1941*, Canberra, 1952, 9–108.

59   Sir Samuel Hoare, the First Lord of the Admiralty, informed his cabinet colleagues that he was prepared to keep the Dominion representatives guessing at the forthcoming Imperial Conference of July 1937 as to what the British would do in an emergency. In the notes he prepared for his cabinet speech, he wrote the following: "I suggest that on no account should I say anything that would imply that we shall not have a fleet capable of action in the East as well as in the West, but that I should emphasise the almost intolerable strain that such a fleet imposes upon us...." Templewood Papers, IX2, Cambridge University Library, Notes for Cabinet Speech, March–April 1937. See also PRO, FO371/20649, A5460/6/45, Defence Plans (Policy) Sub-Committee 2nd Meeting, (DP(P)), 11 May 1937.

60   H. P. Frei, *Japan's Southward Advance and Australia*, 91–159; Robert Menzies wryly observed: "What Great Britain calls the Far East is to us the near north." *Sydney Morning Herald*, 27 April 1939, cited in I. Hamill, *The Strategic Illusion: The Singapore Strategy and the Defence of Australia and New Zealand 1919–1942*, Singapore, 1981, 286.

61   PRO, CAB2/9, C.I.D. 364th Mtg., 6 July 1939; CAB80/1, COS(39)16, 7 September 1939; CAB80/3, COS(39)49, 25 September 1939.

62   M. H. Murfett, "Living in the Past," 94–97; idem., "Australia and the Singapore Strategy," 237–46.

63   John McCarthy's understandably pithy observation of this situation is seen in the following summary: "When required to make defence policy decisions between the wars, successive Australian governments suffered from a chronic lack of self-reliance. The advice of the United Kingdom was usually sought and often followed without serious critical thought. The most important result of this policy was the trust placed in the ability of the United Kingdom to send to Singapore a naval force of sufficient strength to protect Australia from direct Japanese attack." J. McCarthy, *Australia and Imperial Defence 1918–39*, 148.

64   R. J. Bell, *Unequal Allies: Australian-American Relations and the Pacific War*, Melbourne, 1977, 27–28; J. Beaumont, *Australia's War 1939–45*, St. Leonard's NSW, 1996, 26–33; D. Day, *The Great Betrayal*, 20, 186–256; P. Hasluck, *The Government and the People*, Canberra, 1952, 338, 356–57, 541–58; A. Watt, *The Evolution of Australian Foreign Policy 1938–1965*, Cambridge, 1967, 5.

65   M. H. Murfett, "Australia and the Singapore Strategy," 246.

CHAPTER 12

Australia and the Singapore Strategy

by Peter Dennis

In the latter half of the nineteenth century, the doctrine of imperial defence had come to be accepted as the basis for the security of the British Empire. It rested on several assumptions: that command of the sea through the supremacy of the Royal Navy provided the first line of defence; that the colonies and Dominions should provide such forces as were necessary to ensure defence against local attacks; and that in the event of a general war or major international crisis, all parts of the Empire would cooperate in the common cause. Inevitably there were tensions between these assumptions, especially as the Dominions sought a greater degree of autonomy from the centralized approach that underlay the concept of imperial defence, and as perceptions of priorities varied between the metropolitan centre and the far-flung reaches of Empire. Yet these tensions should not be exaggerated. In the final analysis, Dominions such as Australia had no realistic choice but to be part of a wider defence scheme, and to depend on what came to be called in the Australian context "our great and powerful friends." The question was over the degree of that dependence.

In 1920, in the immediate aftermath of the Great War—surely a testament to Australia's willing adherence to the third plank of imperial defence—the Minister for Defence, Senator George Pearce, convened a meeting of the most senior Army generals to develop proposals for the postwar Army. Pearce emphasized that he wanted "not counsels of perfection, but counsels of practicability," and that fiscal restraint was to be the overriding principle.[1] In a little over two weeks—spurred on by the fact that, until the government decided on the basic structure of the Army, even administrative processes could not operate efficiently—the conference drew up an extensive plan. Its recommendations proceeded from two fundamental observations: that notwithstanding the establishment of the League of Nations, Australia's defence basically rested on its own willingness to provide the necessary forces, and that Japan constituted "the only potential and probable enemy" to Australia's security.[2] The generals recommended a nine-stage development that would, in their view, provide Australia with the necessary forces to meet the challenges they foresaw. At the heart of the proposed scheme was the establishment of two cavalry and four infantry divisions, with a fifth infantry division to be dedicated to local defence, together with the subsequent acquisition of the required levels of equipment and supplies. Perhaps because the returning Australian Imperial Force had brought back huge amounts of equipment, and that therefore the recommendations did not involve immediate and undue expenditure, the government formally adopted the generals' scheme in May 1921.

Any sense that the government had accepted the financial implications of the generals' recommendations disappeared when barely nine months later, in February 1922, the government used the necessary reductions in naval forces arising out of the Washington Conference to effect more general savings across the military establishment. Both the small permanent force and the militia were subjected to swingeing cuts in establishment—echoing similar reductions in the British military establishment, especially in the Army. Those reductions were in themselves difficult enough to accept, but in the context of the emerging "Singapore strategy" they posed a real threat to the Army's ability to fulfil its responsibilities.

The basic "Singapore strategy" was accepted by the Dominions at the Imperial Conference of 1923, and its details need not be rehearsed here. What is important to note here is that it *was* adopted by the Australian government, even if on the fundamental question of how the great base at Singapore was to be defended, the Prime Minister, Stanley Bruce, confessed: "[W]hile I am not quite clear as to how the protection of Singapore is to be assured, I am quite clear on this point, that apparently it can be done."[3] From the very beginning, therefore, Australia's political leaders abrogated any sense of responsibility for critical examination of the assumptions underlying the "Singapore strategy." Belief in it became an article of faith, buttressed by the fact that it enabled successive governments to save on defence expenditure, apparently secure in the knowledge that Singapore was the answer to the problems of regional security. Those savings were even greater when the Australian government declined to contribute directly to the cost of the base.

For the Army, the adoption of the "Singapore strategy" heralded a long period of government parsimony, now rationalized not simply on the basis of cutting back on defence expenditure in the wake of a great and victorious war, but justified by an apparently well-argued and well-founded strategic doctrine endorsed at the highest levels of imperial decision-making. It was a formidable obstacle to those in the Army who insisted that the strategy was fundamentally flawed and that it left Australia dangerously exposed if its underlying assumptions proved false. In the same year as the adoption of the "Singapore strategy," the Chief of the General Staff, General Brudenell White, argued that Australia should base its military plans on the assumption of a great war, and successive Chiefs talked in terms of a Japanese invasion of Australia, a decidedly greater level of threat than that suggested by the scenario of "local raids," which the doctrine of imperial defence had always left to small local forces to counter. The Japanese threat was specifically raised in a Defence Committee appreciation in 1928, which concluded that it was "within the bounds of possibility ['although only on a limited scale'] and not so improbable as to allow it being definitely ruled out."[4] In view of the long-standing fear of Japan, the assumptions of the "Singapore strategy" and their implications for specifically Australian concerns raised worrying questions in Army circles. Such was the government's insistence on the primacy and centrality of the "Singapore strategy" to the defence of Australia that to challenge it took courage, not to say foolhardiness.

The succession of financial cuts from 1922 on placed great strain on the Army in its attempts to provide for even a basic capability, however that might be defined. The Royal Australian Navy also suffered severe expenditure cuts, which were materially reflected in the change of name in 1926 from the Australian Fleet to the Australian Squadron, a painful recognition of the reduction in the number of ships that necessarily followed in the wake of economy measures and the outcome of the Washington Conference. There was the additional strain on the budget concomitant with the establishment of the Royal Australian Air Force. Inter-service rivalries did little to enlighten the strategic debate, in which the Navy, by virtue of its close association with the Royal Navy and the now-endorsed "Singapore strategy," had a pre-eminent position.

Within the defence establishment in Australia, the "Singapore strategy" and all that it meant for expenditure allocations had powerful supporters, none more so than Frederick Shedden, who in 1929 returned from a year at the Imperial Defence College (IDC) in London to become Secretary of the Defence Committee. It was the first important appointment in Shedden's career, in which he subsequently became the longest-serving Secretary of the Department of Defence, 1937–56. At the IDC, Shedden had become a convinced disciple of the commandant, Admiral Sir Herbert Richmond, whose firm advocacy of the principles of imperial defence coincided with Shedden's emerging ideas. Shedden gave Richmond copies of various reports on Australian defence, and suggested that the syllabus be expanded to include a series of lectures on economics, which was duly done. When the Minister for Defence visited London, he asked Shedden to prepare a paper on the underlying principles of imperial defence and how they related to Australia's circumstances. With typical application, if not discrimination, Shedden finally produced a paper 120 typed pages in length. It was a comprehensive study, which Richmond told Shedden he regarded as "quite the best analysis of the problem that I have seen."[5]

Despite this endorsement by a powerful advocate of the "blue water" school, Shedden's view did not go unchallenged. His most determined critic was Colonel John Lavarack, a fellow student on the IDC course in 1928. In marked contrast to Shedden, Lavarack was not persuaded by the blue water principles that underlay the "Singapore strategy," and when in 1929 he was commissioned by the CGS to prepare plans to deal with a possible Japanese invasion, Lavarack seized the opportunity and wrote two papers highly critical of the direction of Australian planning. In his first paper, Lavarack argued that the 1928 Defence Committee appreciation underestimated the invasion danger posed by Japan, but did not recommend revisiting the question at that stage because he was not confident his views would prevail, and he was content that at least the possibility of invasion had been acknowledged. His second paper, "A Plan of Concentration," suggested that Japan would wait until the British Empire was so involved in Europe that its capacity to respond to a threat in the Far East would be substantially diminished, and that when those circumstances prevailed, Japan might then seek to exploit British weakness by landing an invasion force at one of three vital places in Australia: Sydney, Melbourne or Newcastle. Whether Australian forces would be sufficient to meet such a threat was the heart of the question, but even more fundamental was Lavarack's direct challenge to the assumptions underlying the "Singapore strategy."

The onset of the Great Depression forced the hand of the new Scullin Labour government, which in February 1930 announced further substantial cuts to defence spending. The Defence Committee—note: Frederick Shedden, Secretary—established a sub-committee to consider how these financial reductions could be accommodated, and appointed Lavarack to chair the sub-committee. Shedden, disappointed that his lengthy examination of the principles of imperial defence—and hence the "Singapore strategy"—had not received greater attention previously, made his paper available to the sub-committee. The move backfired. Lavarack wrote a detailed and stinging critique of Shedden's views, dismissing them as "fallacious" and offering "nothing new." On the question of the guarantee that British naval power afforded Australia, Lavarack wrote:

> The despatch of the British battle fleet to the Far East for the protection of Imperial (including Australian) interests cannot be counted upon with sufficient certainty, and the risk that it will be withheld, added

to the risk of the non-completion, capture, or neutralisation of Singapore, results in a total risk that no isolated white community such as Australia would be justified in taking.

Whereas Shedden argued that if British seapower failed, Japanese economic strangulation of Australia would make invasion unnecessary, and that therefore, from Australia's point of view, military forces to guard against invasion would be superfluous, Lavarack suggested it was more likely that neither the U.K. nor Japan would have complete control of eastern seas, and that Japan's ability to crush Australia economically would be doubtful, thereby making invasion more likely. Lavarack's overall assessment of Shedden's paper was that his ideas were "fallacious" and could not "be accepted as a practical guide to Australian Defence policy."[6]

The sub-committee was divided, the Air Force representative agreeing with Lavarack on the real danger of invasion, while the naval member submitted a dissenting report. That division was mirrored in the deliberations of the Defence Committee, with the Chief of the Naval Staff insisting that "the possibility of invasion [was] so remote that in the present financial state of the country it could not be considered." The bureaucratic solution posed by the Financial Secretary was to recommend that the financial cuts ordered by the Government be spread evenly across the three services. This was accepted by the Minister, who also acceded to the Committee's request that he forward its views to the Prime Minister. There was no response from Scullin.

When Lavarack sent a copy of his paper to Shedden, he sought to minimize any ill-feeling that it might cause, adding that "I don't regard what I have written as the last word by any means." Shedden was not assuaged by this comment, disputing Lavarack's competence to pronounce on matters naval and suggesting that he failed to understand the distinction between the possibility of "raids"—which Shedden accepted—and the likelihood of "invasion." To add weight to his self-perception of authority, and of grievance, Shedden referred Lavarack's paper to his old mentor, Admiral Richmond. He was undoubtedly pleased when Richmond dismissed Lavarack's criticisms of Shedden's arguments as "stupid." Richmond went further, writing that Lavarack's concern that the U.K. might find itself simultaneously engaged in a war in Europe and the Far East, thereby placing real doubts on its ability to send the main fleet to Singapore, was "a hypothetical situation of a highly improbable nature," and adding that "I can imagine no worse way of stampeding a Government into a waste of money."[7] While this endorsement bolstered Shedden's views of his own capacity in strategic matters, it did little to address the questions that Lavarack posed. Furthermore, Richmond's ideas were increasingly at odds with those of the British government and the defence establishment, where there was a growing appreciation of precisely the scenario that Richmond so glibly dismissed, namely a major war in two widely-separated theatres.

Richmond's public statements led to his premature—and forced—retirement but he continued to publish articles on defence matters.[8] One such article, "An Outline of Imperial Defence," published in the *Army Quarterly* in July 1932, provoked a response from Lavarack, now Commandant of the Royal Military College, Duntroon. In his article, "The Defence of the British Empire, with Special Reference to the Far East and Australia," published in January 1933, Lavarack argued that the broad principles laid down so confidently by Richmond paid little attention to the changing realities of the international situation, let alone the circumstances facing Australia. Lavarack's criticisms were shared by other senior Army officers, and when an expanded program of defence expenditure was announced in September 1933, the Chief of the General Staff, Major-General Sir Julius Bruche, successfully argued against Shedden's attempts to have the Army's role restricted to countering raids and persuaded the Defence Minister that planning against invasion should remain central to Army policy. At the same time, Cabinet reaffirmed its basic reliance on seapower to provide security not only against attacks of seaborne commerce and raids on Australian territory, but also against invasion.[9] It seemed that in the absence of a willingness to grapple with criticisms of the "Singapore strategy," the Government preferred to rely on simply reiterating the soundness of the policy to silence its critics.

Two developments further strengthened Lavarack's position on the "Singapore strategy" and its implications for Australian military planning. In late 1934, the long-standing Secretary of the Committee of Imperial Defence, Sir Maurice Hankey, visited Australia to advise on defence matters and specifically to try to reassure the Australian government of the soundness of the "Singapore strategy" and the British government's commitment to complete the naval base to the extent that it could accommodate a major fleet. Shedden was appointed Hankey's assistant during the visit, at Hankey's request, for they were of like minds, Hankey describing one of the briefing papers he had received—i.e. Shedden's earlier analysis of imperial defence—as "this brilliant piece of work" that was argued with "extraordinary brilliancy."[10] Hankey tried to bolster the confidence of the Australian government, but he also admitted to the Lord President of the Council in London, Stanley Baldwin, that "I have made it clear that our government has taken no commitment to send the fleet to Singapore." Nevertheless he acknowledged to the new Australian Defence Minister, Archdale Parkhill, that he had some sympathy with those in Australia who rejected the "extreme application of the 'mere raid' theory," and recommended that on the basis of the protection the Singapore base afforded Australia, the Australian Army could be reduced in size.[11] Hankey then continued his Empire-wide visit, having privately recommended that Shedden become the next Secretary of the Department of Defence. Shedden's hour was about to arrive, and even before he became Secretary, in November 1937, he consciously modelled himself on Hankey, thereby earning himself the nickname "pocket Hankey."[12]

Lavarack's star was also in the ascendant. He was now Chief of the General Staff-designate, and increasingly well-known for his opposition to prevailing government policies on defence. Hankey was aware of his opposition, and took time during his visit to engage Lavarack in detailed discussions, and recommended that the next Chief—i.e. Lavarack, although Hankey was probably too discreet to name him—should undertake a year's study in the United Kingdom, where broader views of imperial defence might offset what Hankey thought was an extreme position on the "Singapore strategy" and its implications for the defence of Australia. It was a forlorn hope, for though the Defence Commitee had apparently acquiesced in Hankey's recommendation that the Army should be reduced from seven divisions—five infantry and two cavalry—to three, it was only a matter of politeness in the presence of the eminent Hankey. The Army completely rejected the proposal, and after Hankey left, the long-standing divisions between the Navy and the Army re-emerged.

A brief word is necessary here to explain the position of the Air Force. On one level, it should have been the natural ally of the Army in urging a move away from the overwhelming reliance on the naval solution that the "Singapore strategy" offered. However, its voice in strategic discussion circles was muted by its fight for survival in the face of overwhelming hostility from the other two services, its struggle to establish itself in the face of heavy expenditure cuts—having, because of its youth, much less of a base from which to rebuild—and the ongoing bitter rivalry between its two most senior officers, Richard Williams and Stanley Goble, who alternated as Chief of Air Staff in the 1920s and 1930s. Preoccupied as he was with these pressing matters, and working under the weight of two largely adverse reports on the Royal Australian Air Force from senior Royal Air Force figures, Williams contributed little to the debate.[13] Indeed, one historian has commented that "it is difficult to know precisely what Williams thought; there is a certain timidity in his appreciations."[14]

As CGS-designate, Lavarack wrote a detailed and stinging critique of Hankey's paper, which raised exactly the problem that the Defence Secretary, M. L. Shepherd, foresaw when he stressed that those appointed to be Chief of Staff of any of the services should be made aware that "the appointment is offered to them only on an unequivocal assurance that they will loyally seek to carry out the Policy of the Government."[15] Lavarack felt no inhibitions in dismissing Hankey's paper as containing "nothing new." It was, he said, the product of a mind "obsessed with the idea of obtaining from all parts of the Empire forces which can be employed in the solution of the *general* defence problem [emphasis added]...[I]n such a matter as the detail of Australia's defence system [i.e. the local problem], Sir Maurice Hankey is not qualified to give an opinion."[16] Lavarack went on to argue for a reduction in spending on the navy to below 50% of the overall defence budget, and a corresponding increase in the army and the air force for local defence, i.e. against both raids and invasion. He concluded by suggesting that if his objections were not accepted, nothing should be done to implement Hankey's recommendations until the British government gave firm and satisfactory answers to the central pillars of the "Singapore strategy": when would the base be completed; what size naval force would the British send; and how long would it take to arrive.[17] These, of course, were essentially the very concerns Hankey had known, before leaving London, he could not answer, and which, in the absence of any answers, his mission to Australia had been designed to allay by smooth talking and a resort to "long-standing principles."

For the next two years, Lavarack pushed his agenda in the face of sustained opposition from Shepherd and Shedden and to the growing displeasure, and finally, bitter condemnation of the Minister for Defence, Archdale Parkhill. Parkhill has had a uniformly bad press in historical accounts, and there seems little to commend his performance. He was acknowledged by his own cabinet colleagues to be vain and arrogant, and on questions of government policy he was not prepared to countenance opposition, no matter how well-founded the contrary arguments. In terms of parliamentary democracy and what that means in the realm of civil-military relations, it was surely correct that Parkhill should insist on the primacy of government policy where there was disagreement, but he showed little regard for professional opinion and expertise in areas that were central to national security. That intolerance was underpinned by a streak of vindictiveness in his pursuit of another advocate of the Army position, Colonel H. D. Wynter, who, not surprisingly, was close to Lavarack. The Wynter case showed that the Government was not prepared to tolerate dissent from its policy, nor was it prepared to have that policy debated, and certainly not in public, and that it would go to any lengths to silence its critics.

In November 1936, in a speech in Parliament, Parkhill appealed for a bi-partisan approach to defence policy. In reply, the Leader of the Opposition, John Curtin, criticized the government's policy in terms that seemed to echo criticisms that had long been made in Army circles. Closer examination of his remarks suggested that he had quoted at length from Bruche's critique of Hankey's 1934 report. Further investigation revealed that Curtin had also drawn on notes of lectures by Wynter in July and August 1935, which also contained lengthy extracts from Bruche's secret report.[18] Bruche's critique was again the basis of an article in the *Sydney Daily Telegraph*, "How Can We Defend Australia," in April 1936. Parkhill was furious, and instructed the Military Board to find the source of the leaks.[19]

Although Wynter subsequently protested that he had been "most grievously wronged,"[20] it seems clear that he was responsible, at least in part and only if indirectly, in communicating the former CGS's views to the Opposition. Wynter had long dissented from government policy—as had most of the Army—and as early as 1926 had given a lecture to the United Service Institution in Melbourne in which he bluntly questioned the ability of the Royal Navy, in conjunction with Australian naval forces, to provide for the local defence needs of Australia, arguing that only a strong Army and Air Force could fulfil that role.[21] As a student at the Imperial Defence College in 1930, his views attracted the attention of Richmond who advised Shedden of his concern that others at the College "[would] not have the knowledge to confute his assertions."[22] Wynter drafted Bruche's commentary on Hankey's report, and by the mid-1930s was widely regarded as one of the Army's most forceful thinkers.

The initial response of the Military Board to Parkhill's demand was less than satisfactory to the Minister. The Secretary of the Board advised Shedden that the Board found "considerable difficulty in criticizing the article 'How Can We Defend Australia'...as the views expressed almost entirely coincide with those of the Board." In any case, he added, the suggestion in the article that the divergence between those who argued for an increase in naval strength and those who urged greater emphasis on the Army and the Air Force was of recent origin was wrong. There had long been a difference of opinion on this question, but he added that the Board—i.e. the Army—"has always been in favour of a reasonable naval contribution to Imperial Defence, *subject to adequate provision for local defence*" (emphasis added). He concluded by advising Shedden that the Board did not know and could not find out who wrote the article.[23]

Parkhill was furious, not only by what he saw as a less than wholehearted attempt to track down the culprit, but also by the Military Board's virtual endorsement of the *Daily Telegraph* heresy, and he asked the Naval Board for its comments. The Navy's response was an unequivocal re-statement of the principles of imperial defence and a total rejection of any criticism of the "Singapore strategy":

> The Naval Board wish to stress that the temporary decline of British naval strength to a level dangerously low against certain foreign combinations is no argument for abandoning the principles of naval defence.
>
> ...[T]he Naval Board regard this theory of deliberate "isolation" and concentration on "protection against invasion" as a counsel of despair both strategically and politically unsound.[24]

In December 1936, having brewed over the matter for several months, and having spoken in Parliament the previous month to refute Wynter's views, Parkhill demanded that Wynter be disciplined. When the Military Board attempted to excuse Wynter's actions, Parkhill took matters into his own hands, spurred on by Shedden who observed to Parkhill that "I am sure that when you realize the fact that you were really not debating Defence Policy with the Leader of the Opposition but with Colonel Wynter, you will feel that firm action is necessary at this time."[25] Shedden might well have said that Parkhill was really debating Lavarack. When called upon to explain his actions, Wynter argued in a minute to Lavarack that he had not leaked confidential material; that the connection between his draft for Bruche and his lecture was purely a "mental one," his lecture having been prepared as an article for the *Army Quarterly before* he was given the task of drafting Bruche's response to Hankey's paper; that Lavarack had approved the text of his lecture on the condition the press was excluded; and that the only other copies of his lecture that were given out were made available to military men—several of whom were also members of Parliament—who could not attend but who were eligible to do so. As for the *Daily Telegraph* article, Wynter denied any knowledge of its provenance, although he admitted his son was a journalist on the paper and he and his son often discussed strategic matters—but, he added disingenuously, only on a philosophical and abstract plane.[26]

Parkhill would have none of it. He rejected Wynter's explanation regarding his son as "absolutely absurd" and "amazing," and argued that Wynter had displayed a "lamentable lack of discretion and vision." As a result, he recommended that Wynter "should no longer be employed at Army Headquarters."[27] The Army Board duly acted on this advice, and on 21 December it recommended that Wynter be appointed GSO1, 11th Mixed Brigade, Queensland, and that he revert to his substantive rank of Lieutenant-Colonel. It concluded that in view of the financial loss and career setbacks that Wynter would thereby suffer, "no further action should be taken against him."[28]

Wynter was not prepared to go quietly, and in January 1937 submitted to Lavarack a lengthy—15 page—and closely argued reply to Parkhill's views. There was not even a hint of contrition, the overall tone of the reply being summed up by Wynter's statement that to expect any officer to ensure that he never drew on official opinions in the course of giving lectures to professional bodies was an "impractical pedantry."[29] In his minute, Wynter sought to have a legal means of replying to the charges made against him, and on 26 January he formally requested a court martial. In a minute to the Secretary of the Military Board, Shedden wrote of Wynter's "impenitent attitude," adding that "he threatens the Minister with political effects of any trial. This almost sounds like a species of blackmail."[30] Wynter's stated intention of having the whole matter aired publicly, with Parkhill being called as a witness, prompted Parkhill to justify his position even more vigorously, while at the same time ensuring that Wynter's request for a court martial was denied, on the grounds that no charges had ever been laid. Parkhill referred to Wynter's "impractical pedantry" comment, and accused him of "unbecoming language," "a perverse obstinacy," and "criticisms of Government policy...[and] disrespectful observations."[31] For good measure, he sought the views of the Chief of the Imperial General Staff in London, Field Marshal Sir Cyril Deverell, who replied that "the action taken in relation to the nature of the offence is in our opinion one of leniency."[32] He also sent a copy of Wynter's lecture to Hankey, who dismissed it as being "riddled with misconceptions and false premises."[33] Wynter's efforts to have his grievances aired publicly came to nothing. Lavarack did not escape censure either, Parkhill describing his action in approving Wynter's lecture as "imprudent," while his unwillingness to discipline Wynter resulted in Parkhill recommending that the proposed award of the Companion of the Order of the Bath be withdrawn.

This sorry episode is illustrative of the wider question of Australian defence policy between the wars and its relation to the "Singapore strategy." There is little evidence that all three services and the governments they advised grappled collectively with the central issues. Acceptance of the underlying assumptions of the "Singapore strategy" was, for the government and its naval advisors, an article of faith. Were those assumptions to be examined critically, especially from an Australian perspective, the whole edifice might well crumble and Australia be left exposed to the threat of an all-powerful Japan. For most of the interwar period, the Army was the centre of opposition to the prevailing policy, an opposition that met with increasingly political resistance. Future developments showed that while the "Singapore strategy" was fatally flawed, it was surely seapower—American rather than the planned British—that "saved" Australia in 1942. Supporters of the Army's case, however, could well claim an equally important turning point in the New Guinea campaign in 1942. Both sides of the argument could point to a lack of resources in the decade or more before the fall of Singapore, and could lay the responsibility for that squarely at the feet of Australia's political leaders. When then-Prime Minister Paul Keating revived charges of "betrayal" in his ill-chosen comments on the occasion of the 50th anniversary of the fall of Singapore, he might well have pondered the question of who betrayed whom.

Professor Peter Dennis is Professor of History at the Australian Defence Force Academy, University of New South Wales. He has published very widely on twentieth century Australian and British military history, including the volume Troubled Days of Peace: Mountbatten and South East Asia Command, 1945–46.

NOTES—

1. J. Grey, "The Australian Army" in P. Dennis and J. Coates (eds.), *The Australian Centenary History of Defence: Volume 1*, seven vols., Melbourne, 2001, 73.
2. Ibid.
3. Quoted in J. McCarthy, *Australia and Imperial Defence: A Study in Air and Sea Power*, St Lucia, 1976, 47.
4. M. Evans, "From Deakin to Dibb: The Army and the Making of Australian Strategy in the Twentieth Century," in P. Dennis and J. Grey (eds.), *A Century of Service: 100 Years of the Australian Army*, Canberra, 2001, 12–30, at 16.
5. D. Horner, *Defence Supremo: Sir Frederick Shedden and the Making of Australian Defence Policy*, Sydney, 2000, 28.
6. Ibid., 34.
7. B. Lodge, *Lavarack: Rival General*, Sydney, 1998, 17–18; D. Horner, *Defence Supremo*, 34.
8. See B. D. Hunt, *Sailor-Scholar: Admiral Sir Herbert Richmond 1871–1946*, Waterloo, Ont., 1982, ch. 10.
9. J. McCarthy, *Australia and Imperial Defence*, 54.
10. D. Horner, *Defence Supremo*, 45.
11. D. Horner, *Defence Supremo*, 46; B. Lodge, *Lavarack*, 35. Stephen Roskill points out that the British Prime Minister, Ramsay MacDonald, was reluctant to read Hankey's paper on the grounds that "it is typed in a trying way"! S. Roskill, *Hankey: Man of Secrets, Volume III, 1931–1963*, London, 1974, 130–31.
12. D. Horner, *Defence Supremo*, 47; S. Roskill, *Hankey*, 590.
13. The Salmond and Ellington reports on the RAAF are outlined in C. D. Coulthard-Clark, *The Third Brother: The Royal Australian Air Force 1921–39*, Sydney, 1991, chs. 3 and 4.
14. J. McCarthy, *Australia and Imperial Defence*, 60.
15. B. Lodge, *Lavarack*, 39, and see his n. 6, 274.
16. Ibid., 43.
17. Ibid., 45–46.
18. Wynter had sent a copy of his lecture to Parkhill, who wrote back that he would "take an early opportunity of perusing the speech, which I feel sure will contain some valuable views." National Archives of Australia (NAA), A5954.
19. Parkhill's own summary of the case is in Cabinet Paper, The case of Lieutenant-Colonel (Temporary and Brevet Colonel) H. D. Wynter, C.M.G., D.S.O., Australian Staff Corps, NAA, A5954, Item 886/1. Wynter's 1935 lecture, which he delivered twice, in July and August, is in A5954/69, Defence of Australia and its Relation to Imperial Defence.
20. NAA, 5954, Item 885, Wynter to Lavarack, 15 January 1937.
21. NAA, A5954/69, Item 886/2, Lecture on the Strategical Inter-Relationship of the Navy, Army and Air Force, 1 September 1926.
22. B. Lodge, *Lavarack*, 18.
23. NAA, A5954/69, Item 886/1, C. B. Laffan to Shedden, 9 April 1936.

24 NAA, 5654/69, Items 886/1, G. L. Macandie, Secretary, Naval Board, to Shedden, 24 April 1936.
25 NAA, 5954/69, Item 886/1, Shedden to Parkhill, 16 December 1936. Shedden added that the "Military Board's attempt at 'whitewashing' is rather amazing. However, as Colonel Wynter is the mainspring of radical Army thought and propaganda I suppose some obligation is felt to rally to his defence."
26 NAA, 5954, Wynter to Lavarack, 3 December 1936.
27 NAA, 5954, Item 886/1, Appendix C, Minute by Parkhill, 17 December 1936.
28 NAA, 5954, Minute, Secretary to the Military Board, 21 December 1936.
29 NAA, 5954, Item 885, Wynter to Lavarack, 15 January 1937.
30 NAA, 5954, Item 886/1, Shedden to Laffan, 16 December 1936.
31 Parkhill, The case of Lieutenant-Colonel…Wynter, 8 February 1937 (see note 17 above).
32 NAA, 5954, Item AQ25/1, Deverell to Parkhill, 22 June 1937.
33 NAA, 5954, Item AQ25/1, Hankey to Parkhill, 19 July 1937.

CHAPTER 13

Symbol of Imperial Defence: The Role of Singapore in British and American Far Eastern Strategic Relations, 1933–1941

by Greg Kennedy

Singapore was more than a naval base. It was a symbol of British imperial intention and control in the Far East from 1921 until its fall in 1942.[1] As part of the Washington treaty system, the British portion of allowable base fortification following the Four and Nine Power Treaties, Singapore took on many roles over the course of its existence. It has most often been seen as a symbol of British military and imperial arrogance, naval incompetence, a failure in tactical, operational and strategic leadership, as well as a betrayal of the Pacific Dominions by Perfidious Albion.[2] The symbolism of the "Singapore strategy" and the base itself are crucial to understanding its place within the British strategic foreign policy formulation process. Depending on the prism through which that strategy was viewed, Singapore could be, and was, many things to many different viewers. This essay is concerned with answering three questions: what did the British strategic policy-making elite perceive to be the value of Singapore in British-American relations in the period 1933–1941; did that perception of that value change or fluctuate at any time in the period and why; and, last, did British efforts to convince the United States' strategic foreign policy-making elite of that value succeed? In short, did the Americans buy what the British were selling when it came to Singapore and British-American strategic relations in the Far East during the Roosevelt administration? For, if the aim of British strategic foreign policy in the Pacific was to convince the Japanese policy-making elite that an attack on the British Empire would not go unpunished, and that the punishment meted out would be done with American assistance, then the role of Singapore as not only a base, but also as a symbol of resolve, of determination, of cooperation, and of coordination is central to understanding the British-American Pacific strategic relationship.[3] Such an approach also forces a re-evaluation of the "worth" of the "Singapore strategy." When seen in the light of a balance of power security system, Singapore appears to have been a sensible solution to the conditions facing British strategic planners from 1933–1941.

In 1933, Singapore symbolized three things in the minds of Franklin Roosevelt's strategic foreign policy-making elite. To the United States Navy, Singapore was the most modern and the latest representation of the global reach of the Royal Navy. Able to act as a forward base of operations for the Royal Navy's largest warships, when fully completed and equipped, Singapore represented the pinnacle of naval bases and their associated technologies. This professional appreciation had two effects. The first was to drive-on the United States to emulate the British base by the development of their own Pacific facility at Pearl Harbour. Eventually, under the naval preparations made possible by the New Deal, President Roosevelt would give approval for the whole of the west coast of the United States to be mobilized towards supporting Pearl Harbour and the Philippine naval bases and garrisons in an attempt to project American maritime power into the Far East. It was Singapore that acted as a catalyst, and it was the benchmark by which the United States Navy could measure its progress in power projection in the Pacific.

Singapore also had an impact on naval arms control, with all its strategic implications. A greater basing capacity in the Far East had the potential to create serious rifts in British-American naval relations. Due to their lack of adequate basing, the United States Navy argued constantly throughout the 1920s and 30s for their need for larger, heavy 8" gun cruisers, while the British, with adequate basing available, opposed such building programmes, maintaining that their smaller, light 6" gun cruisers were the preferred solution to the cruiser question.[4] Without such bases, the American cruisers would be at a severe disadvantage in the areas of sustainment, reach, fighting power, and poise, unless such elements of naval power were built into the actual ships themselves. If the American heavy cruiser design became the accepted standard, not only would such an event create a greater strain on the British naval building program vis-a-vis the American, but also, in reality it would create a major threat due to Japan's desire to mimic such a class of vessel. The Royal Navy did not fear fighting the United States Navy in the 1930s, but it did have considerable reservations about future relations with the Imperial Japanese Navy. If American demands for bigger vessels created a naval arms escalation, that then led to the Japanese obtaining a number of heavy cruisers, then the entire practice of the British cruiser fleet and its protection of Imperial sea lanes of communication would have to be rethought. Part of that re-evaluation would have to focus on Singapore and what its main role would be: main fleet base or cruiser fleet fortress.[5] Naval and political minds were not the only ones to have to ponder such complex issues. Indeed, in many instances in this process of strategic risk assessment, career civil servants played key roles in painting the mental maps.

For the State Department and their political masters, President Roosevelt and Secretary of State Cordell Hull, Singapore symbolized something else. While both groups were aware of the naval symbolism inherent in the base, they were more conscious of the imperial nature of the base. A guarantor of British dominance in the region, in both fiscal and trade matters, Singapore symbolized the control which the British Empire still exercised, and wished to maintain, in the region. Acting as a shield for the Dominions, Australia and New Zealand, as well as for the vast British trade in China and other areas of the Pacific, the construction and maintenance of Singapore was held to be the key to sustained British influence and dominance in the region in the minds of American observers in the State Department. As long as the British were prepared to utilize the strategic leverage afforded them by the base, the Americans would be content to let them lead in any efforts to contain an aggressive Japan.[6] That American perception, of London's having a greater strategic interest in the Far East than did Washington, had serious implications for the eventual mental map British strategic foreign policy-makers needed to maintain in the minds of their American counterparts. In particular, in the aftermath of Munich and British strategic policies in Europe that indicated appeasement was a central part of British strategic foreign policy, U.S. observers kept a wary eye on British behaviour in the Far East. Would there be a Far Eastern Munich that endangered American interests and security in the region? After Munich, Singapore took on an even greater symbolism in British-American relations, a condition that would eventually lead to the destruction of two British capital ships at the hands of the Imperial Japanese Navy. If any sign of weakness or "scuttle" was detected in the British intentions towards the Far Eastern Crisis, and in particular regarding any issues that had the potential for combined British-American actions, there was a great risk that the Americans would abandon the field to the British alone. Such a course would be a disaster for both parties.

Such was not, however, the American view of Singapore when the newly-elected President Roosevelt began his first term in office. In 1933, the United Kingdom and the United States were locked in a bitter dispute over the payment of debts incurred by the former to the latter during the First World War, as well as over world economic issues in general. Many solutions to the growing tensions between the two nations were put forward.[7] One aspect of a possible solution to the war debt issue was presented to the Foreign Office by the British Secretary of State for India, Sir Samuel Hoare, future First Lord of the Admiralty and Secretary of State for Foreign Affairs. Hoare was approached by unofficial American sources, through a Briton named Findlater Stewart, with a proposal that Singapore be allowed to support the United States Navy and its operations in the Far East, for a specific period of time during an emergency situation, in lieu of a portion of war debt payment.[8] Sir Robert Vansittart, Permanent Under-Secretary of State for Foreign Affairs, and the Foreign Office departments responsible for British Far Eastern policy, met the inquiry with little enthusiasm. The person who had raised the issue with Stewart, a New York lawyer named McIlvaine, while having had some relations with Congress and the American government in the past, was an unknown to all Foreign Office officials and to the British Ambassador to the United States, Sir Ronald Lindsay.[9] McIlvaine felt his concept to be unique, but it was not. Vansittart had earlier fended off such a proposal when discussions surrounding war debts surfaced in relation to other debt issues, particularly those concerning British relations with European nations. As for Singapore itself, the American Department of the Foreign Office highlighted the problems surrounding any American use of the base:

> In its present form there is no mention of any undertaking to afford facilities to the U.S. Navy, only of expansion of the base on a scale which would enable it to serve that navy in case of emergency. But (i) if some arrangement regarding the base were to be part of a favourable debt settlement the U.S. would surely require a definite undertaking; and (ii) we could not affect the necessary expansion of the base without explaining to Parliament and to Japan and other interested powers the reason.[10]

The Foreign Office was clear in its desire not to include American basing rights at Singapore as any part of a British-American war debt settlement. Not only would such an agreement arouse greater animosity between the U.K. and Japan, but to pursue such a line would also most certainly end in an embarrassing failure on the shoals of American public opinion, an occurrence that could only deepen British-American imperial and maritime tensions.

In fact, far from wanting a coordinated basing arrangement, the Foreign Office eyed the Roosevelt government's newfound desire to expand its own naval base at Pearl Harbour with great interest, trying to fathom just what such a development might mean for the balance of power dynamic in the Pacific. As well, Foreign Office officials observed Pearl Harbour's development with a view to learning not only more about American intentions in the Pacific and for the U.S. government's support to the priming of the pump of its domestic economy, but also about Japanese reactions to any escalation in base construction aimed at enhancing power projection capabilities in the region.[11] American Secretary of the Navy Claude A. Swanson's acquisition of the enormous sums of money required to reconfigure Pearl Harbour from a class D into a class A harbour, truly able to support "a fleet second to none," in the autumn of 1933, was believed to reflect not just Swanson's desires for a more capable navy, but also those of his President.[12] Paul Gore-Booth, a future Permanent Under-Secretary of State but at the time one of the newest members of the American Department, in cooperation with the Admiralty's Naval Intelligence Department, produced a brief memorandum highlighting the American basing situation and power projection capability in the Far East. Received as being a most informed and enlightened document by the Foreign Office, Gore-Booth's efforts revealed that the United States Navy was improving the Mare Island facility for fleet support on the Pacific coast but made clear that San Diego was the key. Particular improvements and expansion in anchorages at the latter were making it possible for the entire American battle fleet to gather and be sustained on the west coast. As well, the naval infrastructure along that entire seaboard was experiencing a massive upgrade, all in preparation for being able to support a massive fleet effort through operations originating from Pearl Harbour.[13]

At the moment, however, the American ability to project naval power into the region was indeed limited. As Gore-Booth and the Admiralty Intelligence Department pointed out, Pearl Harbour was suitable as a base only for cruiser squadron operations until a channel was cut through the bar across its entrance. With such a channel it would then be able to receive and contain the entire battle fleet comfortably. Guam was defended by fewer than 500 Marines and had only 6" guns for its defence, with no repair facilities. Cavite and Olonpago were well-fortified and defended by 10" to 14" guns, a sizeable garrison and were able to undertake all repairs for the American Asiatic Fleet. The advantage of Pearl Harbour, though, was that:

> Guam and the Philippine Islands being inside the *status quo* area under Article 19 of the Washington Treaty, the United States are not allowed to increase their fortifications. This, however, does not apply to *Hawaii*, which was expressly declared outside this area. It is therefore the only United States Pacific base apart from the mainland which the United States are permitted to fortify...Hawaii is believed by United States authorities to be the key of national defence in the Pacific whose occupation by an enemy would endanger California, Oregon and Washington, and there is no reason to suppose that this view has changed.[14]

The creation of a system of bases adequate for war in the Pacific was a first step by the United States in improving its maritime power capabilities in that ocean. It was an act identical in intent to the U.K.'s first step in preparation for rearming its imperial defence structure in the region: the strengthening of Singapore. Therefore, both nations' strategic decision-making processes were interested in similar issues and were trying to solve common problems with similar solutions. This parallel set of strategic mental maps meant that Singapore would be given a certain symbolism within the American strategic thinking process, one which equated to the role of Pearl Harbour.

The growing international tensions in the Far East were the catalyst for a British re-examination of their defence requirements in 1933.[15] The first step was the creation of the Defence Requirements Sub-Committee. The committee recommended that rearmament should maintain the Far East as its first area of concern. Thus, rearmament was to be aimed at improving the Royal Navy's capability and sustainability in operations for that region. The first priority was, therefore, to increase Singapore's defences and repair facilities.[16] The First Sea Lord, Sir Ernle Chatfield, pointed out to the Committee of Imperial Defence in November 1933 that Singapore was the first step in a long and arduous attempt to restore the Empire's global defences.[17] For the Admiralty and the Foreign Office, the increases to Singapore's capacities had two audiences. The first was any power, like Japan, that doubted British resolve to defend their Far Eastern interests. The second was any potential ally in the Far East that was also determined to resist any aggressive, forceful expansion by Japan. In particular, the United States, as well as China, were the targets of this act of determination.[18] The American decision to invest in Pearl Harbour was seen as an indication that there was in Washington a parallel, though not joint, perception of the strategic situation in the Far East.[19] To British policy-makers in the Admiralty and the Foreign Office, the idea that American and British governments should each have independent naval base expansion programmes was a hopeful sign for the future.[20]

The Roosevelt government's decision to commit the United States to developing a Pacific base equal to Singapore created the opportunity for the Foreign Office to observe reactions in that region: "It will be interesting to see if the Japanese are as upset by this move as by our Singapore base."[21] With powerful Cabinet members, such as the Chancellor of the Exchequer, Neville Chamberlain, still hoping for a return to a pre-World War I British-Japanese strategic relationship, the Foreign Office was particularly concerned at the time to ensure that any British-American naval interaction did not send the wrong signal to Japan: that the two English-speaking nations were working towards a formal alliance aimed at limiting future Japanese expansion in the Far East.[22] While happy to have the uncertainty of such an occurrence playing in the minds of Japanese officials, the Foreign Office was trying to avoid any formal or real manifestation of such an alliance being present in official representations observable by Japan. Such "evidence" in the hands of expansionist Japanese naval and Cabinet officers could be used to make a final case for the end of the Washington treaties and signal a return to unrestricted naval building.[23] Therefore, such events as an American request to have United States Navy warships visit the Royal Navy's Home Fleet in 1934, with the British returning the visit to Balboa in 1935, while innocent enough on the surface, made the Foreign Secretary, Sir John Simon, nervous about the interpretation Japan would put on such an exchange. When asked by the Admiralty for their opinion of such visits, the Foreign Office reply was, "With a view, however, to preventing misinterpretation of the visit in Japan, Sir John Simon would suggest that it should be emphasized through the Press that the visit is a return of that paid by the flagship of the Atlantic fleet to the United States fleet in Balboa in 1931."[24] Sir Robert Vansittart's opinion on British-American relations and the Far East, which travelled not only through the Foreign Office, but also through the Treasury, the Committee of Imperial Defence, Service Chiefs, and Prime Minister, reflected a desire to avoid antagonizing the Japanese. It also contained a healthy dose of cynicism regarding American foreign policy in that region and its effect on British imperial interests. It was his view that:

> (1) They (U.S.A.) will always disappoint us. (2) We have done quite enough running after them, and should do no more; advances must now come from them. (3) We must therefore beware of any American suggestions that we should cooperate (against Japan) in the Far East. The Americans would let us down, or stab us in the back, after having thrust us forward to our cost. (4) I do not want to sacrifice any of the ground gained with the U.S.A. during the last decade—ground for good relations though not for effective cooperation—by any tardy recovering of Japan (which the BofT [Board of Trade] will anyhow make impossible owing to the internal pressure on HMG.) (5) But we ought, during the coming quinquennium, to be more preoccupied in keeping Japan as friendly i.e., non-dangerous, as possible, than in endeavouring to better our existing relations with the U.S.A., which are as good as that unreliable country will or can allow them to be.[25]

On the other side of the Atlantic, similar strategic assumptions were being made by the American State Department. The American Ambassador to Japan, Joseph Grew, believed that only a strong statement of resolve and a clear symbol of determination to protect American interests in the region would have an impact on Japan's future attitude towards the use of aggression and, in particular, naval aggression in the region. He told Cordell Hull that the only way Japan could be convinced to accept its current naval status was by means of:

> ... the definite assurance of ability and willingness to outbuild on the part of America, and the knowledge that fortifications in the Pacific now held in abeyance under the terms of the Treaties, would be pushed to completion in the event of treaty breakdown. Without these restraining factors, national pride will not permit the extension of the present ratio, nor will the inherent wealth nor the past sacrifices of rival power be accepted as a reason for naval inferiority.[26]

Grew saw the British desire to complete Singapore to its full strength as a first step in London's effort to challenge Japanese aggression and argued that the U.S. would be wise to emulate that policy. He was not alone in that regard. His immediate supervisor, Stanley Hornbeck, Head of the State Department's Far Eastern Division, was the recognized voice of authority on matters concerning that region. Hornbeck, too, believed that a balance of power system was becoming the standard for international relations in the Far East. As the new Roosevelt administration eased into foreign relations during its first term, Hornbeck told William R. Castle, the Acting Secretary of State, that the situation in the Far East had deteriorated to the point where maintaining peace was no longer an option, it was rather how much peace could be saved:

> There is at this moment no question of its 'maintenance', the real question being that of preserving what there is left of it (and later restoring it). It is my opinion that, at this stage, nothing short of a threat by the world (or some two or three major powers) of intervention by the use of some form of force would offer any likely chance of preventing a substantial increase in the near future of the intensity of the hostilities which have been in progress between Japan and China during the past fifteen months.[27]

However, Hornbeck, like Grew, was under no illusion as to which nation was expected to take the lead in any efforts to check Japan. British actions, both in negotiations and preparations for rearmament in the region, would be taken as a benchmark for subsequent American actions.[28] Any sign of British accommodation of Japan, especially on issues related to naval disarmament levels or Japanese aggression towards China, would send a signal to the State Department that Whitehall was no longer even a possible ally in the Pacific. Instead, it would be classified, not as a foe, but certainly as an untrustworthy nation in any further discussions concerning strategic foreign policy and defence policy issues.

British-American Far Eastern strategic relations involved Singapore to a greater degree in 1934. Not only did the continued improvements to the base keep it in the public eye on both sides of the Atlantic, but also the hesitation to involve the United States Navy in British naval affairs decreased. On 23 and 24 January, the Royal Navy, represented by Admiral Sir Frederic C. Dreyer, C-in-C China Squadron, and senior naval officers and staffs from the Dominions, met aboard Dreyer's flagship, HMS *Kent*, to debate whether the British should withdraw from Hong Kong and Singapore. Due to his close working relationship with Dreyer, Admiral Frank Brooks Upham, C-in-C of the American Asiatic Fleet, was privy to those high-level British naval discussions, which were held at Singapore. He duly reported the outcome of that conference to his superior, Admiral William H. Standley, the Chief of Naval Operations.[29] Upham's report outlined what British interests and possible courses of action might be in the Far East and how the United States and its navy fit into that future:

> Rumor has it that the British are contemplating giving up Hong Kong and retiring to Singapore for their last stand in the Far East. Although nothing definite has been planned, or at least announced, the mere fact that the British are considering such a turn-about policy is momentous and indicates the true predicament in which foreigners of all nationalities will soon find themselves if something is not done about it. An event which lends color to this rumor regarding the proposed British withdrawal from Hong Kong is the British naval conference held aboard HMS *Kent* at Singapore on January 23rd and 24th. Admirals of the British, Australian, and New Zealand navies participated in the conference, the keynote of which apparently was the matter of the Singapore naval base. Though unconfirmed, reports state that plans are afoot to complete the Singapore base two years ahead of schedule, i.e., by 1938 or 1939, as a means of alleviating anxiety felt in England, Australia, and New Zealand over Japanese ambitions and aggressions in the East. Other reasons given for proceeding with the base were the apparent collapse of world efforts toward disarmament, and the probable imminence of Philippine independence and the resulting decline of the U.S. as a naval factor in the Far East.[30]

Upham continued to outline the growing evidence for increased Japanese pressure on foreigners and their interests in the region. He questioned whether or not the United States would have the resolve to fight Japan in order to maintain its position in the region, finally deciding that public opinion at home would demand war rather than capitulation. As well, he linked the U.S. Navy's position in the Philippines and an adequate basing facility there to any future deterrence of Japan. He pointed out that, "Were we to defend this island as we are prepared to do in Hawaii, the possibility of war will be appreciably removed."[31] Clearly, within the U.S. Navy and the American policy-making elite, the idea that bases would provide the capability for power projection, as well as act as a measurement of resolve and the willingness to deter Japan, was becoming a common factor in their collective mental map of British-American relations in the Far East.

Information on Singapore and British strategic maritime intentions in the Far East was being carefully monitored by the Americans in preparation for the upcoming 1935 London Naval Conference.[32] In part, these probings and observations by the U.S. government were designed to lay the ground work for the technical aspects of the conference. But more importantly, the discussions were seen by the Americans as the process by which they would gauge British resolve to meet Japanese demands for a larger navy.

On 2 March 1934, Prime Minister Ramsay MacDonald had a two-hour lunch at the U.S. Embassy with the American Ambassador to the U.K., Robert W. Bingham, as well as President Roosevelt's emissary-at-large and chief naval negotiator, Norman Davis, and the U.S. *Chargé d'Affaires*, Ray Atherton.[33] During the luncheon meeting, both sides agreed that there was little or no hope the Japanese would accept any formulae other than parity with the Americans and British. Both also agreed that such an outcome was unacceptable and that Japan should be so informed, although independently through separate channels. There was to be no hint of a united front or collusion on the part of the U.K. and the U.S.[34] Clearly, Japanese actions would determine which way British-American naval cooperation would proceed. If the Japanese demanded parity, then the United States and the United Kingdom would be forced to work together against such a programme. If Japan chose a new ratio system that did not create parity, then it would find the two Western nations eager to accommodate it on an individual basis. Naval basing and the continuance of the Article XIX aspects of the Washington Treaty would, of course, figure into any such agreement and future assessments of the balance of power in the region.

British anxiety not to incur Japan's wrath regarding the naval talks was obvious to the Americans, but that did not deter them from assuming that the first steps towards British-American naval cooperation had been taken in the talks with MacDonald. Davis reported to Roosevelt that the British were desirous of having a British-American agreement in order to check Japanese activities:

> The British are unquestionably disturbed as to the far-reaching effect which the present Japanese activities may have, and they are most

desirous of reaching an agreement with us, if possible, because of the salutary effect which it might have on Japan. I am informed that they are pushing the work at Singapore as rapidly as possible but that this will not be completed until 1937. In the meantime, their policy will, in my judgement, be to iron out their differences with us with regard to the maintenance of naval parity, to reach a common understanding as to the Japanese demands for an increased ratio and even to go further, if we are disposed to do so, for the maintenance of peace and the protection of our respective rights and interests.[35]

Davis and Bingham were convinced the British were predominantly desirous of closer British-American naval relations, but were reluctant to do so until the Singapore base was finished. Once that key element in the British imperial defence structure in the Far East was in place, any Japanese attempts to disrupt the balance of power could be met with greater resolve.

For their part, the British strategic policy-making elite was sceptical of America's continued interest in and resolve to help protect the status quo in the region. The Admiralty and Foreign Office desire to observe Japanese reactions with regard to the American improvements to Pearl Harbour was tempered by their desire not to antagonize Japan. Equally, they realized that future developments regarding the independence of the Philippines could have a drastic effect on not only the status quo and balance of power in the Far East, but also on British-American relations and the question of adequate basing for any fleet trying to contain a Japanese move against those islands.

The Philippine Independence question became a more important aspect of British-American Far Eastern relations throughout 1933. Questions about whether or not a neutralization scheme for the islands was a realistic expectation were being balanced against the possible disruption to "the equilibrium in the Pacific" if such a policy was put into effect.[36] Not only would there be questions concerning who would provide a stable governing body for the islands, which were thought incapable of governing themselves, but also there was the danger that independence would put Japan and the U.K. at odds with one another. If Japan became the overseer of the Philippines, then it could obtain the basing facilities that were situated there. Such an acquisition would put Japanese naval units well within range of Hong Kong and allow for sustained Japanese operations not only in that area of the theatre but also against Singapore.[37] However, and more important, if the United States ceased to administer the Philippines, and the League of Nations proved unwilling to undertake governance, then the islanders were most likely to look to the British to fill that void. Indeed it was thought likely that within months of the U.S. leaving the islands to their own devices, the President of the Philippines, Manuel Quezon, would be asking for Dominion status.[38]

The British were not the only European power to have doubts about American desire to remain a force in the eastern Pacific. In December 1933, Joseph Grew had a long chat with the Dutch Minister to Japan, General Pabst, concerning the possible Japanese seizure of Guam in 1935. Seen as a reputable and reliable source of information and analysis by Grew, Pabst's information was not interesting simply because it addressed the issue of Japanese aggression against American interests in the Far East, but rather because it forced Grew to consider what the Philippines meant both for the U.S. strategic position and for the region's balance of power dynamic.[39] The American Ambassador understood that the question of naval bases was a key element in Japanese strategic thinking:

> ... from the military and naval point of view, an American offensive would be a negligible factor, because they hold that no American fleet could effectively operate in Japanese waters so far from its Hawaiian base and with its lines of communication liable to be intercepted. Once in possession of the Philippines, with unrestricted naval building in view and having eliminated the dreaded threat of an American naval base in eastern waters, Japan believes that she could disregard the United States and proceed with her Asiatic ambitions.[40]

If bases were going to be at the heart of Japanese planning for the conduct of a war in the region, then such considerations were vital for the United States as well.[41]

Grew was not alone in his concerns about the long-term nature of an American presence in the Philippines and its basing ability in the region. Indeed, throughout 1934 and 1935, until the conclusion of preliminary talks for the 1936 London naval talks, the British were most concerned about how the Americans would handle any withdrawal from their position in the islands.[42] Sir Ronald Lindsay reported early in January of 1934 that an unofficial committee made up of academics from Yale, Wisconsin and Harvard Universities, convened by Roy Howard of the Scripps-Howard newspaper group, a man known to at times be a confidant of President Roosevelt, had submitted an outline for an independence settlement to the White House. Lindsay pointed out that this report called for the United States to surrender all naval bases in the islands "to take effect upon neutralization and independence. A Philippine neutralization agreement should be negotiated as part of a settlement of larger Pacific issues at the naval conference to be held in 1935 or later."[43] However, as far as Lindsay was concerned, evidence was mounting that America was perhaps becoming less inclined to "stick it out" in the Far East.[44] For example, in March of that same year, President Roosevelt told Congress that the provisions concerning military bases being retained in the Philippines had been eliminated and the question of the retention of naval bases was to be discussed at a later date between the U.S. and Philippine governments.[45] The Foreign Office as a whole, however, was not convinced that the United States was going to abandon immediately its naval base in the Philippines, although there was some concern about how the U.S. could give up military garrisons and fortifications on the islands and still protect its naval base.[46] By November of 1934, during a meeting of the Committee of Imperial Defence, Sir Bolton Eyres Monsell, First Lord of the Admiralty, questioned whether the United States was willing to "shoulder the financial obligations involved in bringing their defences in that part of the world up to date" if a lack of interest in protecting the Philippines led to the U.S. allowing Article XIX to slip into disuse.[47]

Article XIX of the Washington Naval Treaty was part of the Four Power Agreement that regulated the building of fortifications in the Pacific between Japan, the United States, the United Kingdom and France. As preparations for the London Naval Conference to be held in 1936 progressed, American and British fears of Japan's abandoning the Washington system included concerns about the possible abrogation of Article XIX.[48] By 1936, and certainly by July 1937, Japanese actions in the Far East, as well as the continued rearmament and expansionism of Germany and Italy, caused both the United States and United Kingdom to begin to take their own rearmament and preparations for the use of force more seriously. Indeed, by 1935, construction at Singapore was accelerated, with the new deadline for completion now being 1938.[49] In the Far East, British considerations about basing facilities for fleet operations were now focused on 1936, which was seen by the Foreign Office, the Admiralty, and most members of the Committee of Imperial Defence, to have the potential to be a "critical year" for security issues, particularly in that region. Despite this, by the summer of 1937 British actions in the Far East were under intense scrutiny by American foreign policy-making officials, both in Washington and in the region, as to whether or not some British-Japanese deal would be struck.[50]

In order to understand this fully, it is necessary to consider earlier events. Singapore's most important role in proving continued British resolve in British-American strategic relations in the Far East was dictated by events in 1932, by what has been termed the Simon–Stimson misunderstanding. The British Foreign Secretary and American Secretary of State created distrust, suspicion, annoyance, anger and petulance on both sides of the Atlantic in their handling of Japan's actions in China and over events in Shanghai in particular. The end result was Henry Stimson's belief that Sir John Simon had reneged on a promise for the United Kingdom to join with the United States in imposing punitive sanctions on Japan.⁵¹ This meant that if the British strategic foreign policy-making elite was going to keep America "in play" and not allow that nation to drift into more splendid isolation in Far Eastern matters or, indeed, to seek a favourable agreement with Japan at British expense, then impressing the Roosevelt administration that Perfidious Albion was not part of the British-American relationship in the Far East was paramount. The maintenance of Singapore and providing a fleet to be based there was one way of so doing. Thus, confidence-building measures with the United States involved Singapore. Sending the right strategic signals to the Americans was essential for imperial defence.

One of the more important American policy-makers who was a key target for that British strategic signal was Stanley Hornbeck. ⁵² His views of British willingness to meet the expanding Japanese policy were transmitted to both Secretary Hull and Roosevelt on a regular basis, and formed the intellectual core of America's Far Eastern strategic foreign policy formulation.⁵³ His assessment of the U.K.'s role in the Far East focused on that nation's strategy to maintain Singapore as a major naval base. In Hornbeck's mind the British maintenance of Singapore was a benchmark by which the Americans could measure British resolve. The British move towards security in the region, predicated on naval preparedness, was a theme dear to his own heart.⁵⁴ Therefore, what Hornbeck thought of the "Singapore strategy," even though that was not the name he would have given it, was crucial to how the Roosevelt Administration's mental map of the British role in that theatre was formed. Hornbeck was a Theodore Roosevelt protégé. Believing that the best policy was to "speak softly; and *to carry a big stick*,"⁵⁵ Hornbeck's view on the strategic situation in the Far East was that security in that region was now based on the balance of power. He also believed that this would continue to be the situation for some time. Therefore, American interests would be best served not by treaty but by military preparation. For Hornbeck, that military preparation included the continued build-up of naval forces, including bases, and limited involvement in any international agreements that would tie America's hands over rearmament:

> Any treaties which might be concluded under existing circumstances would consist either of platitudinous phrases and/or equivocal prescriptions and/or well-sounding pledges entered into with definite mental reservations (and with no intention on the part of one or another of the parties of scrupulous observance, such agreements would *solve* no problems). We need to be honest with ourselves and with others, careful, courteous, and above all so strong that no other power—no matter what its necessities from point of view of internal politics or its aspirations in the field of its external relations—will desire to attack us.⁵⁶

As for the United Kingdom specifically, if it were able to show the necessary resolve and parallel interests, then it was his belief that the United States "should cultivate conditions of harmony and practical cooperation between ourselves and Great Britain."[57] Hornbeck's appreciation of the situation in the Far East, and his attitude towards possible cooperation with the British, was supported by the Chief of Naval Operations, Admiral Standley.[58] Both Standley and Hornbeck were aware of the difficulties inherent in trying to establish formal, public relations with British strategic policy-making bodies while at the same time trying not to arouse or provoke Japanese ire because of such contact.[59] British strategic policy-makers, in both the Admiralty and the Foreign Office, understood that fact, not only about Hornbeck himself, but regarding the perceptions of the American Far Eastern foreign policy-making elite in general. Thus, they worked hard to try and remedy a situation in which informal cooperation was the desired goal of both sides, but public perceptions of it were the enemy to further cooperation.[60]

Often, the British solutions involved the use of Singapore, or the suggested use of Singapore in its symbolic role. By 1938, the Foreign Office and Admiralty shared a common goal: to get the Americans to participate in ceremonies, meetings, or demonstrations that took place in or involved Singapore.[61] If such could be arranged, the benefits would be enormous. The Japanese would be uncertain as to how far British-American relations were united in opposing their expansion, and such uncertainty would cause hesitation and a reluctance to challenge such a coalition. Japan's belief in an undeclared and informal British-American alliance could have the calming effect necessary for some sort of stabilization in the region. Sir Robert Craigie, a long-time Foreign Office naval disarmament negotiator, former Head of the American Department, and by mid-1937 the British Ambassador to Japan, outlined the strategic value of that alignment of mental maps. Craigie acknowledged the difficulties inherent with the idea of permanently stationing capital ships in Singapore while the security situation in Europe continued to deteriorate, but he emphasized the need to create the image of Singapore as a dominant factor in the region, which would be easier done if capital ships were permanently based there. It was his view that "we must nevertheless be prepared to face a steady deterioration in our prestige and influence throughout the Far East unless we can do something more to sustain in this part of the world our position and responsibilities as the greatest naval Power."[62] Directly related to that centrality was, as Craigie observed, the link between the British maintenance of a strong presence and the growing importance of the United States in helping the United Kingdom maintain the balance of power in the Far East:

> A new and important factor which seems to justify a reconsideration of this problem [maintaining a viable naval presence in the Far

East while at the same time keeping sufficient naval forces in Europe] is the gratifying tendency in the United States to adopt a firmer policy in its relations not only with Germany but also with Japan. So far as Japan is concerned, the main check to this tendency will always be provided by the thought that America is being utilized to do the work which Great Britain should do for itself. The despatch of even one or two battle cruisers to the Far East, manifesting as it would our determination to play our own part in our own defence, would certainly have an encouraging effect in the United States and would, I suggest, weaken one of the most effective arguments of the isolationists.[63]

Further, from the strictly naval perspective, Craigie was convinced that any Japanese southward advance, because of the less isolationist attitude on the part of the Roosevelt Administration, would prompt an American response entailing sending the Pacific Fleet to Pearl Harbour. The Ambassador advised that such a deployment would be even more likely to occur if a small Royal Navy capital ship squadron was already in place in Singapore. Together, such a coincidence of the positioning of major naval units could deter any Japanese plans for an attack on British or Dutch possessions in the region.[64] However, the balance had to be struck between the desire of elements within both the British and American strategic foreign policy-making elites to use such coercive measures and the fear of others that such overt acts would drive Japan into the arms of Germany and Italy.

It was an imprecise science at best, this British manipulation of the American mental map concerning strategic foreign relations in the Far East. The ideas of joint exercises or American cruisers visiting Singapore in late 1937 and early 1938, in the wake of the Japanese attack on the USS *Panay*, were not carried out, even though the discussions and planning for such events did help highlight shortcomings in British-American coordination for any combined actions in the Far East.[65] Indeed, the U.S. Navy was reluctant to become involved too closely with any initiatives to do with Singapore, particularly regarding information sharing, for fear of the *quid pro quo* the British might expect. In October 1938, the U.S. Navy requested "for planning purposes" statistical data about the supply capability of Singapore. Because they possessed no similar operating base in the United States—San Francisco being in the developmental state at the time—the Americans were cautious in their request. Indeed, such caution was well placed, as the Admiralty approved the request, but only if Royal Navy members were allowed a tour of Pearl Harbour in return. The Americans refused to go along with the exchange, fearing domestic political and Japanese foreign policy reprisals as a result of the establishment of an uncomfortably visible and high level of information sharing.[66] However, the heightened tension in the region, as well as the worsening situation in Europe, prompted the British to offer the use of Singapore to the Americans in the event of any joint actions being required in early 1939. The Americans thereafter for the first time began to consider such a condition seriously.[67]

By the spring of 1939, British-American relations had reached the stage where tangible discussions regarding the use of Singapore by the U.S. Navy were a reality. In March of that year, the British Secretary of State for Foreign Affairs, Lord Halifax, instructed Lindsay to inquire if the United States government were willing to resume an exchange of naval views in a continuation of Captain Ingersoll's mission.[68] Halifax was anxious to have the Americans understand clearly that His Majesty's Government, if it were involved in any conflict in Europe, "might not be able at once to reinforce on a large scale their naval forces in the Far East, and that might affect U.S. naval dispositions."[69] The President was indeed anxious to have the talks resumed, but the open procedure of 1938 could not be repeated.[70] Fears of the press finding out about British-American naval cooperation demanded that the utmost secrecy be maintained. If word of such talks got out, the leak would compromise seriously the pending American neutrality legislation. FDR suggested that an officer ranking not higher than Captain be sent as the Naval Attaché to Washington to conduct the conversations.[71] Secret arrangements were made and the talks did take place, putting Singapore squarely on the table as a chip to be used by the British in the bidding for American support in the Far East.

The talks took place at the home of the new Chief of Naval Operations, Admiral William D. Leahy, on 12 June 1939, involving Leahy, Admiral R. L. Ghormley, Director of Plans, Captain Curzon-Howe, the British Naval Attaché in Washington and Commander T. C. Hampton, the Royal Navy representative sent over in disguise from the Admiralty. No one else, except Sumner Welles and President Roosevelt, knew anything about the talks. Hampton told the Americans that if Japan took aggressive action in the Far East, the Admiralty did not know when they would be able to send a fleet to the Far East, nor what the composition of such a fleet would be. This was a change from the talks held with Captain Ingersoll in 1938. Leahy told Hampton that it was his opinion that, if a war broke out in Europe, it was the President's intention to move the U.S. Fleet to Hawaii as a deterrent to Japan. That action would prevent the Japanese from attacking New Zealand and Australia, said the Chief of Naval Operations, but he agreed that the U.S. Navy was not in a position to conduct offensive operations against Japan itself. Questions about the distribution of signal books and cyphers were also brought up at this first meeting.[72] On 14 June, a second meeting was held, with the same participants. This time, Leahy and Ghormley told Hampton they were satisfied that the exchange of signal books and cyphers that had taken place would "enable all U.S. units to cooperate with British units throughout the world in case of necessity. Some further copies of signal books, codes and cyphers would be required as and when U.S. ships in reserve were brought forward."[73] Leahy then went on to explain his "personal views" of how the two fleets should cooperate in case of a war with Germany, Italy and Japan. The U.S. would concentrate on the Pacific and leave forces in the Atlantic as well. The U.S. Fleet would move to Singapore in sufficient force to defeat the Japanese Fleet, which it was believed would consist of a force of at least 10 capital ships. The Chief of Naval Operations was opposed to sending any weak or small force to Singapore. The size of the U.S. Fleet despatched, however, would depend on the size of fleet that the British were willing to send. American public opinion would not tolerate such actions by the U.S. Navy unless there was a suitable British force in the region as well. That British force did not have to be as large, but it had to be an "adequate token force" containing some capital ships. Ghormley told the British representatives that the American Plans Division was now working on a scheme for the movement of an American fleet to Singapore, as no such detailed plans had existed previously. As for the time needed to collect and transit such a fleet, Leahy informed Hampton that, if the British planned on the Americans relieving Singapore, it would take at least 120 days. The Chief of Naval Operations also suggested that any British units working with the Americans in the Far East should be placed under the strategic control of the American Commander-in-Chief, but did not press the point. Hampton told the American naval officers all he knew about the condition of Singapore in terms of docking and repair facilities, hinting that if the Americans based their fleet there, approximately 2,500 semi-skilled and skilled personnel and labourers would be required. In return, Hampton was informed that the U.S. Navy expected to fight for the Philippines but not hold them, and therefore would not base their fleet in the islands.[74] The talks ended quickly and quietly, as Hampton returned to the Admiralty to report his findings.

Hampton's conversations confirmed information the Foreign Office had been gathering for its assessment of possible American actions and reactions in the Pacific in the case of a general war in Europe. Many indicators pointed to the idea that the U.S. Navy would go to its base in Hawaii upon the outbreak of any such hostilities, acting as a clear deterrent to Japan.[75] From there, the American fleet would move to guard the Philippines, but in all likelihood would use Singapore as the staging area, a concept confirmed by Hampton's talks in the United States. The Foreign Office view was that any war in the Far East would be a British-American affair, "as the present Chief of Naval Operations has stated that he does not consider it likely that the United States would be at war with Japan without the United Kingdom being equally at war with the Japanese, this perhaps explains why the Navy Department do not seem particularly nervous about fortifying Guam."[76] British Naval and Air Attaché reports from Tokyo confirmed the unsuitability of Guam as a forward base of operations for the Americans. They too emphasized the point that efforts had to be made by the British naval and air authorities to prepare Singapore for cooperation with U.S. forces.[77] The outbreak of a general war in Europe brought those hypothetical plans into stark reality in September 1939. Moving forward in time a year, the changes in the situation caused by the war become evident.

By November 1940, the U.S. Navy was in possession of a detailed and extensive amount of information regarding Singapore, its capabilities, capacity and suitability for supporting the U.S. Pacific Fleet.[78] The information Commander Hampton relayed about the need for the U.S. Navy to bring along its own skilled labour force was still a valid concern for the use of Singapore by the American fleet, as the U.S. Navy Strategic Planning report pointed out: *"There will be a serious shortage of skilled labor and supervisors upon any increased demand of output, and no foreseen source of supply. They will expect us to supply it if we make use of the base."*[79] As well, the United Kingdom and the United States were already discussing areas of responsibility and command in any general world war, with the Pacific being the area of the main American efforts. Four months after the Strategic Planning report was published, with British senior military officers in the United States briefing the American service chiefs, State Department and politicians, the worth of Singapore, in the American view, had lessened. Royal Navy Admiral Roger Bellairs reported that the U.S. service chiefs "considered retention of Singapore as 'very desirable' and that its loss would be 'unfortunate' but they hold that its loss 'would not have a decisive effect on the issue of the war'."[80] For the Americans, due to the realities of the war in Europe and fears of a British defeat and the subsequent need to protect the territories of the United States itself, a new policy was needed. The American strategic policy-making elite decided to rule out the possibility of sending American capital ships to Singapore.[81] It appeared that British-American relations and the place of Singapore in that relationship had come full circle.

So, what was the value of Singapore in British-American Far Eastern strategic foreign relations? It is clear that, without a continued commitment to providing for its own defence in the region, the United Kingdom would have lost an already questionable potential ally, the United States. A British failure to portray a strong presence, no matter what the technical reality of that presence, in the Far East, to be seen to be unwilling to invest in the military power required to defend its imperial interests, would have been the signal for the United States to move along an even more unilateral path. In the aftermath of Munich, British resolve and determination to meet aggression with force was a key concern and question in the minds of American strategic planners.[82] Reports from Washington in early 1939 indicated that the American strategic foreign policy-making elite had begun to take greater notice of European affairs instead of the normal priority placed on Far Eastern matters. However, the British Embassy in Washington also warned that this did not mean the Far East and the ongoing problems in that region were ever far from the minds of Roosevelt's administration. This meant that under no circumstances could the British afford to give the Americans any reason to believe there was some British-Japanese arrangement inconsistent with British obligations under the Nine Power Treaty.[83] Indeed, the entire imperial defence system could perhaps be said to hinge on British ability to keep the Americans onside:

> ...if a crisis were to arise in which a genuine threat to Singapore by the Japanese Navy were to develop, I believe that such a suggestion when it became public might call forth a reaction in this country of sufficient strength to make it clear to the Japanese that the United States could not stand idly by.... As long as the Japanese think there is a better than an even chance of the United States taking part in a world war, they are not likely to risk it, and if the Japanese will not risk it, there is a very good chance that Rome and Berlin will not risk it either.[84]

This opinion was widely shared.

The Royal Navy, the other half of the British strategic foreign policy-making team most responsible for the maintenance of British-American relations in the Far East, concurred with the views being expressed by the British embassies in Tokyo and Washington.[85] They considered the deterrent effect of the mental map of Japan containing the perception of close British-American naval operations to be a most useful state of affairs and wished to sustain it.[86] The symbol of Singapore kept the issue of the British role in the Far East at the forefront of American appreciations of the situation in that region, thus making the option of a British-American naval solution a viable, if not always desirable, one. Any decision to cancel the Singapore base program or to decrease its capacity or capabilities would have suggested to a suspicious and wary State Department and U.S. Navy that its mental map needed redrawing, that Perfidious Albion was not a horse worth backing. As well, the ability of British strategic foreign policy to utilize the uncertainty in the Japanese mental map about the state of British-American relations would have lost a great deal of its deterrent effect had Singapore not been given emphasis. The evidence for this can be seen in the Japanese lack of action between September 1939 and December 7 1941.

The role of Singapore was to be a symbol of British resolve and capability. Without the symbolism provided by Singapore, the American move towards closer informal and formal means of cooperating with the British in Far Eastern matters prior to any actual Japanese attack might, in the face of isolationist pressures, have been unattainable. Therefore, even though the eventual story of Singapore was one of defeat and failure, it should be kept in perspective. Closer British-American ties were in good part both a product of the existence of Singapore and one of its strategic legacies. That strategic legacy helped ensure a coalition that would eventually reverse the operational defeat that was the fall of Singapore.

Greg Kennedy is Lecturer at the Defence Studies Department, King's College, London, based at the Joint Services Command and Staff College in Schrivenham. He is the author of Anglo-American Strategic Relations and the Far East, 1933–1939, *and has published widely on strategic foreign policy issues, maritime defence, disarmament, diplomacy and intelligence, including, co-editing with Keith Neilson*, Far Flung Lines: Studies in Imperial Defence in Honour of Donald Mackenzie Schurman.

NOTES—

1 The Washington Treaty has been dealt with in detail in many places. One of the best starting points for tracing Singapore's development and utility from the beginning is E. Goldstein and J. Maurer (eds.), "Special Issue on the Washington Conference, 1921–22: Naval Rivalry, East Asian Stability and the Road to Pearl Harbor," *Diplomacy and Statecraft*, 4, 1993.

2 Two of the best works, with extensive bibliographies listing the other works which are pertinent for this essay, are M. H. Murfett, J. N. Miksic, B. P. Farrell and Chiang M. S., *Between Two Oceans: A Military History of Singapore From First Settlement to Final British Withdrawal*, Singapore, 1999; A. Warren, *Singapore: Britain's Greatest Defeat*, Singapore, 2002.

3 For British-American Pacific relations, see I. Cowman, *Dominion or Decline: Anglo-American Naval Relations in the Pacific, 1937–1941*, Dulles, 1996; D. Reynolds, *The Creation of the Anglo-American Alliance: A Study in Competitive Cooperation*, London, 1981.

4 For British-American naval relations and the cruiser question, see G. Kennedy, "The 1930 London Naval Conference and Anglo-American Maritime Strength, 1927–1930," in B. J. C. McKercher (ed.), *Arms Limitation and Disarmament*, New York, 1992, 149–72.

5 G. Kennedy, *Anglo-American Strategic Relations and the Far East, 1933–1939*, London, 2002; idem., "Depression and Security: Aspects Influencing the US Navy During the Hoover Administration," *Diplomacy and Statecraft*, 6, July 1995.

6 For War Plan Orange, see E. S. Millar, *War Plan Orange: The U.S. Strategy to Defeat Japan, 1897–1945*, Annapolis, 1991; National Archives, Washington, D.C. [hereafter

NA], *Strategic Planning in the U.S. Navy: Its Evolution and Execution, 1891–1945*, Navy Basic Plan-Orange, Vol. IV, on microfilm.
7   A. P. N. Erdmann, "Mining for the Corporate Synthesis: Gold in American Foreign Economic Policy, 1931–1936," *Diplomatic History*, 17, 1993, 171–200; A. Booth, *British Economic Policy, 1931–49*, London, 1989, 1–43; J. Nichols, "Roosevelt's Monetary Diplomacy in 1933," in *American Historical Review*, 56, 1988, 295–317; P. Clavin, *The Failure of Economic Diplomacy: Britain, Germany, France and the United States, 1931–36*, London, 1996.
8   Public Record Office (PRO) [All FO records cited are held at the PRO], Foreign Office (FO), 371/16618/5992/5992/45, letter from Hoare to Vansittart, 11 August 1933.
9   Ibid., P. M. Roberts minute, 12 August 1933; D. V. Kelly minute, 18 August 1933.
10 FO371/16618/5992/5992/45, Roberts minute, 12 August 1933.
11 FO371/16618/7875/7875/45, Roberts minute, 6 November 1933.
12 FO371/16598/4601/6/45, Craigie minutes, 17 June 1933; FO371/16598/5308/6/45, Naval Attaché's report, Capt. Dewar, 18 June, and Vansittart and Wellesley minutes, 29 June 1933; letter from FDR to Rev. Malcolm E. Peabody, in E. B. Nixon (ed.), *Franklin D. Roosevelt and Foreign Affairs*, Vol. I, Cambridge, Mass., 1969, 370; FO371/16618/8168/7875/45, Gore-Booth, 14 November 1933; FO371/16618/7875/45, Robert L. Craigie minute, 8 November 1933.
13 FO371/16618/8313/7875/45, Gore-Booth memo, 3 November 1933.
14 Ibid.
15 The catalyst for the creation of the Defence Requirements Sub-Committee (DRC) is found in Imperial Defence Policy, Annual Review for 1932 by the Chiefs of Staff Sub-Committee, 466–68, and The Far Eastern Situation, memorandum by Chatfield 25 February 1933, prepared for the 107th Meeting, Chiefs of Staff Sub-Committee, CID, 28 February 1933, both in N. Tracy (ed.), *The Collective Naval Defence of the Empire, 1900–1940*, Navy Records Society, 1997. For the complete story of the DRC, see Keith Neilson's forthcoming article in *English Historical Review*, March 2003. PRO, ADM167/88, Minutes of Admiralty Board Meetings, 7 December 1933.
16 For discussions in the Admiralty concerning size, capacity and strategic importance, see: Naval Situation in the Far East, Memorandum by the Admiralty for the War Cabinet, 21 October 1919; Singapore, Development of as Naval Base, Memorandum, by the Overseas Sub-Committee of the CID, summary, signed by Samuel Herbert Wilson, Assistant Secretary of CID, 7 June, 1921; Empire Naval Policy, Brief Summary of the Recommendations by the Admiralty, copy, Admiralty, 11 July, 1921; Minute by Capt. Barry Domvile, Director of Plans Division, War in the Far East, for the Deputy Chief of Naval Staff [Vice-Admiral Sir Roger Keyes], 3 November 1921, all in N. Tracy, *The Collective Naval Defence of the Empire*; PRO, ADM116/2581, Admiralty Case 2052-v.1, Singapore Naval Base, 1937–1930 and ADM116/3112, Singapore Defence, 1932; ADM167/88, Minutes of meetings for 22 June, 1933; ADM1/27408, Defence of Singapore, 1931–32.
17 PRO, CAB2/6, Minutes of the Meetings of the Committee of Imperial Defence, 261st Meeting, 6 November 1933.

18 Ibid., comments by Sir John Simon, Secretary of State for Foreign Affairs.
19 G. Kennedy, *Anglo-American Strategic Relations and the Far East*, ch.1.
20 PRO, CAB4/22, CID Papers, Series B, Secret, Paper 1111, The Policy of Japan, 6 June, 1933 and Paper 1112, Imperial Defence Policy, 12 October 1933.
21 FO371/16618/7875/7875/45, Roberts minute, 6 November 1933.
22 FO371/16610/8770/60/45, Craigie minute, 3 December 1933; FO371/16612/9235/252/45, Vansittart minute, 15 December 1933; FO371/16618/7537/5819/45, Snow despatch, 17 October 1933.
23 G. Kennedy, "1935: A Snapshot of British Imperial Defence in the Far East," in K. Neilson and G. Kennedy (eds.), *Far Flung Lines: Essays on Imperial Defence in Honour of Donald Mackenzie Schurman*, London, 1997.
24 FO371/16618/8576/8576/45, Admiralty note to FO, 28 November 1933. This visit never materialized due to the FO's anger over American preparations for the 1935 London Naval Conference. Objections raised by Vansittart, who wanted to send a strong message to the U.S. about British lack of enthusiasm for its naval negotiation tactics, held the day. See FO371/17593/785/785/45, Vansittart minute, 24 January 1934.
25 FO371/16612/9235/252/45, Vansittart minute, 15 December 1933.
26 *Foreign Relations of the United States: Diplomatic Papers* [hereafter FRUS], Vol. I, General, memo Grew to Hull, 26 July, 1933, 380.
27 FRUS, Vol. III, The Far East, Hornbeck to Castle, 10 January 1933, 43.
28 FRUS, Vol. III, The Far East, memo by Hornbeck, 16 May 1933.
29 Franklin D. Roosevelt Private Secretary Files [hereafter FDR-PSF], Presidential Library, Hyde Park, New York, Folder Navy, Harry Roosevelt, letter from Upham to Standley, 4 February 1934.
30 Ibid.
31 Ibid.
32 For the full study of this issue, see G. Kennedy, *Anglo-American Strategic Relations and the Far East*, chs. 4 and 5.
33 Stanley Baldwin Papers [hereafter Baldwin Papers], University Library, Cambridge, 131, untitled memo by MacDonald of conversation with Norman Davis and Atherton, 5 March 1934.
34 Robert W. Bingham Diary [hereafter Bingham Diary], Library of Congress, Washington D.C., entry for 1 March 1934; PRO, MacDonald MSS, 30/69/1753, MacDonald Diary (Large) [hereafter MacDonald Diary], entry for 4 March 1934; FO371/17596/1938/1938/45, record of conversation, 5 March 1934; FRUS, Vol. I, telegram from Bingham to Hull, 5 March 1934, 222.
35 FRUS, Vol. I, memo from Davis to FDR, 6 March 1934, 22–30; see also Confidential US State Department Central Files [hereafter CSDCF] 741.94/32, despatch from Atherton to Hull, 16 March 1934.
36 FO371/16618/5992/5992/45, Roberts minute, 12 August, 1933; FO371/17576/17/17/45, Craigie minute, 1 January 1934, Wellesely minute, 10 January 1934.
37 FO371/16610/1428/89/45, Haigh memo, 22 February 1933 and accompanying minutes by Craigie, Wellesely and Vansittart.

38 FO371/16611/7649/89/45, Craigie minutes, 23 October 1933; FO 371/16610/1428/89/45, Haigh memo, 22 February 1933.
39 FRUS, Vol. III, The Far East, despatch from Grew to Hull, 12 December 1933, 479.
40 Ibid.
41 FRUS, Vol. III, The Far East, despatch from Grew to Hull, 31 August, 1933, 706; Records of the Strategic Plans Division of the Office of the Chief of Naval Operations [hereafter SPD-CNO], Naval Historical Center, Washington Navy Yard, Washington D.C., Miscellaneous Subject Files, 1917–1947, Box 39, Bases and Base Force Projects, 25 March 1935; SPD-CNO, Box 53 Joint Estimate of the Situation, Blue-Red and Orange, 27 March 1935.
42 G. Kennedy, *Anglo-American Strategic Relations and the Far East*, chs. 4 and 5.
43 FO371/17576/857/17/45, despatch from Lindsay, 19 January 1934.
44 FO371/17588/424/424/45, despatch from Lindsay, 3 January 1934.
45 FO371/17576/2319/17/45, confidential memo, 2 March 1934.
46 FO371/17576/3702/17/45, memo by Gore-Booth and accompanying minutes, 11 May 1934.
47 PRO, CAB2/6, Minutes of 266th meeting of CID, 22 November 1934.
48 For the 1936 London Naval Conference and Anglo-American considerations of Japan's position, see G. Kennedy, *Anglo-American Strategic Relations and the Far East*, chs. 4 and 5.
49 PRO, CAB2/6, Minutes of the 270th meeting of CID, 11 July, 1935; CAB2/6, Minutes of the 271st meeting of CID, 14 October 1935; CAB5/8, CID Papers, Series C, Secret, Paper 408, Singapore: Acceleration of Provision of Defences, 9 July 1935, Paper 409, Singapore Defences, 23 September 1935, Paper 412, Singapore Defences, 20 November 1935.
50 Stanley K. Hornbeck Papers [hereafter Hornbeck Papers], Hoover Institute, Stanford University, Chronological Day File (CDF), Box 456, Folder March–May 1937, letter from Hornbeck to Ray Atherton [*Chargé d'Affairs* US Embassy in London], 1 March 1937.
51 C. Thorne, *The Limits of Foreign Policy: The West, the League and the Far Eastern Crisis of 1931–1933*, London, and New York, 1972.
52 On the role of Hornbeck in the creation of Anglo-American Far Eastern strategic relations, see G. Kennedy, *Anglo-American Strategic Relations and the Far East*, ch. 6.
53 FDR-PSF, Folder Japan, record of meeting between Hull, Phillips, Dunn, Hornbeck, Moffat, Standley, Assistant Secretary of the Navy, Roosevelt and Admiral Greenslade, 26 September 1934.
54 Hornbeck Papers, CDF, Box 454, Folder September–December 1934, letter from Hornbeck to Hull, 31 December 1934.
55 Hornbeck Papers, Box 454, Folder September–December 1934, Hornbeck memo, Far East: United States Policy: Desiderata, 17 November 1934.
56 Ibid.
57 Hornbeck Papers, Box 454, Folder January–April 1935, Hornbeck memo, Relations Between the United States and Countries of the Far East—Especially Japan—in 1935, 3 January 1935.

58 Ibid.
59 Hornbeck Papers, Box 454, Folder January–April 1935, record of conversation between Hornbeck and Lord Lytton on The Far Eastern Situation and Problems Presented Thereby, 11 February 1935.
60 FRUS, Vol. III, telegram from Norman Davis to Hull, 2 November 1937, 145–147; N. H. Hooker (ed.), *The Moffat Papers*, Cambridge, 1956, 162–65.
61 The first suggested use of a base in furthering British-American strategic relations came from retired Admiral Sir Lewis Bayly, who suggested to the Admiralty that Malta and Gibraltar's facilities be offered for the use of the American Squadron in the Mediterranean for free. The Admiralty were very keen to do so, saying that, "In view of the value of Anglo-American co-operation in the cause of world peace and the effect on world opinion which would result from any evidence of such co-operation even though the co-operation remains 'unwritten,' My Lords warmly support Admiral Sir Lewis Bayly's proposal..." FO371/20662/5298/228/45, Admiralty memo, 26 July 1937. The FO were willing to go along with the idea, but cautioned against overuse of the propaganda generated from such a gesture due to backlash in America or Japan that could arise. See FO371/20662/6519/228/45, Cadogan minute, 9 September 1937.
62 *Documents on British Foreign Policy 1919–1939* [hereafter DBFP], Third Series, Vol. VIII, despatch from Craigie to Halifax, 14 December 1938, 320.
63 Ibid., 321.
64 Ibid.
65 I. Cowman, *Dominion or Decline*, 133, n. 63; Hornbeck Papers, CDF, Box 457, Folder January 1938, note from Hornbeck to Hull, 4 January 1938; ibid., Folder February 1938, letter from Hornbeck to Hull, 1 February 1938; William D. Leahy Diary, Library of Congress, entry for 28 November 1937.
66 NA, RG 38, CNO-LNA, Box 11 Folder: Singapore Supply Facilities, letter from DNO to U.S. Naval Attaché in London, 30 June 1938; ibid., letter from DNI to U.S. Naval Attaché in London, 19 October 1938.
67 L. Pratt, "The Anglo-American Naval Conversations on the Far East", *International Affairs*, 47, 1971, 745–63.
68 Ibid.
69 FO371/23560/F2879/456/23, telegram from FO to Lindsay, 19 March 1939.
70 On the Ingersoll Mission, see D. Reynolds, *The Creation of the Anglo-American Alliance*, 60.
71 FO371/23560/2880/456/23, telegram from Lindsay to FO, 21 March 1939.
72 FO371/23561/F7010/456/23, most secret report of meeting held on 12 June 1939.
73 FO371/23561/F7010/456/23, most secret report of meeting held on 14 June 1939.
74 Ibid.
75 FO371/22829/2122/1292/45, Lindsay to FO, 3 March 1939.
76 Ibid.
77 FO371/22830/4619/1292/45, attaché reports, 19 May 1939.
78 SPD-CNO, Box 71, British Empire—Singapore—Naval Base, 23 November 1940.
79 Ibid., emphasized in the original.

80 FO371/26219/1134/384/45, telegram from Halifax to FO, 24 February 1941.
81 Ibid.
82 DBFP, Third Series, Vol. VIII, despatch from Mallet (First Secretary at British Embassy in Washington) to Halifax, 16 February 1939, 447–51.
83 Ibid.
84 Ibid.
85 The issue of the vital strategic relations between the two Treasuries and their officials is acknowledged but not dealt with here. See G. Kennedy, "Neville Chamberlain" in T. G. Otte (ed.), *Makers of British Foreign Policy*, Basingstoke, 2001; idem., "'The Rat in Power': Neville Chamberlain's View of Roosevelt's Administration, 1932–1934," *Diplomacy and Statecraft*, 1, 2002.
86 DBFP, Third Series, Vol. VIII, Appendix I, letter from the FO to the Admiralty, 13 February 1939, letter from J. H. Phillips (Admiralty), 29 March 1939 which is enclosed in letter from Mr. Nigel Ronald to Sir Robert Craigie, 13 April 1939, 542–50; PRO, CAB80/3, War Cabinet, Chiefs of Staff Sub-Committee, Memoranda, Secret Paper COS(39) 52, Sino-Japanese Hostilities, 28 September 1939.

CHAPTER 4

Disaster Foreseen? France and the Fall of Singapore

by Martin Thomas

French decision-makers in Paris and Hanoi were never convinced by the "main fleet to Singapore" idea. Their doubts predated the outbreak of war in Europe in 1939 and were only confirmed after it. Metropolitan defence planners and colonial administrators in French Indochina had unique insights into British Far Eastern strategy. As entente partners and eventual allies, the French General Staff, first under General Maxime Weygand and then, from 1936, under General Maurice Gamelin, was always engaged by the consequences of British defence planning for France's preparations for war. And as a client colonial regime acutely exposed to Japanese expansionism, the Hanoi Government-General had a vested interest in the successful completion of the Singapore base. This essay factors the Singapore naval base into French defensive preparations in Indochina and Southeast Asia before and after the advent of the Vichy regime.

Japan's incursion into French Indochina in September 1940 was the first fruit of the policy of southward advance adopted by the Supreme Command Government Liaison Conference on 27 July. The subsequent deployment of Japanese forces in southern Indochina on 28 July 1941 marked "the fateful step" towards war with the United States and the United Kingdom. These moves followed sustained diplomatic coercion of the Vichy government and its colonial administration under Admiral Jean Decoux in Hanoi.[1] Decoux's submission to Japanese threats was hardly collaboration to match Vichy's deeper ties with Nazi Germany. Indeed, many scholars have been indulgent towards the Vichyite *modus vivendi* with Japan, even though Franco-Japanese cooperation enabled Decoux's staff to apply a uniquely racialized version of Vichy's *Révolution Nationale* to the hapless populations of Vietnam and Cambodia in particular.² All the while, the Hanoi administration was manifestly isolated and outgunned. It lacked airpower or any prospect of reinforcement. Its first priority was the long-term preservation of French colonial interest in Indochina. With this objective in view, French colonial units resisted initial Japanese incursions around Langson in northern Tonkin in September 1940. French forces even briefly defied the Japanese in a final doomed confrontation during the *Meigo Sakusan*—the Japanese takeover in Indochina in March 1945.³

International historians tend to assess the wartime hardships endured by the indigenous populations of Indochina through a geo-strategic prism of Japanese economic plunder. Here they follow historical precedent. Even Rooseveltian anti-colonialists critical of French rule in Vietnam laid the blame for the devastating Vietnamese famine of 1944-45 at Japan's door. Those more interested in French imperialism and Vietnamese popular resistance place the breakdown of colonial control in its local setting, linking it to Decoux's adaptation of *Révolution Nationale* policies and the emergence of the Vietminh coalition in 1941.⁴ None, however, dispute the fact that Vichy's enforced accommodation with Japan resulted from extreme military exposure. If the Vichy authorities in Hanoi had no choice other than compromise with Japan before Pearl Harbour, does this tell us anything about the Vichy perspective on the defence of Singapore? Did Vichy France anticipate a Japanese new order in Southeast Asia much as it expected a Nazi-dominated Europe? And how far did Vichy mark a significant departure in French strategic thinking anyway?

Long before its defeat by Germany, France's imperial defence planning was devised in anticipation of the "Singapore strategy's" failure. This, it appears, was as much the result of the very different military cultures in which French and British strategic planning occurred as it was of detailed French assessment of the progress of Singapore's defences. The "blue water" imperialism that informed British grand strategy found little echo in Paris. In spite of the vast scale of the French overseas empire, prewar strategic planning was consumed by the requirements of land defence against Germany. By the time French rearmament began in earnest in 1936, the General Staff considered Far Eastern imperial defence an unaffordable luxury. With their continental priorities much in mind, French military planners and intelligence analysts viewed the "Singapore strategy" with a combination of reasoned pessimism and mounting alarm.

French Perceptions of the Singapore Naval Base, 1920–39

For many of the French expatriates, business and tourist travellers, naval officers and colonial *fonctionnaires* that passed through Singapore in the interwar years, the port was *la plus belle colonie* of the British Empire.[5] The French presence in Singapore was substantial. Two French-controlled banks, the *Banque d'Indochine* and the *Banque Industrielle de Chine*, served the Chinese community, the luxury tourist trade, and, above all, French commercial interests across Southeast Asia. France consistently featured among the top four importers of Malayan rubber and tin. The Michelin Rubber Company, the dominant corporate power in the plantation system of Cochin China, was also a leading commercial investor in the Malayan economy. French naval vessels, merchant ships and liners en route between France, Saigon and Haiphong were frequent visitors to the port. Colonial bureaucrats from Saigon, Phnom Penh and Hanoi often sojourned in Singapore: The richest used it as a stopping-off point in their journey back to France, the poorest chose it as an affordable alternative to the long voyage home. French naval and colonial Army officers travelling to and from Vietnam were also welcomed at the port, provided that they took their shore leave unarmed. In the early 1920s, the five Catholic Churches in Singapore, the city's convent school, the Penang Seminary College, and the Catholic missions in Malaya were entirely staffed by French priests and nuns of the *Ordre des Dames de Saint Maur*. Two of the city's hotels prided themselves on their French head chefs, and the port fire brigade was, for a time, directed by a Frenchman.[6]

French commercial and cultural interest in Singapore was matched by a preoccupation with British imperial security. French governments drew on a wide range of human intelligence sources and their own parallel experience to assess the progress of Singapore's defences in the 20 years preceding 1942. Their own Mediterranean base modernization programme raised comparable difficulties of long-term expenditure, adequate defence in depth, as well as fuel and munitions stockpiling. Crucially, in 1930–31 the Tunisian port of Bizerta, hitherto the principal French fleet base on the southern Mediterranean perimeter, was downgraded in favour of the more westerly Algerian port of Oran. The Naval Staff's plans section concluded that the threat of coordinated Italian land and air attacks on Bizerta rendered it untenable as a main fleet base.[7] Unbeknown to the French, the British Cabinet's standing defence sub-committee had proposed a similar recommendation in 1919, suggesting abandoning Hong Kong as a main fleet base and concentrating on Singapore.[8]

French naval intelligence advised the Ministry of Marine in November 1923 that four British navy officers had worked incognito in Singapore for over a year readying plans for initial base construction. Additional intelligence regarding fuel stores, oil terminals, and road and rail improvements was sent direct to the French General Staff.⁹ Information such as this, typically gathered from local informants and French visitors to the port, exemplified the patchwork of intelligence on which Paris relied for evidence about the early stages of Singapore's defensive modernization. Direct liaison with British planners was rare. In a decade of virtually continuous defensive retrenchment, much of it formally required under the disarmament provisions of the 1922 Washington Naval Treaty, the British and French naval staffs were largely consumed by the annual inter-departmental contests over naval estimates. From 1921 to 1927, First Sea Lord Admiral David Earl Beatty struggled with cost-cutting governments and Chief of Air Staff, Sir Hugh Trenchard, to safeguard a Singapore base programme founded on deployment of a battleship fleet and coastal artillery batteries rather than powerful air defences. The French Naval Staff fought similar bureaucratic battles in their efforts to ensure continued naval supremacy over Italy after the crippling limitations imposed on French naval construction at Washington.¹⁰ The deep-rooted imperial antagonism of an earlier era quickly supplanted the more transient cooperation of wartime military alliance.¹¹ The rivalries and suspicions that marred Franco-British imperial relations in the early 1920s ebbed in the following decade. From Palestine to Singapore, imperial collaboration increased as colonial dissent and threats of external invasion intensified. Reciprocal inspection visits between regional French and British colonial commands became commonplace. But French knowledge about the progress of the Singapore defence works remained incomplete.

From 1932, French governments had three principal sources of information regarding Singapore. The first were the military intelligence personnel of the Indochina command's *Deuxième Bureau*, a small group of specialist colonial Army officers that compiled regular assessments of internal and external threats to French colonial rule. These were locally distributed to French regional commanders and to the Governor-General's *Cabinet Militaire* in Hanoi. After preliminary collation and analysis in Hanoi, *Deuxième Bureau* intelligence summaries were also sent to the colonial Army inspectorate in the Ministry of Colonies and to the *Section Coloniale* in the Ministry of War. A second source of local intelligence was the French consulate in Singapore. It generally transmitted correspondence direct to the Foreign Ministry's Asian Division. Consular reports of military activity were also sent to the *Section Coloniale*. The third and final key source of information was the French service attachés occasionally invited to view the port's defences. Their analyses were distributed among all three French service ministries.

None of these information providers had regular or unrestricted access to all defensive works or British strategic plans. The Hanoi *Deuxième Bureau* concentrated instead on British budgetary allocation, force strengths, native recruitment, and training exercises. French War Ministry staff were in turn primarily interested in Singapore's fixed defences, the completion of the Tengah air base, and the quality of air cover in general.[12] Consular staff tracked the obvious signs of defensive preparation, notably the reinforcement of the garrison from 1937 and the completion of a string of military air bases between Penang and Johore.[13] Naval observers inevitably focused on the progress of the port dry dock, the central element in Singapore's capacity to serve as an autonomous fleet base.

French colonial officials and economic analysts also studied the social structure and the economic organization of Malaya and Singapore. These observers were envious of Singapore's trading prosperity, whatever their reservations about its defensibility. Buoyant demand for Malaya's strategic raw materials ensured a balance of payments surplus that Indochina would never rival. Yet the comparative wealth of British Malaya fed French bewilderment about the neglect of Singapore's land defences.[14] Surely the population of a wealthy colony prone to attack could be taxed more heavily or, if need be, trained as auxiliary forces to ensure its protection?

Over the summer of 1938, the French government invited public subscriptions to an Indochina Defence Loan. The proceeds were allocated to the fortification of Vietnamese coastal defences and the recruitment of some 20,000 additional colonial troops. Subscribers in the colony of Cochin China provided over 10 million of the 33 million *piastres* raised.[15] French recourse to public loan issues to help fund imperial defence was a well-established practice by the late 1930s. But the *dirigiste* impulses of Colonial Ministry planners and the French tradition of centralized coordination of imperial defence by federal colonial governments did not translate easily to the British Empire. French colonial administration was more visibly militaristic. The Ministry of Colonies maintained its own general staff to coordinate imperial planning for Indochina and sub-Saharan Africa. French colonial officials commonly defended military service and forced labour obligations as part of the overall taxation burden imposed on colonial populations. Whatever the claims of economic modernization, and the celebrations of imperial unity in defence of *la plus grande France*, the exploitative nature of French colonialism remained blatantly transparent.[16]

The French Empire on the eve of war had a more strongly martial aspect than at any point since the initial imperial conquests. The French public took solace in the thought that colonial manpower and resources might narrow the demographic and industrial gap between France and Nazi Germany. Parliamentary resolve to protect French imperial possessions was unanimous.[17] In French West Africa, for example, in 1938–39, the military pomp of armistice commemoration also infused the more ecumenical Bastille Day celebrations on 14 July.[18] These ceremonies revealed another facet of French perceptions about the Empire's defensive contribution—its African orientation. French Africa alone seemed clearly defensible. And French Africa was home to the most admired martial races of the Empire. Troops from North and West Africa had been tested to the limit in the trench warfare of 1914–18. The Vietnamese in France during the First World War were more readily identifiable with civilian labour than frontline combat. And these war workers were victims of widespread racial violence in supposedly "colour-blind France."[19] Eugenic ideas and their military offspring, martial race theory, still informed War Ministry evaluations of colonial forces in the interwar period. The generally low opinion of Vietnamese fighting quality only reinforced the Africanist orientation in imperial defence planning. By 1939, Edouard Daladier's administration looked set to return to the mass conscription of indigenous colonial troops adopted by Clemenceau's government a generation earlier. Behind the parliamentary rhetoric and the new colonial levies, the fact remained that French imperial preparations for war were overwhelmingly concentrated on defence of the metropole and its maritime approaches. The net movement in forces was from the colonies to France, not the other way round.[20]

British colonial investment in South and Southeast Asia was of a different magnitude altogether. In this context, it seemed stranger still that the British had neither raised additional levies in Malaya and Singapore nor significantly increased the tax burden on the indigenous population to fund extra defences. Evidently, the French Ministry of Colonies chose to ignore the donations made by the Sultans of Malaya to help fund the acceleration of defensive works and the maintenance of two RAF squadrons between 1935–37.[21] Nor was the War Ministry *Deuxième Bureau* impressed by information from the Singapore Consulate regarding the recruitment from the non-European population of a fortress company of Royal Engineers to man fixed gun emplacements. The obvious retort that reinforcement from India could be quickly accomplished did not dispel French concerns that Singapore did not have the fixed or mobile defences in place to withstand sustained overland attack.[22]

The British, it seemed, had put all their eggs in the "main fleet" basket. An 18-page profile of the Singapore base, submitted to War Ministry intelligence staff in late February 1938, concluded as follows:

> In sum, however well-organized it may be, the Singapore base is only one element in the overall security of this rich British colony. It would be pointless to have constructed it were the British not in a position, in case of danger, to make it the defensive support for a very powerful fleet.[23]

Six months later in October 1938, the Army Staff's colonial section was altogether more pessimistic. Faced with a spate of Japanese victories over Chinese forces in the Wuhan campaign, its advice on possible British-French cooperation in imperial defence was unequivocal:

> The defence of Indochina and of Singapore form a single whole. It is certain, whatever the attitude of Siam, that the great British base will be close to collapse [près de sa perte] the day that Indochina falls into the hands of the Japanese.

French Imperial Defence Assessments

During the interwar years, Admiral Raoul Castex, former Commander of the French North Atlantic fleet, was the most influential strategist of French imperial defence. He was widely recognized as the pre-eminent theorist of maritime warfare within the upper echelons of the naval command. Castex was ultimately appointed by Edouard Daladier to head the newly established Defence Studies College (*Collège des Hautes Etudes de Défense*).[24] In his five-volume study, *Théories stratégiques*, published between 1927 and 1935, Castex insisted that French naval resources should be devoted to the preservation of Atlantic, Mediterranean and African interests. The Pacific was beyond the reach of French naval power; the defence of Indochina *une chimère absolue*.[25] Castex's viewpoint mirrored the thinking within the Army Staff, whose entire strategy hinged on withstanding an expected German onslaught. In the words of Deputy Chief of Staff, General Alphonse Georges, "the colonies would be defended on the Rhine."[26] Admiral François Darlan was also alert to Castex's views, and to the testing responsibilities of Empire protection. As Naval Commander in Algeria in August 1930, Darlan oversaw the initial extension of the Mer el-Kébir fleet base. As head of the advisory staff to Minister of Marine François Piétri in March 1934, he refined strategic plans for naval war against Italy and Germany that left no scope for Far Eastern operations. And as Chief of Naval Staff in April 1939, he warned against extended Far Eastern commitments that could not be fulfilled.[27]

It was against the background of Castex's influential writing and the imminent replacement of senior figures within the French Army and Naval Staffs that on 1 October 1935 Colonel Henri Roux, French Military Attaché in Bangkok, submitted the most influential prewar report on the defence of Singapore. Roux was no ordinary official. He was the former Head of the Army's secret intelligence service, the *Section de Renseignements*.[28] Backed by a wealth of specialist expertise and a formidable reputation as a strategic analyst, Roux's opinion demanded respect. His 45-page report was based on a tour of inspection that included informal discussions with the GOC, General Lewin, and his two subordinate commanders on station in Singapore. It was distributed to all three Service Ministries and the Indochina command. Roux made three main observations. First, he acknowledged that the modernization of the Singapore base was predicated on a wider defensive scheme covering British interests in Southeast Asia. Second, he recognized that garrison strength and stockpiles of strategic raw materials had to be sufficient to withstand the interval between the beginning of hostilities and the naval reinforcement of the base. Above all, he warned that the entire scheme hinged on the location and scale of fixed defences.[29]

In sum, the attaché was unconvinced. The most "salient fact" was that British defensive organization was based on rigid assumptions about the direction and scale of likely attack. According to Roux, the expectation that enemy landings were most likely on the eastern side of Singapore island stemmed from rudimentary assessment of local topography, suitable beaches in particular, rather than from detailed evaluation of Japanese offensive capability. Most alarming was the lack of defence in depth on the Malayan mainland. Ultimately, defence of the base rested on the success of naval and air operations in keeping a determined attacker at a safe distance from Singapore island. Roux was unimpressed by the uncertainty among General Lewin's staff about whether Japan would attack the Netherlands East Indies prior to striking at Singapore. Insufficient importance was attached to Thailand's vital role as help or hindrance to British plans.[30]

Roux's decisive report illustrated key differences in the military culture of French and British strategic planning. Throughout the 1930s, the French General Staff was perennially led by an Army general, always fixated by the German threat, and accustomed to placing the Army's needs above those of the Navy and Air Force—itself not a fully independent service arm until 1934. Defensive planning in Paris and London was less informed by common assumptions about shared threats than might be imagined. Their strategic priorities differed markedly, their estimates of viable deployments and the defensibility of imperial territory in Asia did not coincide.

Preoccupied by the more proximate German threat, by 1936 General Maurice Gamelin's General Staff simply did not have the global reach of their British counterparts. Furthermore, the Army's predominance in policy formulation was reflected in their assessment of the military situation in the Asia-Pacific region. Put simply, French and British strategic planners read the map from very different perspectives. Where the British service chiefs, the Committee of Imperial Defence and the Cabinet interpreted their defensive options in the Far East by reference to the Pacific Ocean, their French counterparts did not share their "blue water" outlook. Between September 1937 and April 1938, the French General Staff undertook a fundamental review of imperial defence commitments. Two points are of significance to us here. First, the bulk of resources were allocated to African territories. The Naval and Air Staffs initially rejected the proposals, but on the grounds that the Army, as usual, took the lion's share. There was, however, general agreement on a second point. Indochina was chronically exposed. The federation required "defensive autonomy" to survive a Japanese attack.[31] The service chiefs were under no illusions that this could be achieved in the foreseeable future. Protection of the Indochina federation was a victim of the more urgent requirements of metropolitan defence.

With no great reinforcement plan of their own for Indochina, criticism of the "Singapore strategy" in France did not match the grumbling among British naval and air force critics over the high proportion of French defence expenditure allocated to the completion of the Maginot defence line. But French unease over British naval preparations for war with Japan was certainly informed by the adverse impact of higher Far Eastern spending on the modernization of British land and air forces for continental warfare.[32] The French gaze was fixed instead on the East Asian landmass. Seen in this light, after 1937 the overwhelming truth appeared to be that the European colonial position in Southeast Asia would be militarily untenable, should Japan overcome China's resistance. At the start of their imperial defence review in September 1937, the General Staff's Advisory Colonial Defence Committee (*Comité Consultatif de Défense des Colonies*) earmarked two cruisers and two submarines for the Indochina naval forces, in addition to an assortment of poor quality fighters, seaplanes and light bombers for service in Vietnam. But there was no concomitant willingness to risk substantial troop reinforcements sorely needed in Europe. The subtext was clear. Indochina simply could not be defended on land against overwhelmingly superior Japanese forces.[33]

Whether in the years of British budgetary retrenchment and defence cuts or in the post-1936 period of intensive rearmament, the French General Staff detected one key flaw in the Singapore defence scheme. The overwhelming concentration on the support requirements of the Royal Navy tended to obscure the fact that the entire plan demanded the maintenance of a secure defensive position on land. The threat of overland attack on Singapore only became a central element in British strategic thinking as a result of Japan's accelerated rate of advance through South China in 1939–40. The fall of France and, above all, the consequent entry of Japanese forces into northern Vietnam in September 1940 in pursuit of their drive into Southeast Asia lent unanticipated urgency to British defensive preparations. These were too little too late. The British decision to extend the "period before relief" during which the Singapore garrison would be required to hold out in anticipation of the arrival of major naval reinforcement proved the veracity of earlier French military predictions. In 1940–41, the concept of Singapore as an impregnable fortress entered the lexicon of British official statements on Far East defence. What little army, artillery and aircraft reinforcement took place did not lend much substance to the fortress idea.

The French were right all along. From the outset of the Singapore base plan, French observers, intelligence personnel and War Ministry staff estimated that Singapore might be required to serve as a defensive redoubt capable of withstanding prolonged attack. At root, French Army planners thought aspects of the preparations at Singapore unsound because they paid insufficient attention to basic considerations of military defence. Returning our attention to Roux's report, the very fact that a military attaché's advice on the land defence of the Singapore base made a greater impression than the French Naval Staff's views about the "main fleet to Singapore" concept was indicative of French doubts about the defensibility of Singapore Island. The War Ministry intelligence summary of the British manoeuvres held at Singapore between 1–4 February 1937 revealed the same military preoccupations. The centrepiece of these exercises was a simulated naval attack led by a "blue force" composed of vessels from the China squadron, including the cruisers HMS *Cumberland* and HMS *Dorsetshire*, and the aircraft-carrier HMS *Hermes*. Admittedly, naval operations were not within the purview of Army intelligence staff. But the focus on air defences, anti-aircraft installations, shore batteries and the deployment of garrison troops revealed the real source of French unease. Again, the conclusion was that land and air defences were the key element in Singapore's defence.[34] In January 1938, the Indochina command held its own manoeuvres. These assumed that the bulk of the colonial garrison would be required to guard the Cambodian and Laotian frontiers with Thailand. A skeleton force was left to defend the Mekong Delta, Cap Saint Jacques and the Saigon approaches. A mock invasion force attacked these three points and attempted a landing at Camranh Bay on the coast of Annam. Here, too, the lesson appeared to be that seaborne landings were more easily repelled than a steady advance over land.[35]

As familiarity with Japanese combined-operations techniques increased in the early years of the Sino-Japanese war, so these French doubts lingered on. The military intelligence bureaux in each of the French service ministries produced monthly analyses of Japanese operations in China. These reports were distributed to the Minister concerned, to the Army, Navy and Air Staffs and could be relayed to the major civil-military liaison committee in the French defence establishment, the *Comité Permanent de la Défense Nationale*, chaired by Edouard Daladier. Supplementary assessments were also produced regarding Japanese strategy, weaponry and fighting quality. In November 1937, for example, the Director of Police in the French international settlement in Shanghai transmitted two detailed intelligence reports. The first examined the total number of known Japanese air raids on major towns and industrial centres throughout eastern China; the second discussed the involvement of Japan's four aircraft-carriers in the conflict to date.[36]

Mounting evidence of Japanese capacity to penetrate far into East Asia nourished French worries about the "Singapore strategy," but was rarely discussed at ministerial or general staff level. By the time the King George VI dry dock was completed in early 1938, low-level cooperation between the French and British

Admiralties had replaced earlier competition for access to the string of islands between the southern Vietnamese coast and Hainan. Theoretically, a Royal Navy relief force heading for Hong Kong might even refuel with French assent at Camranh Bay or the Paracel islands.[37] By this point, the British service chiefs anticipated joint Allied convoys in the eastern Atlantic, but insisted that reinforcement of Singapore held priority over major naval operations against Germany.[38] These more pressing Far Eastern dangers eroded older imperial Franco-British enmities. There was no adverse comment in Paris equivalent to that in Hanoi over British failure to invite any French naval vessels to the opening ceremonies of the completed Singapore base.[39]

The belated conclusion of the British-French military alliance after the German occupation of Prague was followed by detailed Naval Staff talks between late March and mid-May 1939. The conversations took place against the backcloth of Allied efforts to construct a Balkan "peace front," the centrepiece of which was a tripartite military alliance with Turkey. Their commitments newly extended in the eastern Mediterranean, the Admiralty under Lord Stanhope was particularly reluctant to reveal its hand regarding the battleship force likely to be sent to Singapore.[40] Neither Daladier's government nor General Gamelin backed the Naval Staff strongly in trying to persuade their British partners to rethink their Far Eastern strategy. In the event, the issue was discussed in only one session between the two staffs.[41] Darlan and his chief delegate in London, Admiral Jean Odend'hal, could not extract precise information about the size of the British fleet to be sent to Singapore, or the likely date of its departure from the Mediterranean. They were shocked by British readiness to leave the French Navy severely overextended in Atlantic and Mediterranean waters. Darlan's staff rightly deduced that the Admiralty deliberately downplayed the Italian naval threat to avoid complicating the Singapore reinforcement plan. For Admirals schooled in Castex's vision of imperial defence, neither the defensive posture temporarily recommended in the Mediterranean, nor the protracted deployment of a capital ship force to defend the Malay barrier served French interests. Nor did it make sense as part of an allied strategy. It was madness to risk allied communications in the north Atlantic and Mediterranean in pursuit of illusory Far Eastern security.[42] Darlan remained convinced that assured control of the Mediterranean should precede, not follow, any major deployment to the Pacific. The Admiral made this an explicit objective in his preliminary report to Gamelin on the second phase of staff conversations in late April 1939.[43]

On 17 May 1939, the French *Chargé d'affaires* in Singapore warned Foreign Minister Georges Bonnet that a hostile Japan would probably attempt to isolate French Indochina and British Malaya by seizing control of the Gulf of Siam and raiding allied commerce throughout the South China Sea. In such an eventuality, a British naval counter-offensive from Singapore offered the sole protection for France's Far Eastern possessions.[44] His warning fell on deaf ears. Bonnet was determined to avoid military confrontation. Foreign Ministry efforts to appease Japan persisted into the early summer.[45] And French strategic priorities lay closer to home. As we have seen, Admiral Darlan's negotiators in the Allied staff conversations over the summer of 1939 remained irreconciled to the planned transfer of a British fleet to the Far East. The French Naval Staff was apparently unaware that British Admiralty planners were themselves divided over the viability of the main fleet plan at least in part because of their reluctance to rely on French naval cover in home and Mediterranean waters.[46] For their part, Darlan's Admirals dreaded the idea of British capital ships heading eastwards at the height of a European war.

Part of the explanation for French concentration on Atlantic and Mediterranean defence lay in their interpretation of military intelligence on Japan. By early 1939, the tenor of this material revealed the same contradictions apparent in British strategic assessments of Japan.[47] The margin of Japanese superiority in armaments output, resupply capacity, airpower and heavy weaponry was such that the conflict in China was characterized as "a colonial war" between a front-rank power and ill-equipped opponents. Yet, much like British military observers in China, their French counterparts would damn the Japanese Army with faint praise of the victories won against inferior opponents.[48] French military analysts tended to value firepower and the methodical preparation of battle over the mobility and improvisation that often characterized colonial conflict.[49] Perhaps not surprisingly then, the fighting quality and strategic sophistication of Japanese forces were played down. Japanese pilots were tactically naive and "fatalistically Oriental"; Japanese soldiers were automatons drawn towards frontal assaults like moths to a flame. Crude racial stereotyping was as misleading as it was insulting. Nor did France's defeat and change of regime trigger a fundamental reassessment of Japanese fighting quality.

The first Vichy governmental War Book on the Japanese military was compiled in January 1941.[50] By this point, Japanese coercion of the Indochina authorities had already borne fruit in the cessation of contacts with Nationalist China and Japanese military incursions in Tonkin.[51] Yet still Japanese martial prowess was questioned. The contrast between the high quality of the Japanese naval officer corps, the "sanest" element of Japan's armed forces, and the "slow intelligence" of the stoical Japanese sailor led to doubts that the Japanese Navy could make the most of its newest capital ships. Training was, apparently, far below U.S. or "European" standards.[52] Even more remarkably, such ethnocentrism would survive all the contrary evidence of the impending Pacific war. On the eve of the return of a French expeditionary force to Indochina in July 1945, the Army Intelligence Directorate War Book for Japan contained the following description:

> Overall, the Japanese is inferior to the Chinese, as much from a physical as from an intellectual standpoint. Japanese inferiority emerges most clearly when compared with the stronger and taller northern Chinese. The Chinese is characterized by an astonishing facility for rapid comprehension. The Japanese leaves one disconcerted by his apparent clumsiness (*lourdeur*), his air of irresolution, his indecisive turn of mind (*indécise mobilité d'esprit*), but, above all, by his formality and bureaucratic outlook (*esprit bureaucrate*).[53]

The Cartesian logic with which Vichy and Gaullist officials evaluated military options was, if anything, reinforced by the divisive experience of the Second World War. More emotive appeals to patriotism became inseparable from the two competing visions of "true France"—the cradle of Jacobin republicanism cherished by resisters or the epitome of the traditionalist peasant virtues glorified in Vichy's National Revolution.[54] Vichy military analysts admired the strict hierarchy and cult of sacrifice integral to the Japanese military. But still they dubbed the Japanese racially and intellectually inferior. It is tempting to conclude that racist assumptions remained a more powerful formative influence on French strategic planning in the Far East than empirical observation. But this does not chime with the more balanced assessments of those French observers closest to advancing Japanese forces in 1939—the colonial administration in the Indochina federation.

The Indochina Perspective

After the outbreak of the Sino-Japanese War in July 1937, the French military command in Hanoi had good reason to claim that its opposition to Japanese encroachments in South East Asia was more robust than that of British commanders in Hong Kong and Singapore. But neither French military nor civilian officialdom harboured any illusion that the Indochina federation could be defended. French Far Eastern planning was inevitably dominated by this calculation. What the *Quai d'Orsay*'s East Asian section liked to term a policy of "balance" was a rough mixture of concessions to Japan, abortive efforts to increase Indochina's defences and occasional gestures of support for Chiang Kai Shek. From June 1938, the Daladier government showed increasing public resolve in its condemnation of Japanese expansionism in China. But Foreign Minister Georges Bonnet stifled pressure for any substantial policy shift. If anything, Bonnet initiated a more active appeasement of Tokyo.[55] The vociferous diplomatic protests that greeted Japanese annexation of Hainan and the Spratley islands in late March 1939 were colourful, but ineffective. The islands became the southern-most outpost of the Japanese military, some 350 nautical miles from Annam and 750 nautical miles from Singapore. During 1939–40, aid to the Chinese nationalists, whether through ageing war matériel, transport facilities through Tonkin, preferential credit or sympathetic publicity, was little more than a pin-prick to Japan's southward advance.[56]

On 14 April 1939, the French government requested a ban on the export of Malayan iron ore to Japan. Having imposed an embargo on such exports from Indochina, the French Ministry of Colonies was only too aware that their action was undermined by continued British exports. In similar vein, the Foreign Ministry's Far Eastern section sought British backing for a favourable joint response to Chiang Kai Shek's offer in early April to lend Chinese Nationalist support to the defence of Indochina, Malaya and Singapore. In practice, the Foreign Office fudged both questions, leaving the French in Indochina feeling more exposed than ever.[57]

While Daladier and Minister of Colonies Georges Mandel were genuinely reluctant to bow to Japanese pressure, in Hanoi, Governor-Generals Jules Brévie and Georges Catroux assessed their situation with the brutal realism of the underdog.[58] The desperate attempts made to establish a rudimentary armaments manufacturing industry in Cochin China, and the repeated postponements in the construction of a submarine base at Camranh Bay, underscored the fact that France would never divert substantial military resources from the impending conflict with Germany. Wistfully referred to as "notre Singapour" by French defence planners, Camranh Bay, like the trans-Saharan railway before it, remained a pipe dream of imperial strategists.[59] In June 1939, Minister of Marine César Campinchi finally pledged funding to begin construction of the Camranh base and to enlarge the dockyard facilities at Saigon. Neither promised much for Indochina's immediate defensive prospects.[60] The China campaign revealed that the Japanese Army was capable of devastating amphibious operations that "brought startling success in terms of enemy confusion and demoralization." Japan's seizure of Hainan brought this home to the French administration in Hanoi.[61] Military resistance to a Japanese land invasion of Indochina could be nothing more than a token of France's long-term commitment to retain its colonial presence.

It was with this in view that representatives of the Indochina military command headed for staff talks in Singapore between 22–27 June 1939 with Admiral Sir Percy Noble, Commander-in-Chief of the Royal Navy's China Station. The discussions included over 50 participants, including senior British staff officers from Hong Kong, India, Burma, and Ceylon. Yet behind the warm words characteristic of the first months of the British-French alliance, the Singapore conference promised little.[62] Compared with parallel discussions held in Aden in early June regarding joint action in defence of the Indian Ocean and the Red Sea approaches, the talks in Singapore were inconclusive.[63]

The British were unenthusiastic about pooling facilities or forces involving any commitment beyond the Malay barrier. Historian John Dreifort's withering assessment of the conference captures the dilemma: "The British naturally tended to emphasize the role of naval defense in stopping Japan, but Admiral Sir Percy Noble had no fleet. The French stressed military operations to check Japan but they had no army."[64]

French expectations were, in any event, minimal. The delegation from Hanoi arrived without instructions from Paris regarding coordination of regional defence. In a frank assessment of his exchanges with Noble, Admiral Jean Decoux, Naval Commander in Indochina, advised the French Naval Staff that the British were wholly preoccupied with the defence of Singapore and Malaya. Hong Kong seemed doomed. French pleas that northern Borneo be more strongly defended, and that the British should join them in pressing the Thai government to permit transit rights between Malaya and Cambodia, fell on deaf ears. British reluctance to coerce the Bangkok regime into at least benevolent neutrality suggested that the British strategic horizon ended at the Kra peninsula. Nor did Singapore itself seem impregnable. The Indochina naval command was requested to allocate its two cruisers to help cover the initial reinforcement of the Singapore garrison during the first weeks of war. The one consolation was Noble's pledge that British naval forces would attempt to maintain the communications link between Singapore and southern Vietnam. But where were the ships required to do so?[65] To make matters worse, the bitter truths of the Singapore conference were immediately relayed to Tokyo in a Japanese agent's report.[66]

The colonial regime in Indochina placed less reliance on the deterrent value of British naval power than did their political masters in Paris. Deeply sceptical about the "Singapore strategy," and lacking any equivalent reinforcement plans of their own, the Indochina military command increasingly relied on intelligence-gathering and negotiating guile to fill the void left by inadequate defences. The Ministry of Marine, always the best informed and the least impressed of the three French service ministries regarding British Far Eastern defence plans, liaised closely with Decoux. As Head of the *rue Royale* planning section in 1935–36, Decoux had hoped that Franco-Italian *détente* might release naval units for operations elsewhere. But, from 1937 onwards, Darlan's Naval Staff considered war with Italy their first priority. The three-year fleet building programme approved in May 1938 was entirely geared to eventual conflict with Italy and Germany. An accelerated construction programme, including two additional battleships, was to ensure a margin of superiority over the Italian Navy. There were simply no surplus forces available to defend Indochina.[67] In 1939, Decoux's Hanoi command was left to survive on its wits. Intelligence played a key role in this.

Until June 1940, Decoux received regular updates of the information collated by Tokyo Naval Attaché, Captain J. Rosati.[68] Thus French naval officials in Paris,

Hanoi and Saigon closely monitored the competition between the military factions in the Japanese government establishment. They also took note of the incremental pressure for Japan's strategic turn southwards as German forces achieved their decisive breakthrough in the west during May–June 1940. Rosati highlighted the connection between the slowdown in the Japanese military advance into mainland China and the rising influence of the Japanese naval command in Tokyo decision-making. French naval intelligence paid particular attention to little-noticed aspects of Japan's 1940 budget: the creation of South China Sea bureaux within the Tokyo Foreign and Colonial Ministries, and funding for new civil air routes to the Marshall Islands and Saipan.[69]

Before the battle for France began, the French Naval Staff was convinced that Japan intended to seize the Netherlands East Indies in its quest for essential raw materials. Paul Reynaud's government, the product of an acrimonious and divisive ministerial reshuffle in late March 1940, did not, however, bring about any significant alteration in French strategic policy in Indochina. Still condemned to survive on their wits, the Hanoi authorities continued their protests against Japanese bombardment of the Yunnan railway, near the northern Tonkin frontier. On 25 April, the Hanoi colonial government banned the export of iron ore to Japan.[70]

Vichy and the Fall of Singapore

The survival of French Indochina after June 1940 was still more precarious than before. In 1940–41, the long-term threat of Vietnamese nationalism was obscured by the looming menace of a Japanese takeover. More serious than its limited military resources, the Vichy state lacked the political independence necessary to formulate long-term strategic policy.[71] That is not to say that the Pétainist regime or its loyalist administration in Indochina were mere bystanders to the war in Asia. Decoux's government continued to relay agents' reports on Japanese activity in Indochina and Thailand to British intelligence. And French service attachés remained in Tokyo until July 1942, albeit with much reduced ability to communicate directly with France. Their occasional telegrams on Japan's war effort, high command thinking, and the southward advance indicated that they retained key contacts within the Japanese administration.[72]

Unusually, Vichy also permitted the British to retain consular representation in Saigon, another useful intelligence-gathering point. In return, French colonial officials returning from Indochina were still allowed to pass through British imperial territory. Hence, for example, in April 1941, Louis Castex, a French Air Force officer sent to Indochina in 1940 to study the federation's air defences, travelled to the United States by way of Singapore and Manila. On arrival in Washington, he reported to Vichy on the defensive preparations in both ports.[73] Both Vichy and Saigon consular sources provided intelligence to the British of the Japanese military and air force build-up in Cochin China and Cambodia during November 1941 in readiness for the attack on Malaya.[74] Although this intelligence was critically important, the fact remained that the French administration in Indochina could do nothing to prevent Japan's reinforcement of Cochin China. Bitter proof of this was not long in coming. The bombers and torpedo-bombers that launched the devastating attack on the two battleships of Force Z, HMS *Prince of Wales* and HMS *Repulse*, on 10 December were part of Rear-Admiral Matsunaga's Saigon-based 22nd Naval Air Flotilla.[75]

The concept of a Pétainist "double game" in which the Vichy state supposedly acted as sword and shield to protect the French population from the worst excesses of Nazi occupation has long been discredited. Vichy offered the hand of collaboration willingly, often on its own initiative.[76] But the idea of a double game has some validity when applied to Vichy colonial interest in Indochina. Vichy's parallel dealings with the British and the Japanese certainly revealed this double aspect. Apart from its intelligence exchanges with the Singapore authorities, in December 1940 Decoux's administration sought British mediation of its border conflict with Thailand in an effort to prevent a Japanese-arbitrated settlement. Decoux and Sir Shenton Thomas, Governor of the Straits Settlements, were equally keen to avert a pretext for consolidation of the Japanese military presence on the Thai frontier.[77] These back-channels were important, but they did little to halt further Japanese encroachment into southern Indochina, capped in late July 1941 by the use of airfields around Saigon and the Camranh Bay anchorage. Nor should the Decoux regime's contacts with the British mask the genuine enthusiasm with which it implemented the worst of Vichy's racialist authoritarianism. Yet Charles de Gaulle's Free French movement and its British patron did little to undermine Vichy control of Indochina in 1940–42, conscious that their interference might provoke greater Japanese intervention.

What unites secret links to the British and Vichyite repression in Indochina was the Decoux regime's determination to cling on as colonial master. This was a sentiment shared by the Vichy service ministries. It makes the interpretation of Vichy reportage on Singapore problematic. Incoming intelligence on Japanese advances in the weeks following Pearl Harbour was overwhelmingly hostile. But while Vichy's military intelligence establishment was solidly anti-Japanese, it was hardly pro-British. After Mers el-Kébir, the Royal Navy aroused furious passion among Vichy's armistice forces. The dogma of British naval treachery and the veneration of the sailors killed in the Oran bombardment were integral to Vichy propaganda and the cult of Darlan's Navy. Spurred by the abortive British-Free French assault on Dakar in September 1940, Vichy naval intelligence amassed information on British imperial ports and force deployments.[78] But French naval Anglophobia had little relevance in the South China Sea. British defence of Singapore suited Vichy colonial interest in Asia, even though it was at odds with the undeclared naval and colonial conflicts between the U.K. and Vichy in Africa and the Middle East. Vichy's strategic interest collided with its mounting political animosity towards Churchill's government. The future of France and the U.K. in Southeast Asia was obviously intertwined whatever the political differences between them. On 10 May 1941, for instance, the Tokyo Naval Attaché warned that Japan's decision not to assume full political control in Hanoi reflected the certainty that eventual seizure of Singapore would bring French colonial rule crashing down in its wake. Japan was resolved to "eliminate" European authority in Asia, a fact confirmed by Japanese incitement of Vietnamese anti-colonialism.[79] Three months later in early September, the Shanghai Air Attaché noted that British reinforcement of Singapore and the hasty construction of advanced air bases in the Burmese jungle was part of a "war of nerves" with Japan. The outcome of this conflict would determine the fate of colonial Indochina.[80]

Another aspect of Vichy reportage about Japan's descent on Malaya was the certainty that British resistance would not succeed. One week after Pearl Harbour, French Air Staff intelligence warned that Japanese armaments production could only be sustained by the seizure of Malaya's raw material resources and assured naval supremacy in the western Pacific.[81] In their weekly intelligence summaries in early 1942, air staff intelligence contrasted the sluggishness of Japanese operations in China with the unstoppable momentum of advance in Southeast Asia. In Borneo, Japanese forces achieved stunning breakthroughs with relatively limited resources. But Japanese success in outflanking British defences along the Malayan peninsula drew more comment, notably after the capture on 5 January of the Kuantan air base, some 300 kilometres from Singapore.[82]

On 21 January, the Air Staff were advised that the South China Sea was now "Japan's Mediterranean." In this metaphor, Singapore was Gibraltar: isolated and exposed. In early January, the *Deuxième Bureau* predicted the "neutralization" of Singapore. The conviction that Singapore would fall emerged in reports submitted between 23 January and 4 February. With the capture of Tampin and the link-up of Japanese forces advancing down eastern and western Malaya, Singapore faced disaster.[83] The fall-back of British forces and Japanese crossings of the Johore Straits occasioned little surprise at Vichy. The surrender of Singapore itself confirmed Vichy assessments of the preceding Japanese advance, and the longer-term French view that the base was not impregnable to land attack.[84]

In these gloomily accurate intelligence assessments, the distinct perspectives of Pétain's Vichy and Decoux's Hanoi combined. After the psychological trauma of sudden defeat in June 1940, it was perhaps easier for Vichy's military analysts to envisage the collapse of the Singapore redoubt.[85] After 18 months of bruising negotiation with the Japanese Southern Army command, Decoux's government was well-placed to evaluate Japanese regional power. And as a non-combatant state, Vichy had limited access to both British and Japanese official opinion. Two examples illustrate the point. The first were the unacknowledged diplomatic contacts between the U.K. and Vichy maintained via the two governments' embassies in Lisbon. The British Naval Attache in Lisbon thus provided detailed information about the sinking of the *Prince of Wales* and the *Repulse* on 10 December 1941. He conceded that the land and air defences at Singapore were far weaker than Churchill's government would admit.[86] Vichy naval intelligence drew the following conclusion from this information: "Singapore is capable of holding out for a long time (*de résister longtemps*), but enemy aviation will make this naval base untenable and will effectively neutralize it." The second proof of Vichy's privileged intelligence position was its Tokyo Embassy. In March 1942, Tokyo Naval Attaché Bachy provided detailed assessment of Japanese military training for seaborne landings, specifically the preparations made for the assault on Hong Kong three months earlier:

> Before the war, the Army and Navy established units specially trained for seaborne assaults that could undertake key, difficult operations and establish a beachhead. The first elements often swam ashore. Losses were not apparently taken into consideration and were never notified...The expeditionary force that attacked Hong Kong undertook extensive secret training on a neighbouring island where topographical conditions were exactly like those of Hong Kong.[87]

Unsurprisingly, on 21 February Vichy naval intelligence linked the escape from Brest of Germany's two high-speed 32,000-ton battleships, *Scharnhorst* and *Gneisenau*, to the fall of Singapore a week earlier. The British were losing their naval edge.[88] This might serve Vichy interests in Europe, the Mediterranean and Africa, but it was no cause for celebration in Indochina. The fall of Singapore thus revealed the contradictions inherent in Vichy collaboration. Many of its military practitioners had worked with their British counterparts before the war. Relatively few were unqualified admirers of Nazi Germany. Virtually none showed any liking for Imperial Japan. Though few Vichy officials dissented from the public assertion that British perfidy contributed to French defeat in 1940, most recognized that the sources of that defeat lay in France itself. Indeed, the cornerstone of *Pétainism* and the reactionary authoritarianism of the *Révolution Nationale* was the insistence that republican France had been decadent, corrupt and materially weak. Any *schadenfreude* at the humiliating British capitulation in Singapore was eclipsed by the realization that European imperial power was unlikely to recover in Southeast Asia.

Vichy reactions to the fall of Singapore suggest a need to reconsider common assumptions about the supposedly monolithic nature of Vichy collaboration, the complicity of the French colonial authorities in Japan's southward advance and Pétainist opposition to British imperial rule. There was an obvious dichotomy between Vichy's drift towards greater collaboration with the Axis Powers in Europe and the regime's abiding interest in British efforts to deter further Japanese penetration of Southeast Asia as a whole and southern Vietnam in particular. The fall of France, the abrupt change of régime and the beginnings of Vichy collaboration did not alter the long-term French strategic interest in the preservation of British Singapore.

In early 1941, Japanese encouragement of Thai irredentism further undermined French colonial rule in Indochina and confirmed Japanese strategic plans to utilize southern Vietnam, Cambodia and Thailand as transits to Malaya. More than ever, the preservation of a margin of French authority in Indochina and British ability to defend Malaya became inter-linked. By May 1941, Decoux, Darlan's prime ministerial Cabinet and Pétain's general staff were acutely conscious that should Malaya become an active theatre, the Indochinese territories would fall under *de facto* Japanese military control. There was no way to carve a role for a collaborationist French Indochina in the Co-Prosperity Sphere. Nor was it clear what impact the decline of British authority in Malaya would have upon the consolidation of the Vietminh. The one certainty was that the fall of the Singapore naval base would leave the Saigon administration at the mercy of the Japanese Southern Army command and quite incapable of withstanding the Vietnamese nationalist challenge.

Perhaps more significant than Vichy's calculation of its own colonial interest was the fact the regime was unsurprised by the fall of Singapore. In part, this reflected a brutal realism born of past defeat and current weakness. But it was also of a piece with French strategic assessments of the interwar period. At no point in the decade before 1942 was the French General Staff won over to the "Singapore strategy" or persuaded that it could succeed. Exaggeration should be avoided. For much of the 1930s, the British-French entente was conspicuously devoid of close military liaison. Global strategic planning did not begin in earnest until conclusion of the British-French alliance in 1939. The eastern horizon of French military preparations for war rarely stretched beyond the Rhine, let alone to the Far East. The Navy's horizons were unquestionably broader. But its assessment of France's metropolitan and imperial priorities was equally circumscribed. Insofar as the Naval Staff still adhered to an Oceanic strategy, it was essentially confined to the Mediterranean and the coastal waters of francophone Africa. In the short term at least, the Pacific had all but been abandoned. The French Navy's primary role in the initial conquests of Vietnam in the late nineteenth century was a distant memory. Although an Admiral held the political reins in Hanoi after July 1940, successive French governments before and after the June 1940 watershed applied the Eurocentric logic of the Army command to dismiss the prospects for Far Eastern defence. Darlan's Naval Staff regarded the British "main fleet to Singapore" plan with a mixture of dread and contempt. Finally, French military intelligence offered few crumbs of comfort to those hoping that British Far Eastern defence plans would succeed. The Singapore base was not considered impregnable. The primary French focus on the city's land and air defences rather than on the naval forces to be deployed accounted for the underlying pessimism about Singapore. If this was disaster foreseen, it was also proof of the shortcomings of French-British liaison before the war. Insofar as French and British representatives discussed the defence of their Southeast Asian empires, it was largely a dialogue of the deaf.

Martin Thomas is Reader in International History at the University of the West of England, Bristol. He is the author of Britain, France and Appeasement: Anglo-French Relations in the Popular Front Era, The French Empire at War 1940–45, and The French North African Crisis: Anglo-French Relations and Colonial Breakdown 1945–62.

NOTES—

1   I. Kiyoshi, "The Road to Singapore: Japan's View of Britain, 1922–41," in T. Fraser and P. Lowe (eds.), *Conflict and Amity*, London, 1992; J. E. Dreifort, "Japan's Advance into Indochina, 1940: The French Response," *Journal of Southeast Asian Studies*, 13, 1982, 279–95.
2   E.T. Jennings, *Vichy in the Tropics: Pétain's National Revolution in Madagascar, Guadeloupe, and Indochina, 1940–1944*, Stanford, 2001, 130–98.
3   R. B. Smith, "The Japanese Period in Indochina and the Coup of 9 March 1945," *Journal of Southeast Asian Studies*, 9:2, 1978, 268–301; K. K. Nitz, "Japanese Military Policy Towards French Indochina During the Second World War: The Road to the *Meigo Sakusan* 9 March 1945," *Journal of Southeast Asian Studies*, 14:2, 1983, 328–50; Y. Gras, "L'intrusion japonais en Indochine 1940–1945," *Revue Historique des Armées*, 4, 1983, 86–102.
4   D. Marr, *Vietnam, 1945*, Berkeley, 1995; S. Tonnesson, *The Vietnamese Revolution of 1945: Roosevelt, Ho Chi Minh and de Gaulle in a World at War*, London, 1991; E. T. Jennings, *Vichy in the Tropics*, 163–98; C. H. d'Alzon, "L'évolution des conceptions stratégiques du commandement français en Indochine entre 1940 et 1945," *Revue d'Histoire de la Deuxième Guerre Mondiale*, 138, 1985, 5–20; P. L. Lamant, "La Révolution nationale dans l'Indochine de l'Amiral Decoux," *Revue d'Histoire de la Deuxième Guerre Mondiale* 138, 1985, 21–41.

5   Service Historique de l'Armée Archive, Vincennes [hereafter SHA], Série 7N: Carton 7N2837/D1, Société d'études et d'informations économiques: Guy Lacam, La Malaisie britannique et la base de Singapore, 24 February 1938, 15.
6   Service Historique de la Marine Archive, Vincennes [hereafter SHM], Série 1BB3, Carton 1BB3/45, EMG-2, Renseignement: L'influence française à Singapour, n.d. November 1923; PRO, CO825/26/7, Colonial Office Far East correspondence, Visits of French military personnel to Colombo and Singapore, Colonial Office minutes, 28 December 1938.
7   O. Louis, "De Bizerte à Mers el-Kébir: les bases navales d'Afrique du Nord dans l'entre-deux-guerres," *Revue Historique des Armées*, 4, 1999, 31–45.
8   I. Cowman, *Dominion or Decline: Anglo-American Naval Relations in the Pacific, 1937–1941*, Oxford, 1996, 14–15.
9   SHM, IBB3/45, Etat-Major Général note de renseignement, La base nouvelle de Singapour, 2 November 1923; Ravitaillement en mazout à Singapour, n.d. November 1923.
10 B. M. Ranft, "Admiral David Earl Beatty 1919–927," in M. H. Murfett (ed.), *The First Sea Lords: From Fisher to Mountbatten*, Westport, Conn., 1995, 127–40; J. Blatt, "The Parity that Meant Superiority: French Naval Policy Towards Italy at the Washington Conference and Interwar French Foreign Policy," *French Historical Studies*, 12:2, 1981, 223–48, and "France and the Washington Conference," *Diplomacy and Statecraft*, 4:3, 1993, 192–219.
11 J. F. V. Keiger, "'Perfidious Albion?' French Perceptions of Britain as an Ally After the First World War," and M. S. Alexander and W. J. Philpott "The Entente Cordiale and the Next War: Anglo-French Views on Future Military Cooperation, 1928–1939," both in M. S. Alexander (ed.), *Knowing Your Friends: Intelligence Inside Alliances and Coalitions from 1914 to the Cold War*, London, 1998, 37–40 and 55–56.
12 See, for example, SHA, 7N2837/D2, Troupes de l'Indochine EMA-2, Réduction sur le budget de 1933 des forces britanniques de Singapour, 31 December 1932; EMA SR, Singapour: Renforcement de l'organisation défensive, 23 June 1934.
13 SHA, 7N2837/D2, Consul Singapore to Foreign Ministry: Garnison de Singapour, 24 March 1937; Forces aériennes. Nouvel aérodrome géant, 21 April 1937.
14 SHA, 7N2837/D1, Société d'études et d'informations économiques: Guy Lacam, La Malaisie britannique et la base de Singapore, 24 February 1938, 7–14.
15 PRO, CO825/28/5, C8585/8/17, T. C. Sharman, Saigon, to FO, 16 July 1938.
16 C. Coquery-Vidrovitch, "Mutation de l'impérialisme colonial français dans les années 30," *African Economic History*, 4, 1977, 103–52.
17 C.-R. Ageron, "Les colonies devant l'opinion publique française 1919-1939," *Revue Française d'Histoire d'Outre-Mer*, 77:286, 1990, 67–71; P. Jackson, *France and the Nazi Menace: Intelligence and Policy-Making, 1933–1939*, Oxford, 2000, 318, 333.
18 M. Michel, "'Mémoire Officielle,' Discours et pratique coloniale. Le 14 juillet et le 11 novembre au Sénégal entre les deux guerres," *Revue Française d'Histoire d'Outre-Mer*, 77, 1990, 150–53.
19 J. Lunn, "'Les Races Guerrières': Racial Preconceptions in the French Military about French West African Soldiers During the First World War," *Journal of Contemporary*

History, 34:4, 1999, 527–30; T. Stovell, "Color-blind France? Colonial Workers During the First World War," Race and Class, 35, 1993, 35–55.

20 C.-R. Ageron, "A propos d'une prétendue politique de 'repli impérial' dans la France des années 1939–39," Revue d'Histoire Maghrébine, 12, 1978, 228–37; M. Thomas, "At the Heart of Things? French Imperial Defence Planning in the Late 1930s," French Historical Studies, 21:2, 1998, 326–41.

21 I. Cowman, Dominion or Decline, 23.

22 SHA, 7N2837/D1, Singapore consular report, Garnison de Singapore: Non-Européens, 21 April 1937; Lacam, La Malaisie britannique et la base de Singapore, 15.

23 SHA, 7N2837/D1, Lacam, La Malaisie britannique et la base de Singapore, 18.

24 V. Vascotto, "L'amiral Castex et ses Théories Stratégiques," Revue Historique des Armées, 224:3, 2001, 85–86.

25 J.-B. Duroselle, La Décadence: Politique étrangère de la France 1932–1939, Paris, 1979, 266–67; O. Louis, "De Bizerte à Mers el-Kébir," 36–37.

26 H. Dutailly, "Weaknesses in French Military Planning on the Eve of the Second World War," in B. J. C. McKercher and R. Legault (eds.), Military Planning and the Origins of the Second World War in Europe, Westport, CT, 2001, 95.

27 H. Coutou-Bégarie and C. Huan (eds.), Lettres et notes de l'Amiral Darlan, Paris, 1992, 28–29, 49–53, 95–96.

28 For details of Roux's influential role in French military intelligence, see P. Jackson, France and the Nazi Menace.

29 SHA, 7N2837/D2, no. 118/A, Rapport du Colonel Henri Roux sur l'organisation militaire de Singapore et celle des Straits Settlements, 1 October 1935.

30 Ibid., 2.

31 SHA, 7N4196/D1, EMA-2, Note sur la défense des colonies, n.d., probably August 1938.

32 M. S. Alexander, The Republic in Danger: General Maurice Gamelin and the Politics of French Defence, 1933–1940, Cambridge, 1992, 244–49.

33 SHA, 7N4196/D1, no. 286, Inspection générale des troupes coloniales, General Billottee to General Colson, 12 October 1937.

34 SHA, 7N2837/D2, SHA-2, Empire britannique: Les manoeuvres de Singapour, 1–4 février 1937.

35 PRO, CO825/26/8, C1333/8/17, Consul W. W. Coultras, Saigon, to FO, 25 January 1938.

36 See, for example, the air intelligence reports in Service Historique de l'Armée de l'Air, Vincennes [hereafter SHAA], Série 2B: Carton 2B81/D1, EMAA-2, Synthèses de renseignements sur le conflit sino-japonais, 1939; and 2B81/D2, EMAA-2, Note sur les opérations de bombardement aérien japonais en Chine; Etude sur les opérations des porte-avions, des transports et d'hydravions japonais, both 17 November 1937.

37 I. Cowman, Dominion or Decline, 32–33.

38 PRO, CAB5/8, CID 450-COS Sub-Committee report, Questions relating to general defence problems in the Far East, 4 June 1937, cited in N. Tracy (ed.), The Collective Naval Defence of the Empire, 1900–1940 Aldershot, 1999, 569.

39 PRO, CO825/26/8, C3114/8/17, Coultras, Saigon, monthly report, 11 March 1938. The snub was taken to heart in Saigon as three French cruisers, *Montcalm, Gloire,* and *Georges Leygues,* had only recently arrived as reinforcement.
40 S. Cox, "British Military Planning and the Origins of the Second World War," in B. J. C. McKercher and R. Legault (eds.), *Military Planning and the Origins of the Second World War in Europe,* 116.
41 W. D. McIntyre, *The Rise and Fall of the Singapore Naval Base,* London, 1979, 149–50.
42 R. M. Salerno, "The French Navy and the Appeasement of Italy, 1937–39," *English Historical Review,* 110, 1997, 92–93; I. Cowman, *Dominion or Decline,* 37, 141–45.
43 *Lettres et notes de l'Amiral Darlan,* 90–91, 95–96.
44 SHA, 7N2837/D2, tel. 7, Jacques Pingaud Singapore to Sous-direction Asie-Océanie, 17 May 1939.
45 *Document Diplomatiques Français [DDF],* Paris, 1981 *et seq,* 2nd series, Vol. XVI, Bonnet tel. to Charles-Arsène Henry, Tokyo, 12 May 1939; also cited in J. F. Laffey, "French Far Eastern Policy in the 1930s," *Modern Asian Studies,* 23:1, 1989, 144.
46 C. M. Bell, "The 'Singapore Strategy' and the Deterrence of Japan: Winston Churchill, the Admiralty and the Dispatch of Force Z," *English Historical Review,* 114: 662, 2001, 609–14.
47 Three ground-breaking articles on British perceptions stand out: W. K. Wark, "In Search of a Suitable Japan: British Naval Intelligence in the Pacific Before the Second World War," *Intelligence and National Security,* 1:2, 1986, 189–212; J. Ferris, "'Worthy of Some Better Enemy?': The British Estimate of the Imperial Japanese Army, 1919–41, and the Fall of Singapore," *Canadian Journal of History,* 28, 1993, 223–56; A. Best, "Constructing an Image: British Intelligence and Whitehall's Perception of Japan, 1931–1939," *Intelligence and National Security,* 11:3, 1996, 403–26.
48 SHM, 2BB7/T1, Rosati, Tokyo, Contribution au Livre Vert, 1941; J. Ferris, "Worthy of Some Better Enemy?" 240–43.
49 For contrasting views of French military doctrine, see R. A. Doughty, *The Seeds of Disaster: The Development of French Army Doctrine, 1919–1939,* Hamden, Conn., 1985; E. Kiesling, *Arming Against Hitler: France and the Limits of Military Planning,* Lawrence, KS, 1996.
50 SHM, 2BB7/T1, Rosati , Tokyo, Contribution au Livre Vert, 1941.
51 J. E. Dreifort, *Myopic Grandeur: The Ambivalence of French Foreign Policy Toward the Far East, 1919–1945,* Kent, OH., 1991, 209–12; Admiral J. Decoux, *A la Barre de l'Indochine: Histoire de mon Gouvernement Général 1940–1945,* Paris, 1949, 102–22.
52 SHM, 2BB7/T1, Situation de la Marine Impériale Japonaise, 20 January 1941.
53 SHA, 7P164/D1, Notices concernant l'armée japonaise, 1942-45, EMA-2, Japon: Armée, Les Hommes, n.d. July 1945.
54 A cogent introduction to these competing ideological visions is J. Jackson, *France: The Dark Years, 1940–1944,* Oxford, 2000.
55 J. F. Laffey, "French Far Eastern Policy in the 1930s," 138–46; G. Taboulet, "La France et l'Angleterre face au conflit sino-japonais 1937–1939," *Revue d'Histoire Diplomatique,* 88, January 1974, 126–43.

56   SHM, 2BB7/T1, EMG-2, Attaché naval Tokyo, L'annexation des îles Spratley par le Japon, 1 May 1939; J. E. Dreifort, *Myopic Grandeur*, 149–53.
57   DDF, 2nd series, Vol. XV, Georges Bonnet to Charles Corbin London, 7 and 14 April 1939, and Corbin reply, 14 April 1939, 500–01, 631, 648–9.
58   B. Favreau, *Georges Mandel ou la passion de la République 1885–1944*, Paris, 1996, 42, 334. Mandel appointed Catroux as successor to Brévie on 16 July 1939.
59   SHA, 7N2837/D2, SHA-2, Singapour—La conférence franco-britannique, n.d. June 1939.
60   PRO, CO825/28/5, C10342/249/17, H. F. C. Walsh, Saigon, to FO, 12 July 1939.
61   A. R. Millett, "Assault From the Sea: The Development of Amphibious Warfare Between the Wars—The American, British and Japanese Experiences," in W. Murray and A. R. Millett (eds.), *Military Innovation in the Interwar Period*, Cambridge, 1998, 68–69.
62   DDF, 2nd series, Vol. XVII, final report of Singapore talks, 42–55.
63   SHM, TTD 821/Dossier FNEO, Station navale de l'Océan Indien "Bougainville," Conférence anglo-française, Aden, 29 au 3 juin 1939.
64   J. E. Dreifort, *Myopic Grandeur*, 164.
65   SHM, TTD 821, Marine en Indochine, EMN-3, Decoux, Transmission du rapport de la conférence de Singapour, 22–27 Juin 1939.
66   R. J. Aldrich, *Intelligence and the War Against Japan: Britain, America and the Politics of Secret Service*, Cambridge, 2000, 44.
67   R. M. Salerno, "The French Navy and the Appeasement of Italy," 71–77.
68   SHM, 2BB7/T1, Rosati compte-rendus de renseignements, March 1939 – May 1940.
69   SHM, 2BB7/T1, Rosati compte-rendu, La politique d'expansion économique du Japon dans les mers du sud, 1 January 1940.
70   SHM, 2BB7/T1, Rosati to Marine/EMN-2, 1 May 1940.
71   R. C. Hood III, "Bitter Victory: French Military Effectiveness During the Second World War," in A. R. Millett and W. Murray (eds.), *Military Effectiveness, III: The Second World War*, Boston, 1988, 228–32.
72   See, for example, Tokyo naval attaché reports in SHM, 2BB7/T1. The French Embassy in Tokyo had no diplomatic bag facilities after the June 1940 armistice.
73   SHM, Marine en Indochine, TTD 821/Dossier: Relations franco-japonaises, 1941–1944, Castex report, 21 April 1941.
74   A. Best, "This Probably Over-Valued Military Power," 78–79, 86–87; R. J. Aldrich, *Intelligence and the War Against Japan*, 55. The intelligence was wrongly interpreted as evidence of an imminent Japanese occupation of Thailand.
75   L. Allen, *Singapore, 1941–1942*, London, 1977, 142–43.
76   The concept of Vichy as "sword and shield" was popularized by Robert Aron's *Histoire de Vichy* Paris, 1954. The idea was utterly disproved by Robert Paxton's unparalleled *Vichy France, 1940–44: Old Guard and New Order*, London, 1972.
77   R. J. Aldrich, *Intelligence and the War Against Japan*, 44–45.
78   M. Thomas, "After Mers el-Kébir: The Armed Neutrality of the Vichy French Navy, 1940–43," *English Historical Review*, 112:447, 1997, 649–51; SHM, TTA 44/Dossier FMF-2 Renseignements sur la marine anglaise, 1940–1941.

79 SHM. 2BB7T1, Compte-rendu de renseignements No. 1 Lieutenant de vaisseau Sicard Tokyo to Marine, 10 May 1941.
80 SHAA, 3D324/D1, no. 574/SH, Commandant de la Ferté Seneclère, Shanghai, to EMAA-2, 7 September 1941.
81 SHAA, 3D319/D2, EMAA-2, "La puissance militaire du Japon," 12 December 1941.
82 See, for example, SHAA, 3D319/D1, EMAA-2, Bulletin d'informations 109, 14 January 1941.
83 SHAA, 3D319/D1, EMAA-2, Bulletins d'informations 110 and 112, 23 January, 4 February 1941.
84 SHAA, 3D319/D1, EMAA-2, Bulletins d'informations 113, 114 and 115, 11, 17 and 25 February 1941.
85 The French Air Staff, for example, was warned that Japanese close air support of ground attacks matched that provided by the *Luftwaffe* in May–June 1940: SHAA, 3D324/D1, no. 569/SH, Air Attaché Shanghai to EMAA-2, 8 August 1941.
86 SHM, TTA 44/Dossier FMF-2, CRR No. 9, Opinion britannique sur les premières hostilités en Extrême-Orient, 5 January 1942; regarding the Lisbon diplomatic channel, see R. T. Thomas, *Britain and Vichy: The Dilemmas of Anglo-French Relations, 1940–42*, London, 1979.
87 SHM, 2BB7/T1, tel. 6456, AN Bachy Tokyo to Marine, 14 March 1942.
88 SHM, Cabinet du Ministre, TTA 44/Dossier FMF-2, CRR, Opérations navals — Grande-Bretagne, 21 February 1942.

CHAPTER 5

Student and Master: The United Kingdom, Japan, Airpower, and the Fall of Singapore, 1920–1941

> "Once I was student and you were master. Now student has become master."
>
> Darth Vader

by John R. Ferris

The fall of Singapore was one of the great events of modern history. Often seen as a case of the Imperial Japanese Army (IJA) defeating the Royal Navy (RN), in fact it was a triumph of Japan over the United Kingdom in the air. This paper will discuss the tragicomic roots of this triumph. It will examine how and why the British transferred the techniques and technology of naval aviation to Japan, so forging a hammer to smash its Asian empire. It will discuss how Britons responded to the rise of Japanese airpower, in particular how the Royal Air Force (RAF) assessed the Imperial Japanese Navy Air Force (IJNAF).[1] This paper will examine how ideology and observation shaped perception, why it became so negative and inaccurate, and how it shaped British strategy toward Japan and decisions about Singapore. The theme is oversight—a failure by air authorities to take Japan seriously, and by any authority to take Japan seriously in the air—and its consequences.

In 1920, the Imperial Japanese Navy (IJN) asked the British for help to develop airpower. Many British authorities supported the idea; diplomats to increase their influence, arms firms and the RAF to build a market. The British embassy favoured aid for naval aviation so as to garner influence over the IJN and deny that opportunity to other states; it feared France or Italy might send a naval aviation mission. France had made such an offer, and was training the Imperial Japanese Army Air Force (IJAAF).[2] The Military Attache, General Woodruffe, offered the clearest rationale for aid, one shared by the embassy and the Foreign Office:

> Although Japan is a first-class power, it has never hitherto been possible for her to embark on any large undertaking without direct foreign assistance, necessitating the employment of foreign agents and instructors on Japanese soil; and although, as the undertaking progresses, this direct assistance may gradually be withdrawn, she is still unable to rely entirely on her own skill in any given direction.

French, Italian and American aviation "influence" exceeded British; yet to teach Japan to fly would be to control its wings. Woodruffe, noting "the intimate relationship that exists between teacher and pupil, and the deep veneration in which the teacher is held" in Japan, saw "no reason why the Japanese Air Force should not become as dependent on our Royal Air Force, as the Japanese Navy is dependent on our Royal Navy". Moreover, "The Power who commands the Aerial future of Japan opens for herself an undreamed-of vista of strategic possibilities in the Pacific Ocean and in Eastern Asia." Physical causes—poor reflexes and sense of balance—and "national psychology," "a temperament that gets easily 'rattled' in the face of emergency," would likely prevent Japanese from being excellent pilots, but they could develop a competent air force and become a steady market for British aircraft.[3]

To arms firms, this opportunity was one step toward the heights. Memories moved Vickers—before 1914, it built battleships for foreign governments for £2,000,000 or more, as with the Japanese dreadnought *Mikasa*—as did present connections; in 1919, its largest foreign holdings were in Japan.[4] Though its hopes fell short, between 1919–39 Japan ranked third among Vickers' markets, averaging 8 % of its total sales.[5] In 1921, Handley Page urged the RAF and the air industry to establish "a supremacy for British aircraft" in the world, "on similar lines to the supremacy of the British Navy...the British Empire, whose Dominions extend in all parts of the world, is more or less called upon to organize Aerial communication all over the world." The British should disseminate aircraft technology and help foreign countries establish plant because "as the nucleus would be British they would take material forged by British industry and, in all probability, produce British type of machines. The importance of such a development need not be explained either from the industrial or the political point of view, it is so very apparent."[6] Handley Page viewed the opportunity in Japan as a means toward a monopoly in air sales throughout the world. The RAF too wanted to establish markets for aviation firms, to strengthen their profits and their ability to support British interests. The Air Ministry's files on this matter have vanished, but its thinking can be reconstructed. Opinions differed—most enthusiastic was the Civil Aviation Department (CAD), followed by technical branches, with the Air Staff cooler, though still warm. The Air Ministry favoured the development of aviation abroad. It believed modern aircraft of little use to a non-Western state while "in the event of war foreign countries using British aircraft can be controlled as regards supply of equipment and spares etc" and "small countries are not financially able to create large air forces."[7] By such logic, providing aircraft to Japan would whet a market, not guide design; diplomats agreed. Such thinking was infected by racism. RAF officers doubted "coloured pilots" could be good.[8] They saw Japanese as the most advanced of Asian peoples, but with a genius for copying rather than originality.

The Admiralty, however, opposed this proposal. It regarded the IJN as an able navy and a potential foe; it had no wish to make matters worse. It argued that the RN relied upon superiority in personnel and material. A mission would give Japan all British naval aviation knowledge, therefore none could go.[9] Whitehall found these arguments convincing, and decided the United Kingdom should not help the IJN to develop naval aviation, but control over decisions slipped from its control. The government agreed an "unofficial" civil aviation mission could go to Japan. This decision had a loophole. Since 1918, Japanese authorities had pursued aviation assistance from different British departments. An unofficial mission offered some access and the chance to pursue more, by cooperating precisely with those agencies which most wished to promote aviation ties with Japan. These agencies could do anything they wanted, because no one monitored the matter until it was too late. Thus the British received the worst of both worlds. The mission was not "unofficial"—it had much support from the RAF, even more from arms firms, while its members acted as if their duty was to Japan. Yet the IJN could more easily control such a body than an official mission, charged to work with the embassy and for a British department; and also use the opportunity to acquire information Whitehall wished to deny Japan. As soon as it began to form, the British government lost control over the mission. Working closely with Vickers and the CAD, the Japanese Naval Attache organized a mission of ex-Royal Navy Air Service (RNAS) personnel, 19 officers and nine warrant officers, led by Colonel the Master of Sempill, a leading figure in British aviation.[10] Five officer instructors taught basic flying, while others offered advanced work in deck-landing, fighters, seaplanes and flying-boats. This professional team instructed ground crew in photography, drawing and design, engine maintenance, armament and medical techniques, and the development of an airbase. It carried an almost complete inventory of the equipment of British naval aviation, 113 aircraft of 17 models, five used by the British Fleet Air Arm, seven engines, bombs, torpedoes and wireless equipment. The Air Ministry let firms tender their most modern equipment, so long as they did not refer to RAF specifications.[11] Japanese firms procured patent rights to produce much of this kit in Japan.

When the mission arrived, it found the IJNAF a small and primitive service. Its first visit to the main training station, Kasimaguara, revealed a wild plateau overlooking rock, woods, and a 60-square-mile lagoon. Rice paddies and woods covered the proposed location of the landing strip. Within three weeks, paddies were filled in, stumps uprooted, a good landing strip established and the main buildings almost completed. The base opened on 22 July 1921. An audience of 30,000 Japanese, including a who's who of admirals, witnessed a display of British formation flying and exhibition parachuting. As an admiral placed a propeller on a shrine, a Shinto ceremony cleansed Kasimaguara of whatever evil spirits had not been washed away by the early morning rain. With reluctant Japanese concurrence, the mission replaced the existing syllabus and decided to re-train all IJNAF pilots before starting advanced work with them, or the primary training of new personnel. This hurt Japanese pride and threw the mission's schedule off by eight months; it focused on basic training, but at least this ensured the basis was sound. Members of the mission were dismayed that no senior Japanese officer understood aviation and deplored the quality of pilots. They did not initially recognize the tremendous Japanese desire for self-improvement. Instructors found ground crews committed and sound, if below RAF standards. Seamen and officers under armament instruction were excellent, as was pilots' gunnery. Instructors thought the class of re-training pilots, which began on 1 September 1921, inefficient, and disliked their unwillingness to maintain their own aircraft, but worked hard to strengthen their students. The re-training class received tuition in all advanced work, like torpedo dropping. In the space of one week, aircraft linked the past and future of British-Japanese conflict. On 8 April 1922, the retraining flight flew past Kagoshima, which the RN had bombarded in 1864. Four days later, the mission flew escort for HMS *Renown* into Tokyo harbour, carrying the Prince of Wales on his world tour. *Renown's* first sight of Japanese naval aviation was happier than that of its sister ship HMS *Repulse* off Malaya on 10 December 1941.

Meanwhile, without Sempill or Whitehall realizing it, the IJN seized control of the mission. It asked the mission to extend its contract from March to July 1922, allowing it time to train a new class, and approached a select few to stay on for a further year, without consulting Sempill or including him. The IJN assimilated this skeleton into its organization, acquiring a decent copy of the world's best training facilities for naval aviation. Until it left in early 1924, this skeleton managed the routine training of ground crew, while Japanese graduates steadily took over a larger part of the work. By late 1922, a base of 1,000 square acres was established at Kasimagaura, with landing strips, hangars, barracks, classrooms, machine shops and firing ranges. The crowning achievement of the skeleton mission was preparation for work with aircraft-carriers, which was completed with the first deck-landings on *Hosho* in 1923. The mission, however, had little expertise on the key issues of organizing aircraft-carriers. Ironically, the Admiralty provided more aid in this area when, seeking to mislead the IJN on technical issues, it inadvertently led the Japanese Naval Attache to conclude island-deck carriers were the wave of the future. The Sempill mission gave 18 months of sound basic training to the IJNAF and another 18 months of oversight as it took over the work, and outlined the development of the institution for coming years. At a dinner before the mission left, the commander of the IJNAF, Rear-Admiral Tajiri, toasted "You departing Members, to whose competent efforts we are so much indebted for this great development, and you dear pals, whose kindness has so richly earned our sincere friendly love and esteem, we are so sorry to have to say good-bye to you."[12] These sentiments were sincere. They were justified.

In early 1923, however, the British-Japanese relationship over aviation took a sharp turn. At the IJN's request, two members of the mission, especially Sempill, pressed the Air Ministry to give Japan more information; no doubt the main concerns were about aircraft-carriers. While technical personnel remained helpful, the Air Staff vetoed any further Japanese access to advanced British material about naval aviation.[13] It did so because British codebreaking and security services, the Government Code & Cypher School (GC&CS) and MI5, discovered the IJN was using espionage to augment the aid of the Sempill mission. In June 1922, an ex-RNAS officer, whom the Japanese initially called "Butland" but later identified as Lieutenant-Commander Frederick Rutland, told the Japanese Naval Attache in London he was serving on board the aircraft-carrier HMS *Eagle*, "desired a Japanese engagement," and could provide information on naval aviation. "Rutland of Jutland," so called because he overflew that battle in a seaplane, was among the two or three air officers in the world most experienced with aircraft-carriers. Between December 1922 and February 1923, the GC&CS showed the IJN intended to pursue this chance to acquire intelligence about aircraft-carriers—in which it was vitally concerned, as Japanese carriers and ideas about them were having their first sea-trials. However, since "special secrecy is being observed" about carriers and to hire anyone experienced with them would raise suspicions, the IJN moved discussions with Rutland to Paris, deferred his trip to Japan for a year and warned him to avoid "close relations with Sempill."[14] Rutland followed this proposal, and lived in Japan for several years. The British took no action about him other than to monitor his activities abroad, because they were impossible to stop. This news, however, sharpened suspicions of Japan and the decision to deny it advanced aerial technology. Some years later, the GC&CS found that Sempill was on a retainer to point the IJN toward new aviation equipment, though this was not unusual for an arms salesman, nor treasonable.[15] Rutland, however, was a traitor, and a significant one. The IJN hired him for intelligence about aircraft-carriers, at a time when it wanted to tap British expertise on their internal organization, regarding which only the U.K. had knowledge at this time. The IJN had no experience in this complicated matter, that of the Sempill mission was tiny but Rutland's detailed; it was transmitted to Japan. How much this help mattered is uncertain; after all, a German advisor to the IJN on submarines later complained, "I am tired of this job where I have nothing to do and less to say. My work consists of reporting to my office…and there reading newspapers and the latest novels."[16] Yet when added together, Rutland and the Sempill mission gave the IJN five years of education on all elements of naval aviation, basic to advanced, and together with the Admiralty transferred all British techniques and technology to Japan; there are English roots to Pearl Harbour.

Through shrewd manipulation of Britons, between 1921–25 the IJN overturned British efforts to slow Japanese development of naval aviation, and instead used it to advance. The IJN profited by following the British wake through troubled waters, though at the price of following poor practices as well as good ones. British aid did not end in 1923. Between 1928–32 three missions, one with 10 members and representatives from aviation firms, advised the Japanese air forces on maintenance, tactics, air gunnery and armament. The IJN insisted these officers be combat veterans able to provide advanced tuition, for which it paid a premium.[17] Whitehall tolerated these missions, and sent official representatives with them. Yet their assistance was technical, nor did the IJN need more—it was surpassing the RN in the trajectory of naval aviation. By 1923, the IJN had developed a good foundation for naval aviation, improving its position relative to the United States Navy (USN) and the RN, both of which were running hard. In aircrew and industry, and the ability to design aircraft or advanced equipment, it was years behind the leading edge, but in other areas it was advanced. *Hosho* was the first purpose-built aircraft-carrier to reach the water. The IJN had pulled close to the USN in the development of carriers, though further behind the RN. It was less well placed than its two rivals for the next phase of the race, because its base of training and cadres was less good, but its achievement was remarkable. All the IJN lacked was expertise. The British offered it the chance to leap from 1914 to 1921 in a single bound. The IJN made the leap. By 1926, in crude terms, the IJN's air service matched those of the USN and the RN, and it had narrowed the gap in quality. It had 12 1/2 service flights with 240 aircraft, perhaps a third being seaplanes and flying-boats, 90 training aircraft and 200 obsolescent aircraft in reserve. This shore-based strength was intended to reach 17 squadrons by 1931. It had a seaplane-carrier, *Nagato*, an operational aircraft-carrier, *Hosho*, two more, *Akagi* and *Kaga*, nearing completion, with several squadrons ready for service with them, not far from the USN's position, though years behind the RN. The IJNAF had a proven deck-landing capacity, good aircrew and numerical air superiority over any enemy fleet venturing within range of its air bases. Its training establishments and industrial capacity provided a sound base for expansion, if still below British-American standards. By 1929, the IJN had become second to none in naval aviation. It was led by its admiral who was most authoritative in naval aviation—the first navy on earth where this was the case. Its material and practice equalled any other naval air force, and were central to IJN exercises. The IJNAF's 672 trained and 66 student pilots were 300% larger than the pilot pool of the RN's Fleet Air Arm. The IJN had three aircraft-carriers and over 100 operational carrier aircraft, approximately the RN's strength. It trained its carriers under a separate "Flying Squadron," and was learning the tactical possibilities in the use of several carriers under one command. Its strength in land-based aircraft outweighed that of the RN and USN. The IJNAF's main weakness remained the quality of aircrew and its satellite air industry, which was still below British and American levels, but its relative standing in these areas was rising. Soon, it and the USN led the world in naval aviation, with the British far behind. The IJNAF was the legitimate heir to the RNAS—the only one, since the RAF abandoned that service's approach—and it was the sole navy in the world to emphasize land-based aviation for maritime strikes. Between 7–10 December 1941, the IJN enacted all of the RNAS's ambitions from 1918—its land-based aircraft killed capital ships at sea while a carrier-mounted mission sank battleships in port.

The British helped not just the IJNAF but also the Japanese aviation industry. As the Sempill mission reached Japan, many British aviation experts established plants, trained workforces and transferred technology. Their influence was mother's milk to the infant aircraft industry of Japan. Teams from two British firms reached the Mitsubishi and Yokosuka works, the major naval aviation plants in Japan, each with a designer, engineers and a test pilot; the Vickers group consisted of nine men. Oswald Short of Short Brothers, and perhaps 30 assistants, appeared briefly, to develop a seaplane plant. Three ex-employees of Sopwith received senior positions and three-year contracts in Mitsubishi. They were easy to hire, as their firm had just merged with Hawkers, and ideally suited to develop aircraft along the lines of the IJN's standard model, the Sopwith *Pup*. By 1922, they produced four prototypes, from which stemmed the Mitsubishi I–IV models, standard IJN issue until 1932. These derived from British designs of 1921—as did the RAF's standard naval aviation types of the 1920s. This and other foreign aid advanced the technology and capacity of the Japanese aircraft industry during a formative period, in a complex way. Until 1917, Japanese aviation developed haphazardly, but then a military-industrial complex—two of them—emerged between firms and fighting services. The IJN maintained a productive capacity under its direct control, which built 33% of the 2,000 naval aircraft produced in Japan between 1920–30, including all of its trainers and most of its seaplanes, based on British and German *Hansa* models; conversely, the IJA, which had promoted aircraft design and manufacture between 1910–19, abandoned that enterprise. Between 1921–27, the IJA used copies of French aircraft built under licence while the IJN relied on aircraft designed by foreigners working for Japanese firms—a step the IJA did not take until 1926–28. In turn, businesses had different patterns of relationship with military patrons and foreign firms. Mitsubishi dominated the private production of naval aircraft, relying on British models and aircraft derived from them by British experts, while its aircraft produced for the IJA were licensed French models. Kawasaki, dominant in Army aircraft, relied on French aircraft and from 1926, on models produced by German designers. Both services directed the development of their affiliated industries, the IJN more aggressively, making firms establish relationships with specific foreign businesses and acquire patent rights to particular items. In this context, British influence on the Japanese aviation industry was fundamental, and uniquely so.

  The U.K. played into the IJN's policy of purchasing sample models to guide indigenous design and production. The IJNAF's first units relied on Japanese-manufactured copies of foreign aircraft, replaced by a second generation of native design. These aircraft were effective, if obsolescent. New firms built foreign aircraft and engines on licence, first older British models, then more complex equipment. Established firms moved to design and manufacture their own models, gaining access to foreign technology through piracy or patent rights. Japan bought a copy of every aircraft or accessory which entered production in Europe and the United States. As one Japanese designer said, "Before such divergent solutions of air technique, we are like children before a shop-window of a pastry shop; we want to taste all of them."[18] By 1926–27, Japanese firms and services increasingly liked German technology, which swept away French influence, but still the IJN admired British aircraft and the RAF's policy on technical issues.[19] It procured patent rights to marks of the air-cooled Jupiter and Jaguar engines, and the *Hawk*, *Gamecock* and *Bulldog* fighters. British and German aircraft engines, and Japanese variants, dominated the market. Until 1931, British influence on Japanese aviation matched that of any country, and was fundamental to naval aviation. Between 1921–31, 33% of the 2,000 IJNAF aircraft constructed in Japan were built from British licences and another third from Mitsubishi's versions of British designs, the remainder being trainers and seaplanes.[20] In the late 1920s, despite competition from German and Japanese designers, the IJNAF's second generation "Carrier Attack Airplane" and fighter were licensed from British models. The experimental designs of Mitsubishi and other firms relied on British technology, like the Rolls-Royce Buzzard engine and *Sidestrand* and *Overstrand* aircraft; the Jupiter engine, or copies of it, remained standard on IJNAF aircraft, while British seaplanes and flying-boats remained influential.[21] From 1933, however, British influence collapsed, replaced by American, and Japanese firms produced better naval aircraft than British ones did.

Between 1918–41, Japan acquired access to all the world's aircraft for a small cost, in the most one-sided strategic investment on record. It created a new industry in a short time, with a quality ranging from the poor to the excellent, which matched those of every country except the U.K., Germany and the United States and briefly reached their standard. In this process, British experiences were like those of all advanced states. Foreign firms routinely let Japanese teams into their facilities to watch manufacture. The Japanese manipulated American and German businesses and departments perhaps even more effectively than British ones. They used shrewd negotiating tactics to gain access to American aviation technology. Between August 1936 to April 1938, Japanese firms bought 50 American aircraft or engines, in 25 cases purchasing one item, in another eight instances, just two or three, with occasional orders of up to 20 items. Between 1941–45, they stripmined German aviation technology for free.[22] The Japanese squeezed leading firms and countries, and dropped them when they fell behind, turning to the new leader. For the British, the transaction was not one-sided—probably they gained more than did any other country from their involvement in Japanese aviation. Japanese orders for British aircraft and patent rights may have been the largest aviation sale of the 1920s—in any year between 1922 and 1924, every firm in the United States altogether exported fewer aircraft than the Sempill mission carried to Japan; and it came at a critical moment for the British aircraft industry, helping many firms, especially Vickers, Supermarine and A.V. Roe, survive a period of catastrophically shrinking design. Japan was a sizable component of the international market for British aircraft, though this was a tiny part of its exports of manufactured goods to Japan, smaller than that of bicycles, for example. The Sempill mission did help the U.K.—simply less than it did the IJN.

By 1930, student had become master. British authorities made this possible because they thought it impossible. They regarded British aviation as superior to Japanese by nature. Racism shaped this view, as did hubris, a sense the issue was insignificant, an arrogance doubled in danger because it was unthinking. Almost through oversight, Japan received access to the expertise of the best naval aviation force and industry of the day, in the most significant transfer of military technology and expertise of the interwar era. All that remained was the proof of mastery, of war.

Not merely did Japanese airpower rise; the RAF did not realize this was happening. Its estimate of the matter rose between 1920–41, but then it began from a low level. In its first postwar assessment of Japanese air abilities, the Air Staff stated during 1920, "The Japanese are not apt pilots probably for the same reason that keeps them indifferent horsemen"—presumably referring to the fact that the better pilots of World War One came from social groups acquainted with the horse, whether European aristocrats or Canadian farmers; Japanese farmers were not famed for horsemanship. The RAF pledged to defend Hong Kong with four squadrons against 12 Japanese, which probably was possible at that time.[23] In 1921, it thought Japanese airpower "in a very embryonic state, and the nation seems to have little 'flair' for aerial work, possibly for the same reason that keeps them indifferent horsemen. It will therefore be a comparatively simple task to keep our lead over the Japanese in aerial matters."[24] The RAF maintained few means to pursue that prediction, and usually ignored Japan, though this attitude changed slowly. By 1938, the RAF believed Japanese success in China would lead to its dominance in Asia, with "'deplorable' consequences for Britain."[25] Generally, however, the RAF viewed Japan through the prism of bureaucratic politics. One of its main arguments in inter-service battles was "substitution," the idea that airpower could handle jobs more economically than the Army or Navy, and therefore the RAF should control such tasks and their finances. Though the RAF did not think Japan a threat, it saw the Singapore base as a chance. Control over its defence would feed several RAF squadrons, which could then sustain further substitution. By 1925, it formulated a remarkable theory: that the same squadrons in Asia could simultaneously replace infantry on the northwest frontier of India, cruisers for trade protection in the Indian Ocean, and 15" guns at Singapore, while the mere threat that the U.K. could deploy air forces to Singapore would deter Japan from war.[26] These were key roots for the defence of Singapore in 1941, when the RAF focused as much attention on defeating the Army and the Navy as the Japanese.

The RAF rarely thought about war with Japan, but it did have ideas as to how one would occur. The RAF thought the U.K. especially suited to airpower and Japan uniquely susceptible to it. From 1920, the RAF held that a few aircraft in Singapore "would be of themselves the greatest possible deterrent" to Japan.[27] The IJN would not expose warships to the RAF near Singapore, while the RAF would frighten Japanese in peace and war. This idea stemmed from the RAF's general belief that strategic bombing could break the will of any nation, including their own, and the inchoate concept that Japanese were particularly vulnerable to it. British observers produced several generalizations about Japanese "national character," which shaped Whitehall's strategy. They believed the Japanese soul was characterized by a mixture of repression, tension and unpredictability which would break under pressure. The morale of Japanese, unused to setbacks or defeat, would snap if a sharp reverse occurred when war started; doubly so if, contrary to official propaganda, an enemy struck the sacred land of Japan. In 1921, one Army language officer speculated that "the destruction by aerial bombing" of shrines central to state Shintoism could shatter Japanese nerve.[28] In 1941, the Military Intelligence Department held that Japanese, while tough fatalists, had no experience of defeat, and were apt "to panic in an unforeseen emergency. Air bombing on an intensive basis of Japanese towns might well cause such panic, as incendiaries would be particularly effective against native Japanese houses"; "The best way to attack their morale would be to shake their faith in their own invincibility, and the immunity of their shores from attack" through bombing. It retained these ideas well after war broke out.[29] They were widespread. In 1940, the British Naval Attache in Tokyo argued that in case of war, carrier-borne aircraft should immediately firebomb Japanese cities. This:

> would create such havoc and despair, which might well knock Japan out at once. The cities would be a sheet of flames which no fire brigade could cope with. Machinery would be destroyed which could never be replaced in Japan. The moral effect would be so great, when one considers that it would be the first time that war had been brought to their sacred country, that anything internal might happen.

The Foreign Office thought that to despatch just one aircraft-carrier to the Pacific would deter Japan or destroy it—at a time when the IJN had developed the most dangerous carrier force in the world![30] Naturally, RAF officers shared such ideas. In 1937, Air Intelligence noted how Japan had built a sizable air defence in reaction to a small Soviet air force at Vladivostok, proving its sensitivity to air threat.[31] In 1941, the RAF at Singapore focused on the idea of bombing Japan as soon as possible, if war broke out.

These ideas about Japan rested on assumption above evidence. Between 1919–29, most foreign commentators regarded Japanese aviation with disdain. Members of the Sempill mission offered more favourable views, the most positive of any Western observers before 8 December 1941, though still these were mixed. One told American officers "the Japanese make average pilots, but require a little longer time to train…than the average European or American. He considers the great majority of Japanese pilots as purely mechanical fliers who lose their heads completely when anything unexpected happens," though "extremely courageous" pilots who no doubt would improve.[32] Sempill believed Japanese pilots could become tolerable by European standards, though few were "exceptionally brilliant," most "will be probably lacking in resource and initiative" and all suffered from lack of experience with machinery.

The cult of bushido, education and tradition, aim at producing a racial rather than an individual type. It is not surprising, therefore, that Japanese pilots do not always show that instantaneous and instinctive sense of prompt action under entirely unexpected conditions. Given time, however, they will extricate themselves successfully, and no doubt training and long experience will breed the qualities required. Their courage and determination to carry out orders under any conditions are most notable.[33]

Similarly A. G. Loton, the mission's basic flying instructor, thought Japanese pilots "very good. They are steady and reliable and I think the average is high. They produce very few star turns but also have very few failures. The great failing is that they are not quick enough in an emergency." Another, Vaughan-Fowler, thought Japanese establishments equalled any that he knew, and that Japanese learned as quickly as Britons. "The personnel were very keen and could learn quickly under the most difficult conditions, and although they had certain racial difficulties to contend with, they were likely to turn out very well." He was particularly impressed by the quality of his advanced fighter course, who were brave and good pilots, fast to react, if not to think. This surprised him, since Japanese were poor horsemen, while "it is a well-known fact that nations that are good horsemen make good pilots." This exception he credited to practice in their native arts.[34]

Some Britons did agree that for "racial" reasons, Japanese suffered from poor eyesight or balance, which must affect their military capacity; junior personnel frequently expressed vulgar racism. However, vulgar or scientific racism did not dominate the views of most decision-makers. They used vulgar language more than we think proper, leading us to mistake statements of abuse for the nature of analysis. Observers, commanders and statesmen saw Japanese military forces through the lenses of preconceptions about war, Japan and its military institutions. The great problem with their views was not racism, but ethnocentrism; they treated their own approach to war as the universal means to measure military value. By 1941, they measured Japanese and British quality by the standard of Western Europe rather than Eastern Asia; and assumed these rankings would prevail in Southeast Asia. Military ethnocentrism was the greatest cause for mistaken estimates of Japan, followed by the way Britons conceptualized their understanding. Assessments of likely Japanese performance in combat considered not merely tactical characteristics but "national character." Empirical observation might illuminate the behaviour of Japanese individuals; generalizations alone could explain "the Japanese," and the broader the question, the greater the conceptualization required for an answer. Four intellectual traditions affected these generalizations; classical racism as espoused by such men as Houston Stewart Chamberlain; scientific racism and its bastard child, Social Darwinism; environmentalist thinking; finally, the concept in which all of these traditions tended to be merged, views of "national character."[35] Although each tradition was distinct, generally they hunted in a pack; nor was "racism" always top dog. When defined properly, this term must refer to the idea that notable traits occur, invariably or in some predictable fashion, among people of a given "race" and for genetic—as against cultural—reasons. It was part of the views at hand, powerful on some topics or certain minds—including two key officers in autumn 1941, Air Chief Marshal Robert Brooke-Popham and General Archibald Wavell, Commanders-in-Chief of Far East Command and the Indian Army. Across the board, however, military and cultural ethnocentrism and views of national character were equally important to this bundle of ideas. Neither form of racism distorted assessments of the IJA so far as they did Japanese naval or air forces, and even in those cases what is labelled "racism" usually was cultural ethnocentrism tinged by racist terminology.

Not that ethnocentrism comes for free. It hampers judgement of any group which behaves unlike one's own; its effect can be overcome only by recognizing and correcting one's own biases—easier said than done. Again, ideas of "national characteristics" have power, in alloy with weakness. These ideas produce overgeneralizations, predictions about group behaviour which are wrong about many of their members some of the time, and some of them most of the time. Predictions derived from these ideas are crude: at any time perhaps mostly right, but never entirely so. They are descriptive, fitting behaviour which has been observed, but useless in predicting new forms—despite the treacherous temptation they offer in that direction. These ideas did not prevent people from changing their minds or learning. Observers were able to change their opinions immediately in response to experience or observation. What these ideas did was cause people to make specific—often misleading—predictions in the absence of evidence. For a combination of genetic and environmental factors, Japanese were regarded as lacking aptitude for machines and the capacity for innovation; and yet as having great endurance, obedience to hierarchy and organizational ability. Air and naval officers prized the first set of qualities far above the second; these ideas led them to underrate Japanese pilots and sailors. Soldiers respected the qualities in both categories; this led them to respect the IJA's infantry but criticize its artillery and armour.[36] Japanese infantry and fighter pilots formed the opposite extremes of the spectrum; the one admirable, the other not, for the same reasons. Observers drew less consistently from another set of qualities: most saw Japanese as prisoner to their preparations, unable to learn quickly or improvise, prone to hysteria, while a substantial body of commentators saw Japanese as uniquely quick to learn and to overcome error. The nature and effect of assessment varied with the British service. The Army had good intelligence on Japan which was assessed with excellence, accepted at the highest levels—and ignored in Malaya. The RN's mediocrity in intelligence and assessment was saved by system and circumstances; its strategy, resting on bean counting of warships and a rejection of worst-case planning, was not distorted by its underestimate of Japanese quality; neither was the fate of Force Z.[37] Unlike the RN, the RAF never thought seriously about Japan as a threat nor considered whether it dare rely on unexamined stereotypes. Intelligence and assessment about Japanese airpower were poor, they did affect policy, and they did shape disaster in a direct fashion.

The Air Staff paid little attention to Japan. An Air Attache was first appointed there in 1934, while perhaps five RAF personnel served as language officers with the IJAAF between 1918–39, as against 35 Army officers attached to the IJA. The RAF really had just one Japanese expert, R. W. Chappell, who served as language officer in the 1920s, Air Attache during the 1930s and the senior Air Intelligence officer at Far East Combined Bureau (FECB) in Singapore during 1941. He and other RAF observers were hampered by cultural and institutional ethnocentrism. They believed that because bases were untidy, units must be incompetent; that where the IJAAF differed from the RAF it must be inferior. RAF enlisted men served for twelve years, the IJAAF had short-term conscripts: this explained why equipment was badly maintained in Japanese units, and indicated that failing must continue so long as conscripts did. RAF officers, coming from a socially insecure service, emphasized personal behaviour—sportsman-like behaviour, natty grooming—which IJAAF officers did not, and disliked Japanese professional attributes, seeing studiousness as swotting. They attempted to embody the cavalry spirit, and British chivalry always regarded the Japanese horse with disdain. RAF officers overstated the significance of individualism for air combat; since Japanese culture downplayed that characteristic, while Japanese were bad with machines, they must make poor fighter pilots—not so. Even worse, when RAF observers saw specific weaknesses, they looked for general explanations. Once formulated, the latter took on a life of their own, predicting problems which must emerge in the future. Because Japanese made poor horsemen, they must lack the social classes which alone produced good pilots, because industry was rare in Japan, Japanese must be bad with machines, and unable to make good aircraft or maintain them: therefore, aircrew and equipment must continue to be bad, even if there was no evidence on the matter. When analyzing foreign airpower, RAF officers poured much racism into the bottle of national characteristics. They doubted any non-Western people could develop good pilots and air forces, and used crude forms of national and class stereotyping to assess every country, which affected British strategy toward Germany, France and Italy, not just Japan.[38] These problems were doubled because Japanese air forces and industries were in their infancy, and redoubled because the RAF looked most at the worst of the two air forces of Japan, the IJAAF, a poor service struggling to achieve mediocrity. With many weaknesses to observe, strengths were easy to miss.

Though no Fleet Air Arm personnel were seconded to the IJNAF, British naval and naval aviation officers respected that service, more than any Western observers did the IJAAF, largely because it had been trained on the model of the RNAS. In 1931, one Naval Attaché stated:

> The average pilot appears to be entirely without fear and keen to fly at all times. He would undoubtedly carry out any duty allotted to him to the best of his ability, and would continue as far as possible towards his objective regardless of superior opposition. In air fighting, it is considered that rather than be defeated he would ram his opponent if the opportunity occurred. If either shot through the tank or otherwise incapacitated while over enemy territory, it is highly probable that he would purposely crash and kill himself rather than be taken prisoner. His loyalty and devotion to duty is to be much admired. The average Japanese pilot is perhaps rather lacking in mechanical sense and slow to act in an emergency, but as an opponent should never be underrated. Judging by the present course of officers, with sound training they should make very good air gunners.

In 1934, the naval aviation chief of the China Squadron gave a more mixed view:

> The training of Japanese Naval pilots is based on the British system and is thoroughly carried out. Their discipline is excellent and morale is high but they do not take naturally to flying and are slow in acquiring "air sense". They are safe pilots while everything is going well but unreliable in an emergency. Intensely patriotic they will carry out their orders no matter what the cost may be.[39]

These assessments were similar to those Army officers made about the IJA, though different weights were assigned to characteristics, and the overall estimate was less favourable, and less accurate.

RAF observers were more negative about the IJAAF. Units were well-organized but maintenance shoddy. Pilots were poor to mediocre, marked by energy and courage, but "an Air Force…cannot fly by discipline alone."[40] "Immersed in theory to the exclusion of practical work," officers were "almost entirely lacking in initiative and although he has had no opportunity of proving otherwise would not appear to make a good fighting pilot."[41] Whatever force these views had before 1930, Japanese air forces then rose sharply in quality—the IJNAF surged past the Fleet Air Arm and ran the RAF a race, though the

IJAAF remained inferior—while Japanese firms produced some excellent and original models. By 1936, Japan entered the first rank of airpowers. Foreigners miscalculated this achievement and error was easy. In 1932, the last year when foreigners could freely observe Japan's air forces and industry, they were mediocre. Then, as a revolution in airpower occurred in Japan and the world, observers tried to gauge developments which Japanese tried to disguise. Precisely after the first aircraft of indigenous design entered production, the Japanese prevented observation of later, far better, ones. Chappell noted:

> Secrecy appears to have become a mania and information with regard to aircraft which have already been nearly a year in service is refused...When visiting aircraft factories the procedure usually consists of drinking many cups of unwanted tea with the manager and then being hustled through one or two shops of little interest, and a refusal to see those departments which are engaged on work for the Army.[42]

Forced into guesswork, foreigners doubted that air forces once moving at a sluggish pace could suddenly have picked it up as the Japanese were doing. They failed to appreciate the mature quality of Japanese aviation because they had played nursemaid in its childhood. They retained images true of infancy but not adolescence; generalizations coined to explain old weaknesses predicted future ones. RAF observers guessed slightly worse than usual among Westerners, nowhere more than about aircraft design. Chappell noted that Japanese wished to improve the quality of their aircraft, but "one does not need to be a Sherlock Holmes" to discover almost every model was copied from Western designs. "At present there appears to be no likelihood of Japan producing anything original."[43] British observers assumed Japan could not produce first-rate aircraft in large numbers or match the leading edge of development, precisely when such stereotypes ceased to be true. Given the revolution of the period, this led to exactly the wrong prediction that the relative quality of Japanese air equipment would slide instead of rise. In fact, between 1935–41, Japanese and British aircraft were roughly equal in quality, though ultimately the British industry had far more breadth and depth.

All this was reinforced by observation of the Sino-Japanese War where, until 1939, the IJNAF and IJAAF deployed older equipment, reinforcing the British belief they had nothing else. Their performance was mediocre—but no more so than that of the French, Russian and Italian air forces or of RAF tactical and strategic bombing before 1942. British observers thought this performance incompetent because they compared it to what they imagined airpower and the RAF could do; unfortunately, imagination outstripped reality. In 1937, Wing

Commander Bishop, the senior RAF officer in Hong Kong—and at various points in 1941, Head of the Operations section of the RAF in Malaya and commander of its Northern Area, responsible for tactical air preparation against Japan— thought IJNAF operations against Canton and the railways between Canton, Hankow and Kowloon—easy targets—dismal failures, because pilots, poorly trained and equipped, could not bomb effectively in perfect conditions, concentrate forces, assess vulnerabilities or strike them. "Whether they are learning by experience remains to be seen."[44] His successor answered this question in the negative. Though "very nearly unbelievable" to report, the Japanese had overcome none of their elementary problems, despite 11 months experience. Their campaign was "the classic example of the misuse of airpower."[45] The British Air Attache, Shanghai, thought that despite a "considerable improvement" in its performance and industry, Japan "cannot be considered a first-class air power."[46] Until the summer of 1941, IJAAF and IJNAF in China had few modern aircraft; thus, in 1940, when British and Germans used high-performance monoplane fighters, in China, Japan relied on biplanes, as British air defence had done in 1938. Like British Army observers of the IJA, though to a lesser degree, RAF commentators in Japan and China had different views on their subject. In 1937 Chappell thought IJAAF training "probably varies considerably, excellent in some units and in other cases may be dangerously poor." The IJNAF and the IJAAF could handle Chinese and possibly Soviet air forces, "but cannot be considered a major hazard to any first-class Power fighting under equal conditions."[47] This marked a rise in his estimate, which became even more notable by 1939. Japanese air forces had fought well in China, because their system was sound. The "spirit of readiness to die for the Emperor proved invaluable in maintaining the morale of pilots at the highest pitch." Its aircraft industry was efficient and should soon match "the lesser of the first-class Powers."[48] These were more positive views about Japanese airpower than any British authority had ever uttered; they had no effect.

    Between 1921–41, detailed RAF ideas about war against Japan rested on an unflattering idea of its capacity. In 1922, reflecting initial reports from the Sempill mission, the RAF noted that Japanese pilots were slow to train and "the statement has arisen that the Japanese are not, and never will make good pilots."[49] The RAF maintained this confidence for 15 years, though it also recognized a rise in Japanese airpower. In 1930 an inter-service study concluded three to five RAF squadrons could stop 15 Japanese squadrons at Hong Kong—in effect, that the quality of the RAF against the IJAAF had stayed constant since 1920 or risen! By 1934, given the IJAAF's strength, the RAF thought even five RAF squadrons could merely slow the loss of Hong Kong.[50] By 1938, it conceded Hong Kong was indefensible: "The Japanese can today operate a formidable air striking force," which would rise "very appreciably." Meanwhile, in 1933 the RAF thought Soviet air forces better than

Japanese; by 1939 it no longer assumed this to be so.[51] Nonetheless, it believed Japan had barely budged the ratio of quality against the RAF, which could still match at least twice its weight in Japanese aircraft. By 1937–40, official estimates of Japanese airpower were unfavourable, but not entirely so. The Chiefs of Staff noted that British and Japanese equipment in Asia were roughly equal, and the RAF "greatly inferior" in strength but far better in quality, especially regarding maintenance. Japanese pilots were "fairly good" and their morale "very high"; their "main weakness…is lack of initiative: a plan once made is rigidly adhered to, even when circumstances make an alternative imperative. There is no lack of courage—volunteers would be forthcoming for desperate adventures of any kind."[52] The Joint Intelligence Committee (JIC) thought Japanese pilots and organization "good" but their industry "behind that of other first-class Powers" and their aircraft "slight" variations of foreign designs.[53] The RAF's *Handbook on the Air Services of Japan*, its only official compendium on the topic, stated:

> The Japanese are, and always have been, a race with strong military traditions. They possess fully the virtues of loyalty, physical courage, endurance, and determination. They are very inquisitive, and conscientious and indefatigable imitators, displaying much discrimination in the use they make of the inventions and methods of others. Their facility in cooperation is also remarkable, as opposed to the strong individualism of the Anglo-Saxon. They possess an infinite capacity for taking pains, great powers of organization even down to the most minute detail, and a very definite gift of careful planning. Intensely suspicious and naturally secretive, they are able to put their plans into action at the chosen moment with suddenness, speed and efficiency, but with all their qualities they have a definite lack of imagination. The unexpected and the illogical embarrass them more than other races and when their plans break down they lack the capacity to improvise hurriedly, to grasp a new situation quickly or intuitively to rearrange their minds…Their fighting qualities, the legacy of a mighty warrior caste, are to be respected; they are systematically inculcated by education, precept and example with the traditions of personal honour and self-sacrifice. These together with a distinct touch of fanaticism, combine to make the individual no mean adversary.

Japanese "as a race are accustomed to discipline and to regimentation" and had a "latent streak of savagery and cruelty which war brings to the surface—a phenomenon not confined to the Japanese." Their pilots were brave and disciplined, good at set pieces but, with some "brilliant exceptions," they were "slower witted" than Europeans: "the national tendency to slow thinking and consequent dependence on routine must prove a handicap in turning out young pilots as good as those of the leading European Air Powers." The "standard of flying" had improved and "can now be classed as good." IJNAF pilots were "well trained as specialists," but not IJAAF ones. Enlisted airmen were hardy and eager but still conscripts, which crippled the quality of units and maintenance. In a war, Japanese airpower would erode far more quickly than that of a Western air force, especially when far from its bases. The RAF assessed Japanese operational characteristics well, noting that against China, it had first acquired air superiority by attacking enemy airbases, and then emphasized close air support. "Japan can hold her own in the air against the U.S.S.R., but she cannot yet be considered the equal, in essential respects, of the leading air powers of Europe." Its aviation industry was mediocre, though improving. Its aircraft were efficient, but not "of performance equal to that of the first-class European powers or of the U.S.A.":

> Japanese designers have not yet reached a standard equal to that of the designers of the leading European countries. Hence for aircraft of the highest military performance they have to depend on purchase…As yet the Japanese have shown no national inventive genius in the whole wide realm of mechanics. Their undoubtedly efficient machines derive entirely from Western models, copied or modified. It is not to be supposed, therefore, that in the highly specialized and ever advancing technique of aircraft design they will do more than follow Western ideas for a considerable period. Thus in this particular, their efficiency vis-a-vis Western Power [sic] is limited.[54]

These estimates were wrong; and unofficially during 1940–41 most British observers had worse ones, fed by decades of unfavourable assessment, ethnocentrism, vulgar racism, and overconfidence about themselves. Japanese airpower was believed to have four weaknesses—mediocrity in maintenance, industry, aircrew and air combat, and the nation a psychological inability to withstand strategic bombing, each serious and the whole fatal. In 1940, commanders at Singapore noted:

> Experience in China goes to show that in all cases when determined A.A. fire, even in small volume, was encountered it has had the effect of driving the Japanese aircraft to high altitudes with consequent deterioration in their bomb aiming. We consider it probable that severe casualties inflicted on the Japanese both by fighters and by A.A. defences would cause a serious drop in their

morale. It is further doubtful if their maintenance and supply organization could withstand serious losses operating at such a distance from their factories.[55]

The Air Attache, Chungking thought most Japanese air equipment second-rate. The IJAAF was bad—"a determined defence and the initial infliction of even the smallest loss" would wreck it. IJNAF pilots were better. They would fight to the death, "if he is outclassed, he will ram rather than run." The quality of Japanese fighters was uncertain, but they had been whipped by Russian pilots around Hankow in 1938—whom British observers had disdained.[56] There were "cracks...in this imposing façade" of Japanese airpower. Their staffs could not handle "prolonged or efficient air opposition," they were unused to opposition and "Japanese do not take their defeats very well":

> If the opening Japanese air effort can be thrown back with considerable loss, it will place the Japanese Air Services in a dilemma from which they will take a long time to recover; a well-organized defence which can inflict initial losses disproportionate to the weight of the attack will receive its reward in the form of breathing space, for the Japanese are most religiously "textbook"; they take time to ponder counter-measures; and they are most careful not to venture again into what has proved to be a dangerous area before they are satisfied that they can escape more or less unscathed.[57]

These comments reflect the confidence about airpower which underlay the defence of the British Empire in Asia against Japan. As one leading British air journal, *The Aeroplane*, wrote during the Tienstin crisis, "judging by what one hears, the Japanese Air Force would not be much of a menace to a first-class European Air Force...Sooner or later we shall have to settle who is the boss of the Pacific...we may yet see our Air Force deciding whether the white man or the yellow man is to rule the East."[58] That estimate was prophecy, but double edged.

Twenty years of unflattering assessment of Japanese airpower shaped strategy and operations in Asia during 1939–41. These matters must be placed in context. Singapore fell to more causes than the effect needed. Menace in Europe produced weakness in Asia, miscalculations of Japanese intentions and British airpower led Whitehall to underestimate the danger, and to pursue policies which led Japan to attack and left the U.K. unable to defend. The primary problem was power. More resources would have reduced the effect of intelligence failures about Japan, or eliminated them. The British would have sent more and better aircraft had the global situation not been so dire. Even so they could have improved defences in Malaya: HMS *Prince of Wales* and *Repulse*, 300 *Spitfires* and *Hurricanes*, able pilots, and a good maritime reconnaissance and strike force, might have defeated the attack of December 1941. Instead, Whitehall starved Malaya, because of the second problem, miscalculation, especially of Japanese intentions but also of their airpower—Wavell rated that error "incredible."[59] It had many roots. After the Battle of Britain, authorities had great faith in the RAF—outnumbered two-to-one, it destroyed 1800 German aircraft for 780 British and blocked invasion. This situation seemed analogous to that in Malaya, and could have been, had the RAF been trained and organized as at home. None of these conditions existed. None were created, because Whitehall thought the RAF even better than expected. The standard of comparison rose while the Japanese remained underestimated in air combat, maintenance and equipment.[60] When calculating Malaya needed 552 aircraft in the first line, authorities in Singapore defined "Japanese determination" against air defence as "about 60% of the German"; 72 British fighters could defeat 175/195 Japanese—2.4 to 2.7 times their strength.[61] Churchill and the Chiefs of Staff thought this view "unduly pessimistic." The RAF had just beaten twice its number of Germans and thrice of Italians. "Capacity of the Japanese should not be overestimated."[62] The JIC held, "The operational value of the JAF is probably akin to that of the Italians"; the Chiefs of Staff told the Australian government they were worse.[63] Whitehall ruled that if outnumbered three-to-one, the RAF could defeat Japan and smash invasion. Local authorities agreed.

Britons were optimistic about quality and quantity. In June 1939, 40 operational aircraft were in Malaya, all obsolete, rising to 164 by December 1941, all reinforcements modern—second-rate but thought better than Japanese. Whitehall put special faith in 60 *Buffalo* fighters, expected to deter attack and win that first victory to crack the nerve of Nippon. They were not expected to beat Japanese airpower on their own. Officials assumed that before war came, the British would place 336 aircraft in Malaya, including better fighters.[64] Japan would not attack, certainly not without ample warning, and it could deploy little power against Malaya. From June 1941, British officials held the risk of war with the U.S.S.R. would occupy Japan's air forces. It could strike Malaya only with 323 aircraft, mostly obsolete, suffering a "presumably high rate of wastage" because of poor maintenance and bad bases, against 336 British aircraft—safe odds.[65] Simple intelligence failures about the size of Japanese air forces in southern Indochina and the presence of torpedo bombers and when the enemy would strike crippled British naval and air operations on 7–10 December 1941 more than did those about quality, though they framed those events. Far East Command Headquarters devoted most of its time not to defence but attack. "Japan's collapse will occur as a result of economic blockade, naval pressure, and air bombardment. This latter form of pressure being the most direct, and one which Japan particularly fears, requires careful planning"; thus the British should rapidly develop air bases to strike Japanese forces in China and possibly their home islands.[66] Far East Command even revived an idea dead for a decade— to strike Japan from Hong Kong.[67] It believed that garrison could stand for a long time, securing a valuable base for "taking offensive action at a later stage of the war."[68] Far East Command wished to send four *Buffaloes* to Hong Kong, which, on the analogy of Malta, just might have a "salutory effect" and hold all Japanese airpower in China at bay.[69]

Overconfidence caused these errors; it had substance. Fighter Command could have beaten twice its strength of Japanese squadrons, not because of pilots or aircraft, but system. A web of errors held British authorities from seeing such a system must be created in Malaya. They underrated the IJNAF and IJAAF, concluded these could not beat the RAF at its best and so sent their worst, and in such small numbers. Air defence lacked four essential ingredients: effective radar equipment, a good command and intelligence system, trained pilots and first-rate aircraft. Whitehall created these problems; the RAF in Malaya exacerbated them. It assumed Britons must be better than Japanese by nature, without effort.[70] The RAF fell below its standards and Japanese ones. Yet, precisely those who most underrated Japan most advocated a powerful RAF in Malaya. Authorities in Singapore warned that without half as many fighters as Japan, the RAF might lose.[71] The heartiest Briton would have feared the four-to-one superiority Japan achieved in the air on 7–10 December 1941. That attack might have failed against the 552 first-class aircraft they wanted, possibly even against 336. Nor was the intelligence failure absolute. In 1940–41, the British Air Attache at Chungking provided some detailed reports about the *Zero* aircraft. Wing Commander Warburton's feelings were mixed, but he was the first RAF observer to break from negative assessment of the IJAAF. In a widely circulated and influential assessment of May 1941 that outlined Japanese weaknesses in the air, he still described the *Zero* as "good" by any standard. This information did not affect views in London or the RAF command in Malaya, denied some of these reports due to Far East Command Headquarters disorganization, and possessing a senior officer, Bishop, expert in and contemptuous of Japanese airpower.[72] At the Far East Command intelligence staff, FECB, however, Chappell was predisposed to expect a rise in Japanese airpower. In September 1941, after examining two Japanese bombers in Thailand, he noted "obviously a great improvement has been made in the manufacture of aircraft by the Japanese." Air Vice-Marshal Pulford, Commander RAF Far East, soon agreed that Japan possessed a bomber-type equal in quality to a good British model, the *Whitley*. Brooke-Popham too accepted some of the reports on Japanese aircraft, though racism influenced his views more than most, while his senior air staff officer despised Japanese airpower. In August, these reports led Brooke-Popham, for the first time, to question the RAF's ability to defend Malaya— to know defeat in the air, though not immediate disaster, was possible.

He outlined a slow-motion version of what occurred in December—two months for two days. He had half the first-line aircraft he needed, 30% of their immediate reserves, and might lose up to 33% of his pilots per month—perhaps 66% the rate expected against Germans. If these losses were not replaced immediately, his power would erode fast. In particular, anti-shipping forces, poor in quantity and quality, might not stop amphibious forces from capturing the airfields on the east coast, wrecking the defence of Malaya. "Not only is our ability to attack shipping deplorably weak but we have not the staying power to sustain even what we could now do. As our air effort dwindles (as it would if war came now) so will the enemy's chances of landing increase."[73] Hence, the Army must be Malaya's main line of defence for some time. Concerns stemmed not only from good intelligence, but bad. British authorities accepted inaccurate reports indicating an imminent rise in Japanese airpower: that a training mission of up to 180 German pilots was in Japan, where large numbers of ME 109s and ME 110s were being manufactured, and some of which were in service. [74] Just before the war, Far East Command raised its estimate of Japanese airpower, which affected planning; the estimate, alas, still was wrong, and the planning executed badly. Only had Whitehall accepted far better views far earlier could this material have reshaped events on 7–8 December 1941.

One should not overstate the impact of intelligence and assessment; Singapore fell to power and policy. Japan would have taken Singapore had it wanted, no matter British deeds; Whitehall made the correct decision in focusing on Western theatres and running risks in Asia. Japan lost and the British won the Second World War, which one might not have predicted in July 1940. The problem was not the policy, but its formulation and execution. In 1941, several fatal shots were fired into the British Empire; had one missed, another would have struck. But in the world as it was, the fatal shot was fired by a British hand, and the bullet was a complex idea: that Japanese leaders were cautious and would not risk war with stronger states, while airpower would deter attack or defeat it. This was wrong. Commander Genda, key to the attack on Pearl Harbour and the senior IJNAF officer in London in 1940, reported home that the Battle of Britain proved the RAF bad and the Luftwaffe worse! He underrated the British as much as Britons did Japan, but his errors sapped the deterrent capability which their mistakes led Britons to think they had.[75] Again, in December 1941 the RAF in Malaya failed in every way—to stop invasion, detect the enemy, sink transports at sea, protect British warships and soldiers, or achieve air superiority. Mistaken faith in airpower cascaded through every other British decision, shaping four fatal flaws in policy. Whitehall believed a few obsolescent aircraft with green aircrew could deter Japan, or defend Malaya and crack Japan like an egg; while pilots need not train for a hard war; nor soldiers, since they need just defend RAF bases. Only had Britons understood the balance of airpower, and of how Tokyo perceived the matter, could they have appreciated that a policy of deterrence and defiance must fail; only then could they have assessed Japanese calculations correctly and made good decisions about the deployment of force, and their defensive and offensive value. Even then, the British merely could have smashed the first attack on Malaya and lasted some months longer. Proper intelligence could have affected only the margins of events, the difference between risk-taking and recklessness, strategy and fantasy, defeat and humiliation. These differences are significant.

John Ferris is Professor of History at the University of Calgary, where he has taught since 1987. He was a leading member of the Anglo-Japanese History Project, and has written widely on strategy, intelligence, the formulation of British strategic policy, British signals intelligence, British-Japanese relations and the background to the fall of Singapore.

NOTES—

All material from AIR, CAB, FO, HW, PAREM and WO files are held by the Public Record Office, London; that from D. Hist. may now be found in the RG 24 series at the National Archives, Ottawa; that from the RG 38 and RG 165 series, at the National Archives, Washington; that from the AWM, at the Australian War Memorial, Canberra; that from the AA material, the Australian Archives, Canberra; and that from SHAT at le Service Historique de l'Armee de Terre, Chateau de Vincennes. The papers of Captain Bottomly, Messrs. Handley-Page and Air Vice-Marshal Maltby are held by the RAF Museum, Hendon; the Vicker's Collection, by the Cambridge University Library; and the Brooke-Popham papers, by the Basil Liddell Hart Centre for Military Archives. All of this material appears with permission of these institutions, and of the copyright holders.

1 [Editor's note:] The editorial policy of this volume is to minimize the use of acronyms as much as possible. But due to the nature of this topic the author had no choice but to refer to services as institutions so many times that in this essay that policy had to be set aside.
2 SHAT 7N 3322, Military Aviation Attache, Tokyo, to French Ambassador, Japan, 5 June 1920.
3 FO371/3819, Military Attache, Memorandum No. 44, 30 June 1919.
4 Vicker's Papers, Cambridge University Library, Historical Document No. 534, Memorandum by unknown author, Foreign Investments, 1 June 1919; B. Nagura, "A Munition-Steel Company and Anglo-Japanese Relations Before and After the First World War: The Corporate Governance of the Japan Steel Works and its British Shareholders", in J. Hunter and S. Sugiyama (eds.), *The History of Anglo-Japanese Relations, 1600–2000*, Vol. IV, *Economic and Business Relations*, London, 2002.
5 Historical Document No. 536, Foreign Business Expenses, London Office Armament Contracts and London Representative and Agency Expenses Including Demonstrations and D.O. Expenses, 31 March 1934.

6   Handley-Page Papers, RAF Museum, Hendon, AC/70/10/77, Handley Page to Air Ministry, 21 July 1921.
7   AIR5/274, Air Staff Views, undated and no author but probably Burnett and circa January 1924.
8   AIR8/46, Minute by Bullock to Secretary of State, 24 November 1926.
9   FO371/5358, Minutes of inter-departmental conference, 22 October 1920.
10 J. Ferris, "A British 'Unofficial' Aviation Mission and Japanese Naval Developments, 1919–29," *The Journal of Strategic Studies*, V, 1982, 416–39. Except where otherwise stated, all citations on the Sempill mission may be found in this article.
11 AC/70/10/77, Director of Aircraft Supplies to Handley Page, 6 January 1921.
12 RAF Museum, X001-2315/024, Speech by Rear-Admiral Tajiri, 7 July 1922.
13 F. N. Brackley, *Brackles*, 1952, privately printed, copy in British Library, 159–72.
14 HW12/42, No. 12246, 9 January 1923; HW12/43, No. 102469, 2 February 1923.
15 HW12/78, No. 022075, 5 January 1926.
16 RG38/E 7C 11942, Memorandum for the DNI, W. G, Sebald, 4 November 1928.
17 HW12/129, Nos. 937869, 037919; HW12/134, No. 039484; HW12/135, 039918, undated.
18 Anonymous "View of the Japanese Air Force," *L'aeronautique*, No. 77, 10 February 1925; J. Ferris, "A British 'Unofficial' Aviation Mission and Japanese Naval Developments, 1919–29."
19 HW12/78, No. 022253, 27 January 1926; HW12/79, No. 022388, 9 February 1926; HW12/79, No. 022481, 25 February 1926.
20 These figures are derived from those on the production of aircraft scattered through the pages of R. C. Mikesh and S. Abe, *Japanese Aircraft, 1910–1941*, Annapolis, 1990.
21 RG165, 2085-852, Memorandum by U.S. Military Attache, London, No. 31380, 25 November 1931, No. 31439, 1 January 1931; RG 165, 2331-H-56, 21 February 1923, U.S. MA, Visit to Mitsubishi and Kawasaki Aircraft Plants; RG 165, 2085-956, SD 130, *Handbook on the Air Services of Japan*; R. C. Mikesh and S. Abe, *Japanese Aircraft, 1910–1941*, 125, 135, 167–72.
22 HW12/43, No. 102700, 27 February 1923; RG165, 2085-913, Licences Issued for Export of Aircraft and Aircraft Engines to Japan, 16 August 1936, to 20 March 1937, Licences Issued for Export of Aircraft and Aircraft Engines to Japan, 31 March 1937 to 14 April 1938; H.-J. Braun, "Technology Transfer Under Conditions of War: German Aero-Technology in Japan During the Second World War," in N. Smith (ed.), *History of Technology*, Eleventh Annual Volume, 1986, London, 1986, 11.
23 CAB5/3, CID Paper 120-C.
24 Ibid.; CAB5/4, CID Paper 156-C.
25 CAB53/42, COS 798; CAB53/10, COS meeting, 23 November 1938.
26 AIR8/45, Lecture by CAS on the employment of airpower on overseas defence, January 1925.
27 CAB5/3, CID Paper 120-C; CAB5/4, CID 156-C.
28 FO371/6681, Memorandum by K. S. Morgan, undated but circa Spring 1921.

29 FO371/27890, Memorandum by MI2c, Japanese Morale, 31 March 1941; WO208/2059A, MacKensie to White, undated, but June–July 1942 according to internal evidence.
30 FO371/24711, F 5308, Minutes by Ashley Clarke, 19 November and R. A. B. Butler, 21 November 1940.
31 AIR9/23, Memorandum by A.I. 2.c, S/L Pelly, Japan's reaction to the threat of bombing by Soviet aircraft, 4 November 1937.
32 RG165, 2085-224, Memorandum by U.S. Military Attache, Japan, Aviation, Tokyo, 31 January 1922.
33 "The British Aviation Mission in Japan," a lecture by Colonel the Master of Sempill, *Transactions and Proceedings of the Japan Society*, Vol. XXII, 1924–25.
34 AIR5/358, Memorandum by Vaughan-Fowler, 1924.
35 J. R. Ferris, "'Worthy of Some Better Enemy?': The British Assessment of the Imperial Japanese Army, 1919–1941, and the Fall of Singapore," *The Canadian Journal of History*, August 1993.
36 Ibid.
37 C. M. Bell, "The Royal Navy, War Planning and Intelligence Between the Wars," in P. Jackson and J. Siegel, *Intelligence and Statecraft: The Use of the Limits to Intelligence in International Society 1870–1970*, Westport, 2002.
38 D. Edgerton, *England and the Aeroplane: An Essay on a Militant and Technological Nation*, London, 1991, 18–59.
39 FO371/12523, Naval Attache, Report No. 5, 11 June 1927; FO371/15520, British Embassy, Tokyo, Japan, Annual Report, 1930; RAF Museum, Hendon, Bottomley Papers, AC 71/9/66, Appreciation of the Situation on 3 March 1934.
40 FO371/21037, Memorandum No. 2, by Air Attache, 9 February 1937.
41 RG165, 2085-647, McLaren to Baldwin, 30 September 1926; FO371/10309, in Tokyo Embassy Despatch No. 23, 18 January 1924, F/L Bryant, A Few Notes on the Japanese Army Air Corps, undated, circa January 1924; AIR 5/756, Military Attache Tokyo, Report No. 16, 27 May 1926, and Tokyo Embassy Despatch No. 443, 13 August 1927; FO371/13246, Tokyo Embassy Despatch No. 639, 20 December 1927, F/L Chappell, Report on the Participation of Aircraft in the Japanese Grand Manoeuvres, 1927, undated, circa December 1927; FO371/21027, Memorandum No. 2, by Air Attache, 9 February 1937; FO371/21037, Tokyo Embassy Despatch No. 84, Memorandum No. 2, by Air Attache, 9 February 1937.
42 FO371/20284, Air Attache, Tokyo, Report No. 20, 19 December 1935.
43 AIR2/2008, Annual Report on the Air Services of Japan, 1936, by Chappell, 28 January 1937.
44 D. Hist., Memorandum by Bishop, General Remarks on Japanese Air Bombardment of Canton-Hankow and Hankow-Kowloon Railways, 16 November 1937; Memorandum by Bishop, Sino-Japanese Hostilities, Conditions in Canton, passim, 24 March 1938.
45 D. Hist., The Bombing of the South China Railways, W/C Walser, 23 August 1938.
46 AIR2/35, British Air Attache, Shanghai, Memorandum on Air Operations During Sino-Japanese Hostilities, 1938, 58.

47 AIR2/2008, Annual Report on the Air Services of Japan, 1936, by Chappell, 28 January 1937.
48 FO371/23570, Air Attache, Tokyo, Annual Report on Aviation in Japan, January 1939.
49 AIR5/810, RAF Monthly Intelligence Report, No. XIII, May 1922.
50 CAB53/24, COS 344; CAB53/4, 96th and 116th meetings of the COS, 9 December 1930, 24 January 1934; CAB53/23, COS 318.
51 CAB16/109, Third meeting of the Defence Requirements Sub-Committee, 4 December 1933.
52 CAB53/32, COS 596.
53 CAB54/6, DCOS 103 JIC.
54 RG165, SD 130, *Handbook on the Air Services of Japan*, 2085-956/2.
55 AWM113/MH/1/95, Report of Singapore Defence Conference 1940, 31 October 1940.
56 D. Hist., Bishop, Report on Military Information Obtained at Hankow, 5 February 1938, covering Boxer, same date, Report on Military Information Obtained at Hankow, 16–26 January, 1938.
57 WO208/722, Hong Kong Naval, Military and Air Force Intelligence Report No. 4/41, 1 May 1941.
58 Anonymous, *The Aeroplane*, 19 July 1939, 78.
59 PREM3/168/3, Memorandum by Wavell, 30 May 1942.
60 PREM3/156/2, COS(40)592, 31 July 1940.
61 AWM113/MH/1/95, Report of Singapore Defence Conference, 1940, App. F, 31 October 1940.
62 AA, A1608/AA 27/1/1, Dominion Office to Australia/New Zealand, telegram No. 49, 26 January 1941.
63 CAB81/102, JIC(41)175 Revise; D. Gillison, *Royal Australian Air Force 1939–1942*, Canberra, 1962, 157.
64 CAB54/8, DCOS 126; AIR23/3575, Memorandum by A. G. Bishop, 9 October 1941; AA, A5954/555/5, Advisory War Council Minute, 16 October 1941.
65 CAB81/103, JIC(41)327, 13 August 1941; WO106/2496, War Office to C-in-C Far East, No. 84981, 19 August 1941.
66 J. R. Ferris, "The Singapore Grip: Preparing Defeat In Malaya, 1939–41," in I. Gow and H. Yoshi (eds.), *A History of Anglo-Japanese Relations: Military Dimensions*, Palgrave, 2002.
67 C. M. Bell, "Our Most Exposed Outpost: Hong Kong and British Far Eastern Strategy," *The Journal of Military History*, 60/1, January, 1996, 33–35.
68 J. R. Ferris, "The Singapore Grip."
69 AIR23/1863, N Section to C of S, undated; AIR23/1870, Memorandum by Joint Planners, Appreciation of Strength of RAF Required in Far East, 3 September 1941; AIR20/291, 243/6, C-in-C Far East to War Office, 24 November 1941; D. Gillison, *Royal Australian Air Force 1939–1942*, 171.
70 RAF Museum, Hendon, AVM Maltby Papers, AC 73/15/22, Memorandum by Maltby, undated, Original, Operations in Malaya and N.E.I.

71 AIR23/3575, Tactical Appreciation of Defence Situation in Malaya, 16 October 1940.
72 WO208/772, Hong Kong Naval, Military and Air Force Intelligence Report No. 4/41, 1 May 1941; AC73/15/22.
73 Brooke-Popham Papers, V/4/26, 359/4, Far East Headquarters to War Office, 20 August 1941; AIR20/289, 305/4, Easfar to Air Ministry, 15 August 1941; AIR23/3575, Pulford to Brooke-Popham, 13 August 1941; FO371/ 31858, Memorandum by Air Attache, Bangkok, No. 1, 26 September 1941; AWM 67/3/220 C, Long to Fairfax, 9 November 1941, quoting Pulford.
74 AIR40/2618, Air Intelligence Reports, from SIS, A.I. No. 32201, 15 July 1941, 33811, 17 October 1941; AWM 54/423/6/17, Memorandum by MI IA, A Review of Japan's Position, undated but circa November 1941, according to internal evidence; AWM 67/3/220 C, Long to Fairfax, 9 November 1941. These reports help to explain why in December 1941, British air officers in Malaya concluded they were being attacked by Germans rather than the Japanese.
75 T. Cook, "The Japanese Perspective," in P. Addison and J. Crang (eds.), *The Burning Blue: A New History of the Battle of Britain*, London, 2000, 108–20.

CHAPTER 16

The Evacuation of Civilians From Hong Kong and Malaya/Singapore, 1939–42

by Kent Fedorowich

Until recently, the trials and tribulations of European civilians interned by the Japanese in the Asia-Pacific region between 1941–45 have received little attention from scholars. Despite the publication of a number of personal accounts from former internees between the mid-1940s and early 1960s,[1] academics have been preoccupied with the larger geo-political, strategic and military issues that unfolded in the Far East during the Pacific War. However, the resurgence in prisoner-of-war studies, in part stimulated by end-of-war anniversaries or campaign commemorations has, since the mid-1980s,[2] prompted renewed interest in the parallel plight of civilian internees.[3] Public interest has also been sparked by the vociferous campaign undertaken by former Allied POWs and internees seeking an official apology and financial compensation from the Japanese government for the horrendous treatment many received during captivity. Revelations over enforced prostitution of mostly Korean "comfort" women—but some European females as well, as dramatically sensationalized by Hollywood in the star-studded movie *Paradise Road*—has kept civilian internment in the public eye. Finally, the release of intelligence records, POW interrogations and war crimes files in a number of Western democracies has, in turn, inspired a new generation of scholars interested in oral history, colonial elites, race, and war and memory to re-examine this hitherto forgotten episode of human endurance.[4]

A number of questions remain unanswered. Why, for example, were so many civilians captured? Were there not contingency plans for the evacuation of European civilians from British Far Eastern colonies? What plans, if any, had been made for important members of the Asian population to flee Japanese aggression? The purpose of this chapter is to examine these and other questions. Using a comparative framework, it analyzes the relative success of the Hong Kong government in getting as many of its European civilians out of the exposed colony with the disastrously ad hoc and last minute policies of the Singapore government. One of the more interesting facets is the tension that existed between civilian and military authorities over the formulation and execution of these policies; and the recriminations which were unleashed during the secret wartime post-mortems—especially over Singapore between the former Commander-in-Chief Far East, Air Chief Marshal Sir Robert Brooke-Popham, and the Governor of the Straits Settlements, Sir Miles Shenton Thomas.

In July 1938, as war clouds gathered on the diplomatic horizon, Brigadier A. E. Grasett was selected as the new General-Officer-Commanding (GOC) Hong Kong. The appointment of this Canadian-born officer dovetailed neatly with the War Office's growing concern over Hong Kong's defensive capabilities. The conundrum for British military planners, as one naval historian has pointed out, was to "strike a balance between the Colony's equivocal wartime role and the resources devoted to its protection."[5] In other words, London had to find a cost-effective way to protect the colony so it could play its dual role in defending British interests in southern China and, if possible, thwarting Japanese incursions southward towards Malaya and Singapore.

Three options concerning the future of Hong Kong were discussed: demilitarization in peacetime; evacuation on the eve or outbreak of hostilities; or to stand fast and defend it. Although the first two options were attractive—not least of which they would release troops for duties elsewhere and allow a welcome reallocation of precious fiscal resources for other military projects—they were quickly dismissed on the grounds they were short-sighted, premature and unnecessarily defeatist. Moreover, if the colony was either demilitarized or abandoned, it would seriously undermine British prestige and influence in China.[6] Nonetheless, the question remained of how best to defend an increasingly isolated outpost of Empire. In the end, the British Chiefs of Staff opted for the cheapest of the three standards proffered by the Joint Overseas and Home Defence Sub-Committee. The Chiefs of Staff recommended to the Committee of Imperial Defence that the best way to defend the colony was to abandon the mainland territories and fortify Hong Kong Island, thus denying the anchorage to enemy forces. This complete recasting of the colony's defence scheme also made it essential to evacuate all European civilians "at a precautionary stage or before it...other than those essential to the defence of the Island."[7]

Under this contingency, it was projected that if the island garrison could hold out for 90 days—later revised to 180—this would allow the Admiralty time to assemble naval relief forces to evict the Japanese from the surrounding mainland. Once secure, the Royal Navy could then use Hong Kong as an advance base to harass Japanese forces, especially the long and precarious lines of communications between Japan and Southeast Asia, which would help it regain the military initiative in the region. How ironic that the strategic illusion of a besieged island garrison supposed to hold out for months while a naval task force steamed to its rescue was not confined to Singapore! For high-ranking officers, such as Air Vice-Marshal J. T. Babington, Air-Officer-Commanding Far East from September 1938–April 1941, this over-reliance in British Far Eastern planning on contingencies connected with the fleet was dangerously myopic. A lot could happen in six months during a so-called period of relief. "It is indeed this continued reliance upon a doubtful contingency," he complained to a confidant in London, "which has all along messed up defence measures in the Far East." Further discussions ensued over the course of 1938–39 as to how best defend Hong Kong. In the end, it was decided not to abandon the mainland defences, known locally as the Gin Drinkers Line, but instead fall back to the island if the garrison was pushed out of the New Territories and Kowloon.[8]

By June 1939, the imperial authorities had prepared contingency plans for the evacuation of non-combatants from Hong Kong in the event of war breaking out. They involved the removal of 5,000 British women and children and 750 other European nationals who would be sent to destinations in India, the Philippines, and Australia.[9] Such precautions seemed fully justified when in mid-August an estimated 15,000 Japanese soldiers, supported by tanks and heavy field artillery, were deployed in the hinterland between Hong Kong and Kwantung province. This caused great anxiety in the colony, as the size of this force—twice that of the 7,000-strong British garrison—was deemed well above that required for simple policing duties along the colony's landward borders. Fearing an imminent attack, the frontier districts on the British side were evacuated, European women and children were advised to leave the colony and the garrison put on a war footing. Despite these contingencies, and the appointment on 4 September 1939 of a Director of Evacuation, the Hong Kong government failed to prepare the necessary evacuation measures. In part, this can be explained by the easing of tensions in the region when, with the shock announcement of the Nazi-Soviet Pact on 23 August, the majority of the Japanese troops along the Hong Kong frontier were hurriedly redeployed north to counter a possible Soviet incursion into Manchuria.[10] Lulled by the false dawn of an "improving" diplomatic situation in the Far East, the failure of the colonial government to implement its evacuation measures during August 1939 proved dangerously short-sighted and would have serious repercussions when the diplomatic climate in the Far East worsened the following year.

The fall of France in June 1940 had direct consequences for the tenuous British position in China. The elimination of France provided the Japanese with an opportunity to consolidate their position in Peking and the treaty ports of Shanghai and Tientsin. With the loss of French support, British influence and prestige was undermined to Japan's advantage.[11] Becoming increasingly strident, Japan demanded the British withdraw their token forces from these three northern cities. Isolated, and of no military consequence, the garrisons were eventually withdrawn to bolster defences in Malaya and Singapore.[12] Meanwhile, concern was voiced regarding the vulnerable position in southern China, especially Hong Kong. In a secret memorandum submitted to the War Office by the newly appointed Chief of the Imperial General Staff, General Sir John Dill, it was re-emphasized that in the event of war with Japan, "Hong Kong would be isolated and the garrison would have very little hope of being relieved." The colony therefore should not be reinforced; it being recognized "that in the event of war it would almost inevitably fall."[13] But what about the safety of the estimated 7,000 European women and children who resided in the colony? What was to be done with them in the event of an attack?

When Grasett received War Office instructions to undertake precautionary measures in the colony on 19 June 1940, he recommended that for defensive purposes the maximum number of women and children be withdrawn to the Philippines or Australia. The Chiefs of Staff concurred, arguing that an evacuation might not be possible in the event of a surprise attack by the Japanese. In addition, the presence of large numbers of British women and children in Hong Kong would be a "serious embarrassment" to the government.[14] If thousands of British civilians were allowed to remain and were interned, not only would untold and unnecessary suffering occur, but the Japanese would also be handed an immense propaganda windfall. No action was to be taken, however, until the Foreign Office was consulted. In the meantime, Hong Kong's Governor, Sir Geoffrey Northcote, agreed that all necessary preparations short of evacuation would be made.

The decision by the Foreign Secretary, Lord Halifax, not to recommend an evacuation was based on the supposition that it might be misconstrued by the Japanese as a sign of weakness. In his opinion, the "whole situation hinged on the attitude of the Japanese." As a result, the War Cabinet decided on 22 June not to evacuate European civilians for the time being. The Secretary of State for War, Anthony Eden, was invited to make the necessary preparations, including the provision of shipping, for the future evacuation of wives and children of service personnel. But a mere three days later, as tension mounted in the Far East, the War Cabinet reviewed the evacuation proposal. At that meeting, Eden challenged Halifax's earlier supposition. Apart from the direct military advantages accrued through evacuation, he suggested that such action demonstrated the U.K. was intent on defending its interests in the Far East. Far from being misunderstood by the Japanese, the evacuation would have a "steadying effect" on Tokyo.[15] The Chiefs of Staff supported Eden. They argued that the Japanese would not "interpret this step as a sign of weakness, rather the reverse." Esler Dening, a senior Foreign Office Consul, concurred. "The Japanese are easily impressed by realities. Measures to evacuate Hong Kong and to defend both Hong Kong and Singapore are realities. A German failure to swamp Great Britain would be the most impressive reality of all." After further consultation with Northcote, Halifax changed his mind and endorsed the evacuation order on 26 June. Two days later, the Foreign Office instructed the Hong Kong authorities to initiate the compulsory evacuation of European women and children.[16]

The announcement caught the colonial government off-guard and completely unprepared. Nevertheless, on 1 July the Hong Kong authorities proceeded with the evacuation order. By 3 August, all the service families had been withdrawn to the Philippines as well as the remainder of the registered non-service British women and children, making a total of 3,474 evacuees. In addition, the War Office refused to grant exit permits to women and children wanting to travel to Hong Kong from the United Kingdom.[17] On the surface, it appeared that the Hong Kong government had responded effectively and efficiently to the evacuation order. But the hurried preparations and the imposition of compulsory registration for evacuation angered many evacuees, their husbands and employers who felt it was premature and unnecessary. The Philippine authorities were not happy either about the way in which the Hong Kong evacuees were "unloaded" on them.[18]

The following sequence of events demonstrates how swiftly the evacuation was conducted. On 29 June, the colonial government was given the authority to order any individual not essential to the defence of the colony to leave. On 2 July, all women and children of European descent were told to report for registration. No exceptions were to be allowed apart from those in essential services such as nursing. However, large numbers of women were exempted when it was suddenly realized that government and commercial business would grind to an immediate halt if deprived of all female clerical staff. Many others simply did not register because they were awaiting notification that their nursing applications had been processed. Some, like the Director of Medical Services, Dr. P. S. Selwyn-Clarke, were simply cunning. Using the cover story that his family was visiting friends in nearby Canton, Selwyn-Clarke contrived the absence of his wife and child on the day of registration and hence avoided his family's compulsory evacuation. In other cases, motivated either by a sense of duty or a determination to be with their loved ones, women themselves immediately challenged the evacuation order. Take the case of the two female missionaries who insisted on staying behind to continue their work. Until their appeals had been decided, these women refused to leave.[19]

Opposition to the evacuation order remained resolute. One Hong Kong newspaper claimed it was "clumsily carried out and entirely unaccompanied by any shock-absorbing arrangements to reduce its effect."[20] At Westminster, the Under-Secretary of State for the Colonies, George Hall, was asked in Parliament if he would comment on the "great distress" caused by the compulsory evacuation order.[21] Throughout July 1940, local Hong Kong newspapers printed scores of letters from angry colonists disgusted by what they saw as the unfair and disorganized manner of the first stage of the evacuation to the Philippines. According to Arthur Jefferies, an employee of the Hong Kong Radio Service, stories had reached the colony about how evacuees had to queue for hours outside the British consul in Manila just to be processed for re-evacuation to Australia. He also told his wife how two naval ratings had received letters from their wives who reported that the situation at Fort McKinley, where they had been quartered in Manila, was frightfully grim. It pained him, he told his wife Kitty, to hear of stories of women and children "[l]ining up for food with tin mugs and plates." In fact, Jefferies had much to be concerned about as his wife and family had been amongst the first wave of evacuees sent to Australia via Manila. "Everybody agrees that the only way in which this evacuation was at all necessary was as a 'Gesture' to the Japs that we would try to hold this place, not that they have shown any inclination to attack. In other words, your 'bit' in this war is as a sacrifice on the Altar of Diplomacy."[22]

For many Europeans, the Hong Kong authorities had simply bungled the entire affair; especially over the apparent sub-standard treatment their loved ones had received while in Manila. Others charged the government with favouritism as some wives and daughters of prominent officials or businessmen were allowed to stay behind on the slimmest of pretences. Jefferies recalled that it was alleged that the Commissioner of Police, T. H. King, used his influence to get his wife and two daughters jobs in the government's censorship branch the day before they were to be evacuated.[23] The Hong Kong General Chamber of Commerce and D. C. Edmonston, the influential manager of the Hong Kong and Shanghai Banking Corporation, lodged robust protests. The latter threatened to take the case to the Judicial Committee of the Privy Council. One embittered woman, who had been evacuated to Manila, "returned and unsuccessfully contested the legality of the evacuation proceedings in the Supreme Court."[24]

The Chinese and Eurasian communities were equally vociferous in their condemnation of the evacuation order, claiming that it was a blatant example of racial discrimination. Furthermore, why should the Hong Kong taxpayers finance the evacuation of a small and privileged section of the white colonial elite when it was apparent that the vast majority of the colony's citizens would be neglected and left undefended when the Japanese invaded?[25] The colonial government realised that if these charges were left unanswered, they might have a serious effect on the morale of the Eurasian and Chinese populations. Authorities responded by enlisting the help of the Colonial and Foreign Offices. In July 1940, the Hong Kong government informed London that it was considering the evacuation of those wives and children of Chinese and Eurasian residents with a faithful record of service "thought to justify exceptional treatment." These would be families of past and present members of the Legislative Council, Justices of the Peace and members of the Hong Kong Volunteer Defence Corps. The maximum number was estimated at 1,500, later revised upwards to 3,400; half of which were British subjects and the majority of whom would be from the "educated class, possessing ample means."[26]

Appeals were made to colonial administrations in Mauritius and Fiji for help in taking small numbers of non-European evacuees. The Foreign Office attached great importance to this request in order to "avoid [the] appearance of discrimination in favour of European women and children" who had already been evacuated, mainly to Australia.[27] Sir Mark Young, the new Governor of Hong Kong who had arrived in September 1941, reinforced this point just days before the Japanese attack in December: "It is considered politically the most desirable to give the Chinese population an equal opportunity with Europeans to leave Hong Kong under prevailing conditions." The Colonial Office was equally sensitive to this most delicate of issues. It agreed with the Foreign Office that there were obvious political implications to get some Chinese out of Hong Kong, however small their numbers, so as to avoid charges of racial discrimination. Nonetheless, Young's request that immigration regulations be waived to allow those Chinese wanting to go to Singapore was adamantly opposed by Governor Shenton Thomas. This was no surprise to the Foreign Office. "Singapore running true to form!" commented one junior official.[28] A similar request had also been forwarded to the Australian government in July 1940 but was immediately refused.[29] Determined to maintain the sanctity of the "White Australia" policy, no Asians would be allowed to land in Australia for an indefinite period. This included Chinese *amahs* and non-white domestics in the service of the recently evacuated European women and children who had landed in Australia from Hong Kong between July and September 1940. All Asian servants were denied permanent entry. However, using loopholes within the existing immigration regulations, as many as 130 *amahs* were granted temporary landing rites for periods of six months. This procedure was subject to an ongoing review, and even with the outbreak of hostilities in the Asia-Pacific region, Commonwealth immigration authorities maintained a watching brief on this seemingly innocuous issue.[30]

In the end, very few Chinese were evacuated to neighbouring colonies by the Hong Kong government despite the political importance the British government seemingly attached to it. Fiji agreed to take 500 Chinese women and children who were to be sponsored by the Hong Kong authorities, while it was hoped that the 1,405 Portuguese women and children, largely of mixed parentage, would find sanctuary in nearby Macao. The majority of Chinese who left willingly did so on their own accord using their own financial resources; the colonial authorities assumed correctly that those who vacated the colony were from the wealthier commercial classes.[31]

It was the Evacuation Representation Committee (ERC), established in November 1940 and comprised largely of rancorous elements from the business community, which conducted the most determined campaign against the government's evacuation policy. Indeed, it was a partially successful campaign, which persisted up to the Japanese attack in December 1941. Furthermore, the overall power and influence of the European community within Hong Kong was not to be underestimated either, as Brooke-Popham noted after one of his inspection tours to the colony shortly after the ERC's inception.[32] In August 1940, the number of women granted exemption was 950, of whom 500 were deemed essential wartime personnel. As pressure on the government mounted, official resolve began to weaken slightly. In late July, the Colonial Office noted that the Foreign Office, which had been "rather negative" towards the evacuation scheme from the outset, had accepted advice from locally-based observers in Hong Kong to proceed more slowly with the remainder of the evacuation scheme now that the bulk of it had been carried out.[33] This move failed to mollify an embittered European community. For the next three months, the recriminations against the Hong Kong administration continued unabated. Now sufficiently worried about the legality of the original order, the new military Governor, Lieutenant-General E. F. Norton, who succeeded the ailing Northcote in August 1940, terminated compulsory evacuation on 6 November.[34] Approximately 200 evacuation orders were cancelled and the individuals concerned were allowed to stay provided they volunteered for duty in one of the auxiliary services.

This concession did not mean that evacuation was now a dead issue. Convinced that a contingency plan should remain in place, the government announced a voluntary evacuation scheme in early December 1940, which it hoped its European citizens would heed. Colonial authorities were adamant, however, that restrictions on the re-entry of women and children would continue; a point reiterated by George Hall almost a year later. The re-admission of British women, but not children, might be allowed, but it was strictly conditional on the needs of the defence and other public services in Hong Kong.[35] This did not stop Arthur Jefferies from venting his displeasure. Feeling victimized for obeying the government's evacuation order, in March 1941 he complained to his wife that when he went out to the theatre or a night spot he could not help "seeing so many white women...[It] made me boil and brought back with a rush the realisation of the deprivation we have been subjected to in the middle of our lives."[36] The now-ill Governor Norton was still feeling the pressure over this divisive issue. While on a stopover in Hong Kong in early March 1941, Governor Shenton Thomas recorded that Norton remained "very worried over the women palaver."[37]

The evacuation issue continued to plague the Hong Kong administration on two fronts. In September 1941, the ERC petitioned the Hong Kong government to remove the re-entry ban. It was denied, as was their request to see Governor Young, who had recently arrived in the colony without his wife and family. Appeals to senior cabinet ministers in London from women evacuated to Australia made little impression either, as did requests made by several Westminster MPs in mid-November 1941 that in light of the improving political situation in the Far East, the Colonial Office consider overturning the banning order.[38] Entwined within the campaign to overturn the government's banning order were the parallel issues of medical care, remittances, and allowances for those who had already been evacuated.

Many families were finding it extremely difficult to make ends meet in their adopted countries. For those women without relatives or friends to help cushion the emotional and financial upheaval experienced during the evacuation, many found their new environments unforgiving. Others experienced a host of problems ranging from accommodation, education, and employment to bureaucratic infighting over which government or department was ultimately responsible for the long-term upkeep of these families. At one stage in May–July 1941, the Hong Kong authorities contemplated the cancellation of remittances to 367 women and children who had been evacuated to Canada and the United States. Valued at $HK110,000 per month, the colonial government complained that the exchange rates were crippling them. However, for political reasons, it was decided not to implement the plan. Governor Northcote had just succeeded, albeit temporarily, in calming down agitation regarding the evacuation of Europeans to Australia. Not only would the cancellation of remittances reopen the entire evacuation controversy, it would also discriminate against those families who had dutifully complied with the government's 1940 edict. The Treasury reluctantly agreed to allow the remittances to continue owing to the fact that the majority of the evacuees were in Canada and given the unsettled condition in the Far East.[39]

Families with substantial private means had little to worry about, while those from the fighting services were maintained under agreements brokered between the British, Dominion and colonial governments. Wives of former government officials, like Pat Walker-Taylor, whose husband Basil had been an Assistant Food Controller in the Malayan state of Kedah, discovered upon arrival in Fremantle that she was entitled to an allowance of £7/10s per week. This was a temporary arrangement until permission was granted for the wives of these officials to receive half their husbands' salaries.[40] However, it was those families with limited means which found the going tougher, especially women with large broods of young children who were struggling to make ends meet, dependent as they were upon variable exchange rates, allowances from their husbands or remittances from relatives overseas. The establishment of evacuee committees in Australia, Ceylon, India, and South Africa went some way to alleviating a few individuals' particular financial worries. And there is no question that the Dominion and colonial authorities involved were most sympathetic to the plight of these people.[41] Nonetheless, there were others who found the demands of their new situation difficult if not unbearable, a situation aggravated by the duress of separation.[42]

The strain of prolonged absence was, however, picked up by one senior Colonial Office official who remarked that the friction created in Hong Kong over evacuation could have serious and long-lasting effects on the colony's war effort. The Taikoo dockyard was full with shipbuilding contracts, but morale was low because the men were suffering from the enforced absence of their wives and families. This was affecting the efficiency of the dockyard. What harm could be done if wives, but not the children, were allowed to return? Governor Young, who was sympathetic to the distress caused to the Hong Kong community over the evacuation order, took up the cudgel. Aware that the departure of so many families had been the subject of the "most bitter recrimination," he discussed with his superiors in London the further need to alleviate distress. He also announced that his administration had recently established a committee to investigate and facilitate the return of evacuees.[43] A relaxation of restrictions was not a good idea, replied the War Office on 4 December 1941. For one thing, it could lead to more trouble. Reaffirming that the decision to evacuate was a necessary and "prudent wartime measure," the War Office agreed to reconsider the compulsory evacuation order only if there was some "radical change in the political atmosphere of the Far East."[44]

The attack launched on Hong Kong three days later by battle-hardened forces of the Imperial Japanese Army confirmed that there was not. On Christmas Day 1941, Hong Kong surrendered. By early January 1942, approximately 2,800 men, women and children, mainly British, were relocated to Stanley peninsula on the southeast corner of Hong Kong island. The swiftness of the colony's capitulation struck a bitter blow to British influence and prestige in southern China. Moreover, the high number of interned women and children—858 women and 286 children below the age of 16 years—proved highly embarrassing for the British government. George Hall, when probed in Parliament about the colony's prewar evacuation measures, stated that longstanding arrangements had been available for all women and children who wanted to leave Hong Kong. However, he was forced to admit that the difficulty had been to get them to leave.[45]

As is well-known, the fall of Singapore on 15 February 1942 was one of the blackest moments in twentieth century British history.[46] Therefore, it should come as no surprise that the abject failure to evacuate European civilians from Malaya and Singapore prior to the outbreak of war in the Far East has been shrouded in similar controversy. Unlike Hong Kong, there was no compulsory civilian evacuation scheme for the 31,000-strong European population in Malaya and Singapore. Secure in the "impregnability" of fortress Singapore, the colonial officials *in situ* and most of their military counterparts did not see the need to make such prewar contingencies. Put simply, the decision to evacuate European civilians prior to the outbreak of hostilities was viewed as defeatist.[47] The view that the Japanese simply did not have the resources or capacity to launch a sustained offensive against Malaya and Singapore was also commonplace. This gross underestimation of Japanese military prowess, combined with an equally ossifying overestimation of British defensive capabilities, compounded the shock in official circles when Lieutenant-General Yamashita's Twenty-Fifth Army attacked in December 1941.

This misplaced optimism permeated much of the European community as well. Take Eileen Niven, for example, the American wife of a Scotsman who worked for the Public Works Department (PWD) in Singapore. Writing to her parents in Seattle, Washington, four days before the outbreak of the Pacific War, she wrote:

> The political situation...seems to be simmering along nicely, and for all I know it may be approaching a boil now. But that doesn't mean Singapore itself by any means and certainly nobody here seems the least bit alarmed. I think that if the Japs really do decide to make another military move, it will be one of the other places mentioned, not here. With all the strength that has been poured into this place, I think it would be just a little bit *too* difficult, and that they will at least try going round it first. So what I said about this time last year...still holds good. Singapore isn't for it yet, and nobody is moving out of *here* yet.[48]

Nonetheless, there were other forces at work that contributed to the panic and chaos which engulfed all civilians living on the peninsula in the ten weeks prior to capitulation.

In July 1941, Prime Minister Winston Churchill appointed Duff Cooper, the Chancellor of the Duchy of Lancaster and former Minister of Information, with the all-important task to investigate how best to improve the coordination and control of government policy, in particular defence planning, in the Far East. Arriving in Singapore in early September 1941, Cooper reported back to London in late October of a disparate number of government departments working within their own sphere, independent of one another and sometimes in ignorance of each other's actions. This did not make for sound government or effective coordination between the various civilian and military departments. Nor did it provide London with an accurate or complete picture of what was happening in such a vital region of the empire. As a result, Cooper argued that the War Cabinet was presented with the "component parts of a jigsaw puzzle many of which are missing and all of which are supplied and painted by different hands."[49]

According to Churchill's protégé, some of the senior government officials and military commanders in Singapore did not inspire much confidence either. Cooper recommended that Brooke-Popham, who had a reputation of falling asleep during dinner parties, be relieved immediately. His age and "failing powers renders him jealous of any encroachment on his sphere of influence." Fearing that Brooke-Popham had always viewed him with great suspicion ever since his arrival, Cooper noted that the ageing C-in-C Far East had fiercely resisted his idea to create a War Council. His appraisal of the Governor was equally negative. After three months of working with him, Cooper vilified Shenton Thomas as "one of those people who find it quite impossible to adjust their minds to war conditions. He is also the mouthpiece of the last person he speaks to."[50] The GOC Malaya, Lieutenant-General A. E. Percival, who had taken command in May 1941, reached a similar conclusion. Percival claimed that Shenton Thomas, although an expert minute writer, lacked leadership and never really grasped the respective responsibilities of the military and civil arms during the Malayan campaign.[51] Megan Spooner, the wife of Rear-Admiral E. J. Spooner, who commanded the naval establishments in Singapore, came to a similar conclusion about the Governor: "A nice man but not a leader of men with I should say a rather rigid insensitive brain."[52]

It was not all one-way traffic. The news of Duff Cooper's appointment initially received a lukewarm reception in Singapore, not helped by the allegation that, according to Shenton Thomas' biographer, the personal luggage he and his socialite wife brought with them on this wartime mission seemed highly inappropriate at 100 pieces! Initially, Shenton Thomas liked the Coopers, and was instrumental upon their arrival in stifling biting editorials in the local press on the need for Lady Cooper to accompany her husband to a war zone.[53] The critics did not stop there. When Cooper visited the Australian headquarters at Kuala Lumpur shortly after his arrival, one staff officer remarked that he was not particularly impressed with Churchill's envoy, "mainly because he was wearing a pansy hat—wide brimmed straw, with a multi-coloured scarf around it."[54]

The unrelenting tensions and embittered rivalries, which existed between high-ranking government officials and their military advisors in Malaya, had a direct impact on government planning and efficiency. Constant infighting between politicians, senior members of the armed forces and influential civilians, such as the highly critical chief editor of the *Straits Times*, G. W. Seabridge, not only contributed to a spiralling decline in morale, but also indicated just how rule-bound and lethargic the Malayan Civil Service had become. In the end, it appeared that more energy was being expended on settling personal scores or preserving bureaucratic fiefdoms than fighting the Japanese. As a result, government responses in the areas of civil defence, such as air raid precaution and the auxiliary fire services, were both apathetic and archaic.[55] The controversy surrounding the colonial government's lacklustre response to a coordinated civilian evacuation plan best illustrates how the convergence of poor leadership, personal vendettas, and the colonial executive's shortcomings led to such unnecessary suffering.

The Japanese attack on the northern Malay states began in earnest on 8 December 1941. Two days later, Duff Cooper was appointed Resident Minister for Eastern Affairs and convened the first War Council. Meanwhile, in northwest Malaya, III Indian Corps under the command of Lieutenant-General Lewis Heath was under intense pressure. The island of Penang was heavily bombed for several days, serious damage was inflicted on Georgetown and civilian casualties were heavy. On 13 December, the Fortress Commander, Brigadier C. A. Lyon, and the Resident Counsellor, Leslie Forbes, ordered the evacuation of all military personnel and all European women and children. Despite the effect this might have on morale throughout Malaya and Singapore, Heath was ordered to abandon the island if dictated by military necessity.

Douglas Sturrock, the Registrar of Imports and Exports, noted in his diary that when the evacuation order was given on 14 December, the entire European community, which had been given one hour's notice, was ordered to assemble in the lobby of the Eastern and Orient hotel. After being divided into groups, they set off in sections for the harbour where they embarked on a rag-tag flotilla of four ships bound for Singapore. Originally placed on an old ferry, Sturrock's party had to be transferred mid-voyage to another vessel after the first ship developed engine trouble. The second vessel now held 570 people. Thirty-six agonizing hours later it reached Singapore.[56] For Mrs. L. M. Gray, who had been recovering in hospital after giving birth to their second daughter seven days earlier, her journey was less eventful but equally long. She and her two daughters were taken by ferry to the mainland where they boarded a train at Prai. Limited to two small cases, "plus a knife, fork and spoon," her luggage was filled mostly with napkins for the baby. Twenty-eight hours later she reached Singapore, where, after a short interval she, her two daughters, and 900 other female evacuees with children embarked on the SS *Duchess of Bedford*, which slipped anchor on 31 December 1941, bound for England.[57]

As the military crisis deepened, on 17 December, Heath ordered that all European women and children should be evacuated from the state of Perak. When Stanley Jones, the "sinister" Colonial Secretary, heard of this he immediately informed Shenton Thomas. Warning the governor that the withdrawal of European women and children from nearby Penang several days earlier had been a public relations disaster, which had seriously undermined the morale of the Asian population in Singapore, he reminded Shenton Thomas that Heath's order ran contrary to the civil government's policy of no racial discrimination vis-à-vis evacuation. Prior to the War Council the following day, Shenton Thomas issued a notice to the effect that Heath's order was unauthorized. Astonished, Cooper wrote Churchill:

> ...no evacuation was to be permitted, that trains travelling south were forbidden to carry passengers who appeared to be evacuees, that first-class carriages were to be taken off the trains in order to prevent Europeans from travelling, that motor cars travelling south were to be turned back, that petrol should not be supplied to private individuals and that they should not be allowed to telephone long distance....He announced that he had taken these steps with an air of triumph, expecting to be congratulated on having been so quick off the mark. What, however, terrified me most of all was that no member of the Council including General Percival, General Heath's immediately [sic] superior officer, said a word or raised an eyebrow— until I suggested that it was the first time in the history of the British Empire when it had been our policy to evacuate the troops first and to leave the women and children to the tender mercies of a particularly cruel Asiatic foe.[58]

The War Council quickly sided with Cooper and overturned the Governor's draft order. Not only was it wrong, argued Cooper, that civilians behind the lines countermand a field officer's operational order, but it defied logic. Heath's intentions were perfectly clear, as they were responsible. He needed to get the civilians out of harm's way in order that they did not hinder the movement of his troops. According to the War Council, whatever the short-term impact this measure had on Asian morale, the decision not to evacuate European women and children from forward areas was "not only bad in principle but might lead to serious trouble and react on our prestige." This point was reiterated by C. W. Dawson, the Secretary for Defence, when he told the War Council on 22 December that it was profoundly wrong to think that abandoning the Asian population would have a deep effect on their resolve or confidence in their European masters. The future of Malaya, argued Dawson, was "infinitely small" compared with the ultimate objective of winning the war. Hence a sense of proportion was required when comparing the situation in Malaya with the larger war effort.[59]

Cooper's appeal for common sense was supported by Captain L. P. Young of the 9th Gurkha Rifles who criticized the civilian authorities for not having the proper evacuation orders in place well in advance. He claimed that during the Malayan campaign no civilians were evacuated until the battle actually reached an area.[60] General A. P. Wavell, Supreme Commander of the ill-fated American-British-Dutch-Australian Command in Southeast Asia and the Southwest Pacific, reached a similar conclusion. The preponderance of British, Chinese and Indian civilians in the Malayan towns during operations was, he claimed, an unnecessary complication which impeded military efficiency. Instead of making their own arrangements, it was these "foreigners" who looked on the government to arrange for their removal in the event of bombing or invasion. Under these circumstances, the absence of a prewar civilian evacuation plan made it difficult to see how the debacle at Penang, whatever the implications for British prestige, could have been averted.[61]

It was clear that Shenton Thomas—who was described by Percival as a "slippery Welshman," who did his utmost to "pass the baby" to someone else[62]— had no idea of how quickly the military situation had deteriorated. Others did. When the first bombs fell on Perak's capital, Taiping, on 18 December the British Resident, N. F. H. Mather, noted that the surprise and nature of Japanese air operations hastened its evacuation. For several days "women and children of all nationalities had been going quietly away, so that practically none [were] left" in the city.[63] The Perak episode and the clash between Cooper and Shenton Thomas highlights two important problems: the Governor's poor judgement in matters which did not pertain to him; and how the increasingly acrimonious relations between him and Duff Cooper threatened to paralyze civil defence policy.

As the military situation worsened in northern Malaya, there was constant reference in the War Council to the proposed evacuation of European civilians. Jones' duplicity in this episode was bad enough, but what really angered Duff Cooper was that the civil administration had been completely inept despite the fact that it was supposed to have organized a special committee to formulate these contingencies 12 months earlier.[64] Nonetheless, Shenton Thomas remained unrepentant. In his version of events, he maintains that the War Council eventually agreed that the civil government would not order compulsory evacuation of civilians from any sector. If, however, a field commander considered the military situation justified, he could implement compulsory evacuation. "Meanwhile evacuation of European women and children from such [a] large area as Perak, far from the front line, *with no mention of Asiatics*, must have a deplorable effect."⁶⁵ He reiterated this when he told the Colonial Office "we are not going to have any discrimination of race in evacuations nor is the Civil Government going to issue any orders as to who should stay and who should not. I have made it clear that if the military order an area to be evacuated, then the order applies to everyone."⁶⁶

The prickly question of evacuation continued to inflame relations between Cooper and Shenton Thomas. The Governor was insistent that if the British community disappeared at the first sign of trouble, Asian morale would evaporate. He was steadfast in his call for no racial discrimination and insisted that in future, some civil officers remain behind to look after their Asian charges. Once again, white paternalism and British prestige had reared their ugly heads. On 21 December, after another arduous day in the War Council, Shenton Thomas vented his anger at Duff Cooper's intransigence over discrimination. "It is very difficult when men, who know something at least of the country and people, are obstructed by one who knows nothing." His wrath grew when 10 days later he confided in his diary that Cooper's strings were being pulled by his two most outspoken critics—Seabridge, of the *Straits Times*, and F. D. Bisseker, a prominent businessman from Penang.⁶⁷

Fortunate Singaporeans in one of the few air raid shelters, 1941

Meanwhile in London, the Chiefs of Staff advised the War Cabinet that steps be taken to evacuate *bouches inutiles* (useless mouths) from Singapore. It recommended that all civilians regardless of race who were not taking part in the defence of Malaya and Singapore be evacuated, "a measure of compulsory evacuation being desirable," but not obligatory. However, the War Office insisted that the evacuation of European service families, including those locally enlisted, would be "compulsory and without exception" provided they were not given such "undue priority of shipment as would amount to racial discrimination." Other civilians, including families of local volunteer forces, were to be settled by those colonial governments concerned. For instance, men in the Straits Settlements Volunteer Force would be the responsibility of the Straits Settlements authorities. Stressing that these measures were at the discretion of the Resident Minister, the Chiefs of Staff also drew Cooper's attention to the cable from Shenton Thomas that in any withdrawal of the civilian population there should be no distinction on racial grounds. Reaffirming that it was "most important to avoid racial discrimination," the Chiefs of Staff recognized that it would not be easy to implement since Chinese, Indians and Malays would not be permitted to land in many countries. Undoubtedly, the debate over compulsory evacuation in Hong Kong the previous year was still fresh in their minds. The availability of shipping was another problem. The War Cabinet reaffirmed the principle that there must be no racial discrimination in the evacuation of Malaya's civilians, and requested that Duff Cooper sound out the authorities in the Netherlands East Indies as to possible arrangements and closer cooperation on this matter—in particular, the evacuation of the Asian population.[68]

On 23 December, the Colonial Office cabled Singapore outlining the War Cabinet's decision. In his own words, Shenton Thomas was "tickled to death" with its contents, crowing that it confirmed that any civilian evacuation should be made *without* racial discrimination. He gleefully confided in his diary: "I am sure Duff Cooper thinks I prompted it!"[69] If Shenton Thomas thought he had been vindicated and the discrimination issue was finally dead and buried, he was badly mistaken. At another War Council five days later, Cooper noted how indignant Vice-Admiral Sir Geoffrey Layton, C-in-C Eastern Fleet, became over the sub-committee set up to deal with the evacuation of women and children from Singapore. The War Council discovered that the committee, chaired by Mr. Justice J. Aitken, had never sat because the Governor "had been endeavouring to settle the whole matter without allowing the committee to meet, and behind their backs." Shenton Thomas said that the committee was meeting later that morning, which Cooper afterwards found out was not true![70] The atmosphere within the War Council was fraught, and relations between the Resident Minister and the Governor were now irreconcilable. Paralysis gripped the civil administration. Even the belated appointment of the highly capable Brigadier Ivan Simson as Director-General of Civil Defence (DGCD) on 31 December did not escape the machinations between Cooper and Shenton Thomas.[71] Perhaps more controversial was the installation of Bisseker as Simson's deputy. As General Manager of the Eastern Smelting Company, Penang, in 1940 he was elected to the Straits Settlements Legislative Council and soon became the senior unofficial elected member of that body. A forthright critic of the colonial government's unsatisfactory preparations for war, this influential businessman and labour expert had most recently tangled with Shenton Thomas when the former led a delegation criticizing the government's hurried evacuation of Penang. Not surprisingly, Shenton Thomas despised Bisseker. This did not augur well for the future.

Meanwhile, as the debate within the War Council was waged over compulsory evacuation, many civilians had been leaving Singapore voluntarily. Prior to the investiture of the island on 31 January, ships that brought supplies and reinforcements to the island, including the ill-fated 18th Division, departed with hundreds of civilian evacuees and wounded service personnel. On 21 January, Percival cabled London that 5,200 European women and children had been evacuated so far. However, 4,800 remained; 4,200 of which had applied for passage. The War Office was told that every available berth in all ships leaving Malaya had been filled. But, as Peter Elphick has commented, many more could have been jammed onboard. Indeed, he claims that in the last week of December 1941, several large transports actually left port either empty or half-full.[72]

As the Japanese advanced steadily down the Malayan peninsula, the colonial administration singularly failed to invoke a compulsory evacuation order. For those civilians who escaped the Japanese onslaught on the peninsula, it was largely through the intervention and improvisation of local district commissioners and officials from the PWD, the FMS Railways, and the Post and Telegraph Services.[73] Once in Singapore, colonial authorities continued to rely on the individual to make the necessary passage arrangements, including paying for their own ticket. Such incompetence was unacceptable and drew the ire of Mrs. E. G. V. Day, whose New Zealand-born husband had, until recently, been the British Adviser in the northern state of Perlis. "We have lost everything like thousands of others" she wrote to Lady Diana Cooper in mid-January 1942. "That is nothing, but the muddle and unnecessary loss and suffering caused by indecision and muddled orders is heartbreaking. Thousands of women and children are here [in Singapore], when a little imagination and foresight could have saved the situation. The muddle in Penang has been repeated everywhere in the country and if it is to be repeated in Singapore then we must be in Hell."[74]

Government paralysis was made worse as Singapore became congested with thousands more refugees. As people and vehicles fled southward through Johore— "rubbing each other like potatoes being washed"—officials on the mainland seemed overwhelmed by the situation.⁷⁵ Once in Singapore, the need to evacuate the *bouches inutiles* became even more urgent. As the colonial government pushed on with its voluntary evacuation procedures, Shenton Thomas remained steadfast to his principle of no racial discrimination. On 23 January, he cabled London that he hoped that between 4,000 and 5,000 Indians would be leaving Singapore for the sub-continent "very shortly." Not more than 50 percent were women and children, "but if useless men wish to go and there is accommodation, there is no objection." The Colonial Office noted, however, that Indian women had been generally unwilling to sail without their menfolk. There was the added complication that the Government of India itself was unprepared or unwilling to take large numbers of Indian evacuees unless they were from Indian service families, were people of independent means, or possessed a government guarantee. Efforts by the Colonial Office to mobilize the Secretary of State for India and Burma, L. S. Amery, and get him to "stir up" Viceroy Linlithgow and his officials in Delhi fell on stony ground.⁷⁶

Chinese and Eurasian evacuees were even more problematic. Facilities were being provided for Chinese to get away to China via Burma, but few wanted to go. After an initial refusal, Ceylon agreed to admit 500 Asians on residential visas only if priority was given to Malayan Ceylonese. Shenton Thomas pinned his hopes on Australia, which up to now had allowed only 50 Chinese and 50 Eurasian women and children entry into the Commonwealth. Australia's intransigence over asylum issues had caused "acute bitterness and uneasiness" amongst Singapore's Chinese community; a community that had been giving invaluable assistance in bolstering civil defence. At the end of January, the Straits government cabled Canberra seeking to increase its Asian intake, albeit on a temporary basis, to 5,000 refugees. The Colonial Office, despite the obvious humanitarian appeal, did not think the proposal had much chance knowing how entrenched the "White Australia" policy was in that Dominion's political fabric. They were right.⁷⁷ In the end, the only territory which welcomed small numbers of Chinese evacuees was the nearby Netherlands East Indies.

The exodus continued. On 6 February, 2,400 civilians were evacuated to Bombay in *Convoy Emu*. Once again, Peter Elphick has charged that the authorities could have packed more in. Unfortunately, the P&O Company, which had been given the task of arranging passages, were forced, because of the intense bombing, to relocate from their city centre offices. This caused confusion and inevitable delays in obtaining a berth, which were aggravated by profiteering. Compounding the bedlam was the colonial government's insistence on maintaining passport controls. Tragedy turned into farce when it was revealed on 8 February that one vessel in the last convoy had left port without being completely filled owing to the unnecessary restriction of embarkation hours. Shenton Thomas asked Rear-Admiral Spooner that in future he give more notice about the departure of evacuation ships. This edict was pointless; having all the hallmarks of closing the door well after the livestock had bolted from the barn. Fed up with official bungling and red tape, some civilians with the help of equally desperate military personnel took drastic measures during the final days of the battle and commandeered several ships in their bid to avoid capture.[78] W. A. Baker, a former ship's captain retired by the Straits Steamship Company in December 1941, observed during those final chaotic days that ships "leaving for anywhere were filled with women and children. Passages were impossible to get except for women and children. All the same, many husbands seeing their wives off forgot to come ashore again!"[79]

Pandemonium was exacerbated by official incompetence at the highest levels. Four days before the surrender, J. T. Rea, a Chinese Protectorate officer serving as deputy head of the Singapore immigration office, was ordered to join his Volunteer unit. To Rea, who had been busy renewing passports and dealing with emergency travel documents, the mobilization order seemed fantastic. To replace an experienced official who was providing an essential service at such a crucial juncture during the final stages of the evacuation seemed ludicrous.[80] Meanwhile, unbeknownst to Simson or Percival, the Governor had ordered the withdrawal of all the European technical harbour staff, further aggravating what now became a desperate free-for-all on the congested docks.[81]

On "Black Friday," 13 February 1942, the last official civilian evacuation from Singapore was carried out. Simson, as DGCD, was allotted 300 of the 1,200 places earmarked for young civilian technical staff from the Malayan Civil Service, especially the PWD, whose experience was deemed vital for war work elsewhere. Thirteen of the 40 vessels remaining to the civil authorities were also allocated to Simson for this task. Only five hours notice was given to evacuate. With the inevitable disruption to communications, compounded by an ever-changing military situation on the island itself, people were naturally compelled to move from their normal work and residential addresses. Many were therefore nowhere to be found when the order to evacuate was given. As a result, Simson and Bisseker were forced to take the initiative and issue their own permits, even if this meant filling the quota with older men, women, and children without first consulting the Governor or the Aitken committee. In all, 320 hand-written passes were issued.

According to one embittered ex-internee, these passes were not allocated fairly; many going to "unofficial civilians of [Bisseker's] own delection."[82] The calamity was further complicated by charges from another group of ex-internees that Bisseker left the colony without official permission. More damning still were Shenton Thomas's allegations that Simson never had the authority to issue these passes, and that he deliberately ignored the civilian chain of command. Simson disputed these and other allegations. First, Bisseker had left the colony on his express orders. Second, the DGCD had been given the authority to issue these passes. And finally, the hasty evacuation of the colony's civilians had been entirely unnecessary if these people had been obliged to leave much earlier. This last point was especially poignant when Simson sombrely recalled that all 13 vessels assigned to him were later sunk by the Japanese with heavy loss of life. Many others who survived the sinkings were later killed or captured in Sumatra; only a few reached sanctuary in India.[83]

The acrimony aroused by these conflicting stories over inelastic evacuation procedures and clashing jurisdictions rumbled on for years, especially stories of alleged desertion by high-ranking European government officials and senior members of the Malayan Police force. In one instance, Assistant Superintendent F. I. Tremlett took personal responsibility for the men under his immediate command. Ignoring the Inspector-General's edict of 11 February that all police were to disarm and offer their services to the Japanese, he ordered his party of nine men to leave Singapore. Six were members of the Malayan Special Branch. Of these, two were Chinese operatives involved in counter-espionage work, key personnel whose capture by the Japanese would have been disastrous and whose services were essential to the renewal of Special Branch activities after the war. For many more, especially the younger European officers, they simply ignored the order because they wanted to continue to fight against the Japanese elsewhere. Who could blame them? Although this was technically-speaking an act of desertion, as one observer minuted: "This is a very difficult matter and calls more for a Solomon than a Judge Jefferies to pass judgement."[84]

There are numerous escape stories that highlight the complete breakdown of authority during those final days prior to surrender; but one in particular involving the Malayan Survey Department illustrates the chaos that existed at dockside. On 11 February, officers with wives were told to get them out on any available ship. When a small party from the department, including six or seven wives, arrived at the docks they found the SS *Empire Star* about to depart. "The ladies of our party were put on board," recalled one employee, "but were immediately ordered off again by the Chief Officer who said that he would not allow anyone on board without a special permit for his ship. He added that he had already sent off about 40 women and children for that reason." Undaunted, Mr. C. Noble set off for town to the shipping agent's office to try and get the permits. He returned to the wharf empty-handed. Noble then went deeper into the dock area and found the *Ipoh* in the process of coaling. Its captain, whose crew had deserted him earlier in the day, raised no objections to taking women and children on board without permits, provided the men helped crew the ship. He recalled that there "seemed to be no naval control and no permits were necessary either to enter the wharf area or to board the ship."[85]

When Singapore surrendered on 15 February 1942, over 10,000 women and children had been evacuated from Malaya: 7,174 Europeans, 2,305 Indian and

1,250 Chinese. At the time of capitulation, about 200 British women and children had been left behind.[86] As British authorities grappled with how to deal with these refugees scattered as they were throughout the Empire,[87] a more immediate but parallel task was to find out exactly how many British and Commonwealth citizens were in Japanese hands, their location and condition. Indeed, a sense of urgency gripped Whitehall as atrocity stories filtered back to London from Hong Kong as early as January 1942. Eager to confirm these and other incidents, in early February the Foreign Office also set in motion the machinery for the reciprocal evacuation of its diplomatic officials and their families.[88]

Recriminations were swift to follow the humiliating defeats at Hong Kong, Malaya, and Singapore. From Watford, one private citizen found it strange that so many civilians, "many not British subjects, should have been left in Hong Kong only to read afterward that there [were] not enough supplies to go round and that to a considerable extent the fall of the Colony was hastened" because of their presence. The reference here was mainly to the huge influx of Chinese refugees from outside the colony which the colonial authorities seemed unable to control and which was a huge burden on the colony's resources prior to the Japanese offensive.[89] Similar questions were being raised in the Stanley internment camp by many of the male internees, some of whom deeply resented the presence of so many women and children in the camp. How were they going to feed so many useless mouths?[90]

The post-mortem after the fall of Singapore was even more cutting. Brooke-Popham was scathing about the civil defence authorities in Malaya and their lack of urgency and preparedness. As expected, Shenton Thomas responded equally vigorously in defending his administration. Denying that his government had been apathetic towards the 5.5 million Asians in Malaya, he thought the government concessions given to the officers and men who were lavishly catered for with canteens, dances, duty-free cigarettes, tobacco, beer, and spirits may have contributed to the military's poor performance during the campaign.[91] As far as the charges that compulsory evacuation should have been implemented well before hostilities, there was a strong divergence of opinion. Simson was trenchant concerning the lack of an obligatory evacuation scheme. Surely, as in Hong Kong, military necessity dictated the evacuation of the civilian population. However, from the outset, the "chairbound" civil administration had singularly failed to realize the grave military situation facing them in Malaya.

It was not just a lack of imagination that permeated the highest levels of government, most notably the Governor, which led to the colony's swift conquest, argued Simson. Complacency was an equally important factor. "To put it bluntly," recalled Layton, "the civil population had taken the optimistic public statements before the Japanese attacks at their face value; they were shattered by the gulf between them and reality...As it was, things went downhill too fast and too inexplicably for a community which normally lived a life of complete security and unnatural luxury."[92] Leaving these claims of inertia and decadence aside, there were practical issues that confronted British officials during their deliberations whether to impose a compulsory evacuation scheme. As the former curator of the herbarium at the Botanical Gardens in Singapore pointed out, despite the obvious dangers of staying behind, it had been very difficult to persuade many European women to leave. They "felt it their duty to stay and to help the Asiatics, who looked to us for the protection they did not get."[93]

Shenton Thomas remained adamant that his insistence on no racial discrimination during the civilian evacuation had been vital for the maintenance of British prestige.[94] However noble the sentiment, it is misplaced. Official compulsion would have saved lives in Singapore, a point emphatically made in mid-1942 by Sir George W. Maxwell, former Chief Secretary of the Federated Malay States, 1920–26. In a sweeping condemnation of civil defence policy made on behalf of the Association of British Malaya, he charged that it was the European community that had been discriminated against. Indeed, during the height of the civilian evacuation from Singapore, the Colonial Office made an interesting observation. It commented that although there was no racial discrimination in the allocation of shipping passages, except that priority be given to women and children, in practice there was an even more "objectionable type" of discrimination being implemented—that of personal wealth. Put simply, it might appear to people in the United Kingdom that rich Chinese could leave Singapore whereas the subordinate classes of Europeans could not.[95]

In the final analysis, the compulsory evacuation of Hong Kong in July 1940 had been a relative success, despite a fierce rearguard action fought by the European business community to get the order overturned. In Malaya and Singapore, on the other hand, however admirable Shenton Thomas's stand on racialism, his obsession to preserve British imperial prestige blinded him to the cold political realities. Asians, if evacuated, were not welcome in large numbers in other parts of the British Empire and/or were unwilling to travel too far. Therefore, by default, those who were evacuated were largely European.

Kent Fedorowich is Senior Lecturer in British Imperial History at the University of the West of England, Bristol. He is the author of Unfit for Heroes: Reconstruction and Soldier Settlement Between the Wars, *and co-editor and author of other volumes on twentieth century military history, including, with Bob Moore,* The British Empire and its Italian Prisoners of War.

NOTES—
1. The most well-known contemporary works, largely written by women, are, G. Dew, *Prisoner of the Japs*, London, 1943; P. Harrop, *Hong Kong Incident*, London, Eyre and Spottiswoode, 1943; G. Preistwood, *Through Japanese Barbed Wire*, London, 1944; F. H. Stevens, *Santo Tomas Internment Camp, 1942–1945*, privately published, 1946; E. Hahn, *Miss Jill*, New York, 1947; A. N. Keith, *Three Came Home*, London, 1948; B. Jeffrey, *White Coolies*, London, 1954; J. E. Simons, *While History Passed*, London, 1954; J. Bowden, *Grey Touched With Scarlet*, London, 1959; E. Field, *Twilight in Hong Kong*, Hong Kong, 1960.
2. There are hundreds of stories, diaries and first-hand accounts concerning the surrender, captivity and repatriation of POWs and civilian internees in the Far East during World War II. Indispensable are the reference works by Van Waterford, *Prisoners of the Japanese in World War II*, Jefferson NC, 1994; S. P. MacKenzie, 'Prisoners of War and Civilian Internees, The Asian and Pacific Theaters', in L. E. Lee (ed.), *World War II in Asia and the Pacific and the War's Aftermath, with General Themes: A Handbook of Literature and Research*, Westport CT, 1998, 172–82; and J. F. Vance (ed.), *Encyclopedia of Prisoners of War and Internment*, Santa Barbara CA, 2000.
3. Since the mid-1970s, there has been a resurgence in the publication of civilian internee material including first-hand accounts and diaries, as well as the republication of those produced in the immediate postwar era. See C. Lucas, *Prisoners of Santo Tomas*, London, 1975; L. Warner and J. Sandilands, *Women Beyond the Wire*, London, 1982; J. Gittins, *Stanley, Behind Barbed Wire*, Hong Kong, 1982; C. M. Petillo (ed.), *The Ordeal of Elizabeth Vaughan: A Wartime Diary of the Philippines*, Athens GA, 1985; S. F. Huie, *The Forgotten Ones*, Sydney, 1992; S. Allan, *Diary of a Girl in Changi 1941–1945*, Kenthurst NSW, 1994; J. Ruff-O'Herne, *50 Years of Silence*, Sydney, 1994; G. Wright-Nooth with M. Adkin, *Prisoner of the Turnip Heads*, London, 1994; J. Mathers, *Twisting the Tail of the Dragon*, Lewes, Sussex, 1994; P. Abkhazi, *Enemy Subject: Life in a Japanese Internment Camp 1943–45*, reprint Stroud, Gloucestershire, 1995; H. Colijn, *Song of Survival: Women Interned*, Alexandria NSW, 1996; A. M. Bowman, *Not Now Tomorrow—Ima Nai Ashita*, Bangalow NSW, 1996; G. Bossard, *POW: One Girl's Experience in a Japanese POW Camp*, Auckland, 1999. For a scholarly approach, see J. Kennedy, *British Civilians and the Japanese War in Malaya and Singapore, 1941–45*, London, 1987; M. Brooks, "Passive in War? Women Internees in the Far East 1942–45," in S. Macdonald, P. Holden and S. Ardener (eds.), *Images of Women in Peace and War*, London, 1987, 166–78; B. Archer and K. Fedorowich, "The Women of Stanley: Internment in Hong Kong, 1942–45," *Women's History Review*, 5, 3 1996, 373–99; B. E. Archer, "A Study of Civilian Internment by the Japanese in the Far East 1941–1945," PhD thesis, University of Essex, 1999; F. B. Cogan, *Captured: The Japanese Internment of American Civilians in the Philippines, 1941–1945*, Athens GA, 2000; T. Kaminski, *Prisoners in Paradise: American Women in the Wartime South Pacific*, Lawrence KS, 2000.
4. G. Hicks, *The Comfort Women, Sex Slaves of the Japanese Imperial Forces*, St Leonards, NSW, 1995; H. Nelson, "A Map to Paradise Road, A Guide for Historians," *Wartime: Journal of the Australian War Memorial*, 32, 1999, 1–20. For war crimes, atrocities and

the use of POWs for sources of military intelligence and propaganda, see Y. Tanaka, *Hidden Horrors: Japanese War Crimes in World War II*, Boulder CO, Westview Press, 1996; A. B. Gilmore, *You Can't Fight Tanks with Bayonets: Psychological Warfare Against the Japanese Army in the Southwest Pacific*, Lincoln NE, 1998; S. C. Smith, "Crimes and Punishment, Local Responses to the Trial of Japanese War Criminals in Malaya and Singapore, 1946–48," *South East Asia Research*, 5, 1, 1996, 41–56; P. Towle, M. Kosuge and Y. Kibata (eds.), *Japanese Prisoners of War*, London, 2000; S. J. Flower, "British Prisoners of War of the Japanese, 1941–45," in I. Nish and Y. Kibata (eds.), *The History of Anglo-Japanese Relations, 1600–2000: Volume 2: The Political-Diplomatic Dimension, 1931–2000*, London, 149–73. See R. Bickers, *Britain in China: Community, Culture and Colonialism 1900–1949*, Manchester, 1999, and S. Wolton, *Lord Hailey, the Colonial Office and the Politics of Race and Empire in the Second World War: The Loss of White Prestige*, London, 2000 for two recent examples of studies on race, empire and colonial elites.

5   C. M. Bell, "'Our Most Exposed Outpost': Hong Kong and British Far Eastern Strategy, 1921–1941," *Journal of Military History*, 60, 1 1996, 71; G. R. Perras, "'Our Position in the Far East Would Be Stronger Without This Unsatisfactory Commitment': Britain and the Reinforcement of Hong Kong, 1941," *Canadian Journal of History*, 30, 2 1995, 231–59. Also see C. M. Bell, *The Royal Navy, Seapower and Strategy between the Wars*, London, 2000.

6   C. M. Bell, "Our Most Exposed Outpost," 70–73. For the importance of maintaining British prestige in southern China and its impact on inter-allied relations during the Second World War, see K. Fedorowich, "Decolonisation Deferred? The Re-Establishment of Colonial Rule in Hong Kong, 1942–45," in K. Fedorowich and M. Thomas (eds.), *International Diplomacy and Colonial Retreat*, London, 2001, 25–50; A. Whitfield, *Hong Kong, Empire and the Anglo-American Alliance at War, 1941–1945*, London, 2001.

7   Public Record Office (PRO), War Office Papers, WO106/2366, secret notes for Brigadier Grasset, The Future Policy for the Defence of Hong Kong, 26 August 1938; Cabinet Office Papers, CAB21/2427, Joint Defence Committee and Overseas Defence Committee papers, Hong Kong, Defence Questions 1938–39.

8   PRO, Admiralty Papers, ADM116/4271, War Cabinet discussions of COS39176 and PDC3921, Hong Kong-Period Before Relief, Port Defence Committee, 28 December 1939; Minutes by R. H. Lenses, Local Defence Division, and Rear-Admiral Tom S. V. Phillips, Deputy Chief of Naval Staff, 3 and 8 January 1940; Colonial Office Papers, CO967/70, Sir Geoffrey Northcote, Governor of Hong Kong, to Lord Moyne, Secretary of State for the Colonies, 6 June 1941; Foreign Office Papers, FO371/27622/F 10344/G, Minute by J. C. Sterndale Bennett, Head of the Far Eastern Department 1940–42, 6 October 1941; Air Ministry Papers, AIR2/4218, Babington to Group Captain J. C. Slessor, Director of Plans, 16 August 1939.

9   National Archives of Australia, Canberra [hereafter NAA], CRS A1608, item B39/1/3, part 1, Geoffrey Whiskard, British High Commissioner to Australia, to Prime Minister R. G. Menzies, 16 June 1939; Menzies to Whiskard, 22 June 1939.

10 National Archives and Records Administration, College Park NARA, State Department Records, RG 59, Decimal Files-Hong Kong 1930–39, 846G.00/47 F/B, Addison E. Southard, American Consul-General, Hong Kong, to State Department, Washington, 1 September 1939.
11 For an assessment of British-Japanese relations, the impact of the fall of France and Japan's quest for strategic resources, see P. Lowe, *Great Britain and the Origins of the Pacific War*, Oxford, 1977; C. Thorne, *Allies of a Kind*, London, 1978; A. Best, *Britain, Japan and Pearl Harbor: Avoiding War in East Asia, 1936–41*, London, 1995; N. Tarling, *Britain, Southeast Asia and the Onset of the Pacific War*, Cambridge, 1996; M. Thomas, *The French Empire at War, 1940–45*, Manchester, 1998; S. Hatano and S. Asada, "The Japanese Decision to Move South," in R. Boyce and E. M. Robertson (eds.), *Paths to War: New Essays on the Origins of the Second World War*, London, 1989, 383–408; and J. Marshall, *To Have and Have Not: Southeast Asian Raw Materials and the Origins of the Pacific War*, Los Angeles, 1995.
12 PRO, WO193/866, Grasett to War Office, 26 June and 5 August 1940. Although recognizing British vulnerability during this crisis, the Chief Clerk at the Foreign Office, Henry Ashley Clarke, minuted that they, not Japan, should decide when to withdraw the troops: "We shall want to withdraw the garrisons but should try to choose our moment," FO371/24666/F 3542, Minute by Ashley Clarke, 11 July 1940.
13 PRO, WO193/864, War Office memorandum, Military Situation in the Far East in Relation to Possible Japanese Demands, 20 June 1940. For a recent reappraisal of the decision to reinforce Hong Kong and its impact on British-Canadian wartime relations, see K. Fedorowich, "'Cocked Hats and Swords and Small, Little Garrisons': Britain, Canada and the Fall of Hong Kong, 1941," *Modern Asian Studies*, 36, 1 2002.
14 PRO, CAB65/7, WM 1754011, 22 June 1940; CAB66/9, WP(40)222, COS report, Immediate Measures Required in the Far East, 25 June 1940.
15 PRO, CAB65/7, WM 181407, 25 June 1940.
16 PRO, FO371/24666/F 3479, Minute by Dening, 2 July 1940; CAB65/7, WM 1754011, 22 June 1940; CAB65/7, WM 1834013, 26 June 1940; CAB66/9, WP(40)222, 25 June 1940; WO193/864, War Office notes on previous cabinet paper, 26 June 1940. For the Colonial Office analysis of the evacuation issue, see CO323/1808/6, Minutes of July–November 1940.
17 On 1 July, of the 1,833 service wives and their offspring, 1,640 were sent to Manila. Four days later, a further 1,779 non-service British women and children, out of the 2,129 who registered on 2 July, also embarked for Manila. PRO, WO193/866, GOC Hong Kong to War Office, 24 June 1940; G. B. Endacott, *Hong Kong Eclipse*, Hong Kong, 1978, 14. For the discussion on the banning of European women and children from Hong Kong and other potential war zones, see CO273/664/1, Memo for Under-Secretary of State, War Office, 9 August 1940.
18 PRO, CO323/1808/6, Minute by W. B. L. Monson, Acting Principal Secretary, August 1940.
19 G. B. Endacott, *Hong Kong Eclipse*, 14; B. E. Archer, "A Study of Civilian Internment by the Japanese in the Far East, 1941–1945," 45–46; P. S. Selwyn-Clarke, *Footprints*,

Hong Kong, 1975, 63; PRO, CO129/587/12, Minute by Monson, 7 July 1940.
20   Quotation cited in G. B. Endacott, *Hong Kong Eclipse*, 15.
21   *Hansard*, House of Commons, fifth series 1939–40, Vol. 363, Cols. 1246–7, 31 July 1940.
22   Australian War Memorial (AWM), PR 84/317, Arthur E. Jefferies Papers, Jefferies to his wife, 11 and 23 July 1940.
23   Ibid., Jefferies to his wife, n.d. probably mid-July 1940.
24   G. B. Endacott, *Hong Kong Eclipse*, 16–17. For a discussion of the financial role played by interned bank officials and their experiences in Hong Kong, see F. King, *The History of the Hong Kong and Shanghai Banking Corporation*, Vol. 3, Cambridge, 1988, 570–630.
25   *Hansard*, House of Commons, fifth series 1939–40, Vol. 363, Col. 1246, 31 July 1940; H. J. Lethbridge, "Hong Kong under Japanese Occupation: Changes in Social Structure," in I. C. Jarvie and J. Agassi (eds.), *Hong Kong: A Society in Transition*, London, 1969, 91–2.
26   PRO, CO129/589/17, Minute by Monson giving categories and numbers of non-Europeans the Hong Kong authorities wished to evacuate, 12 February 1941; Dominions Office Papers, DO35/721/M 681/5, Officer Administering Government of Hong Kong to Colonial Secretary, 10 July 1940.
27   PRO, FO371/27622/F 1808, Foreign Office to Governor B. E. Clifford of Mauritius, 15 February 1941.
28   PRO, FO371/26622/F 13400, Young to Colonial Secretary, 2 December, Thomas to Colonial Secretary, 3 December, and Colonial Secretary's reply, 4 December, with minute by A.L. Scott, 13 December 1941; CO129/590/1, Minute by Monson, 3 December 1941. Norton only lasted as military governor for eight months when Northcote replaced him on medical grounds in April 1941. Brooke-Popham had been impressed with the teamwork of Grasett and Norton, but Northcote's resumption of the governorship worried the C-in-C as Northcote, according to Brooke-Popham, lacked the personal drive and administrative grip of his predecessor. Young's appointment in September, along with several other key replacements, was another attempt by London to rejuvenate local trust in the civil government. LHCMA, Brooke-Popham Papers, 6/2/7 and 10, Brooke-Popham to Ismay, 28 February and 19 April 1941; PRO, CO967/69, Young to Parkinson, 14 October 1941.
29   NAA, CRS A1928/1, item 520/36, Senator H. S. Foll, Minister of the Interior, to Menzies, 13 July 1940; and report of conference concerning Hong Kong evacuees written by Dr. F. McCallum, Senior Medical Officer, Department of Health, 28 August 1940; AWM 60, item 336/40, Department of the Army memo, Evacuees - Hong Kong - Medical Attention and Pay Facilities, 9 September 1940; CRS A1608, item B39/1/3, part 1, Prime Minister's Department to Governor of Hong Kong, 25 July 1940.
30   For the intriguing discussion of this issue, see the correspondence in NAA, CRS A433/1, item 49/2/44, Memos by A. R. Peters, Department of the Interior, 29 July 1940, 10 April, 22 May 1941; Minutes by B. Lawrey, 4 September 1942, and A. Bryan, 9 May 1946.

31 PRO, CO129/589/17, Minute by Monson, 12 December 1941. In August 1939, many prominent Chinese residing in Hong Kong responded to the deteriorating diplomatic situation in the Far East by removing their families to Manila and Singapore. NARA, RG 59, Decimal Files-Hong Kong 1930–39, 846G.00/47 F/B, Southard to State Department, 1 September 1939.
32 LHCMA, Brooke-Popham Papers, V/1/4, Brooke-Popham to Ismay, 6 January 1941.
33 G. B. Endacott, *Hong Kong Eclipse*, 16–17; PRO, CO323/1808/6, Minute by A. H. Poynton, Principal Secretary, 26 July 1940.
34 LHCMA, Brooke-Popham Papers, 6/2/4, Brooke-Popham to Ismay, 6 January 1941. According to Brooke-Popham, Norton "brought tremendous drive and energy to bear on all the problems of civil defence" since his appointment. The arrival of a military governor was not lost on the local press or Consul-General Southard who reported to Washington that opinion in Hong Kong saw Norton's appointment as a "commendable step and probably implies that this colony will be ruled as a fortress." NARA, RG 59, Decimal Files-Hong Kong 1940–44, 846G.001/14, Southard to State Department, 3 July 1940. Southard also forwarded copies of editorials from the *South China Morning Post* and the *Hong Kong Daily Press*, 6 August 1940. Ibid., 846G.001/16 F/FG, Southard to Washington, 7 August 1940.
35 Special Memo. #50 of 1940 - Government Evacuation Scheme, 4 December 1940, cited in B. Archer and K. Fedorowich, "The Women of Stanley," 376; *Hansard*, House of Commons, fifth series 1941–42, Vol. 374, Cols. 2067–8, 11 November 1941; ibid., Vol. 376, Cols. 295–6, 19 November 1941.
36 AWM, PR 84/317, Jefferies to his wife, 25 March 1941.
37 PRO, CO967/76, Shenton Thomas to Parkinson, 16 March 1941.
38 PRO, CO129/589/18, petition from ERC to Colonial Secretary, Hong Kong, 20 September 1941; letter to Duff Cooper, Chancellor of the Duchy of Lancaster, from evacuees in Australia, n.d.; *Hansard*, House of Commons, fifth series 1941–42, Vol. 374, Cols. 2067–8, 11 November 1941; ibid., Vol. 376, Cols. 295–96, 19 November 1941.
39 PRO, CO129/589/17, Northcote to Moyne, 13 May 1941; FO371/27622/F 7264, Northcote to Moyne, 20 July 1941; ibid., F 8316, W. B. Douglas, Treasury, to Ashley Clarke, 23 August 1941; ibid., F 8968, Moyne to Northcote, 30 August 1941.
40 IWM, 01/24/1, Lt. Basil Walker-Taylor Papers, wife Pat's diary, 19 March 1942.
41 For the extensive documentation involving Hong Kong evacuees and their upkeep in Australia, see NAA Melbourne, MP 729/6, item 16/401/335 and MP 1587/1, item 334; also see PRO, CO825/47/14, representations by evacuees in Australia to British Parliamentary Delegation, 1944. Arrangements for Malayan evacuees in South Africa can be found in CO825/31/1, Report on the Malayan Government Agency for Evacuees, Union of South Africa, 10 April 1943; CO825/33/15, Report by the UK High Commissioner in South Africa, Lord Harlech, 1943. Work done by the Ceylon Evacuees Committee can be found in CO980/140. Similarly, post-liberation welfare issues, repatriation and the reunion of the Far Eastern evacuees is in CO980/169–72 and 174. For the wartime financial problems experienced by government

employees of Eurasian and Chinese extraction that fled to Macao, see CO825/30/12, Minute by Monson, 13 May 1942.

42 For an insightful analysis of how the British government grappled with the entire issue of pay and allowances for prisoner-of-war families, in particular the Far East, see B. Hately-Broad, "Prisoner-of-War Families and the British Government During the Second World War," PhD thesis, University of Sheffield, 2002, 106–23 and 135–51. Australian scholars have led the way on the issue of family separation, POWs, repatriation, and the emotional responses that resulted. See M. Reeson, *A Very Long War: The Families Who Waited*, Melbourne, 2000, and M. McKernan, *This War Never Ends: The Pain of Separation and Return*, St. Lucia, Qld., 2001.

43 PRO, CO129/589/17, Minute by G. E. J. Gent, Assistant Under-Secretary of State for the Colonies, 29 November, Young to Colonial Office, 27 November 1941. Arthur Jefferies wrote to his wife that two days after Young's arrival in Hong Kong, the Governor made a radio broadcast in which he tried to reassure those who had parted with their families that he was sympathetic to their problems and would give the issue his undivided attention with a view of reuniting these families as early as possible. "The way he spoke was encouraging, it certainly did not sound like empty promises. Everybody is feeling most optimistic about it especially in view of the improved war situation generally." AWM PR 84/317, Jefferies to his wife, 12 September 1941.

44 Ibid., F. C. Scott, War Office, to Gent, 4 December 1941.

45 B. Archer and K. Fedorowich, "The Women of Stanley," 379; *Hansard*, House of Commons, fifth series 1941–42, Vol. 377, Col. 701, 28 January 1942.

46 There is a growing literature on the British failure in Malaya and the fall of Singapore. The standard texts remain S. W. Kirby, *The War Against Japan: Volume 1: The Loss of Singapore*, London, 1957, and his *Singapore, The Chain of Disaster*, London, 1971. Also see L. Allen, *Singapore 1941–42*, London, 1977, and R. Callaghan, *The Worst Disaster: The Fall of Singapore*, London, 1977. For new research on British prewar planning, the land campaigns, inter-allied cooperation, intelligence gathering and political intrigue, see J. Pritchard, "Winston Churchill, the Military, and Imperial Defence in East Asia," in S. Dockrill (ed.), *From Pearl Harbor to Hiroshima*, London, 1994, 26–54; Ong C. C., *Operation Matador: Britain's War Plans Against the Japanese, 1918–1941*, Singapore, 1997; M. H. Murfett, J. N. Miksic, B. P. Farrell and Chiang M. S., *Between Two Oceans: A Military History of Singapore From First Settlement to Final British Withdrawal*, Singapore, 1999; J. Ferris, "'Worthy of Some Better Enemy?': The British Estimate of the Imperial Japanese Army 1919–41, and the Fall of Singapore," *Canadian Journal of History*, 28, 3 1993, 223–56; A. Best, "'This Probably Over-Valued Military Power': British Intelligence and Whitehall's Perception of Japan, 1939–41," *Intelligence and National Security*, 12, 3 1997, 67–94; and R. J. Aldrich's superb *Intelligence and the War Against Japan*, Cambridge, 2000.

47 P. H. Kratoska, *The Japanese Occupation of Malaya 1941–1945: A Social and Economic History*, London, 1998, 48. The population figures are from CO273/669/10, The Civil Defence of Malaya, Report by Sir George Maxwell, 1942.

48 Rhodes House Library, Oxford RHL, Eileen Mills Niven, Mss Ind Ocn s99, folder 2, Eileen to her parents, 4 December 1941.

49 PRO, CAB66/20, WP(41)286, British Administration in the Far East, 29 October 1941. Papers relating to his appointment, conduct and powers while Minister for Far Eastern Affairs see PRO, ADM116/4334 and Prime Minister's Office Papers, PREM3/155, coordinating authority papers, June 1941–March 1942.
50 PRO, CO967/77, Cooper to Churchill, 18 December 1941; LHCMA, Megan Spooner Papers, 1/2, Singapore diary, 24 November 1941, makes reference to Brooke-Popham's party trick.
51 IWM, Percival Papers, P23/F48, Percival to Maj.-Gen. S. W. Kirby, 3 and 22 November 1954.
52 LHCMA, Spooner Papers, 1/2, Singapore diary, 8 September 1941.
53 B. Montgomery, *Shenton of Singapore*, Singapore, 1984, 87; PRO, CO967/76, Shenton Thomas to Parkinson, 19 October 1941. In his biography of Duff Cooper, John Charmley vigorously contests Montgomery's allegation concerning over-packing: *Duff Cooper: The Authorized Biography*, London, 1986, 154–62. Cooper makes no reference whatsoever to the estrangement and then the intense conflict that raged between Shenton Thomas and himself. D. Cooper, *Old Men Forget: The Autobiography of Duff Cooper*, London, 1953, 289–305.
54 AWM, PR 00683, Capt. H. E. Jessup Papers, folder 2, Jessup to his wife, 20 September 1941. Jessup was taken prisoner and has left a detailed and insightful account of his POW experiences.
55 PRO, CAB66/22, WP(42)92, memo by Duff Cooper, 19 February 1942; S. W. Kirby, *Singapore, The Chain of Disaster*, 190–94 and 227–33; P. Elphick, *Singapore: The Pregnable Fortress*, London, 1995, 402–05. For an embittered account of the machinations which occurred between the civil and military authorities prior to the Japanese attack, see the memoir by C. A. Vlieland written in 1965. Vlieland had been Secretary for Defence, Malaya, 1938–41, but was dismissed as a result of ongoing intrigue in the colonial government and pressure from Brooke-Popham and Layton. LHCMA, C. A. Vlieland Papers, Disaster in the Far East 1941–42. Also see PRO, WO106/2609B, Seabridge report, 28 February 1942.
56 S. W. Kirby, *Singapore, The Chain of Disaster*, 156; RHL, Douglas Sturrock Papers, Mss Ind Ocn s189, diary, 16 December 1941. Captain A. W. Rogers, Australian Army Medical Corps, remarked in his POW diary how one family from Penang had told him "stories of muddling and inefficiency by the local officials [which] were absolutely blood-chilling to us." AWM, PR 85/145, Capt. A. W. Rogers Papers, folder 1, diary, 9 July 1942. A question was later raised in Parliament on the number of non-European inhabitants evacuated. The answer was a "small number," according to Duncan Sandys MP, Financial Secretary at the War Office. He also added that "there was no general desire on the part of the Asiatic community to leave the island." *Hansard*, House of Commons, fifth series 1941–42, Vol. 377, Cols. 950–1, 29 January 1942. Questions over the treatment of U.S. citizens on Penang in conjunction with Asian evacuation were raised. Ibid., Cols. 1779–80, 18 February and Vol. 378, Cols. 353–5, 26 February 1942.
57 IWM, 99/50/1, Maj. W. Gray Papers, which contains a three-page typescript by his wife on her evacuation from Singapore, n.d.

58 PRO, CO967/77, Cooper to Churchill, 18 December 1941. Kirby, who had access to these documents when writing the official history, used the Cooper–Churchill correspondence but obviously was not allowed to reference it when he wrote *Chain of Disaster*. See 188–96.
59 For the debate in the War Council over the evacuation of Penang, see PRO, WO106/2568, War Council minutes, 13–22 December 1941, especially Dawson's argument in minutes of 22 December 1941.
60 PRO, WO106/2579C, Notes on Malayan Campaign by Capt. Young, n.d. The recriminations over the evacuation of Penang, the panic and resulting loss of prestige as well as the disagreements over who actually had the jurisdiction to give evacuation orders was keenly debated after the fall of Singapore. See PRO, WO208/1529, Report by Maj. H. P. Thomas, Indian Army, Malaya and Singapore, May 1942; CO273/669/10, The Civil Defence of Malaya. Despite being a public relations disaster, several former government officers who had served with the Malayan Civil Service on the island at the time defended the decision made by local officials to evacuate Penang. R. Heussler, *Completing a Stewardship: The Malayan Civil Service, 1942–1957*, Westport CT, 1983, 36, n. 1.
61 PRO, CAB66/26, WP(42)314, Wavell's despatch on operations in Malaya and Singapore, 8 September 1942.
62 IWM, Percival Papers, P23/F48, Percival to Kirby, 3 November 1954, commenting on a draft of volume 1 of Kirby's *The War Against Japan*. Also see C. Kinvig, *Scapegoat: General Percival of Singapore*, London, 1996, for Percival's role in the defence and fall of Singapore.
63 RHL, N. F. H. Mather Papers, Mss Ind Ocn s205, *Changi Guardian*, 10 April 1942.
64 Churchill College Archive Cambridge (CCC), Duff Cooper 1st Baron Norwich Papers, DUFC 3/7, diary entry, 19 December 1941.
65 B. Montgomery, *Shenton of Singapore*, 96. Unclear if emphasis in original or added by author.
66 PRO, CO967/76, Shenton Thomas to Parkinson, 17 December 1941.
67 B. Montgomery, *Shenton of Singapore*, 98–99; PRO, WO106/2568, War Council minutes, 19–21 December 1941 outline intense discussions over civilian clearance orders and who had jurisdiction to issue them; RHL, Sir Miles Shenton Thomas Papers, Mss Ind Ocn s341, box 1, diary, 31 December 1941.
68 PRO, CAB65/20, WM133414, 22 December 1941; WO106/2534, War Office to GOC Malaya, 28 December 1941; War Office memo, Evacuation of Civilians from Singapore, 22 December 1941.
69 B. Montgomery, *Shenton of Singapore*, 99. Both Duff Cooper and Shenton Thomas make fleeting references in their respective diaries to the intense battle being waged in the War Council over civilian evacuation and the issue of racial discrimination. Montgomery, as the official biographer and apologist, seems to have had access to the originals, which were not released when the Governor's papers were deposited in Rhodes House Library. Instead, an annotated diary in notebook form containing short entries was catalogued and not the meatier diary used by Montgomery, the brother of Field Marshal Bernard Montgomery of Alamein. RHL, Shenton Thomas

Papers, Mss Ind Ocn s341, box 1, diary entries for 21 and 23 December 1941. Compare these with B. Montgomery, *Shenton of Singapore*, 98–99.

70   CCC, DUFC 3/8, diary entry, 28 December 1941. The War Council agreed with the committee in principle on 23 December. Chaired by Mr Justice Aitken, it included E. G. V. Day as secretary, representatives from the three Services, Paymaster-Captain Jolly, RN, Brigadier Newbigging and Air Commodore Modin, as well as members from the Asian communities. Another Malayan Civil Service official, S. M. Middlebrook, was later added to assist with the Chinese community. RHL, Shenton Thomas Papers, Mss Ind Ocn s341, box 2, file 1, statement made by Governor Thomas while in Changi, 8 May 1942; and PRO, WO106/2568, War Council minutes 23, 24 and 26 December 1941. CO273/673/7, Minute by W. S. Morgan, a former internee, 11 January 1946, makes a brief mention of the Aitken committee during postwar discussions on alleged desertion of government officials and Malayan police during the last days of siege.

71   S. W. Kirby, *Singapore, The Chain of Disaster*, 191–92; B. Montgomery, *Shenton of Singapore*, 104–06; PRO, PREM3/161/1, Moyne to Churchill, 6 and 22 January 1942 discussing cables from both Cooper and Shenton Thomas, each criticizing the other for inadequacies in civil defence provision. Also see I. Simson, *Singapore, Too Little, Too Late: Some Aspects of the Malayan Disaster in 1942*, London, 1970.

72   PRO, CO273/669/6, GOC Malaya to War Office, 21 January 1942; P. Elphick, *Singapore: The Pregnable Fortress*, 400; I. Simson, *Too Little, Too Late*, 100–01. Elphick uses a summary of extracts found in Seabridge's baggage now in PRO, WO106/2579C, distributed by the Chief Censor, India, to the Director, Post and Telegraph Censorship, London, 11 April 1942; and WO106/2609B, Seabridge report, 28 February 1942.

73   S. W. Kirby, *Singapore, The Chain of Disaster*, 188, singles out these officials for praise. Evacuation reports from government officials can be found at RHL, W. F. Wegener Papers, Mss Ind Ocn s50, Report of Evacuation from Malaya by W. F. Wegener, Chief Mechanical Engineer FMS Railways, 1942; J. Kennedy, *British Civilians and the Japanese War in Malaya and Singapore, 1941–45*, 19–40.

74   CCC, DUFC 3/8, Mrs. Day to Lady Cooper, 12 January 1941.

75   Quotation cited in P. H. Kratoska, *The Japanese Occupation of Malaya 1941–1945*, 41.

76   PRO, CO273/669/6, Shenton Thomas to Cranborne, 23 January, Minute by Maj. W. R. Rolleston, Colonial Office, 12 January, C-in-C India to War Office, 9 January, Minute by Gent, 23 January, Amery to Moyne, 26 January 1942; WO106/2568, War Council minutes, 24 January 1942; RHL, Shenton Thomas Papers, Mss Ind Ocn s341, box 2, file 1, statement by Shenton Thomas made while interned in Changi, 8 May 1942.

77   PRO, CO273/669/6, Minutes by Gent, 19 and 23 January, Shenton Thomas to Cranborne, 24 January, Australian High Commission, London, to Dominions Office, 1 February 1942.

78   P. Elphick, *Singapore: The Pregnable Fortress*, 400; PRO, WO106/2568, War Council minutes, 8 February 1942.

79   IWM, 01/24/1, Capt. W. A. Baker Papers, account written while in Changi Prison, 25 May 1942.

80 R. Heussler, *Completing a Stewardship*, 31–32.
81 C. Kinvig, *Scapegoat*, 212.
82 PRO, CO273/673/7, Minute by W. S. Morgan, 11 January 1946.
83 I. Simson, *Too Little, Too Late*, 102–03; B. Montgomery, *Shenton of Singapore*, 168–71; RHL, Shenton Thomas Papers, Mss Ind Ocn s341, box 2, file 1, statement by Thomas, 8 May 1942.
84 PRO, CO273/673/7, Minutes by J. J. Paskin, Assistant Secretary and Head of the Colonial Office's Eastern Department 'A,' 19 January and 11 August, Minute by Monson, 26 October 1945; CO273/669/7, statements by Tremlett and D. Neville Turner, FMS Police, 20 February and 3 April, H. W. Nightingale, Malayan Liaison Officer, British Consulate-General, Batavia to Chief Secretary, Ceylon, 13 April 1942, Minute by Morgan, 25 October 1945. The failure of the civilian and military authorities to clearly demarcate their jurisdictions, and above all, work together, also informed wartime discussions on postwar colonial reform in Hong Kong, Malaya, and Singapore. PRO, CO967/80, Colonial Office report by W. D. Battershill, Assistant Under-Secretary of State, Gent and Rolleston, 4 December 1942.
85 RHL, Lt.-Col. C. Noble Papers, Mss Ind Ocn s199, typs. of the evacuation of the Malayan Survey Department 1942.
86 PRO, CO537/1251, Hist. DD1, Report by Sir Robert Brooke-Popham on his Command in Malaya, 27 May 1942. This 78-page report, which was published for internal consumption, was discussed by the Chiefs of Staff and presented to the War Cabinet as COS(42)336, 8 July 1942. The PRO did not release this controversial report until 1995. Churchill, for one, demanded that it have a "most restricted circulation" and that questions about its publication be "severely resisted." "I do not wish it to be known outside our own War Cabinet circle," commented the Prime Minister, "that there are such Despatches in existence." Office of the War Cabinet to Miss M. R. Malleson, Assistant Private Secretary, Colonial Office, 25 September 1942.
87 PRO, CAB66/23, WP(42)135, Position of Civilians Evacuated from the Far East to the Dominions and India, Memo by Clement Attlee, Secretary of State for Dominions Affairs, 26 March 1942; CAB65/25, WM38425, 30 March 1942; *Hansard*, House of Commons, fifth series 1941–42, Vol. 378, Cols. 2189–9, 26 March 1942.
88 K. Fedorowich, "Doomed from the Outset? Internment and Civilian Exchange in the Far East, The British Failure over Hong Kong, 1941–45," *Journal of Imperial and Commonwealth History*, 25, 1 1997, 113–40. Also see P. S. Corbett, *Quiet Passages: The Exchange of Civilians between the United States and Japan During the Second World War*, Kent OH, 1987.
89 PRO, CO129/589/17, J. S. Henney, Watford, to Moyne, 27 January 1942.
90 B. Archer and K. Fedorowich, "The Women of Stanley," 379.
91 PRO, CO537/1251, Brooke-Popham report, and Shenton Thomas's rebuttal, 13 March 1946.
92 I. Simson, *Too Little, Too Late*, 81–87; PRO, PREM3/168/4, war diary of Vice-Admiral Layton, 1 June 1942. Wavell reinforced this point in PREM 3/168/3, Wavell to General Sir Alan Brooke, CIGS, 18 May 1942 and by Lt.-Commander H. Ainslie

who commanded the Controlled Mining Party, Singapore: ADM199/357/ TO 6281, debriefing paper, 29 April 1942.
93   P. Elphick, *Singapore: The Pregnable Fortress*, 401; PRO, CO980/65, M. R. Henderson to Colonial Office, 21 September 1942.
94   He was unrelenting on this theme in his postwar papers when corresponding with the staff of the official history. RHL, Shenton Thomas Papers, Mss Ind Ocn s341, box 3, file 4, Comments on the Draft History of the War Against Japan, October 1954; box 2, file 5, comments on Percival's despatch on operations of Malaya Command.
95   PRO, CO273/669/10, Maxwell report; CO273/669/6, Minute by Gent, 15 January 1942. Maxwell had a long and distinguished career in Malaya between 1909 and 1926. He retired from the Malayan Civil Service in 1926 but maintained an active interest in its affairs. See R. Heussler, *British Rule in Malaya*, Oxford, 1981.

CHAPTER 17

Churchill and Singapore

by Raymond Callahan

A statue of Winston Churchill broods over London's Parliament Square. Ivor Roberts-Jones' interpretation of this most remarkable man is a sombre one—he stands in a greatcoat, leaning on his walking stick, seemingly braced to endure a storm. It embodies a judgment Churchill himself rendered on his wartime record: "In war, you must have the capacity to endure defeat and disaster and survive mistakes."[1] Nothing during his five years as Prime Minister and Minister of Defence better illustrated the truth of this proposition than his part in what he described as "the worst disaster and largest capitulation of British history."[2] His role in the Singapore debacle did not end with the fall of the city, however. After the war, his memoirs shaped the story of the British war effort for a generation, and they still remain extremely influential. This essay will address both aspects of Churchill's involvement in the fall of Singapore: his actions as a wartime policy-maker—in many ways *the* policy-maker as far as Singapore was concerned—and the way in which his memoirs then shaped the story.[3]

A discussion of Churchill's part in the saga of Singapore's fall might well begin with a memorandum he wrote early in 1912, a few months after becoming First Lord of the Admiralty. "If the power of Britain were shattered upon the sea, the only course open to the 5,000,000 of white men in the Pacific would be to seek the protection of the United States," he wrote.[4] Churchill's realization that British naval power alone made possible the strategic security it guaranteed its Australasian Dominions was certainly clear enough, but it was also at that point rather theoretical. When he wrote it he was, in fact, arguing that Australia and New Zealand were best protected, not by the creation of "local" naval forces, but by contributing to the Royal Navy's ability to confront the challenge of the German fleet in the North Sea, thus helping to maintain its worldwide supremacy. The thought that British seapower might be shattered in other ways had simply not occurred.

By the time Churchill had occasion to revisit the issue, however, during Stanley Baldwin's 1924–29 government, in which he served as Chancellor of the Exchequer, the world had changed dramatically. The United Kingdom had indeed defeated the German challenge but had then been forced—by the state of its finances, the mood of its much enlarged electorate, and the clamant necessity of good relations with the United States—to accept limitations on the size of the Royal Navy. These in turn made it a one-hemisphere navy, albeit with responsibilities in both. At the same time, Japan, while not yet hostile, had to be moved from the "friendly" to the "doubtful" column. The same American pressures that compelled the British to accept a cap on naval strength also led to the cancellation of the 1902 alliance with Japan. The Japanese, in any case, were clearly developing ambitions in East Asia that brought them into potential conflict with long-established British interests there—and the Admiralty had in fact begun to think of Japan as a potential enemy during the latter stages of World War I. These changes posed the question of how a British fleet, based in home waters and the Mediterranean, was to protect the Empire's interests in the Far East. This particular circle was neatly squared by the decision to create a great fleet base on the north shore of Singapore Island, to which the Royal Navy could redeploy in the event of a serious challenge to British interests by Japan.

There was always a large element of fantasy about the "Singapore strategy," for it assumed that Japan would be accommodating enough to mount its challenge at a moment when the U.K. was free to respond. Of course, the reverse was most likely to be true, something that a number of critics immediately pointed out.[5] The most likely case was, however, also an insoluble problem—so everyone tacitly agreed to the proposition that the worst possible situation was unlikely to arise. Churchill was certainly a party to this fantasy, which was a convenient one for an economizing Chancellor fighting a major battle to hold down the naval estimates. In the era of the Locarno and Kellog pacts it was, moreover, relatively easy to believe that the world was becoming a safer place. Churchill's personal radar, which, at other points in his career, alerted him to approaching danger, gave no warning. It is a bit hard to blame him for that.

By the time Churchill returned to the centre of events in 1939, another strategic revolution had occurred, and the unlikely had become all too probable. A resurgent Germany, a hostile Italy—its considerable military weaknesses as yet unrevealed—and a Japan clearly bent on eradicating Western influences in East Asia had, between them, undermined the "Singapore strategy." To avoid confronting the issue, a new fantasy was put in place to cover the destruction of the old—the "period before relief," the time the Singapore "fortress" was expected to hold out before the arrival of the fleet, began to climb sharply. Seventy days had been the long-standing figure. In July 1939, it was raised to 90 days; in September to 180. The reason was that London was unwilling to accept the risks to its Mediterranean position that the diversion of considerable naval forces to the Far East would entail.

The change in Singapore's real—as opposed to its theoretical—position in British strategic priorities occurred before Churchill returned to office, but it accorded with his thinking. Even out of office, and out of favour, he was always well-informed. He also had a career-long habit of sharing his views on great issues with the government of the day. In March 1939, he sent Chamberlain a lengthy memorandum on naval strategy, which made absolutely clear what his priorities were: the Royal Navy's position in the Mediterranean must at all costs be maintained. "On no account must anything which threatens in the Far East divert us from this prime objective," he added, even if this meant accepting "losses and punishment" in the Far East. His view of how to explain this to the increasingly anxious Pacific Dominions was certainly robust: "tell them the whole story and they will come along."[6] There are a world of assumptions in that sentence and the document as a whole provides a key to much that would subsequently happen.

The successive strategic transformations that affected the "Singapore strategy" since its initial formulation were as nothing compared to the cataclysm of May–June 1940. Almost literally overnight, the British Empire found itself faced with a German-controlled Europe, a war with Italy in the Mediterranean—and, of course, the rapidly deepening hostility of Japan. Air assault and invasion loomed. The British Army had been, temporarily, both disorganized and partially disarmed. Worst of all, the U.K. did not have a single major ally, only its Dominions, India and its vast but militarily ill-organized dependent Empire. It was in these parlous circumstances that Churchill put his impress on British grand strategy—and remained thereafter totally consistent in his commitment to his design. The U.K. itself had to be defended—this, the decision that the British would remain in the war, may well be the single most important of his contributions to Germany's ultimate defeat. But survival, although necessary, was not sufficient. Victory was the goal, and to that end, the United States must be brought into the war—at almost any price. But victory would be meaningless unless the U.K. emerged with its Great Power status intact. All this pointed to the importance of the Mediterranean—holding it meant access to oil, confirmation of continuing status as a Great Power, and a clear signal to all neutrals, especially the vital one across the Atlantic—that the British both intended to fight on and could do so vigorously and successfully. This, in turn, led to the British assault on the French fleet in July 1940 and on the Italians thereafter. Relatively little of this new strategic outlook was original with Churchill. The clear-eyed ruthlessness with which operational decisions followed strategy was. The situation demanded hard choices, and Churchill made them. The British would fight the war they had on hand—and in which, for the next 18 months, they barely held their own. The "Singapore strategy" essentially ended in May 1940. In the Far East, the British would bluff, and hope the United States would deter Japan. In his first letter to Franklin Roosevelt after becoming Prime Minister, Churchill made that hope brutally clear: "I am looking to you to keep that Japanese dog quiet in the Pacific ...."[7] Anyone in a key position in the U.K. ought to have been very clear what Churchill's priorities were—he never concealed them, and most of his colleagues shared them, if not the single-mindedness with which the Prime Minister pursued them.

All that said, however, important questions remain. Even within his strategic priorities, could Churchill have seen that Malaya was better defended? Did he make clear to his Australian allies that the "Singapore strategy" had, in effect, been cancelled? Once the war broke out and he was forced to confront the looming calamity in Malaya, were his interventions of any help? The answers to these questions, this essay will suggest, were "probably," "no," and "probably not."

When the "Singapore strategy" finally collapsed with the fall of France, it left a vacuum that needed to be filled—not least because Australia and New Zealand were making major commitments to the Middle East. The filler, put in place over the ensuing summer, was a new strategic fantasy. Now airpower was to protect the naval base until such time as a fleet could be sent, which meant a much enlarged garrison would be required, in order to hold all of Malaya, so that airfields could be built at what the RAF deemed optimal locations. The policy and an accompanying command reorganization that put in place as "Commander-in-Chief, Far East" an Air Chief Marshal recalled from retirement, given limited powers and virtually no staff, would only have produced results if an air force of appropriate size and quality had been provided and if all the clashing local interests—the military, the civil administration, and the business community—had been forced, as they were at home, to work together. Churchill opposed the first and did not have time to address the second.

As one works through Churchill's wartime papers—now published for the period September 1939–December 1941—one is repeatedly struck by the utter consistency with which the Prime Minister stuck to his priorities. Nothing substantial could be diverted to Malaya and Singapore from the war against Germany and Italy. "I do not take an alarmist view about the defence of Singapore, at the present time," he wrote in a January 1941 minute, refusing to allow any considerable reinforcement of the tiny, and obsolete, RAF force in the Far East.[8] It turned out that the time would never, in fact, be propitious for the despatch to the Far East of modern aircraft. The demands of home defence, the Battle of the Atlantic, and the deepening conflict in the Mediterranean and Middle East would, in any case, have left very little, even if Churchill had been willing to part with it. The decision to supply Russia, virtually inevitable in the circumstances, ended any prospect of a substantial upgrade for Malaya's defences—even though the commitment to do so remained official policy. As usual, Churchill was crystal clear about it—to his inner circle in London. In mid-September 1941, in a note for the Chiefs of Staff about the movement overseas of troops, equipment and aircraft, he simply decreed: "Malaya can wait ...."[9] Underpinning Churchill's refusal to take any steps to improve the defences of Malaya was the conviction that to do so in any significant way was to court disaster somewhere much more important, and the equally strong belief that a Japanese attack would, in fact, bring in its train what he most sought—American belligerence. "I must repeat my conviction that Japan will not declare war upon us at the present juncture," he wrote in a "Most Secret-Action This Day" note in July 1941. "If, contrary to the above view, Japan should attack us, I am of the opinion that the United States would enter the war as the weight upon us would clearly be too great."[10]

Churchill never repented about the priorities he established and enforced. In his secret session speech on 23 April 1942, he devoted one paragraph, in what was one of his longer war speeches, to an account of Singapore's fall, and then, almost with relief, moved smartly westward—"I now leave the lesser war...and come to the major war against Germany." He admonished his listeners that "the war cannot be ended by driving Japan back to her own bounds and defeating her overseas forces. The war can only be ended by the defeat in Europe of the German armies...."[11] After the war, reflecting on the whole story in a note written in 1949–50 while the drafting of the fourth volume of his memoirs was in process, he was still adamant: "The major dispositions were right," he wrote, adding a bit defensively "I had not the life and strength to light up the field of interest with the same intensity after I had done all I could in the West and in Africa." Then came a restatement of his July 1941 view of the absolutely crucial factor: "I consoled myself by feeling the Americans would be in it, and that would make amends for all." He closed with unshakable conviction: "...if I had known all about it then as I know now, there were no substantial resources which could have been diverted from home defence, from the Desert, or from Soviet Russia."[12]

In view of Churchill's very candid admission that London simply could not provide adequate resources, it is interesting that, reflecting on the defeat in Malaya and Singapore's fall, he then noted, "Of course, the reason was that the people we sent out were an inferior troop of military and naval men."[13] This would be a theme his memoirs would develop: resources were scarce, but local leadership was inept. The "we" of course included him, and clearly he made no greater effort to supply effective leadership—and organization appropriate for war conditions—than he did to provide quality aircraft or troops. But nor did anyone else in London. Again the impression that no one had time to deal with Malaya is overwhelming. Churchill did not make time to see Air Chief Marshal Sir Robert Brooke-Popham before his departure for Singapore to take up the job of Commander-in-Chief, Far East. Nor did the Chiefs of Staff as a group. The Royal Air Force, having attained a primacy in the Far East, gave little thought to its problems thereafter. There is no evidence that either Air Chief Marshal Sir Cyril Newall or his successor as Chief of the Air Staff, Sir Charles Portal, ever argued seriously with Churchill about either the numbers or quality of the aircraft available in the Far East.[14] The Chief of the Imperial General Staff, General Sir John Dill, played an ambivalent, but similarly ineffective, role. He named Lieutenant-General A. E. Percival General-Officer-Commanding Malaya, a reasonable enough appointment in the circumstances, and he had a major clash with the Prime Minister in April–May 1941 over the degree to which the Mediterranean and Middle East were absorbing resources while Singapore—still officially ranking second only to the United Kingdom itself in priority—was not yet at the agreed minimum strength. This clash, according to Churchill's senior military aide, Hastings Ismay, writing after the war, was the decisive moment in Churchill's loss of confidence in Dill.[15] It would therefore seem that Dill, at least, was a strong supporter of improving Malaya's defences. Yet when, in the late autumn, he briefed his successor as Chief of Imperial General Staff, Sir Alan Brooke, on the state of British defences in the Far East, Dill "told me frankly," as Brooke recalled after the war, "that he had done practically nothing to meet this threat. He said that we were already so weak on all fronts that it was impossible to denude them any further to meet a possible threat." Brooke added, "I think he was quite right...."[16] The curious will note that Brooke does not say that Dill blamed the lack of preparedness on Churchill—and Brooke was hardly a "Churchillian." In view of the Churchill–Dill clash, ostensibly over this issue, in May 1941, what can be made of Dill's admission to Brooke? Possibly Dill was less worried about Singapore than about the absorption of resources by the Mediterranean war and found Singapore a useful counter-argument? We may never know, Dill having largely slipped through the meshes of the historians' nets.[17]

We do know, however, that Dill did nothing to correct one of Churchill's most fundamental misconceptions—that Singapore was a fortress capable of all-around defence, which it was not and had never been intended to be. From the summer of 1940 onwards, Churchill's minutes consistently refer to Singapore as if it were a true fortress. Neither Dill nor anyone else ever corrected him. Why? Here Churchill's anger both at the time and later is more understandable.[18]

The pattern of denial of resources, inattention to local realities, and reluctance to spare even some talent for the Far East persisted to the end. When the inadequacies in civil-military coordination in Malaya became clear, Churchill's solution was to send Duff Cooper, a second-tier politician—but definitely a Churchillian—who was in need of employment, on a mission of inquiry. When the overdue decision to replace Brooke-Popham was taken, a very capable soldier, Lieutenant-General Bernard Paget, was first named, then held back in case he was needed to command a British force cooperating with Russia in the Caucasus, and finally replaced by Lieutenant-General Sir Henry Pownall. Pownall, in turn, was available because the Prime Minister wanted to bestow his current position as Vice-Chief of the Imperial General Staff on Major-General Archibald Nye. As a result of all this, Pownall only reached Singapore on 23 December 1941.

Pondering on Singapore's fall while preparing his memoirs, Churchill commented on the whole question of Far Eastern defence: "If it had been studied with the intensity with which we examined the European and African operations, these disasters could not have been prevented, but they might at least have been foreseen."[19] No one in London, however, had time for this sort of focus in 1940–41.[20] Still, it is hard not to conclude that decisions on coordination and senior appointments could have been better handled by the Prime Minister.

If Churchill's priorities were clear and largely shared, except perhaps by Dill, in London, did he convey those priorities with equal clarity to his Australian allies? He had, after all, in March 1939 told Chamberlain that he had only to be candid with the Australians and they would support a shift in strategic priorities. It was advice that he himself found difficult to follow, however. The reason was the same one that had led to the demise of the original "Singapore strategy": the importance of the Mediterranean and Middle East. Three Australian divisions were serving in that theatre by 1941—indeed India, Australia, New Zealand and South Africa provided most of the divisional formations there, something of which the Prime Minister was uncomfortably aware. The Australians knew of course that "main fleet to Singapore" had been postponed indefinitely, and that a new airpower-centred strategy had replaced it. They knew that a troop build-up was underway in Malaya, to which they were contributing a division. But the degree to which British policy-makers had relegated Singapore to the back of their minds and the bottom of their priorities does not seem to have become fully apparent to the Australians—and neither Churchill nor the British Chiefs of Staff ever candidly said so. It is, nevertheless, odd that the Australian Prime Minister, Robert Menzies, who made an extended visit to the U.K. from February to April 1941 and who was certainly not an uncritical admirer of Churchill, failed to realize just how little real interest there was in Malaya and Singapore among British policy-makers.

As the situation in the Far East worsened in the second half of 1941, so did feelings in London about Australia. This was driven largely by the insistence of the Australian government under Menzies' successors, Arthur Fadden and John

Curtin, on the relief of the 9th Australian Division, the backbone of the besieged Tobruk garrison. Churchill, bending his energies to launching a major offensive against Rommel on which he pinned very considerable hopes, saw this as a distraction and disruption, as did General Sir Claude Auchinleck, the Commander-in-Chief, Middle East. Despite their appeals, however, the Australian government stood firm and the division was withdrawn. The whole episode foreshadowed what would later happen when Curtin exploded over first, the destination of the 18th British Division, and then Churchill's attempt to divert the homeward-bound 6th and 7th Australian divisions to Rangoon—fury in London, followed by grudging compliance with Australian demands. By the eve of the war in the Far East, Churchill's view of the Australian government was a harsh, almost hostile one: "I feel this Australian Government is out to make the most trouble and give the least help," he told the Chiefs of Staff two weeks before Pearl Harbour.[21] It was an atmosphere in which candid discussion between the two governments was simply not possible, and set the stage for the crisis in British-Australian relations that the Malayan campaign and the fall of Singapore would bring, a crisis whose echoes linger still.[22]

That said, however, questions remain, as they do about Dill's role. With the access he had in London, why did Menzies fail to grasp that the airpower strategy for Malaya was as much a fantasy as the abandoned "main fleet to Singapore" had been? What would have happened if the Australian government had been as determined about adequate airpower in Malaya as they were over the relief of the 9th Division? Would they have discovered they had more leverage than they thought—or would the crisis in British-Australian relations that followed Pearl Harbour have preceded it instead?

Once Japan attacked both the British and the Americans simultaneously, Churchill's greatest objective had been achieved—America was in the war. His thoughts turned immediately to a conference in Washington to shape Allied strategy. He pursued this goal with his usual relentlessness, undeterred by the unfolding disaster in the Far East, whose most dramatic moment, for him at least, was the loss of *Prince of Wales* and *Repulse*. In January 1950, he wrote a four-page memo for the "syndicate" of assistants on his war memoirs, defending Tom Phillips' handling of his ships. It was more than he did for anyone else involved in the campaign—but, of course, he had known Phillips well.[23] His only attempt to influence the conduct of the campaign came on 15 December. He was already on his way to Washington on a voyage that, slowed by gales, would take 10 days. Much of that time was consumed in preparing a remarkable series of memoranda on future strategy in preparation for his first wartime summit with his long-sought American allies. On the 15th, however, he sent the Chiefs of Staff in London a warning message:

> Beware lest troops required for ultimate defence Singapore Island and fortress are used up or cut off in Malaya Peninsula. Nothing compares in importance with fortress. Are you sure we have enough troops for prolonged defence? Consider...moving 1 Australian Division from Palestine to Singapore.[24]

Four days later he reverted to the same point in another message to the Chiefs of Staff.[25] Writing to his wife on the eve of his arrival in the United States, he assumed an orderly withdrawal to Johore was, in fact, underway. He then added, expressing the theme his memoirs would embody, that "we must expect to suffer heavily in this war with Japan, and it is no use the critics saying 'Why were we not prepared?' when everything we had was already fully engaged."[26] Caught up in the *Arcadia* conference, Churchill did not thereafter revert to the question of the speed of the withdrawal from northern Malaya. Unfortunately, in this case, he had been right—but unable to make an impact on events.[27]

There was, however, one action Churchill took while in Washington that had a considerable impact on the latter stages of the campaign as well as on the way its history took shape. Bowing to American wishes, he agreed to the war's first unified theatre command and accepted the American nomination of Sir Archibald Wavell—not one of his favourite generals—to head it. ABDA (American-British-Dutch-Australian) Command was doomed from the beginning, but Wavell, whose reputation remains high—perhaps, in part, because he was useful as a cudgel with which to belabour Churchill—managed to make an impact on the final stages of the campaign in Malaya, and the defence of Singapore itself, that was, at the very least, unhelpful. His role in the Burma campaign was similar—but that is another story. He would also help position Percival as the principal blame-carrier, as well as powerfully enhance the "blame the Australians" explanation for the city's rapid fall, an issue that still reverberates.[28] As in so many cases, Churchill did what the pressure of events constrained him to do, but the result was to put the last act in the drama of Singapore under the direction of a commander who, years later, during a round of golf in New Delhi, admitted to one of his partners, "I misjudged the Japs. I did not realize for quite a long time what terribly efficient and serious soldiers they were."[29]

The record seems clear. Churchill did what he did in relation to Far Eastern defence with his eyes open and fully cognizant of the price that might have to be paid. He chose to fight the war his nation's future depended on and hoped to sort the rest out in the aftermath of victory. The hope was, of course, vain, but it is hard to see what other choice there was, although it is possible to imagine someone less clear-sighted and determined than Churchill trying to avoid making it—with fatal consequences. He certainly never repented his priorities and decisions. In a note written during the production of his war memoirs, he put it as clearly as language can: "...it must be admitted I did not attempt to turn my mind on to the situation until after the Japanese had declared war and the Americans were our Allies. Then I did, and it was too late for [massive?] adjustments, *but even if it had not been too late, it would have been right not to do it.*"[30]

This note introduces the second theme of this essay. Churchill not only dominated policy on Far Eastern defence in 1940–41 and remained thereafter firm in his belief that it had been correct, but also got to shape, to a remarkable degree, how posterity would see his wartime stewardship. It is to his treatment of the defeat in Malaya and the fall of Singapore in his memoirs this essay must now briefly turn.

Marshal of the Royal Air Force Lord Tedder describes, in his aptly-titled memoir *With Prejudice*, Churchill's response to some criticism of his war memoirs by Field Marshal Jan Smuts, his much admired South African friend: "These are *my* stories," Churchill declared. "If someone else likes to write *his* story, let him."[31] Churchill's six-volume telling of his story, which began to take shape shortly after his electoral defeat in 1945, bore the impress of his mind and style, but was also the product of a cottage industry. That in turn may have had a significant impact on how the story of Singapore's fall was told.

Churchill had become adept at using teams of assistants, his usual method of composing his multi-volume works from *The World Crisis* on. For the Second World War, the team was F. W. Deakin, Denis Kelly, the indefatigable proofreader C. C. Wood, and a group of military advisers, the most important of whom for purposes of this essay was Pownall. Sir Edward Marsh and Lord Ismay were on call—as, of course, was nearly anyone else Churchill wished to consult. The memoirs were as much "syndicate productions"—albeit with much better prose—as were the Cabinet Office official histories that limped after them. The fourth volume, *The Hinge of Fate*, took shape in 1949–50, with Pownall playing a major role in composing the two chapters, "Penalties in Malaya"—the title was Denis Kelly's, and an improvement on the original "Shock at Singapore"—and "The Fall of Singapore." Pownall would, in fact, receive a unique acknowledgement in the text of the latter chapter. A talented staff officer who had been on the Committee of Imperial Defence staff before the war and Chief of Staff to the British Expeditionary Force in 1939–40, Pownall finished the war as Chief of Staff to Mountbatten in Southeast Asia Command. Crucially, he had been tapped to succeed Brooke-Popham in late 1941 and actually did so for about two weeks before being absorbed into the new ABDA command as Wavell's Chief of Staff. As readers of his published diaries know, Pownall could be both perceptive and acerbic, and was certainly not dazzled by Churchill.[32] Over the 1948–49 holiday season, he began to work on Malaya and Singapore. In an early note to Churchill he remarked:

> If there was lack of foresight the commanders on the spot were not the only ones to blame. In this I do not exclude myself, as I was in the War Office in 1938/39 and again in 1941. I do not recall that defences on the North Shore were ever mooted whilst I was there. In those years there were so many more urgent and dangerous problems nearer home that Singapore did not, I fear, get a high priority in our thoughts or in our working time.[33]

A few days later he sent Churchill a copy of a paper he had done, "largely to clear my own mind," on the changes in Far Eastern defence policy over the two decades 1921–41. It cannot have been entirely comfortable reading. Referring to the airpower strategy adopted in August 1940, Pownall pointed out that "because of overriding commitments in other theatres of war, the RAF did not get within sight of the strength needed to carry out the new policy." The army that was to hold the undermanned airfields that protected the empty naval base looked better on paper: "...reinforcements to Malaya were considerable in strength, if not always in quality."[34] One of the areas where quality was most lacking was at the top, where Pownall felt Percival, whom he had seen in action as Brigadier General Staff to I Corps in the British Expeditionary Force, was simply not up to the demands of commanding an army in the field. Indeed, Churchill's view of the mediocrity of the commanders in Malaya may have owed much to Pownall.

As he turned his mind to how to present this episode, Churchill himself acknowledged that lack of attention had been the Far East's lot in 1940–41, telling Denis Kelly about the mistaken belief that the northeast monsoon made campaigning impractical: "It is not to our credit in the highest circle at home that we did not know more about the actual climatic conditions in Malaya...."[35] At some point in this process, Churchill dictated a note to his team that outlined his approach to the story:

> I did not intend to pass judgement on the behaviour of generals or troops at Singapore. Forgive us our trespasses. I considered that an inquiry during the war was impossible for reasons of public safety. I always intended to have one on Singapore and Tobruk after the war was over. This is still my opinion. I am not going into details at all on this subject.

One detail in particular he wished to avoid: "One must avoid all squabbles with the Australians and their beastly general (Bennett) about it."[36]

The great problem with the idea of a Royal Commission or similar high-level inquiry had already been identified, however, in 1946 by the Joint Planning Staff in a report to the Chiefs of Staff. A complete examination of the circumstances of Singapore's fall, the planners pointed out, would have to range very widely, taking in policy, command and administration in London as well as on the spot, and could not avoid touching very sensitive issues, not least in British-Australian relations.[37] The Attlee government, in the face of this, made no move to institute an inquiry—nor, despite what he had written, did Churchill when he returned to office in 1951. Some of the same concerns prompted the sequestration for a half century of Wavell's 1942 report on the fall of Singapore—which, when finally released in the early 1990s, provoked an explosion in Australia.

The end product of all these competing pressures was the shape of the two chapters dealing with the campaign in Malaya and the fall of Singapore. In the chapter on his post-Pearl Harbour trip to America—"A Voyage Amid World War" in *The Grand Alliance*—Churchill devoted a mere page-and-a-half to the December fighting in Malaya, highlighting his warnings of 15 and 19 December about fighting too far forward. "Penalties in Malaya," in *The Hinge of Fate*, follows the same pattern—a brief narrative, drafted by Pownall, of the fighting on the mainland is followed by a focus on Churchill's exchanges with Wavell, especially on Wavell's 16 January 1942 telegram that finally exploded the "fortress" idea. Churchill noted on the draft of this chapter: "My immediate reaction was to repair the neglect so far as time allowed. But I was also angered."[38] That anger is fully apparent in the published text.[39] The other issue highlighted in the chapter, despite Churchill's proclaimed "no squabbles with Australia" rule, is the exchange with John Curtin over the destination of the 18th British Division, then en route to Singapore. Churchill had come back from America, as he told Wavell, strongly impressed with the importance of China to Roosevelt. After Wavell's 16 January message, the Prime Minister, sensing Singapore's impending doom, began to focus on saving Rangoon and, with it, America's access to China via the Burma Road. News that this was under discussion in London led to Curtin's famous "inexcusable betrayal" telegram of 23 January, which Churchill printed. His gloss on it—"It is not true to say that Mr. Curtin's message decided the issue"—is one of the least convincing statements in the entire six volumes.[40]

The "Fall of Singapore" chapter is more of the same—except that Pownall's role is openly acknowledged. The Churchill additions to Pownall's draft were largely messages exchanged with Wavell, himself increasingly out of touch with events on the island—to which he managed only one brief visit, 10–11 February, during its final agony.[41] Interestingly, the chapter concludes, not with any summing up by Churchill, but with a condolence message from Roosevelt on Singapore's fall: "I hope you will be of good heart in these trying weeks, because I am very sure that you have the great confidence of the masses of the British people."[42]

That, perhaps, catches the essence of the matter. Churchill did have the unshakable trust of the British public during the war, and after it, virtually iconic stature for the rest of his life. As his notes and observations during the building of his memoirs indicate, he realized—and was reminded by his advisers—that the responsibility for the debacle in the Far East was widespread. Nonetheless, while a very careful reading of his memoirs can piece together both his priorities and how he enforced them, the Malaya–Singapore chapters had the effect of focusing attention on the local commanders and their conduct of the battle. Was it Pownall's influence that allowed the far-from-flawless Wavell, twice sacked by Churchill, largely to escape criticism? Taken together with the decision by the Attlee government, left undisturbed by Churchill, not to open the can of worms that was the Singapore story, the local focus in Churchill's account helped to shape perceptions of the campaign for a generation.[43] Not until the 1970s and the opening of the archives could Churchill's version begin to be seriously critiqued. To have dominated the historiography of his war—and particularly of one of its most controversial chapters—for so long is not the least of Winston Churchill's many remarkable achievements.

What then can be said in conclusion? Churchill, in common with the rest of the post-1918 British policy-making elite, relegated the problem of imperial defence in the Far East to the back of his mind, perhaps because, as Geoffrey Best has so insightfully suggested, there may have been "a wish, a yearning, not to have to face up to this ultimate challenge to imperial security because of some sense that the problems looming in the mists of the future were going to be, in the last resort and the worst case, insoluble."[44] In 1940–41, this inattention became even easier as everything had to be subordinated to the struggle for British survival in Europe. Afterwards, Churchill's memoirs shaped the story into an account that, although not untrue, subtly shifted much of the responsibility elsewhere, while simultaneously regretting the lack of a "formal pronouncement by a competent court," a court he knew would never sit.[45]

To tweak the record, some 60 years on, is not to deny Churchill's essential greatness. It is, however, to do justice to the complexity of the circumstances and the intensity of the pressures within which all of the actors in the drama of Singapore's fall had to perform—as well as perhaps to acknowledge how very difficult it always is to carry out von Ranke's command to his professional successors to explain "how it really was."

Professor Raymond Callahan is Associate Dean of Arts and Science at the University of Delaware, where he has been teaching since 1967. In addition to his work on the Malayan campaign, he has published studies of the origins of the East India Company's army, the 1942–45 Burma campaign, Churchill's war leadership, and the Normandy campaign. He is a Fellow of the Royal Historical Society.

NOTES—

1 Winston S. Churchill [hereafter WSC], Note on Burma, CHUR 4/261, f 197. Undated but 1949, when the relevant volume of his memoirs was under construction. The Churchill Papers are held by the Churchill Archive Centre, Churchill College, Cambridge [hereafter CCC]. I would like to acknowledge the generous help of Mr. Allen Packwood, Acting Keeper of the Churchill Archive Centre, and his staff during a very productive and enjoyable research visit to the CCC.
2 WSC, *The Second World War IV: The Hinge of Fate*, Boston, 1950, 92.
3 There is another "Churchill and Singapore" story, and that is the Prime Minister's attempt to efface the events of February 1942 by bending British strategy against Japan to achieve its reconquest. This led in 1944 to the longest sustained argument of the war between him and the Chiefs of Staff, with threats of resignation by the latter hanging in the air by the summer of 1944. Even the ever-emollient Ismay was at the end of his tether over the matter. The whole episode has been discussed in H. P. Willmott's *Grave of a Dozen Schemes: British Naval Planning and the War Against Japan, 1943–1945*, Annapolis, 1996, but a closer examination of Churchill's role is needed.
4 WSC, Memorandum, undated, but January/February 1912, quoted in R. S. Churchill, *Winston S. Churchill: Companion Volume II*, Boston, 1969, iii, 1511–12.
5 Certainly the flaw in the logic was noted in Australia at an early date. L. Wigmore, *The Japanese Thrust*, Canberra, 1957, 7–8. The Australian official history is very frank, although naturally seeing things from an Australian perspective. Since the archives began to open in the 1970s, there has been a steady stream of books analyzing the origins, development and collapse of the Singapore strategy. One of the earliest was R. Callahan, *The Worst Disaster: The Fall of Singapore*, Newark, Del. & London, 1977, reprint Singapore 2001; one of the most recent is the excellent collaborative work by M. H. Murfett, J. N. Niksic, B. P. Farrell and Chiang M. S., *Between Two Oceans: A Military History of Singapore From First Settlement to Final British Withdrawal*, Singapore, 1999.
6 This paper is in CCC, CHUR 4/96, ff 57–65. M. Gilbert, *Winston S. Churchill, Companion Volume V*, London, 1982, iii, 1414–17 has printed it in full.
7 WSC to Roosevelt, 15 May 1940, M. Gilbert (ed.), *The Churchill War Papers, Volume II: Never Surrender May 1940–December 1940*, New York, 1995, 46. It is interesting that this 1300-page volume does not have a single index entry for "Singapore."
8 WSC to Lord Cranborne, 5 January 1941, M. Gilbert (ed.), *The Churchill War Papers, Volume III: The Ever Widening War, 1941*, New York, 2001, 25, cited hereafter as CWP3. Cranborne, as Dominions Secretary, was responsible for relations with Australia and New Zealand.

9   CWP3, WSC to Hollis for COS, 17 September 1941, 1223.
10 CWP3, WSC to Eden and Ismay for COS, 16 July 1941, 949.
11 C. Eade (compiler), *Secret Session Speeches*, London, 1946, 65, 73.
12 CCC, CHUR 4/255, WSC, Note, undated but 1949/50, ff 118, 123–4.
13 Idem. f 122. Churchill, of course, knew none of the commanders involved except Admiral Phillips—but Pownall, who played a significant role in the composition of Churchill's memoirs, did. Percival's biographer, Clifford Kinvig, in discussions at this conference, argued that Churchill had met Percival twenty years before, when, as a relatively junior officer, Percival accompanied the Commander-in-Chief, Ireland, to a Cabinet meeting at which Churchill was present, and saw him before he left for Malaya. The evidence for any 1941 meeting is indirect and unsupported by anything in the Churchill Papers. Churchill's 1941 appointment diary, oddly, records only one engagement—and that not with Percival. In any case, even if Churchill remembered an officer he briefly encountered two decades previously and a 1941 meeting could be firmly proven, it does not alter the fact that fundamental inattention was Malaya's and Singapore's lot until the eleventh hour—something Churchill himself admitted in a postwar note (see note 30 below).
14 In an excellent essay included in this book, essay number five, John Ferris has argued that British assessments of Japanese airpower were based on erroneous assumptions rather than, as is often alleged, dismissive racism. He makes a compelling case that helps in explaining—but certainly does not explain away—the Air Ministry's attitude.
15 Ismay to John Connell, n.d., in R. Wingate, *Lord Ismay: A Biography*, London, 1970, 57. Connell was Wavell's official biographer.
16 A. Danchev and D. Todman (eds.), *War Diaries 1939–1945: Field Marshal Lord Alanbrooke*, London, 2001, 203. The quotation is from the postwar notes, written 1951–56, that Lord Alanbrooke—as Alan Brooke had become—added to his wartime diaries.
17 Alex Danchev has done as much as can be done to rescue Dill from oblivion, but unfortunately there is simply not enough material for a full-scale study. In many ways the best account of Dill's stormy tenure as CIGS remains B. Fergusson (ed.), *The Business of War: The War Narrative of Major General Sir John Kennedy*, New York, 1958. Kennedy was Dill's Director of Military Operations.
18 Curiously, at least one member of Churchill's staff, Lt.-Col. Ian Jacob, claimed—in a postwar note to Ismay—that he had never envisioned Singapore as a fortress in the true sense of the term. Perhaps he assumed everyone else understood it as he did and so said nothing at the time.
19 CCC, CHUR 4/255, WSC, Note, undated, but 1949–50, f 122.
20 The belated attempt to redeem the promise of a Singapore-based fleet, the despatch of *Prince of Wales* and *Repulse* on their doomed voyage, was in fact less about providing significant naval strength in the Far East than about influencing American and Australian opinion, allied with an unrealistic—because outdated—belief in the deterrent value of capital ships. Churchill knew that, if war came, Force Z could only survive by making itself very scarce very quickly.
21 CWP3, WSC to Ismay for Chiefs of Staff, 24 November 1941, 1505.

22 D. Day, *The Great Betrayal: Britain, Australia and the Outset of the Pacific War, 1939–1942*, New York, 1989, is an interesting—if not totally convincing—Australian view of all this.
23 CCC, CHUR, 4/253A, WSC, Note, January 1950, ff 133–36.
24 WSC to Ismay for Chiefs of Staff, 15 December 1941, CWP3, 1630. This was an indication of his belief that the Australian forces were a freely disposable reserve force—an attitude that produced a sharp clash with the Australian government when he attempted to send Australian troops to Rangoon in February 1942.
25 CWP3, WSC to Ismay for Chiefs of Staff, 19 December 1941, 1647.
26 CWP3, WSC to Clementine Churchill, 21 December 1941, 1663.
27 See the careful recent account of the campaign by Brian Farrell in M. H. Murfett et al., *Between Two Oceans: A Military History of Singapore From First Settlement to Final British Withdrawal*, 180–215. Churchill's analysis coincided with that of the commander of the principal operational formation in Malaya, Lt.-Gen. Sir Lewis Heath, whose III Indian Corps bore the brunt of the fighting in northern and central Malaya. Unfortunately Percival was on poor terms with Heath, whose views therefore were discounted. Percival's conduct of the campaign, which led to the defeat in detail of III Indian Corps, was however approved by the Chiefs of Staff in London, presided over by Alan Brooke.
28 Wavell's official biographer, John Connell, produced a well-written hagiography that has kept Wavell's stock perhaps undeservedly high. R. Lewin, *The Chief: Field Marshal Lord Wavell, Commander-in-Chief and Viceroy 1939–1947*, London, 1980, is much more critical. The assessment by Brian Farrell, "The Dice were Rather Heavily Loaded: Wavell and the Fall of Singapore," in B. P. Farrell (ed.), *Leadership and Responsibility in the Second World War: Essays in Honour of Robert Vogel*, forthcoming, Montreal, 2003, is excellent and long overdue.
29 CCC, Slim Papers, 5/4, Davies to Lewin, 15 May 1974.
30 CCC, CHUR 4/255, WSC, Note, undated but 1949–50, f 118. The italicized words have been struck through in the original typed text and a final, handwritten sentence added: "The major dispositions were right."
31 Arthur, Baron Tedder, *With Prejudice*, New York, 1966, i; italics in the original.
32 B. Bond (ed.), *Chief of Staff: The Diaries of Lieutenant-General Sir Henry Pownall*, two vols., London, 1973–4. One well-informed study of the campaign argues that one of Wavell's worst mistakes was not sacking Percival and replacing him with Pownall: see B. P. Farrell, "The Dice were Rather Heavily Loaded." Pownall's role in the composition of Churchill's memoirs can be tracked through the pages of M. Gilbert, *Winston S. Churchill, Volume VIII: Never Despair 1945–1965*, London, 1988. Gilbert does not, however, go into detail about how the treatment of individual episodes was shaped. The index contains no entry for "Singapore."
33 CCC, CHUR, 4/255 a, Pownall to WSC, 30 December 1948.
34 CCC, CHUR 4/258, Pownall to WSC, 2 January 1949, ff 14–15. An expanded, and blander, version of this appeared as an appendix in *The Hinge of Fate*.
35 CCC, CHUR 4/255 a, WSC to Denis Kelly, 7 August 1950, f 92.
36 Ibid., WSC, Note, undated but 1949–50, ff 118–19.

37   B. P. Farrell, "The Dice were Rather Heavily Loaded." See also Farrell's Appendix 3 in *Between Two Oceans*, 247, n. 117.
38   CCC, CHUR, 4/235b, WSC, Note, f 266.
39   WSC, *The Hinge of Fate*, Boston, 1950, 48–50.
40   WSC, *The Hinge of Fate*, 55–59. The quoted sentence is on page 58.
41   See Brian Farrell's comments on Wavell's role during the fighting on the island in "The Dice were Rather Heavily Loaded."
42   Roosevelt to WSC, 19 February 1942, *The Hinge of Fate*, 107.
43   It is interesting that in their 1946 report on the implications of an inquiry into Singapore's fall, the Joint Planning Staff recommended that, if one had to be held, it should focus on events after the withdrawal onto Singapore Island. This focus on the local commanders is, in fact, what Churchill achieved. PRO, CAB119/208 Malayan Command—Implications of a Public Inquiry. This JPS file, which ends with a document dated 15 May 1946, was closed until 1997.
44   G. Best, *Churchill: A Study in Greatness*, London, 2001, 127.
45   The phrase appears at the beginning of the "Fall of Singapore" chapter in *The Hinge of Fate*, 92. It is probably not Pownall's.

CHAPTER 8

1941: An Overview

by Brian P. Farrell

December 7 1941 was famously described as "a date that will live in infamy," after the Japanese surprise attack on the United States naval base at Pearl Harbour. But war came to Singapore a few hours earlier, in an air attack carried out by that same navy. The relationship between the two events sums up at a glance the tumultuous events of one of the most dramatic years in world history, 1941, and the place of the struggle for Malaya and Singapore in those events. For the attack on Singapore was both intertwined with the strike against the U.S. Navy, and overshadowed by it. The year 1941 marked the transformation of two Great Power wars, one in Europe, another in Asia, into a true world war—and the stakes matched the scale. In the biggest picture, 1941 was the year the war went beyond the power of the British Empire to remain a principal belligerent. It had no choice but to fight. But for it to keep fighting on this level, at this intensity, something had to give. That is where Malaya and Singapore came in. The question this paper asks is the following: When examined from the vantage point of the "big picture," the global war, what conclusions can we draw about why Malaya and Singapore proved to be so vulnerable?

After the Great War a generation before, the world's strongest powers erected a new order, to be based on new principles, that was to prevent any such conflict from ever erupting again. The peace settlement of 1919 established a League of Nations, to put an end to the selfish pursuit of national interest and replace it with general cooperation to maintain collective security. The principle of self-determination was to ensure that all distinct peoples gained the right to pursue their own destiny; general disarmament by agreement was to rid the world of the scourge of aggression; political trusteeship was to put an end to colonialism;

and a multilateral world economy was to bring about a freer flow of goods and services, to the general enrichment of all. This agenda was far too ambitious for the twenty-first century, let alone the twentieth, and its very ambition was perhaps bound to make the crash all the harder. But right from the start it was doomed by the reactions of most of the Great Powers, without whom no viable world order could ever be built.

Germany, beaten in war and punished in peace, felt no great attachment to a settlement it saw as directed against it, and many Germans yearned from the start to regain their lost lands, power and prestige. Japan left the peace conference frustrated by what it saw as a racially-based refusal by the Western powers to treat it with the respect it craved. Worse, China was divided and weak, but aroused and ambitious, and its relationship with Japan had already provoked concerns in the West about the future of East Asia. Russia, wracked by revolution and civil war, was treated as an outcast by the other powers, who tried indeed to destroy its Bolshevik government in the cradle; it reciprocated by opposing the settlements reached in Paris and the world order they envisaged. Most damaging of all, the United States, now the wealthiest and strongest power in the world, its President the chief architect of this bold new framework, opted out of its own creation from the start. The U.S. Senate rejected the peace settlement, the Americans turned to military isolationism and never joined the League of Nations. That in practice left only two Great Powers, the British and French Empires, committed to defend the new world order sketched out in Paris. But both were weakened by the strain of a costly victory, neither was very keen to dismantle colonialism in order to assist self-determination, and both were now forced to protect empires larger than the resources they felt they could spare to do the job—let alone to police the world. The story of the next two decades was far from a simple progression from vulnerability to collapse, but the instability at the very core of this would-be new world order was the crux of the matter. The house of cards did have to be pushed, but it remained a house of cards.

After economic disaster and despair pushed two unsatisfied powers, Germany and Japan, into unprecedented extremism, a crisis developed in the 1930s. Germany and Japan were determined to use military force to build an entirely different vision of world order, one based on agendas of empire-building and assumptions of racial superiority. They wanted to smash the existing international framework of politics and economics and put their own in its place. These aspirations brought on a war with the British and French in Europe, and with China in Asia. The Germans forced France to its knees but could not compel the British to make peace. The Japanese won victory after victory in China, but could not find a way to make it yield. The Axis powers were riding high, but the key fact of the war at the beginning of 1941 was that the world's *greatest* power centres remained, as yet, uncommitted. The United States and the Soviet Union, the great continental land mass economies, the industrial giants of the world, the absent titans of the 1919 settlement, were not yet in the fight. In 1941, Germany and Japan deliberately forced them both into it by attacking them. That triggered a fight that could not be anything but a struggle over the future direction of world order—a true world war. The British Empire was not sidelined in this fight, but rather swept up by it. For the hard fact was that by 1941, the United Kingdom, supported by its Dominions and colonies, was fighting for its very survival as an independent state—fighting a stronger enemy, and not winning.

Of the three most historic decisions of 1941, the British government was a party to only one. Pride of place must go to Adolf Hitler's decision to start a war to the death against the Soviet Union. "When operation *Barbarossa* begins, the world will hold its breath," the German dictator boasted some weeks before his forces invaded the USSR on 22 June—and so indeed it did. Not much less pivotal was the Japanese decision to attack the strongest power in the world, rather than be forced by economic strangulation to give up the dream of creating a new imperial order in Asia. This swept the British up in a larger conflict, one in which they were more in the way than on the bull's-eye. The struggle was over who would determine the future international order in Asia. The decision the British did share was the American-British agreement that if—read when—America did enter the war, and there was *never* any question on whose side it would, then the alliance of the English-speaking powers would concentrate their combined might to defeat Germany first, because it was the most dangerous threat. The confirmation of this decision after the attack on Pearl Harbour, despite the fury that attack aroused among the American people, was President Franklin Delano Roosevelt's most important command decision of the war—and a great British victory! It was also a decision that, in retrospect, underlined why the Western Allies were soon to suffer so many defeats, as their forces in Southeast Asia buckled under the Japanese onslaught. With the Soviets reeling back on Moscow and fighting for survival, the Western empires either prostrate or distracted, and the U.S.A. only really beginning to mobilize for a global war, the Japanese saw a historic now-or-never opportunity to strike in Asia while most of their rivals were vulnerable. But while the Axis powers had for the moment caught their enemies off-guard, they had also in fact already signed their own death warrant. The Japanese advance in Malaya and Singapore, dramatic as it was, in fact reflects only the former point—and we should be careful not to let it obscure the latter. The reason it sometimes does is that Allied vulnerability at that time was on display for all to see—but the correlation of forces all but bound to shift so heavily in favour of the Allies was already taking shape, even if that was harder to see at the time.

This disconnection between the underlying realities of power, and how the facts of power appeared at the time, is, when you look at the biggest picture, an important reason why the weakness of the British Empire's defences in the Far East seemed so shocking in 1941. Things were, indeed, not altogether as they seemed, from a global perspective. Two accusations have been made against the British government, blaming it for not doing enough to make Malaya and Singapore more defensible while there was time. One is unanswerable, and we have heard much about it today. The "Singapore strategy" was indeed all that it has been called—a strategic illusion, a non-starter, a bluff. A one-ocean navy, lacking a modern and effective air arm, or land-based air support, was never likely to be able to protect a colony that would probably only be attacked when the main forces were already engaged elsewhere. This dilemma was grave indeed, but only a fundamental shift in imperial policy, perhaps before 1935 at the latest, might, in retrospect, have made enough of a difference—and at what cost elsewhere? The other accusation deserves more attention, and fittingly we have heard it discussed here today as well. From May 1940 the United Kingdom and the Empire finally did abandon all qualms, and mobilize seriously for total war. It was late and desperate, but it was now serious. From that point forward, the Churchill government has been taken to task for making choices in grand strategy that made Far East Command weaker and more vulnerable than need have been the case. This is the issue that deserves our closer attention, the point that needs to be pursued. Here too, we have heard already today the outlines of the argument. It is one that brings together the long-term problem of the "Singapore strategy," and the immediate but very broad problem of coping with a war expanding to become a global conflict. From the vantage point of a global overview, what can we see? Just how defensible were Malaya and Singapore, and what more, in all fairness, could or even should have been done?

Four issues related to developments from May 1940 need further exploration here. First, there is the charge that too much emphasis was placed on home defence, leaving too little for anywhere else. Second, there is the argument that too much reliance was placed on the Americans in the Far East. Third, there is the charge that the Japanese were underestimated in almost cavalier fashion. Finally, there is the argument that resources desperately needed in the Far East, where they might have been very important, were wasted on assisting the Soviets, where they were swallowed up to little effect. The first charge is misdirected. The second is unfair. The third is absolutely right. The last one is unconvincing.

By the autumn of 1941, there were very large armed forces indeed concentrated in the United Kingdom. More than 100 Air Force squadrons, some 25 Army divisions, and half the battle fleet was guarding the homeland and its approaches.[1] These forces included some of the best equipped and trained formations in the Empire, especially in the Air Force. The British Chiefs of Staff had agreed the year before that the Far East required at least 336 frontline aircraft to be properly defended. RAF Far East had barely 180 aircraft of all types when war broke out in December, and almost none of them were top-of-the-line.[2] All these facts have led to the charge that far too much emphasis was placed on home defence, leaving other areas avoidably weak. Two considerations make that charge misdirected. First, what was really needed overseas were formations, not just equipment. Moving aircraft and tanks alone was not enough. Full-strength squadrons and brigades, cohesive combat-ready units, were the only reinforcement that was really useful. But moving the men and their machines took a great deal of shipping, and a lot of time. The cold truth was that the British just did not have the shipping to move many divisions, and the ground equipment of squadrons, out of the U.K. in the second half of 1941. As it was, to move *two* divisions overseas they had to borrow the shipping from the Americans, by direct appeal from Prime Minister Churchill to President Roosevelt. One of those divisions, the 18th, in the end wound up in Singapore.[3] Only more formations could have been decisive help for the Far East, and these could not then be moved. The second consideration is that the British high command had been traumatized by the beating the Army suffered at the hands of the Germans in France in 1940, plus the difficulty all services experienced fighting the Germans in the Mediterranean theatre in 1941. The Chiefs of Staff did not then expect the Soviets to survive the German onslaught. They were wrong, but that does not change how they felt then. They were loathe to send too many formations out of the U.K. for fear the Germans might again be able to concentrate for an invasion.[4] In retrospect this fear looks exaggerated, but that is not quite fair. The trauma was real, as was later underlined by the continuing difficulty the Allies faced fighting the German Army in 1944. The absolute numbers look bad: so many in the U.K. in 1941 not fighting, so few elsewhere and all hard-pressed. But the numbers, when set in context, do not tell the whole story.

By the end of 1940, at the latest, there is no doubt the Churchill government had all but abandoned an independent policy towards Japan and resorted to following the American lead in the region. The unavoidable repercussion for grand strategy was to leave all British defence plans, and forces, ultimately depending on the Americans to quickly soak up any Japanese attack on the Western powers. This has been criticized as short-sighted, based on such considerations as the reluctance of the Americans to make prior concrete commitments to joint plans, the general unpreparedness of the United States for war in 1941, and the disagreement over priority areas to defend. None of these considerations was decisive, and the criticism is unfair. Whether the U.S. was ready for war or not, the British Empire was not going to prevail against Germany and Italy, let alone Japan as well, unless the Americans intervened on the Allied side. As Raymond Callahan rightly noted, Churchill's global priority in grand strategy in 1941 was to do whatever would accelerate American entry into the war, and nothing that might hinder it.[5] There was no escaping the ramifications of that policy, which itself was the only sane one to pursue under the circumstances. The British could not send decisive reinforcements to the Far East while so hard-pressed in Europe. They could not take the lead in deterring Japan. They were too weak. They could plead with the Americans to make joint plans, argue about priorities, and urge them to mobilize—and they did all those things, and more. The ill-fated decision to send a small naval force to Singapore in autumn 1941 was very much done to impress the Americans, among other reasons. The two things the British could not do were to demand, or to go it alone. The physical strength was just not there. The British did not blindly fall in behind Uncle Sam, they did so with eyes mostly open.[6] This criticism is unrealistic. Worse, it is heavily influenced by considerations after the fact, by how rapidly the Allies were swept out of Southeast Asia, making some feel it had been wrong ever to rely on the Americans. That is unhistorical. In December 1941, there was no choice.

Critics are on much stronger footing when they blame the British, at all levels in the chain of command, for widely underestimating the Japanese to an almost absurd degree. There is much to this charge. This is not a simplistic matter of blind racial arrogance, "we are white, they are yellow, they are not as good as us." There was of course some of that, but the Japanese gave as good as they got in that respect. No, this is a more complicated picture of different British images of the Japanese largely giving way to one far too complacent perception, propelled by ethnocentrism and laced with wishful thinking. Thanks to the work of colleagues such as our own John Ferris, we know that some British authorities were very impressed by Japanese fighting power indeed.[7] But in London and Singapore, a more complacent image did undoubtedly settle in. The Japanese did not do things the same way we did, nor use the same equipment, so they could not be as efficient as us. Forget the nonsense about not being able to see in the dark, or being no good with machines. The assumptions that did settle in decision-making circles were bad enough. From the Prime Minister on down, a common view was that the Japanese might prove to be a problem because they could take advantage of the world situation and attack by surprise, with great numbers—but there seemed to be a good chance they could be held before they did irreparable damage, because on the battlefield they would probably be about as efficient as the Italians, which in British eyes in 1941 was an insult. This image helped justify the decision to take a calculated risk with the Far East.[8] The Japanese exposed it brutally from December 1941, and this time there are grounds for criticism. The British had alternate views available and could have reconsidered more rigorously. One is left with the impression that an ethnocentric-based intelligence assumption was used to justify a policy driven more by other factors. This act of self-deception was compounded by the real intelligence failure here: The British overestimated their own forces. It would have been daunting and difficult to face up to a more grim estimate of the Japanese in late 1941, but it cannot have led to any outcome worse than the one finally endured. This mistake was avoidable, and it did matter.

The same cannot be said for the final criticism, the argument that supplies sent to the Soviet Union did little good, whereas they might have had a disproportionately positive effect on the defence of the Far East. This is unconvincing on two grounds. First, as I argued earlier, formations, not equipment, were what the Far East needed. The British did not start sending major equipment to the U.S.S.R. until very late in September 1941. Very little would have reached the Far East, had it been directed there, before the Japanese attacked. Nor did the British send top-of-the-line equipment.[9] *Valentine* tanks may have been of some use to Malaya Command, had they arrived in time, but the men to crew them would still have needed time to learn the terrain and fit into the force. They would not have had it. That argument is admittedly influenced by hindsight, by knowing when the Japanese did attack. The second reason to reject this criticism is not, and it ties us into the broadest point we need to consider here, in this overview of 1941. Things can be relative as well as absolute. And those responsible for the biggest decisions of grand strategy and national policy can never forget that, and must always weigh and balance conflicting pressures. The British government and its military advisers were not optimistic about Soviet chances before December 1941, but that certainly did not mean they could lightly afford to write them off. The Soviets provided something that was absolutely necessary in order to win the war: a continental army that could pin down the main force of the main enemy, the German Army. The Chiefs of Staff flatly refused to confront the German Army on the continent again until it was very considerably worn down. It was in the highest national and imperial interest for the British government to do whatever it could to keep the Soviets in the fight. All it could do in 1941 was offer equipment and words, but both it had to offer.[10]

The Eastern Front, not the Pacific, was the centre of gravity of the expanding war in 1941. Here was the only slight chance the Axis had to derail the Grand Alliance before the Americans were ready to fight at full strength. Had the Germans been able to break the Soviet state and push it out of Europe, the German Army might have been able to shift massive forces back to the west long before the Americans were ready to lead the counterattack. This clash of titans was simply beyond the strength of the British Empire. Churchill rightly saw the German invasion of the Soviet Union as a godsend, and immediately understood that the longer the Eastern Front lasted, the more the war must turn in favour of the Allies. This had nothing to do with the nature and character of the Soviet regime; it was a matter of sheer survival. Other critics have charged that Churchill did nothing but doom the Empire, and open the way for Soviet expansion, by fighting Nazi

Germany to the death.[11] What an absurd, even obscene argument. Nothing could be done about Soviet expansion, it was far too late for that. By 1941, the question was whether the world could tolerate the very existence of the far greater evil, Hitler and his atrocious regime. Churchill got it right. Helping the Soviets was the right choice at the time, in the real world. Breaking the strength of the British Empire was a small price to pay in return for helping to forge the alliance that destroyed Nazi Germany and Imperial Japan. But in 1941, having to deal with the accumulated shifts in world power over two decades meant making very hard choices indeed. Singapore, and the Far East, did pay part of the price.

In conclusion, the decisions made by the British government and high command regarding the defence of Singapore and the Far East need to be seen not only in a long-term perspective, as we have been doing today, but also, for the year 1941, in a global and comparative one. Only then can the realistic range of choices then available, and the stakes riding on everyone's decisions, be fully appreciated. Underestimating the Japanese can be explained but not really excused, especially given how much it rested on overestimating yourself. That was a costly mistake, and it raises a vital point. I am not arguing that the British did nothing wrong, or that they were absolutely helpless. The story of arrangements made for imperial defence after the First World War is one of failure, and nowhere was that more dramatically underlined than in Singapore. But I am arguing that the problems they faced by 1941 were close to insoluble if the solution *had* to include a successful defence of Singapore. And the main reason for this is that you need to make global decisions to fight a global war, and you had better get your priorities right. When you consider the hard facts of the military, economic and logistical situations, and compare how all the major powers settled those priorities, the British did not fail the test.

The very survival of the nation, let alone the Empire, rested entirely by 1941 on forging an alliance with powers strong enough to defeat the Axis. Making peace with Hitler was indeed unthinkable, and defeating him, let alone the Japanese, without stronger allies was impossible. Churchill did nothing to prevent nor even dilute that alliance, and much to bring it on. The calculated risk was that Singapore might be lost and the war still won. That proved to be correct. There is no way, of course, that we can know what would have happened elsewhere had more forces been sent to Singapore. But as I argued earlier, the means needed to send what might have made a difference were not really available anyway. The British Empire was not winning the war. It could not have done much more than it did at the time to defend Singapore. And it got the biggest decision of all absolutely right. Compare that to the fateful decisions made that year by its main enemies. Hitler launched his war of enslavement and extermination against the largest land mass and army in the world, an army the Germans grossly underestimated in both quantity and quality. His armies provoked a war of no quarter, which gave the Soviet peoples little choice but to stand and fight to the death under the Stalin regime or be enslaved at best. This war to the death was to be won in four months; Hitler actually *reduced* war production, and the size of his army, just as he sent it into total war. When *Barbarossa* died in the snow before Moscow, Germany was finally forced to enter the race to mobilize for total war. It would prove to be too late. To compound the error, the German dictator declared war on the U.S.A., removing a domestic headache for President Roosevelt. As for the Japanese, they decided that, rather than relinquish their dream of hegemony in China and ascendancy in Asia, they would attack an economy ten times their own size. Their plan was not bold, it was reckless. While most of their army carried on the war in China, and watched the Soviets in the north, the remaining *one-fifth*, with the navy, was going to throw the Americans and their Western friends out of Asia, then dig in and fend off all counterattacks until the American people grew weary of the fight and forced Washington to sue for a peace that would leave Japan dominant in Asia. Talk about intelligence failures! The Japanese persuaded themselves to adopt this fantasy because they concluded the Americans did not have the stomach for total war. The Imperial Japanese Army and Navy barely bothered to align their operations, and certainly did not integrate them in any national grand strategy. They did not even bother to prepare their navy to convoy the raw materials they were running such a risk to seize from Southeast Asia to Japan; it would not be necessary, the Americans would never get through the protective cordon of Japanese-held islands and bases. Corregidor surrendered in May. The Imperial Japanese Navy lost the war in the Pacific the next month, near Midway. Japanese miscalculations make British mistakes look trivial.

The year 1941 was indeed the year that, in retrospect, revealed to the world that the British Empire could not stand on its own in a world war. Singapore and the Far East were indeed the theatre that would pay the highest price for this. But when you take everything into consideration, and compare with others, an even more important fact in world history stands out. When the stakes were the highest and the balance of forces at its most dangerous, the British did not make decisions that were likely to lead to their final destruction. Singapore was swept up in a global war, but its defenders made largely sensible global decisions. Germany and Japan, driven by ambition and self-delusion on the grandest scale, brought about the very coalition bound not just to defeat but to destroy them. This is the central fact of 1941. The apparent vulnerability of Singapore revealed only a window of opportunity that was in itself an illusion. It could only be opened by bringing on the very clash of titans all but certain to destroy those who dared try.

NOTES—

1. B. P. Farrell, *The Basis and Making of British Grand Strategy 1940–1943: Was There a Plan?* Lewiston, N.Y., 1998, Book 2, appendix B.
2. M. H. Murfett, J. N. Miksic, B. P. Farrell and Chiang M. S., *Between Two Oceans: A Military History of Singapore From First Settlement to Final British Withdrawal*, Singapore, 1999, chs. 7–8.
3. B. P. Farrell, *The Basis and Making of British Grand Strategy 1940–1943*, Book 1, ch. 4; M. H. Murfett et al., *Between Two Oceans*, ch. 8.
4. B. P. Farrell, *The Basis and Making of British Grand Strategy 1940–1943*, Book 1, passim.
5. Essay number seven in this volume.
6. B. P. Farrell, *The Basis and Making of British Grand Strategy 1940–1943*, Book 1, ch. 4.
7. Essay number five in this volume.
8. M. H. Murfett et al., *Between Two Oceans*, ch. 7.
9. B. P. Farrell, *The Basis and Making of British Grand Strategy 1940–1943*, Book 1, ch. 4.
10. Ibid.
11. The various works by John Charmley are noteworthy in this respect.

Part Two

The Malayan Campaign and the Fall of Singapore

CHAPTER 19

General Yamashita Tomoyuki: Commander of the Twenty-Fifth Army

by Akashi Yoji

The Tiger of Malaya

On 15 February 1942, Lieutenant-General Yamashita Tomoyuki, Commander of the Twenty-Fifth Army of the Imperial Japanese Army, accepted the surrender of the British forces defending Singapore from Lieutenant-General A. E. Percival at the Ford Factory at Bukit Timah. The defeat of the British forces was "the worst disaster and the largest capitulation of British history," as wartime Prime Minister Winston Churchill recorded in his memoirs. Yamashita's conquest of the British fortresss, fighting his way along the length of 1,100 kilometres of the Malayan peninsula in only 70 days after his troops landed at Kota Bahru in the northwest of the peninsula and Singora and Patani in southern Thailand on 8 December 1941, was one of the most brilliant campaigns of modern military history. For this feat, Yamashita earned the sobriquet, "Tiger of Malaya."[1]

Yamashita was born on 18 November 1885, the second son of a country physician in a farming village of Kochi prefecture in South West Shikoku. He was not a diligent pupil at school but in 1904 he enrolled at the Military Academy and graduated 16th of 920 cadets in December of the following year. With his appointment as a cadet officer, he began a chequered military career that lasted 40 years.[2] His performance as a regimental officer was outstanding and he gained admission to the War College at the second attempt. Three years later, he graduated with honours, ranking sixth in his class of 56 officers, and received a sword from the Emperor as a mark of distinguished performance. Captain Yamashita thus became an officer of the elite, with every expectation for a bright career ahead of him and was rewarded by a posting to study European affairs in Switzerland and Germany, from 1918 to 1922.

During these years Yamashita and Tojo Hideki, his future rival, struck up a close friendship. After returning to Tokyo, Yamashita twice served in the Military Affairs Bureau of the War Ministry, a much-coveted appointment, from 1922 to 1927 and from 1930 to 1932. At War Minister Ugaki Kazushige's direction, Yamashita carried out the "Ugaki Army Reduction Programme," which abolished four divisions and retired 30,000 officers from active service. In his second tour of duty in the Bureau, Yamashita helped draft a number of reform plans, aimed at streamlining Army organization, in the face of strong opposition from within the Army itself. While serving in these appointments, he gained political skills that earned him a reputation as a capable military bureaucrat. About this time, Yamashita became a member of the *Ichiyukai/Futabakai*, an association of which Tojo was also a member. This was organized by middle-ranking elite officers to reform the Army and aimed at getting rid of the *Choshu* clique that had dominated the Army since the 1880s.

Yamashita served as a military attache in Austria from February 1927 to August 1930, and was then promoted to the rank of Colonel and posted to command the elite 3rd Regiment of the Imperial Guards Division. He succeeded Colonel Nagata Tetsuzan, who was a charter member of the *Ichiyukai/Futabakai* and leader of the *Toseiha* (*Control*) faction. This rivalled the *Kodoha* (*Imperial Way*) faction, whose reform-minded radical young officers looked upon Yamashita as their leader. In April 1932, War Minister Araki Sadao, the leader of the *Kodoha*, made Yamashita Chief of the Military Service Section, another stepping stone to higher rank. He again succeeded Nagata with whom he shared a mutual respect, although they were ideologically incompatible. Promoted to Major-General in 1934, Yamashita succeeded Tojo as Chief of the Military Investigation Bureau of the War Ministry. By this time, he was regarded as the spokesman of the *Kodoha*, although he never identified himself with it publicly.

The assassination of Major-General Nagata in his office at the Military Affairs Bureau in August 1935 by a *Kodoha* officer intensified the

Toseiha-Kodoha rivalry and sparked the *coup d'etat* on 26 February 1936, engineered by young *Kodoha* officers of the 1st and 3rd Regiments of the Guards Division. Yamashita had commanded the latter six years before. He was suspected of having instigated the coup because of his sympathetic statements and behaviour prior to and during the four-day insurgency, during which rebel troops occupied the heart of Tokyo and killed or wounded the Emperor's trusted officials.[3] Yamashita understood and sympathized with the young officers at an emotional level but did not support their attempt to overthrow the government by resorting to violence. When the coup turned out to be a lost cause, Yamashita tried to distance himself from them, lest he be further implicated. Yamashita, the able bureaucrat, knew how to "swim with the current" in order to protect himself and was quick to read the situation. When the Emperor branded the soldiers as rebels, declaring that he would personally command troops to quell the mutineers, Yamashita saw the writing on the wall. He asked the young officers to commit suicide by ceremonial disembowelment, but he promised that an imperial representative would be dispatched to honour the ritual of their suicide. The Emperor, enraged by the assassination of his close confidants, was angered by the War Minister and Yamashita when they presented a petition for His Majesty's representative to be sent and flatly turned it down. Yamashita was overawed by the Emperor's wrath and realized that he had lost the Emperor's trust. He decided to resign from the Army.

Yamashita's superiors dissuaded him from resigning but he was subsequently relegated to a post in Korea, to command a brigade. For the remainder of his career, Yamashita was burdened with expiating the offence that incurred the Emperor's wrath. He was prepared to die for the Emperor and, no matter where he was, always arranged his office desk so as to face toward the Imperial Palace, as if he were in the Emperor's presence. In battle, he commanded his troops from the forefront, always in the face of enemy fire, almost as if seeking a chance to die in action.

Brigade command was a leisurely appointment in peacetime, and Yamashita had an enjoyable time in Korea with his family. His biographer said that Yamashita mellowed in character, having time to reflect on his conduct during the attempted coup and to study Zen Buddhism. He took up the practice of calligraphy, taking the *nom de plume Daisen* or "Giant Cedar." It was said that he gave a fine example of sincerity and selfless devotion to his country.[4]

In his private life, Yamashita was a good-natured man who enjoyed his share of domestic chores. His habit of taking a nap at any time—and snoring loudly—even at critical moments, was well-known throughout Army circles. He was extremely aware of hygiene: he would not eat fruit unless thoroughly cleaned, nor drink ice water. He gave soldiers an order not to drink unboiled water, to prevent an epidemic in the last days of war in the Philippines. He always carried a fly swatter and slept under a mosquito net during the Malayan campaign. He was careful of his appearance, always kept his boots well-polished and sported a small black moustache. Yamashita was a man of simple tastes with no particular hobbies but was fond of children and thoughtful in his behaviour towards other people. He was a large man, of imposing appearance, weighing nearly 100 kilograms and standing 180 centimetres tall. With his glaring eyes, Yamashita looked manly and indomitable. He was scrupulous in his attention to minute detail, to the point of being regarded as a perfectionist. He was of uncertain temper and would sometimes explode in rage if his officers did not meet his standards. That all said, Yamashita possessed a personality that attracted the loyalty of officers who served under him; they trusted his leadership and generalship.

With the outbreak of the Sino-Japanese War in July 1937, Yamashita's brigade was deployed to north China. He led his troops from the front, often exposing himself to enemy fire as he sought, unsuccessfully, to atone for the events of February 1936. The Emperor, however, remained displeased with him and not only refused to sanction his appointment to command the Garrison Army in Mongolia in December 1937, but turned down a proposal that he be appointed Vice-War Minister in August 1939.

Yamashita served in a number of posts overseas in the period between 1936 and 1940 before returning to Tokyo. He had by then been promoted to the rank of Lieutenant-General. In July 1940, he assumed the post of Superintendent of Aviation Headquarters, succeeding Tojo, who became War Minister. The Emperor reluctantly sanctioned Yamashita's appointment only following a unanimous recommendation from War Minister Hata Shunroku, Vice-Chief of Staff Sawada Shigeru, and Military Counsellor Sugiyama Hajime. However, Yamashita hardly had time to get acquainted with his new post when he was ordered to head a six-month mission to Germany and Italy.

While in Berlin, Yamashita had talks with Hitler on 16 June 1941.[5] The *Fuhrer* requested that Japan attack Siberia, should Germany declare war on the Soviet Union. Yamashita assured the *Fuhrer* he would do what he could to satisfy Hitler's wishes but turned down outright a request that Japan declare war on the United States and United Kingdom, because Japan's policy priority was to bring the Sino-Japanese War to an end and reform the armed forces. Yamashita cautioned mission members not to express any opinion in favour of expanding the alliance with Germany and Italy, nor to suggest that Japan should declare war on the United States and United Kingdom.

The Yamashita mission, forewarned by Hitler and Herman Goering of operation *Barbarossa*, the invasion of the Soviet Union, hastened to leave Berlin on 18 June and wired an urgent telegram to Tokyo, outlining the German invasion plans. Tojo was sceptical of the authenticity of these reports, saying that Hitler would not divulge such highly classified information to Yamashita. Yamashita was furious at Tojo's reaction and said, "What did Tojo think of me? How could Hitler tell a lie to the general who is the head of the mission? As the War Minister, Tojo ought to evaluate the information with much seriousness."[6]

Once back in Tokyo on 7 July, Yamashita presented his report on the inspection tour at a meeting with top Army leaders and emphasized the urgency of preparing plans for war against the Soviets. Subsequently, on 6 August, the army in Manchukuo mobilized huge forces for a military exercise to check Soviet Army movements in eastern Siberia. Yamashita also urged the implementation of many of his proposals: to streamline the air arm, to mechanize the Army, to integrate control of the armed forces in a defence ministry coordinated by a chairman of joint chiefs of staff, to create a paratroop corps and to employ effective propaganda. In short, Yamashita was of the opinion that, without change, Japan would not be able to fight a mechanized modern war. At the end of his two-hour report, War Minister Tojo said curtly, "Thank you for your report. I will think about how to implement your proposals," and adjourned the meeting. Asked by a mission member about Tojo's brusque comment, Yamashita said: "He is totally different in outlook to me." Nine days after Yamashita presented his report, he was abruptly transferred, allegedly by Tojo's order, to a newly created post as Commander of the Manchukuo Defence Army. This transfer was said to have been made to keep Yamashita out of Tokyo at a time when rumours were circulating in the corridors of the War Ministry and General Staff that Yamashita would soon replace War Minister Tojo.

Yamashita in the Malayan Campaign

No sooner had Yamashita assumed his new post than he was ordered to report to Tokyo. On 8 November, he received orders to assume command of the Twenty-Fifth Army, only three days after the Japanese government arrived at its decision to go to war against the Western Powers, depending upon the outcome of negotiations with the United States. In two days, Yamashita read and digested intelligence reports made available to him before attending a joint Army-Navy conference convened to consider war plans against America and England. These intelligence reports were gathered by the Taiwan Research Institute and by covert intelligence activities in Burma, the Dutch East Indies, Malaya, and the Philippines carried out by officers of the General Staff. At the conference, Imperial Headquarters informed Yamashita that he was to command 5th, 18th, 56th and Guards Divisions.[7] He sat by chance next to Admiral Yamamoto Isoroku, Commander-in-Chief of the Combined Fleet. Asked by Yamamoto about the prospects of the Malayan landing operations, Yamashita said in confidence, "I have studied all intelligence reports about the region. The key to a successful operation depends on whether I can land my troops." He assured Yamamoto that his army would succeed once ashore, because the enemy consisted largely of Indian soldiers. The only problem for successful landing operations would be, he said, the extent of the naval and air support his army could get. That question was yet to be negotiated.

When Suzuki Sosaku, his Chief of Staff, reported to Yamashita problems in securing air support, he told Suzuki that in negotiating with the Air Force he should weigh the importance of losing a score of ships full of troops against losing a few aircraft and pilots. "If air cover cannot be provided," he wrote in his diary, "aircraft are not needed."[8] He was determined to win this battle. Yamashita held a meeting with the commanders of naval and air forces in Saigon on 15 November, to discuss the question of their support. It resulted in their commitment to support Yamashita's landing operations and the three commanders finalized the detailed agreement on the 18th, Yamashita's 57th birthday. In his diary entry of the day, he wrote, "I am [now] confident of victory." So elated was he by the commitment of the naval and air commanders that he boasted of conquering Singapore on New Year's Day 1942. It was perhaps half serious, because he was convinced, after having observed the rubber plantations and jungles outside Saigon, that they would not be obstacles to an assault against the British in Malaya. Only a "driving charge" (*Kirimomi Sakusen*) would do the job of conquering the British fortress, he thought. Nonetheless, he felt he was in an awkward situation; he would earn the jealousy of his rivals, should he succeed in the battle—and he would be booted out of the Army should he fail. The three divisions comprising the Twenty-Fifth Army totalled 60,000. The 5th and the Guards Divisions were mechanized for mobility and the 5th and 18th Divisions were battle-tested in China. The 5th Division had been trained for assault landings. The Twenty-Fifth Army was the strongest mustered by the Japanese Army and its staff were said to be top-notch officers, commanded by one of Japan's most outstanding generals. However, Yamashita had hardly acquainted himself with most of them, because they were hastily recruited, and it was up to him to bring out their individual talents and capabilities.

The invasion forces of 26,000, of which 17,230 were combat troops available at the initial stages of war, assembled at Sanya in Hainan Island, and Yamashita's first order to them was "no looting; no rape; no arson." He made it clear that any soldiers committing such crimes would be severely punished and their superior officers held accountable. Throughout the Malayan campaign, Yamashita enforced strict military discipline.

An armada of 27 transports departed Sanya on 4 December for their destinations in southern Thailand and at Kota Bahru. On board, soldiers received the pamphlet *Read This Alone And The War Can Be Won*. At midnight of the 7th, the convoy divided into six groups for landings. The *Takumi* Detached Force of the 18th Division succeeded in its assault landing at Kota Bahru at 0130 hours on the 8th but sustained heavy casualties. The main force of the Twenty-Fifth Army, together with Yamashita and Matsui Takuro, Commander of the 5th Division, landed at Singora and Patani. Yamashita wanted to share the fate of the frontline troops at landing and the whole army was informed that the commanding general was on board the *Ryujo Maru*. The spirit of Yamashita's leadership, from that time on, was one of the causes of the success of the units under his command. His troops ran into a skirmish with Thai soldiers because of a misunderstanding, but no more. The sinking of HMS *Prince of Wales* and HMS *Repulse* on 10 December removed a major threat to the invading forces. Sir Shenton Thomas, the Governor, and most British military leaders in Singapore did not take the Japanese invasion seriously at first. The Governor's first reaction when he was informed of the Japanese landings at Kota Bahru was, "Well, I suppose you'll shove the little men off."[9] In the morning, "he and his wife had breakfast in the balcony of the Government House, enjoying the last glimpse of Singapore at peace." Many other Singapore residents were as complacent and continued as normal, dancing at Raffles Hotel while others went to the movies or played bridge.

The British high command underestimated the Japanese ability to carry out assault landings. Percival's misgivings about the *Matador* plan for an advance into Thailand and Brooke-Popham's hesitation and delay at the eleventh hour, before cancelling *Matador* and giving the new orders to the 11th Indian Division, "had a great psychological effect on the troops."[10] Brooke-Popham, Commander-in-Chief Far East, made his decision not to implement the plan on the grounds that it could not be effective unless put into effect 24 hours in advance of enemy landings. This immediately changed things for the British, forcing them from an offensive to a defensive campaign.

Yamashita had not much more than one-third the total manpower of the opposing British-led forces, so his strategy was to conquer Singapore in the shortest time possible in order to overcome his numerical disadvantage. He intended to drive hard against the enemy with a *Kirimomi Sakusen*. The strategy was well-described by orders given by one of his battalion commanders: "Do not stop but charge forward no matter what happens and do not respond to fire from behind." Yamashita concentrated the 5th and Guards Divisions on the west coast where the land was flat and the roads well-paved and made them compete, one against the other, in their advance. His first objective was to break through the Jitra line and secure intact the bridges at Kuala Kangsar over the 400-metre-wide Perak River. True to the *Kirimomi Sakusen*, only two battalions supported by a company of tanks broke through the Jitra line near the Thai-Malaya border on 11 December. The Japanese had achieved their early objectives within 24 hours of the commencement of hostilities, and Percival should already have seen that he was facing a different kind of adversary, skilful in penetration and dauntless in attack, disregarding casualties.

Thereafter, lightly-armed Japanese soldiers captured Alor Star, Benton, Kroh, Penang, and Taiping with a "Bicycle Blitzkreig." The British abandoned Penang without resistance before Japanese troops crossed the channel. Some of Yamashita's fears were realized when Japanese troops occupied Penang on the 19th. Incidents occurred in which some soldiers committed the crimes of looting and raping, despite notice given on 11 December that military discipline would be strictly enforced. Yamashita immediately ordered the soldiers involved to be severely punished and disciplined their regimental and battalion commanders, who were held accountable for the crimes committed by their soldiers. In his diary, Yamashita wrote angrily, deploring the fact that his orders had not been heeded by soldiers and stressing that the re-education of the Japanese in discipline and morality was necessary.

British troops also retreated from the Perak River without resistance, having destroyed the bridges only half an hour before Japanese troops arrived there. Yamashita expected the British to make a stand on the Perak River line, and its abandonment only gave a pause to the Japanese advance until the bridges were repaired. Having sensed the lack of fighting spirit of the British, Yamashita quickly summed up the situation. He concluded the enemy would seek to defend Singapore by making a stand in northern Johore, on the Muar River line.

Yamashita's Engineer Corps repaired the bridges on the Perak River at Kuala Kangsar in three days. He pressed hard on the 5th and Guards Divisions to capture Kuala Lumpur. Despite having made good progress, he was not satisfied with his staff who seemed not really to understand the purpose of the war. He believed it to be a "great sacred war" that the whole world was watching. He was determined to fight it openly and squarely, in such a way that colonized people would look upon the Japanese as "soldiers of justice." Only then, Yamashita believed, would the war have achieved its objective. He believed that his staff did not have the same sense of the mission as he did, as could be seen in the operations plans prepared by Tsuji Masanobu, his Operations Officer. According to these plans, Singapore would be captured on 11 February, the National Foundation Day. That seemed to Yamashita to be playing to the gallery. The more he got to know of the quality of his staff and field commanders after landing in Malaya, the more unhappy he was with them. He jotted down in his diary on 26 December, "They are all stupid." Increasingly, he became irritable.

The driving advance of the Japanese Army was stalled at Kampar, where the British, taking the advantage of a "rocky bastion," resisted fiercely. Troops of the 5th Division, exhausted by battle after battle by day and night since landing at Singora, were unable to dislodge the enemy for six days. Tsuji asked Twenty-Fifth

Army Headquarters to reinforce the struggling division. When this request was overruled by the Chief of Staff on the grounds that the 11th Regiment that Tsuji asked for had been deployed for a seaborne operation to attack the British at Kampar from the rear, he demanded that he be dismissed and withdrew from the staff. Yamashita's irritation at Tsuji's defiance and outrageous behaviour may be seen in his diary entry on 3 January 1942: "This man is egotistical and wily. He is a sly dog and unworthy to serve the country. He is a manipulator to be carefully watched." Yamashita attributed Tsuji's undisciplined conduct to defects in his education.[11] Yamashita was sometimes too harsh in his judgement of his officers. When the battle at Kampar came to a standstill, he was critical of division and battalion commanders whom he believed to lack fighting spirit. "It is egregious folly on their part to be unable to defeat the enemy for six days while sustaining a few hundred casualties," he wrote in his diary on 6 January. The British retreated from Kampar on 2 January when Japanese seaborne troops attacked them as ordered by Yamashita, overruling his staff's objections. He now drove on to Kuala Lumpur which was entered by Japanese troops on 11 January, without much resistance, the British having withdrawn during the night. Yamashita was put out that they had been allowed to escape. Recording his displeasure, he wrote, "I don't want them pushed back—I want them destroyed."[12] On occupying the Federal Capital, Yamashita again ordered his garrison army to enforce strict discipline, to prevent looting and violence. A number of areas were declared off limits and no incidents were reported.

Yamashita's *Kirimomi Sakusen* charged forward with no let-up, overrunning defence lines at Gemas, Muar, and attacking the enemy behind their positions by a further sea borne operation. Allied troops were hard-pressed as they retreated to Singapore, but inflicted heavy casualties on Japanese troops at Gemas. Commenting on the fighting capabilities and poor tactics of his frontline commanders at Gemas, Yamashita recorded in his diary on 16 January "that they were careless in their tactics, concentrating on frontal attack on the enemy, that resulted in an unnecessary great loss of soldiers' lives." By this time, the main force of the 18th Division, commanded by Lieutenant-General Mutaguchi Renya, had arrived at Yamashita's tactical headquarters. The 18th Division's arrival made the Twenty-Fifth Army nearly up to full strength. The three divisions converged on Johore Bahru on the last day of January 1941.

On the same day, Governor Thomas and Lieutenant-General Percival jointly issued a statement to the citizens of Singapore: "The battle of Malaya has ended and the battle of Singapore has begun. Today, we are trapped in this fortress. Our duty is to hold onto the fortress until reinforcements arrive. Of course, they will come."[13] The statement came as something not far from a bolt from the blue, because the citizens had scarcely been informed of the war situation. Thomas and Percival had kept much unfavourable battle news from the public for fear it would have an adverse effect on citizens' morale. Many were therefore unpleasantly surprised when the Japanese troops reached the doorstep of Singapore, just across the Johore Straits, and were poised to assault the fortress.

Yamashita's Assault on Singapore

Setting up his tactical headquarters at Skudai, Yamashita carefully studied the defences of Singapore in the minute detail necessary for planning an assault on the island. Elaborate measures were taken to conceal his plans. He ordered the removal of local residents from troop concentration areas, banning daylight movements of troops and imposing communications silence while transmitting false telegraphic messages. Arrangements for one-way traffic made for the efficient transportation of ammunition and materials. Furthermore, each division was ordered to take special precautionary measures to keep the plans under wraps. One regiment had meals prepared eight kilometres away from the Straits and had them carried forward at each mealtime. Another regiment that assembled its troops at a location 10 kilometres away from the waterway took pains to have meals prepared further inland in order to prevent wisps of kitchen smoke being observed.

Yamashita also ordered the Guards to manoeuvre in the eastern part of Johore Bahru, to persuade the enemy that he was assembling large forces there, to assault the eastern end of Singapore Island. The Guards ran scores of trucks eastward by night, with horns blaring and headlights on, and drove them back in silence with dim lights. They set up a fake communications centre, to suggest that a superior command post was there. All these elaborate deception measures were intended to disguise the real landing operations aimed at the northwest of Singapore by the 5th and 18th Divisions. Yamashita believed the siege of Singapore was his own battle, different from the Malayan operations, the plans for which were developed and laid down by the General Staff. He had implemented these plans accordingly. The General Staff, however, left it to Yamashita' s own discretion to assault Singapore. Thus the assault upon Singapore was the battle in which Yamashita could demonstrate his ability as a tactician.

When Yamashita gave his orders for the landings, he was hopeful the enemy would surrender on 11 February, the National Foundation Day, but for different reasons from the battle schedule drafted by Tsuji. The four days' stocks of food supplied to his soldiers would be exhausted by then. Short of food and ammunition, his troops, stranded and exposed to enemy fire, could face serious problems in Singapore. He had also been informed that the Guards Division would be deployed to Sumatra and the 18th Division to Burma as soon as Singapore capitulated.

Without the slightest warning, Southern Army Headquarters withdrew a major part of the 3rd Air Group from the Twenty-Fifth Army, despite the fact that the decisive battle was about to take place. The air corps deployment to Sumatra would seriously deprive his army of air support. When Southern Army Headquarters informed Yamashita of this reduced air support, he blew up and asked, "Who is going to take the responsibility should Singapore not capitulate on schedule?"[14]

Tearing up voluminous papers brought to him by Tsukada Osamu, the Chief of Staff, Southern Army, on how to capture Singapore, Yamashita reflected crossly in his diary that "whenever there are two alternatives, the Southern Army always chooses the worse one."[15] There had always been chilly relations between the two headquarters. The visit of Tsukada with unsolicited advice and his departure without thanks for the lunch Yamashita had given him irritated Yamashita so much that he was ready to explode.[16]

Besides his infantry, Yamashita could rely on the barely adequate firepower of 440 large and small artillery pieces, but ammunition was in gravely short supply. It was reported they could possibly run out of ammunition in any artillery duel lasting a few days. Yamashita also faced the problem of transporting troops of the 5th and 18th Divisions across the kilometre-wide Straits. It was estimated that it would take seven to 10 hours to complete the landings. Reduced air support, exhausted soldiers, shortage of ammunition and food supplies, and time-consuming landing operations—none of these factors was encouraging for Yamashita. Under the circumstances, there was no alternative but to attack relentlessly and bring the enemy to surrender in the shortest time possible. The outcome of the battle depended upon a successful landing assault. And that gave rise to his strict order to maintain the utmost secrecy about the landing plans. On the eve of the assault, Yamashita was tormented by all sorts of uncertainty and was on "the verge of mental explosion."[17]

Percival was certain that the Japanese would hit the northeast, and that his army could hold the invading enemy at the water's edge. There were 88,000 soldiers and 226 guns at his command, which his superiors felt should enable him to hold the enemy for two months. His artillery could pose a serious threat to the Japanese if used efficiently. In reality, Percival had been negligent in failing to construct defensive positions in the north and northwest and was hesitant in destroying the causeway, which was only partially blown up. Morale was low among his troops: Gurkhas and Indians did not get along well and British and Australians did not see eye-to-eye. Most important of all, Percival and Major-General H. Gordon Bennett, GOC of the 8th Australian Division, disagreed with each other about almost everything. City life was incongruous. With the battle about to commence, on the one hand citizens were in panic and older people, women, and children were evacuating the island; on the other, many people, with nowhere to escape, crowded movie theatres.

On 8 February, despite the objections of his staff, Yamashita moved his tactical headquarters forward to the top of the tower of the Palace of the Sultan of Johore. This was an excellent location providing him with a view overlooking Singapore but was also a conspicuous target for enemy shelling. That did not prevent him from taking a catnap for a half hour. As the landings began, he watched their progress, waiting for flares to signal success. Around 2240 hours, Yamashita saw red and blue flares signalling successful landings by the 5th and 18th Divisions and his staff cheered *Banzai*. Without pausing to build a beachhead, the assaulting troops charged the enemy with *Kirimomi* and drove them into retreat.

Yamashita had just moved his tactical headquarters forward to the north of Tengah aerodrome on the morning of 10 February when a staff officer from rear command headquarters burst in and told Yamashita that an entire Guards regiment had been incinerated by burning oil, leaking from tanks along the Straits. For a moment, Yamashita turned blue. The panicky report turned out to be inaccurate, a result of misunderstanding when Nishimura, Commander of the Guards Division, and his Chief of Staff accepted an engineer's report without verifying it. Later, Nishimura sent a staff officer to see Yamashita, who snapped, "Go back to your divisional commander and tell him the Imperial Guards can do as they like in this battle." Nishimura's troops landed between the Kranji River and the causeway.[18] Yamashita's army drove hard toward Bukit Timah, Bukit Panjang, and Mandai from three directions: the Guards from the north, the 5th from the west to the centre, and the 18th along the southern edge of the island close to the sea. Yamashita's frontline troops were to reach the reservoir section near Bukit Timah by the night 10 February. Assessing the battle situation, Yamashita hoped the British would surrender on the following day, the National Foundation Day, and he had a surrender appeal dropped from the air, but no response came by nightfall. When Colonel Iketani Hanjiro, a senior planning officer, suggested to Yamashita that the assault be halted because supplies of shells, gasoline, and food were dangerously low and further supplies were unlikely, Yamashita insisted on maintaining pressure on the enemy. He said, "The enemy is also going through a hard time. If we halt now, we will lose the initiative over the battle and the enemy will discover our shortage of supplies and counterattack us!"[19]

Japanese control of the reservoirs and their cutting of the water supplies delivered a serious blow to the morale of the British command. Once more, Yamashita ordered an onslaught of artillery attack to create panic in the city. On 15 February, Percival and his generals unanimously agreed to surrender and he sent Brigadier Newbigging, accompanied by Major Wild as interpreter, to Yamashita's headquarters to suggest that truce negotiations be held at City Hall. Yamashita thought this could be a trap. To test Percival's sincerity, he sent

Lieutenant-Colonel Sugita Ichiji, an intelligence officer, with a demand that Percival himself be present at negotiations at the Ford Factory. The two generals met for negotiations at 1830 hours. With his massive physical appearance and glaring eyes, Yamashita overpowered a nervous and indecisive Percival at the negotiating table and forced the British commander to surrender with a bluff.[20] It was the moment of brilliant victory for Yamashita whose name now became a matter of public acclaim. He accomplished a military feat in 70 days with three divisions that German generals had told him would probably take nearly a year and a half with five divisions.[21]

The fruits of Yamashita's victory were overwhelming. The Japanese captured 740 artillery pieces of all kinds, more than 10,000 vehicles, 3.38 million rifle bullets and a vast store of foods and materiel. In addition, they captured more than 130,000 prisoners of war. The price of the Japanese victory, however, was no less light: 5,240 died and 9,528 were wounded during the campaign. Of these 1,713 died and 3,378 were wounded in the battle for Singapore. About two-fifths of those casualties were believed to have occurred during the final assault landings.

About five months after the fall of Singapore, Yamashita wrote an assessment of his victory. He thought the British would surrender when his forces carried Bukit Timah. In the face of strong resistance, he exerted more pressure on the enemy, by cutting water supplies, by artillery barrage and aircraft bombing. These were very effective in persuading the British to surrender. He also noted other factors that contributed to the British debacle, including inadequate defence preparations and delay in carrying out a counter-attack, which should have been launched when the British were still holding fast at Bukit Timah and when the Japanese forces were short of ammunition. Yamashita noted also the effectiveness of his diversionary tactics masking the decision to make the landings in the northwest and the effective deployment of the 5th and 18th Divisions. He considered that senior British generals, whose prejudice encouraged them to underestimate Japanese military capabilities, ought to be held responsible for the debacle at Singapore. They were all "out-generalled, outwitted and outfought."[22] Specifically, he concluded that Percival was responsible for a large share of the defeat. He was a "nice good man" who was neither a dynamic leader nor an inspiring general. "He was good on paper but timid and hesitant in making command decisions." Furthermore, Percival overestimated Yamashita's landing forces at five to six divisions totalling about 100,000 men. In short, he and others concluded that Percival was a staff officer *par excellence* but a poor commanding general. In contrast, Yamashita was seen by a contemporary witness as a brilliant professional soldier "absolutely up-to-date in the science and technology of [modern] war."[23]

Aftermath

In the immediate aftermath, Yamashita was overwhelmed by emotion. He wept in silence and found it impossible to sleep on the night of the capitulation. Several times he left his bedroom in the early morning hours of 16 February and wandered alone in the grounds of his headquarters, bowing deeply and ceremoniously in the direction of the Imperial Palace to the northeast and praying. The Japanese people and German military leaders showered congratulations upon Yamashita, acclaiming his military feat. In Japan, flag-waving citizens organized a victory march to the Imperial Palace and shrines. Yamashita's staff also requested a triumphant entry into Singapore City but he turned down their request: It was "not the time to be intoxicated with victory in the early stages of war" for, in truth, the Malayan Campaign had been no more than a prelude.[24] He issued a precautionary order that troops, except authorized soldiers, be kept outside the city limits until peace and order were restored. A nightmare recollection of looting, rape, and massacre committed by Japanese soldiers in China was in his mind when he did so. He had little trust in the behaviour of soldiers intoxicated with victory. For this reason, prior to the siege of Singapore, Yamashita had requested that the War Ministry augment military police units in order to maintain strict military discipline. In his postwar memoirs, Percival acknowledged Yamashita's appropriate measures for maintaining law and order, especially for protecting women and children.

Yamashita gave priority above all to holding a memorial service for fallen soldiers and attended services observed by each one of the three divisions he commanded. He had a small statue made of the God of Mercy and offered a daily prayer. Thereafter, he held a memorial service each year on 15 February, in Manchukuo and the Philippines where he was later stationed. He was also concerned about wounded soldiers and prisoners of war and civilian detainees and visited the wounded in hospital. Where the treatment of prisoners of war was concerned, he was strict in observing the rules of war he had studied when he was a military attache in Austria. He reprimanded soldiers mistreating and insulting prisoners of war, saying that in their countries it was not a matter of shame for them to become prisoners after having fought gallantly and done their duty. He was disappointed by what he regarded as unbecoming behaviour by his own staff officers who were disrespectful towards captured British officers and demanded that they change their attitude. "I regret that staff officers today have no sense of propriety," he said in his diary.[25] While he was in Singapore, Yamashita treated prisoners of war humanely and refused to use them for labour, disregarding a demand from the War Ministry.[26] He showed consideration for the Governor, for captured British generals and for women detainees. Yamashita sent gifts of food and liquor to Thomas and presents to the generals on their birthdays. He also sent cartons of milk to women in a detention camp.[27] The General Staff and the War Ministry were critical of Yamashita's humane treatment of prisoners of war and of his punishment of an officer for ill-treating British soldiers.[28]

A series of incidents that left a deep scar in occupied Malaya and Singapore was the interrogation and execution of Chinese residents, atrocities that have been the subject of many studies. It has been said that Tsuji Masanobu was the primary culprit and Asaeda Shigeharu and Hayashi Tadahiko, Twenty-Fifth Army staff officers, were the instigators. Ian Ward's study concluded that Yamashita should not be held responsible for the atrocities. He did, however, hold him responsible "for failing to guard against Tsuji's manipulation of command affairs."[29] According to Major-General Kawamura Saburo, the *Syonan* Garrison Commander, Yamashita gave him an order on 18 February that his garrison army should carry out a military mopping-up operation without delay. This was to remove "hostile Chinese," to free the army from concerns about internal security. Yamashita had been ordered to deploy his forces immediately to Sumatra and Burma but there were believed to be many hostile Chinese still hiding in the city and planning to obstruct future operations. After telling Kawamura briefly about the need to maintain law and order in general terms, Yamashita said that Suzuki, his Chief of Staff, would provide the details of the mopping-up operation. Suzuki gave Kawamura concrete details, calling for a *genju shobun* (severe disposal) at once of hostile Chinese. Kawamura was taken aback by the term *genju shobun*, which in a military parlance meant execution without trial. He sought clarification of the term but Suzuki broke in saying, "You may have your own opinion on this matter and it has been decided by the commanding general. It is essentially a military mopping-up operation. See that the work is duly carried out."[30]

Oishi Masayuki, Commander of the 2nd Field *Kempei-tai* unit, also queried the *genju shobun*, and Kawamura and Oishi agreed to carry out the interrogation with "fairness and prudence," according to the rules of war. However, the first and second interrogations took place over the next two weeks in a slovenly fashion, despite the instruction requiring fairness and prudence. Perhaps inevitably, the interrogations lacked discrimination, because the *Kempei-tai* were short-handed. To identify "hostile Chinese" from among tens of thousands in a limited time was not possible. Consequently, untold numbers of Chinese were executed. Yamashita may be judged guilty of the massacre to the extent that he authorized the mopping-up operation, ordering the *genju shobun* of "hostile Chinese." However, under the rules of war, a mopping-up operation was legitimate.[31] Though he issued the order, Yamashita was not aware of the indiscriminate way in which the examinations were carried out.

After this, Twenty-Fifth Army troops were redeployed to the Malayan Peninsula, Sumatra and Burma. Yamashita spent some time in drawing blueprints for the construction of a memorial monument for fallen soldiers and a *Syonan*

Shrine and whiled away more time inspecting troops and facilities, receiving visitors, and attending social functions. On one occasion, he attended a meeting at the Adelphi Hotel with Malay, Chinese, Indian and Arab leaders. Addressing them, Yamashita said, "It is my pleasure to celebrate His Majesty's birthday with you, *who have now become citizens of Imperial Japan*. I hope that you, the people of Malaya and Sumatra, *moved by becoming new citizens of Imperial Japan*, will do your best in honest calling." Newspaper reporters flashed his remarks to Tokyo where the government was embarrassed by them. His speech was regarded as improper and out of step with government policy on nationality for occupied countries. Prime Minister and War Minster Tojo and others were displeased by Yamashita's remarks and considered him to be arrogant. In late June, Yamashita received secret orders to assume command of the First Area Army. He was to proceed immediately to Manchukuo without stopping in Tokyo. This was an unusual way, to say the least, for a distinguished general to be treated. Under normal protocol, the Emperor would accord such generals the honour of an audience to present his "memorials." The War Ministry's order deprived him of the honour that he had hoped for. He said no more about presenting his "memorials," which he packed, ready for his departure to Manchukuo on 12 July 1942. His appointment remained veiled in secrecy until October 1944 when he assumed command of the Fourteenth Area Army in the Philippines, to wage a hopeless defensive war against the Allies. The War Ministry imposed strict censorship on his whereabouts from July 1942 until October 1944.

Many believed that Tojo was behind Yamashita's appointment to Manchukuo. He was said to be jealous of Yamashita's distinguished military achievements and of his popularity. By contrast, Tojo had scarcely any battle experience, nor achievements as a field commander. He was nervous about Yamashita, whose name was often mentioned as a possible War Minister or Prime Minister, and fearful of a return to power of the *Kodoha*.[32] Former Prime Minister Prince Konoye Fumimaro, a supporter of the *Kodoha*, was foremost of those pressing for Tojo's replacement. It can, however, be argued that keeping Yamashita out of Tokyo had nothing to do with Tojo's alleged jealousy. His new appointment was of critical importance, given the threat posed across the border in northern Manchukuo by the Soviet Army. There, the presence of a renowned general of Yamashita's reputation would add weight to the defence. It was more appropriate for him to command an elite army of 300,000 troops than to attend to routine administrative matters in *Syonan*, with which he was reportedly becoming increasingly tired and irritable.

As for his audience with the Emperor, Yamashita was not the only general of distinction not to be given the honour of presenting "memorials" at that time. Even Anami Korechika, a trusted general of the Emperor, was denied that honour in similar circumstances. That Yamashita's appointment to his new post was a scheme to keep him out of central Army circles seems far from the truth.³³ No one really knows what was on Tojo's mind when he approved Yamashita's appointment. Nonetheless, it was his masterstroke that the most renowned general was appointed to the post of defending northern Manchukuo against the Soviet Army. Even the Emperor, who had unpleasant memories of Yamashita since the 26 February incident, found it difficult to disagree with the appointment of Japan's most outstanding general to the defence of Manchukuo, where tension was heightening in Japan-Soviet relations. Nonetheless and perhaps coincidentally, Yamashita's appointment did keep him out of Tokyo.

Yamashita was promoted to full General in February 1943, a promotion every one expected but thought overdue. Meanwhile, Tojo had been losing support in the corridors of the Army and in political circles. Yamashita's name came up twice, in November 1942 and September 1943, as a possible candidate for the post of War Minister or Premier. In July 1944, when the Tojo cabinet resigned, he was again seriously considered for appointment as War Minister.³⁴ Yamashita's appointment as Commander of the Fourteenth Area Army in the Philippines was made public in October. People pinned high hopes on him to turn the tide of the deteriorating war situation. Yamashita regarded it as his last duty to his country, to which he would not expect to return alive. Before proceeding to the battlefront, he had a long wished-for audience with His Majesty on 30 September. With the Emperor's words that "the fate of the Empire rests upon your shoulders," Yamashita felt that the Emperor's displeasure with him had at last been dispelled and the burden he had been carrying was finally lifted.

The Philippine war situation was, however, hopeless. The only thing Yamashita could do was hold off the enemy forces as long as possible by inflicting casualties on them in order to gain time for the defence of the homeland. His army surrendered to the U.S. forces on 2 September 1945, and he signed the Instrument of Surrender on the following day at Baguio. Much to Yamashita's humiliation, Percival, who had nothing to do with his defeat, was present at the surrender signing ceremony. Percival's presence was seen by Yamashita as an obvious measure of revenge, intended to humiliate him. Recalling that unbearable humiliation, Yamashita told a chaplain just before his execution that the thought of committing suicide crossed his mind for a moment then.³⁵

On 9 October 1945, the U.S. Army South West Pacific Command indicted Yamashita as a war criminal on charges of serious negligence in observing the rules of war, and of allowing his troops to commit atrocities. He pleaded his innocence of the atrocities committed by troops in the battle for Manila, but on 7 December the military court sentenced him to death by hanging. His defence lawyers brought the case to the U.S. Supreme Court but it rejected the appeal. Two associate justices, however, wrote a minority opinion, opining that Yamashita was denied a fair trial as guaranteed by the American Constitution, and that the trial was conducted with prejudice. His lawyers petitioned President Harry Truman for a reduced sentence but he turned down the appeal. General Douglas MacArthur ordered the execution carried out.[36] Before the execution itself, Yamashita took a nap, requesting one of his defence lawyers to wake him up one hour before the execution. It was carried out at 0305 hours on 23 February 1946. Yamashita asked a chaplain to convey a message as his will to bereaved families and to the Japanese people.[37] Apologizing to the bereaved families for the lost lives of husbands and sons as a result of mistakes made in commanding his forces, Yamashita asked them to register three things in their memory: "Do your duty; give priority to education in science; raise children with *chibusa kyoiku* [breast-feeding education from babyhood]." He asked the Japanese people to remember these homely messages as the last words of the man who had taken away the lives of their children.

Conclusions

A renowned general is often misunderstood and portrayed in a manner that does not do justice to the real man and Yamashita was no exception. Without doubt, he was one of the most outstanding generals in modern Japanese military history. His fame derives from the fact that he, as the commander of Japanese forces, conquered the British fortress of Singapore in the most dramatic victory of the Imperial Japanese Army during the Asia-Pacific War. Everyone remembers the scene in which Yamashita, leaning his huge frame on his sword, demanded Percival's surrender at the Ford Factory.

Yamashita gave the impression of a brave, swaggering general. In reality, he was far from that image; he was an able and diligent military bureaucrat to the point of scrupulousness and was a rational man, unlike many of his colleagues who believed in spiritual superiority over rational thinking. This irrational mode of thinking prevalent among some Japanese officers saw expression in a tendency to denigrate the importance of logistics. Instead, such officers would employ soldiers in hand-to-hand fighting, regardless of casualties, in order to make up for weaknesses in logistics. Speaking of the battles at Kampar and Gemas, Yamashita was critical of the weak performance of frontline commanders and of Tsuji Masanobu. They, believing in spiritual strength over material superiority, led their soldiers in reckless frontal attacks, into close combat that resulted in heavy casualties on the Japanese side.[38] Yamashita did not share such beliefs, that spirit would overcome material odds. Overruling the objections of his staff, he ordered an attack on the enemy's rear by a seaborne operation that forced the British into retreat. His remark, "They are all stupid," in assessing their weaknesses is indicative of his untraditional but rational thinking. It underlined his view of military science and his scathing criticism of those who believed spiritual superiority would overcome materials odds and modern technology. He rejected the outdated military tactics of hand-to-hand fighting in which they were trained.

Yamashita was strict in enforcing discipline and would not tolerate anyone who violated it in any way, as was demonstrated by his first order given to his troops before landing at Singora. Throughout the Malayan campaign, he insisted on uncompromising enforcement of discipline not only on his staff, field commanders, and soldiers but also on civilians. He also made it clear that not only the soldiers who violated discipline, but also their superior officers, would be held accountable. When three soldiers looted the Palace of the Sultan of Kedah, they were executed and their officers disciplined. As noted, Yamashita sentenced regiment and battalion commanders to a 30-day house detention when their soldiers looted and raped, following the occupation of Penang. When soldiers were caught looting a shop in Singapore and it was reported to Yamashita, he ordered a parade of all officers and, standing in the scorching sun, gave a scathing address on the enforcement of military discipline.[39] He read a report of the unlawful conduct to the officers, deploring the instances of indiscipline committed by soldiers, despite his warnings. He had a low opinion of the moral fibre of Japanese soldiers. He attributed such immoral conduct to failures in education in military barracks and, especially, in education at home. In his diary, Yamashita made frequent reference to the importance of moral education at home from childhood, stressing the vital role of the mother in child-rearing, as he said in his last message to the Japanese people.

Though Yamashita was strict in enforcing discipline, he was sensitive and compassionate not only towards his own soldiers but also to his foes. Throughout the Malayan campaign, he always had his command post set up in an ordinary house, unlike other commanders who chose large houses with amenities as their tactical headquarters. He was mindful of the example that a superior officer should set to his subordinates. He always gave priority to receiving an officer visiting from the battlefront, regardless of his rank. Yamashita would personally instruct his adjutant to arrange bedding, should the visitor stay overnight at his tactical headquarters. He personally wrote a letter of commendation to Major-General Takumi Hiroshi of the 18th Division for his gallantry in successful landings at Kota Bahru and, in an unusual demonstration of thoughtfulness, had his staff officer deliver it to Takumi by hand. He was genuinely concerned with the fallen, with wounded soldiers and with the conditions of captured Allied military and civilian personnel. Not only did he hold the memorial service for fallen soldiers soon after the fall of Singapore, he also visited hospitals to comfort wounded soldiers.

Yamashita endured the remaining days of his life in humiliation after he surrendered to the U.S. forces in the Philippines and told a chaplain how difficult it was for him to endure that. His Chief of Staff feared that he might take his own life the day after the military court sentenced him to death by hanging and ordered Yamashita's adjutant to keep an eye on the general all night. Yamashita, however, did not chose *seppuku* (self-disembowelment) as many generals did after Japan surrendered, as a way of taking responsibility for defeat. Instead, he met his fate in resignation, suffering humiliation until the end of his life, because, he said, his last duty to his soldiers was to see every one of them going home safely.

Yamashita had every credential necessary for success in military life— education, ability, matrimonial support[40] and an imposing physical appearance. These qualifications alone did not make him a general. In addition, he displayed a shrewd ability to identify change and to cope with it. He demonstrated this by his recommendations for radical reform of the armed forces after his return from his inspection tour of Germany and by his insistence on educational reform. Until 1932, Yamashita's military career had been promising but Army politics and rivalry between factions changed the course of his career and of his life. After Yamashita became associated with the activities of reform-minded colonels and majors, he stood out among his fellow members for his political sense and acumen. Young officers of the *Kodoha* began to look upon Yamashita as their leader because of a sympathetic attitude to their "pure" motives for radical political change, even though he had not declared himself a *Kodoha* member.

When the 26 February 1936 *coup d'etat* was seen to have failed, Yamashita sought to extricate himself from the position he found himself in. His habit of "swimming with the current" was noted by others and he incurred the Emperor's long-lasting displeasure. Thereafter he carried the burden of making amends for his imprudence. Judged by his behaviour before and during the incident, Yamashita was seen as a braggart and as an agitator with political ambitions. It was, however, a turning point in his career. Much of the remainder of his life was spent seeking the opportunity to die in action, to reverse the Emperor's displeasure. Thereafter, he became modest and thoughtful and avoided politics. Through the experience of his spiritual agony, he mellowed in personality. Many officers who served under Yamashita later looked upon him as an ideal model of the commanding general. His life encompassed moments of pride and of disappointment. Up to the last moments of his life, Yamashita stressed the importance of the education of the Japanese people. He pointed out defects in education in the past that brought the Imperial Army and the nation to ruin. He had himself been nurtured for most of his military life in that tradition, and he accepted his death, resigned to his fate. His death not only symbolized the tragedy of the Imperial Army but also that of Yamashita's own glorious military career. That is why he is remembered as a *higeki no shogun*, a tragic general.

Professor Emeritus Yoji Akashi received his PhD from Georgetown University and taught at Geneva College, Nanzan University and Aichi Shukutoku University. He is currently Emeritus Professor at Nanzan University. His work includes volumes on the Malay military administration and on the Japanese Occupation of Malaya and Singapore and has been widely published.

NOTES—

1. Yamashita did not like the sobriquet. When a German military attache congratulated Yamashita on the fall of Singapore by addressing him as "General Tiger," Yamashita replied, "*Nein, ich bin nicht der* Tiger," and he explained that "the tiger attacks its prey in stealth but I attack the enemy in a fair play."
2. When asked why he chose a military career, Yamashita said that it was "fate because I was physically sturdy and was not as good as my elder brother in school."
3. Yamashita provided housing in a barrack of the 3rd Regiment of the Imperial Guards Division for one of the radical young *Kodoha* officers when he was its commander. The night before the coup was to take place, a group of *Kodoha* officers visited Yamashita at home, when he reportedly incited them to "kill Okada." Prime Minister Okada Keisuke was one of their assassination targets. Some young officers accused him of aiding and abetting the coup.
4. He took *Daisen* (Giant Cedar) as his *nom de plume* after the tree that stood skyward in front of his house in childhood and this was a guiding motto for his life. He meant by it that he wanted henceforth to be a man of upright character and bearing, looking up skyward like the giant cedar.
5. T. Shinobu, *Sanbo honbu sakusenka*, 39–62; O. Shuji, *Yamashita Tomoyuki*, 167–71; J. D. Potter, *Marei no tora. Yamashita Tomoyuki no shogai*, 37–51. (The original title is *A Soldier Must Hang.*) Assessing Hitler's personality, Yamashita said, "He does not impress me much. On the platform he may be a good orator with exaggerated gestures. He was more like a bank clerk when I had a talk with him face-to-face."
6. T. Shinobu, *Sanbo honbu*, 60–61. Asked to comment on the Yamashita-Tojo relations, Tanaka Shinichi, the Chief of the Planning Bureau, General Staff, said, "They did not get along well for many years because of personality differences. Tojo was an able man, but he kept away from him such capable men as Ishihara and Yamashita who opposed him."
7. Originally, four divisions were to be placed under his command, but Yamashita declined the fourth one, insisting that three divisions were enough to conquer British Malaya and Singapore, leaving the 56th in Japan.
8. Yamashita diary, 10 November 1941.
9. N. Barber, *Sinister Twilight: The Fall & Rise Again of Singapore*, London, 1968, 28.
10. C. Lee, *Sunset of the Raj: Fall of Singapore 1942*, London, 1994, 17.
11. Yamashita appreciated Tsuji's ability as a planning officer. Though other senior officers were reluctant to deal with this eccentric officer, Yamashita was confident of bringing out the best in him.

12   K. Caffrey, *Out in the Midday Sun: Singapore 1941–1945*, London, 1974, 97.
13   K. Noboru, *Shisetsu Yamashita Tomoyuki*, 196–97.
14   Ibid., 203.
15   Yamashita diary, 23 January 1942.
16   A. Swinson, *Yonin no samurai* [A Quartet of Japanese Army Commanders in the Second World War], trans, 121.
17   Ibid.
18   Tsuji Masanobu, *Singapore: Britain's Greatest Defeat*, Sydney, 1960, 256. Relations between Yamashita and Nishimura were severely strained and there had been little personal contact between them throughout the Malayan campaign. The rift occurred at the battle of Muar when Yamashita went over Nishimura's head in appointing a new regimental commander to succeed wounded Colonel Iwakura Hideo. Yamashita originally planned to use the Guards for the second wave of the landing assault, but unsatisfied with the decision, Nishimura requested that his division lead the attack together with the 5th and 18th Divisions. It looked to Yamashita that Nishimura's Guards Division showed no disposition to fight hard at the battle of Bukit Timah, despite coaxing and cajoling. I. Ward, *Snaring the Other Tiger*, Singapore, 1996, 22, 52; J. D. Potter, *Marei no tora*, 101, 105–06; K. Caffrey, *Out in the Midday Sun*, 159–60.
19   K. Noboru, *Shisetsu Yamashita Tomoyuki*, 215–16. Major Kunitake Teruto, junior planning officer in Yamashita's headquarters, felt that the Japanese might be on the brink of surrender. Kunitake Teruto "*Watashi wa ano hi mosho Yamashita ni eikan wo sasageta*," *Maru*, No. 324, August 1973, 80.
20   So much has been written about the "Yes or No?" surrender negotiation. It remained on Yamashita's mind for years and he wanted to correct erroneous reports of the negotiations scene, at which he looked as though he behaved arrogantly. His "Yes or No?" demand was not directed at Percival but at his interpreter, a newspaper reporter who did not understand military terms. Having lost patience with the interpreter, Yamashita demanded that he ask whether Percival was ready to accept surrender in a simple answer, "Yes" or "No." Yamashita saw that Percival was dallying to gain time. It was imperative for Yamashita to bring the enemy to surrender at the negotiating table before the British might discover the weaknesses of his own army—the extremely fatigued troops, shortage of artillery ammunition, and no single reserve to throw into the battle. He wanted to avoid, by all means, being engaged in a street fight that would result in a battle of attrition. At the end of the negotiations, Yamashita wanted to say a few kind words to Percival but was unable to say them in English. He thought that these words were not to be conveyed through an interpreter. When Yamashita was stationed in Manchukuo and his old 3rd Regiment held an outdoor play presenting a "Yes or No?" stage show, he walked out of the show quietly, not wanting to see the replay of the scene. O. Shuji, *Yamashita Tomoyuki*, 260.
21   Tsuji Masanobu, *Singapore*, 215; T. Eitaro, *Sanbo Tsuji Masanobu, Denki*, 131; I. Morrison, *Malayan Postscript*, London, 1942, 131; C. Lee, *Sunset of the Raj*, 12, 18; K. Caffrey, *Out in the Midday Sun*, 38–39; R. Callahan, *The Worst Disaster: The Fall of Singapore*, London, 1977, 249, 254, 270.

22 R. Callahan, *The Worst Disaster*, 270.
23 I. Morrison, *Malayan Postscript*, 131.
24 Tsuji Masanobu, *Singapore*, 275.
25 Yamashita diary, 16 February 1942.
26 J. D. Potter, *Marei no tora*, 105.
27 B. Montgomery, *Shenton of Singapore—Governor and Prisoner of War*, Singapore, 1984, 160, 163; K. Noboru, *Shisetsu Yamashita Tomoyuki*, 221.
28 J. D. Potter, *Marei no tora*, 129.
29 I. Ward, *The Killer They Called A God*, Singapore, 1992, 237.
30 K. Saburo, *Jusan kaidan no nobura—shokeisha no kiroku*, 163–68.
31 This last judgement reflects the personal views of the author, without prejudice to those of the editors of this volume.
32 K. Noboru, *Shisetsu Yamashita Tomoyuki*, 140, 225; O. Shuji, *Yamashita Tomoyuki*, 171; H. Kazutoshi, *Nippon sanboron*, 80.
33 Nugata, *Rikugunsho jinjikyokucho*, 413–14.
34 K. Noboru, *Shisetsu Yamashita Tomoyuki*, 247; O. Shuji, *Yamashita Tomoyuki*, 267.
35 K. Noboru, *Shisetsu Yamashita Tomoyuki*, 312.
36 F. Reel, *The Case of Yamashita*, Chicago, 1949. Reel was Yamashita's defence lawyer.
37 K. Yoshihisa, *Unmei no Yamashita heidan. Fuirippin sakusen no jisso*, 307–15. Forty minutes before his execution, Yamashita orally communicated his last words to the chaplain.
38 Yamashita diary, 3 January 1942.
39 Tsuji Masanobu, *Singapore*, 279.
40 His wife was the daughter of Maj.-Gen. Nagayama Motohiko, of the *Saga* military clique led by General Araki Sadao who promoted Yamashita in the early 1930s.

CHAPTER 10

Allied Prisoners of War: The Malayan Campaign, 1941–42

by Sibylla Jane Flower

For most commentators, the history of prisoners of war (POWs) captured by the Japanese in the course of the Malayan campaign begins after 15 February 1942 in Singapore with the march to Changi or with the assembly of the Indians at Farrer Park. This emphasis on the POWs on Singapore Island has obscured the fate of those captured on the mainland. In fact, Allied POWs were taken by the Japanese within hours of the first landings in Thailand and Malaya and stragglers were still being captured as they emerged from the jungle months after the surrender.

This paper will examine the capture, interrogation and incarceration of POWs from the time of the Japanese landings on 8 December 1941 until the arrival of their troops opposite Singapore Island 54 days later on 31 January 1942. Over 11,000 POWs were detained by the Japanese in Malaya during this period. They included over 10,000 Indian officers and men and approximately 1,200 officers and men of other nationalities—British, Australian, New Zealander, Dutch and Anglo-Indian. These POWs belonged to units of the British Army, the Indian Army, the Volunteer Forces of the Federated and Unfederated Malay States, the Straits Settlements Volunteer Force and the air forces of Australia and The Netherlands. There were also 13 officers of the Special Operations Executive (SOE) captured by the Japanese during operations behind the lines.

In examining the nature of the actual surrender of the POWs, their interrogation—where this occurred—and their subsequent treatment, the first and most obvious point to stress is that there were false expectations on both sides. The Allied forces were instructed that the moment a soldier, whether a combatant or not, puts up his hands or casts aside his weapons as a means of indicating surrender, he automatically becomes a prisoner of war with all the safeguards enshrined in the Conventions. No guidance had been offered by Allied commanders to their men other than the requirement to declare name, rank and number. The exception here was those who were trained for operations behind the lines where the "normal" rules of warfare did not apply. In turn, the Japanese had not expected soldiers—let alone officers—to surrender. But there was also a presumption on the part of the Allies that whatever atrocity the Japanese had perpetrated against the Chinese—soldier or civilian—similar retribution would not be accorded to "us."

One need only look at the reaction in the Foreign Office in London during the first week of February 1942 to the earliest reports of Japanese brutality towards soldiers, medical officers, nursing sisters and people in the service of the Church during the invasion of Hong Kong. The first report was greeted with disbelief and, because it was written by a woman, more easily dismissed as unreliable. And when corroborative evidence appeared from an impeccable source, the first inclination was to attempt to suppress it.[1] This desire to suppress disturbing and unwelcome news took account not only of the obvious threat to morale—with Singapore on the brink of surrender—but also of the enormous rebuff this development represented to the two distinct but irreconcilable strands of thought about Japan and the Japanese. On one side were ranged the ardent Japanophiles of Foreign and War Office, academe and elsewhere and, on the other, those who saw the Japanese soldier as ineffective and myopic with buck-teeth and bandy legs—a stereotype widely promoted among the Allied troops.

The Japanese saw captured Allied POWs as the means to three distinct ends: first, to elicit information of an operational or strategic nature; second, to undermine morale among the fighting troops by the use of "frenzied brutality" against surrendered personnel; and third, to take hostages to use as bargaining counters. In the Malayan Campaign, there was a further dimension to Japanese objectives and this was the attempt to subvert the loyalty of the Indians in the service of the British. The operation was directed by a Japanese staff officer, Major Fujiwara Iwaichi, who arrived in Thailand on 1 October 1941 following a report sent by the Military Attache in Bangkok, Colonel Tamura Hiroshi, to Tokyo on the feasibility and advantages of supporting nascent Indian nationalism in Thailand and Malaya.[2] The circumstances surrounding the recruitment to the Japanese cause of Indian officers serving in northern Malaya in the weeks before the outbreak of war are obscure, as is the extent of their treachery in revealing early operational plans. But after the catastrophe at Jitra, there was little difficulty in promoting the Indian National Army among the POWs.

By no means were all POWs interrogated at the time of capture. The Japanese obviously targeted officers for information about strategy, but Allied soldiers of all ranks would have been party to information of an operational nature and attempts were made to extract this by torture or at the point of bayonet or gun. There is ample evidence to show the extent of the interrogations during the Malayan Campaign and Japanese assessments exist of the intelligence received by these means. Indeed, Colonel Tsuji Masanobu, Chief of Operations, Twenty-Fifth Army, claimed that the interrogation of POWs up to the end of January induced the Japanese to revise their estimates of the Allied defences and strengths in Singapore.[3]

When considering the subject of interrogations of POWs in Malaya, it is worth glancing briefly to compare and contrast the campaign in Hong Kong. There the path of the Japanese invasion had been prepared so thoroughly and was over so quickly that the taking of prisoners for interrogatory purposes was virtually unnecessary. The careful intelligence work undertaken by the Japanese in Malaya prior to the outbreak of war is well-known. But it must be borne in mind that a constant re-evaluation of intelligence was necessary given the speed and distance—nearly 1,000 kilometres—of the Japanese advance. In Malaya, as in Hong Kong and the first Burma campaign of 1941–42, the Japanese employed the same deliberate and highly successful method of undermining Allied morale by the brutalization, mutilation and murder of POWs. No one who has interviewed veterans of the Malayan campaign is left in doubt that memories of Japanese behaviour in the field particularly towards the wounded are frequently more painful than recollections of the subsequent captivity. Havildar Nehrmal Singh, 2/16 Punjab Regiment, told British investigators of six British soldiers tied to trees near Penang in December 1941 and bayoneted after they refused to give information and there are many similar instances to be found in the records.[4] Another recurring theme is the manner in which the Japanese tortured their captives to death by binding them together tightly with rope.[5]

Once the Japanese became aware of the fundamental sense of obligation the Allied forces had towards their wounded comrades, the opportunity to use the latter as bargaining counters during the campaign became irresistible. Both Lieutenant-Colonel Charles Anderson, 2/19 AIF, at Parit Sulong and Lieutenant-Colonel Philip Toosey, 135 Field Regiment, RA, on Singapore Island were faced with demands to surrender in return for the release of hostages. Toosey later described the incident when he was forced to reject the offer of a safe passage for a group of 10 or 12 British gunners as "the worst...of his wartime career"—and he commanded camps on the Thailand-Burma railway.[6] This ultimatum is fully documented in the affidavit of the soldier who brought it to Toosey, returned to his party and survived the subsequent massacre. But there is oral evidence of other instances indicating that the Japanese used this technique throughout the Malayan Campaign and with increasing frequency once they had landed on the Island.[7]

The Japanese invasion force which landed just north of Kota Bahru in northeast Malaya and at Singora in Thailand on 8 December 1941 captured one British Army officer and the crews of two *Blenheims* of the RAF within the first four days. The starkly contrasting experiences of these men are worth examining in detail for the light they apparently cast on the attitude of the Japanese to their captives in the early stages of the campaign. Captain John Close, whom the Japanese labelled "Capture No. 1," was commanding an anti-aircraft battery on the airfield near Kota Bahru when he was captured on 8/9 December. He was of particular interest to the Japanese because he belonged to one of the regiments of the Hong Kong and Singapore Royal Artillery—the only ones in the British Army at that time with Indian troops. Close resisted their inquiries about the defences of Singapore and the dispositions of his Indian troops with the result that his arms were tied behind his back with wire and, for four or five days, he was given neither food nor water. Realizing that Close had information which could be of use in the attack on Singapore Island but lacking skilled interrogators, the Japanese despatched Close to Saigon where he was questioned and tortured at the HQ of the Southern Expeditionary Army. After the surrender of Singapore, he was sent to Changi where he was debriefed by Major-General Key.[8]

In Saigon, Close was joined by the crew of a *Blenheim* of 60 Squadron, RAF, which flew out of Tengah on 8 December with instructions to bomb the Japanese-occupied airfield near Singora. The crew which comprised the captain (Sergeant A. McC. Johnstone), an observer (Pilot Officer P. N. Kingwill) and a wireless operator/air gunner (Flight Sergeant G. W. Gregory) were flying a *Blenheim Mk IV* for the first time, armed with five .303 Brownings and loaded with two 500-pound bombs. As they approached their target near Singora, a large formation of Japanese fighters appeared and, veering towards the coast, Johnstone spotted part of the invasion fleet. Twice Kingwill pressed the button to release the bombs and both times the mechanism failed. With 1000 pounds of bombs still on board, one engine extinguished and losing height, evasive action was impossible and they were forced to crash land on the jungle canopy with the Japanese fighters continuing to fire into the wreckage. The bombs subsequently exploded, but not before the crew managed to escape. The three were arrested by Thai police on the following day near Haadyai and handed over to the Japanese.[9]

At Singora, they underwent interrogation with torture. Johnstone, the captain, was ordered to stand trial for the capital offence of taking up arms against the Imperial Japanese Army and was sentenced to death, a sentence later commuted to three months' imprisonment. The crew was then taken to Saigon where they remained in the hands of the *Kempei-tai* for over 60 days before being sent to Changi. During the initial interrogation of the crew at Singora, their captors were at pains to establish whether Japanese lives and property had been lost. They accepted the fact that the bombs had not been released and had exploded only after the crash. Subsequently the crew learnt of the fate of their three comrades in 60 Squadron which strengthened their belief that it was the chance failure of the release mechanism to work which had saved their lives.[10]

This other *Blenheim* was shot down in the same vicinity but three days later. The fate of the crew was apparently a subject of speculation at a reception held by the Japanese for Thai notables in Singora on the following day. The senior judge of the Singora High Court, Nai Vichitra Krairiksh, later recalled the manner in which the Japanese Vice-Consul, Katsuno Toshio, had boasted at the reception, "Why should we not kill Allied airmen, it is the only way to get rid of them."[11] The Thai policeman who brought the crew to Singora on 12 December testified in 1946 that about a week after he had done so, he saw these same men taken to the beach near his house and beheaded.[12] This was interpreted by Allied investigators as an indication that their bombs had indeed destroyed Japanese lives or property.[13]

In the initial stages of the campaign, captured British officers of the Indian Army were targeted. They belonged to the senior regiments in action, they knew their Indian troops and many of them held the key to divisional plans. There was a concerted effort on the part of the Japanese to deprive the Indian Army of its officers. Ten Indian Army officers of field rank survived capture and interrogation on the mainland: four lieutenant-colonels and six majors.[14] When Captain Ian Wethey, 5/14 Punjab Regiment, was captured north of Slim River Village on 8 January 1942, he was taken to Ipoh where he underwent interrogation at the hands of senior Japanese staff officers and *Kempei-tai*. His captors, anxious to discover the whereabouts of the Australian infantry battalions, varied sadistic beatings with attempts to make him drunk on *sake*. When it became clear that neither the beatings nor the alcohol would loosen his tongue, the Japanese condemned him to death by beheading. Wethey requested and was granted leave to be shot by firing squad but, to his surprise and relief, he was later gagged and bound, thrown into the back of a truck and transported to the jail at Taiping.[15]

Captain Charles Wylie, Adjutant, 2/1 Gurkha Rifles, spent four days after the battle at Slim River in the jungle in the company of a small group of British troops and Gurkhas. He was captured by a patrol on the night of 12/13 January and taken to Kuala Lumpur where he was interrogated in front of approximately nine senior Japanese officers. He was confronted with an elaborate map depicting the defences of Singapore and had considerable difficulty convincing his interrogators he had never been there. Fortunately for Wylie, the Japanese became aware during the course of these interrogations that many of the Indian Army officers stationed in northern Malaya prior to the outbreak of war had no occasion to visit Singapore. He was fortunate to leave his interrogation having experienced no more physical damage than a chop on the neck by guards which rendered him only briefly senseless.[16]

When the Japanese realized there was intelligence potential among Allied officers and men, they organized a framework in which to conduct the interrogations. The swiftness of the campaign required a mobile force of skilled interrogators assisted by the *Kempei-tai*. These interrogations were conducted by Japanese staff officers attached to the Headquarters of the Twenty-Fifth Army including Lieutenant-Colonel Sugita Ichiji, Chief Intelligence Officer, who spoke good English and admitted in 1946 to questioning "one or two" European prisoners.[17] Sugita's role is easy to establish because he was later well-known to the POWs in the early weeks at Changi. After the war, Colonel Hongo Takeshi identified other staff officers who interrogated POWs including Colonel Tsuji Masanobu, Major Asaeda Shigeharu and Major Hayashi Tadahiko.[18] After the war, Asaeda was charged with the murder of the *Blenheim* crew at Singora but by that time he was himself a prisoner in Russian hands. Lieutenant-General Yamashita must surely have been aware of the aircrew's fate as his headquarters during the first days of the campaign was at Singora where he lodged in the residence of the Thai governor.

The Japanese staff officers either spoke English or were attended by reasonably competent interpreters. But such interpreters were few and far between and by the time the armies reached Johore and the POWs were numbered in their hundreds, this deficiency became critical. In the Allied forces, there were apparently no more than three or four Japanese speakers and these were attached to divisional or brigade headquarters. One of these British officers, Lieutenant O. M. Wynd, Intelligence Officer 22nd Indian Brigade, had been born and brought up in Japan and was fluent in the language. He was detained at Gemas for 10 days and forced to interpret at interrogations of Allied personnel.[19]

The interrogations were far from inevitably fatal, many of the Allied personnel involved were subsequently removed to one of the civilian jails which housed the POWs in Malaya. The fact that a comparatively small number of men wounded in battle survived to enter Pudu Jail in Kuala Lumpur—the major holding camp—reflects the contempt of the Japanese for the wounded, who were generally dispatched by bayonet or bullet on the battlefield. The senior medical officer at Pudu did not see a POW with gunshot wounds until late February.[20]

But there are other facts to be taken into account, not least the attitude of the individual Japanese officers into whose hands the POWs fell. Two contrasting examples illustrate this point. On 25 January 1942, Captain R. B. C. Welch RAMC found himself near Senggarang with a party of 20 wounded men unable to proceed because the road south had been cut. Here he was joined by Captain J. A. Mark RAMC and Padre J. N. Duckworth, 2nd Battalion, The Cambridgeshire Regiment, and their party of 60 or 70 stretcher cases. Realizing that motor transport was out of the question, the wounded were given the choice of remaining behind or making an attempt to escape through the jungle. Forty-five patients remained, together with the RAMC orderlies and drivers. When a Japanese officer arrived on the 27th, he held out his hand to the British officers and ordered his troops to distribute tinned foods, water and cigarettes. Watches and medical supplies were confiscated but the party was otherwise unmolested. The orderlies and drivers were removed and the two medical officers were taken to Batu Pahat, questioned at length by two English-speaking Japanese and returned to their party in a staff car. On 12 February, all the survivors were taken by lorry and rail in stages to Kuala Lumpur, their number increasing as other POWs were picked up along the route.[21]

The background to the second example—the massacre of approximately 150 Australian and Indian wounded men after the withdrawal of the force commanded by Lieutenant-Colonel Charles Anderson, 2/19 AIF, from Parit Sulong on 22 January—was pieced together by POWs while still in captivity. The only officer to witness the massacre and to escape, Lieutenant Ben Hackney, 2/29 AIF, described the appalling scenes he witnessed at Parit Sulong to many of his fellow captives in Pudu Jail and later in Changi. What, they wondered, could have provoked the "frenzied brutality" of this particular attack on wounded men? The action was not designed to shatter the morale of fighting troops because the intention on the part of the Japanese was clearly to kill the entire party and leave no witness. It was evident to Hackney that the order for the massacre came from a senior officer and was a considered response rather than the action of troops in the heat of battle.

Light from two sources was cast on the motivation of the Japanese officers who ordered the massacre. Later in 1942, Anderson found himself in Burma as a POW, and conversation with one of the Japanese officers in command frequently turned to the battles of the Malayan campaign. Anderson discovered that one of these Japanese officers (Lieutenant Shiina Hirayasu) had been in the reserve Guards battalion at Muar, one of the few actions in the Malayan Campaign where the Allies inflicted serious losses on the Japanese forces. Anderson wrote later in a letter to Lieutenant-General Percival, "He told me that in the engagement we killed a Japanese Brigadier and two Regimental Commanders and admitted to heavy casualties."[22] Further information was gleaned by one of the British officers who heard Hackney's story in Pudu and reluctantly found himself engaged as an extra in a re-enactment of the Battle of Muar for the Japanese cinema. He asked one of the Japanese officers why the POWs at Parit Sulong had been massacred. "The answer was that a Regimental

Commander (Colonel) had been killed in action and that the troops were told to take no prisoners, in revenge."²³ In a rare moment of personal reflection in his account of the Malayan campaign, Tsuji refers to the bitterly fought action between 16 and 23 January and the annihilation of a Japanese tank company at the Parit Sulong bridge. One of the young officers, Captain Miura, had been taught by Tsuji at the Military Academy. "In imagination I can see him now," he wrote, "undaunted by a serious wound, going into action like a demon—and to a heroic death on the battlefield."²⁴

After capture, the officers and men of Indian origin, numbering approximately 10,000, were separated from their British officers and assembled at the police barracks at Kuala Lumpur where some chose to join the Indian National Army and others were coerced into doing so. The POWs of other nationalities captured in northern Malaya in late December and early January numbered about 390 and were held in civilian jails or police barracks at Penang, Alor Star and Taiping. They were later concentrated at Taiping until their removal in late June–early July to Pudu Jail in Kuala Lumpur, which had become the principal holding camp for the POWs of the Malayan Campaign after the fall of the city on 11 January.

The first group of British POWs—13 officers and 43 other ranks—arrived at Pudu from the police barracks on 22 January to establish the camp which eventually held approximately 1,200 men.²⁵ The majority remained until October 1942 when they were handed over to the newly established Japanese POW Administration, Malaya, and dispersed: those who belonged to the British forces and the European officers of the Indian Army who were, in the eyes of the Japanese, fit enough to work were sent directly by rail to Thailand to join the labour battalions building the Thailand-Burma railway; the Australians, the sick and those who had lost limbs went to Changi. A British group of five officers and 95 men—mostly belonging to two battalions, the 2nd Loyals and the 2nd East Surreys—were detained in Malaya for a further two months. They were sent to Malacca in November and, wearing captured British uniforms and equipment, acted reluctantly as extras in a propaganda film on the campaign, the "action" taking place at Malacca, Muar and Johore Bahru.²⁶

Pudu Jail was a massive structure of stone and concrete built in 1895, but the area initially allotted to the POWs was the original women's block, a walled area 60 yards-square containing only six cells and two small rooms. A belt 20 yards broad surrounded the building which had to suffice for cooking, latrines and exercise. The majority of the first POWs at Pudu belonged to the 11th Indian Division and had spent 10 or more days in the jungle and rubber plantations in an attempt to catch up with the retreating forces. The men came into Pudu "tired, half starved, in rags and with morale at its lowest."²⁷ All were suffering from exposure and septic sores and had been stripped of their possessions upon capture. Tsuji commented, "We had noticed that when the enemy's front was broken their troops took refuge in the jungle, but finding they could not escape through it, were driven by hunger to surrender after two or three days."[28] On the other hand, POWs captured south of Kuala Lumpur—the Australians, and soldiers of the 9th Indian and 18th British Divisions—were better clothed and many arrived with money or possessions such as watches or fountain pens, a huge advantage at the start of captivity.

POWs arrived daily. On 9 February, they totalled 446, by the 18th there were 550 and in late March, 724. With minimal food supplies, only two taps to supply water, no medicines, no lighting and contact with responsible Japanese impossible to establish, conditions reached a critical point. By April, the Japanese became alarmed at the increasing number of deaths and more accommodation was made available in the vast almost-empty jail. By the time the camp closed, the introduction of working parties and wages for labour had enabled the POWs to harbour enough resources to alleviate the worst suffering.

Much of the evidence concerning Japanese atrocities in the Malayan Campaign is oral. The investigations undertaken in Hong Kong in the months after hostilities ceased enabled surviving witnesses to reconstruct fairly accurately what occurred along the paths of conquest. Indeed, there were witnesses who escaped from Hong Kong and published accounts in books and newspapers as the war continued. But it was different in Malaya. The traces had disappeared, particularly in the more remote districts, as had so many of the witnesses when the war crimes investigators began their work. And in Malaya it is evident that the sufferings of the various nationalities during the Japanese occupation were given higher priority for investigation than the treatment of the surrendered personnel of four or five years before. As a melancholic footnote to the story of the Indian National Army, much of the evidence gathered by the Allies in Burma in 1944 about the fate of soldiers in the Malayan Campaign came initially from Indians who had—willingly or not—renounced their earlier allegiance.

Sibylla Jane Flower has been engaged in research on the history of Allied POWs since 1991 during which time she has carried out extensive documentary research and has interviewed key survivors throughout the world. She has been instrumental in securing the release of many government files of relevant papers. Jane Flower is writing a history of POWs in Burma, Thailand, Malaya and Singapore which will be completed in 2003.

NOTES—

1. Phyllis Harrop escaped from Hong Kong to Macao on 27 January 1942; for the reaction to her statement forwarded by the British Vice-Consul, see PRO, CO980/52, Foreign Office memorandum signed by Lt.-Col. S. J. Cole, 4 February 1942.
2. Fujiware Iwaichi, F. *Kikan: Japanese Army Intelligence Operations in Southeast Asia During World War II*, Hong Kong, 1983.
3. Tsuji Masanobu, *Singapore: The Japanese Version*, London, 1966, 182–83.
4. Imperial War Museum (IWM), CSDIC Report No. 15, 1 August 1944, 10.
5. J. H. Marsman, *I Escaped from Hong Kong*, Sydney, 1943, 65–66.
6. P. N. Davies, *The Man Behind the Bridge*, London, 1991, 56–57.
7. PRO, WO311/562, Affidavit, Gunner Robert Edward Pate, 135 Field Regiment, RA, Lancaster, 30 August 1946.
8. *Royal Artillery Institution, Lieutenant John Christopher Close MC, Royal Artillery*, privately printed, London, 1946.
9. Interview, author with Wing Commander P. N. Kingwill, August 1993. He recounts the story of the crash, interrogation and initial imprisonment in *"Johnnie"*: A Tribute by 30 Squadron RAF Association, privately printed, n.d.
10. Interview and correspondence, author with Wing Commander Kingwill.
11. PRO, WO325/75, Sworn statement of Nai Vichitra Krairiksh, 20 February 1947.
12. PRO, WO325/75, Sworn statement of Sgt.-Maj. Chamnarn, Singora, 17 July 1946.
13. Information from Wing Commander Kingwill.
14. Papers of the late Maj. J. A. Gardner, 2nd Loyals, in private possession. Gardner was adjutant at Pudu Jail.
15. Typescript, I. H. Wethey, "Reminiscences of Life as a Prisoner of War (January 1942–August 1945)," n.d. [c.1994], by courtesy of Dr. R. J. Pritchard.
16. Interview and correspondence, author with Lt.-Col. C. G. Wylie, July 1994.
17. PRO, WO325/75, Summary of Examination of Sugita Ichiji, 6 November 1946, 2.
18. PRO, WO325/75, Summary of Examination of Hongo Takeshi, 19 March 1946, 1–2.
19. PRO, WO325/31, Affidavit signed by Lt. O. M. Wynd, London, 29 April 1946.
20. Interview, author with the late Capt. J. A. Mark RAMC, November 1992.
21. IWM, Diary of R. B. C. Welch, typescript.
22. IWM, Percival Papers, LMH 7, Letter, Charles Anderson to Percival, 12 August [n.y.].
23. IWM, Percival Papers, C. H. D. W[ild], Notes on Proposed Interrogation of Japanese General Officers in Japan, Singapore, 9 November 1945.
24. Tsuji Masanobu, *Singapore*, 170.
25. PRO, WO222/1388, [Lt.-Col. J. C. Collins RAMC], Prisoner of War Camp, Kuala Lumpur, January/October 1942, typescript. Collins was the senior medical officer at Pudu.
26. Interview, author with G. S. Mowat (formerly Lance Corporal 4th Bn, SSVF), April 1997.
27. PRO, WO222/1388, Collins, 1–2.
28. Tsuji Masanobu, *Singapore*, 150.

CHAPTER 11

The Island Battle: Japanese Soldiers Remember the Conquest of Singapore

by Henry P. Frei

Few campaigns have been more covered, explained and analyzed than the Malayan campaign. Much is known about the traumatic fall of Singapore, above all from the British and Australian sides and, to a lesser extent, from the Chinese, Indian, and Malay sides. What strikes one as odd in the fascinating Western-oriented literature is the paucity of detail about the Japanese soldiers in the field who may be regarded as the *raison d'être* of the campaign and fall of Singapore. They remain altogether a largely faceless mass, bicycling their way down to Singapore. It is timely now to review the fall of Singapore from the Japanese perspective and focus on the psychology and motivation of the Japanese infantryman who shaped that momentous event in modern world history.

This paper draws on Japanese war memoirs and autobiographies, supplemented by interviews with five soldiers of the three divisions that made up Japan's Twenty-Fifth Army. Machine-gunner Ochi Harumi and Private Miyake Genjiro were from the 5th Division, Sergeant Arai Mitsuo from the 18th Division, Corporal Tsuchikane Tominosuke from the Imperial Guards Division and Lieutenant Onishi Satoru from the military police. The paper presents excerpts from a longer manuscript, aiming to show the heroism and cowardice, humanity and barbarity of the Japanese soldier, as he fought his way down the Malayan peninsula to conquer Singapore. This was the battle of the century, or, if not that, at least the worst military defeat in modern British history, as Churchill himself noted. How did it look to the enemy?

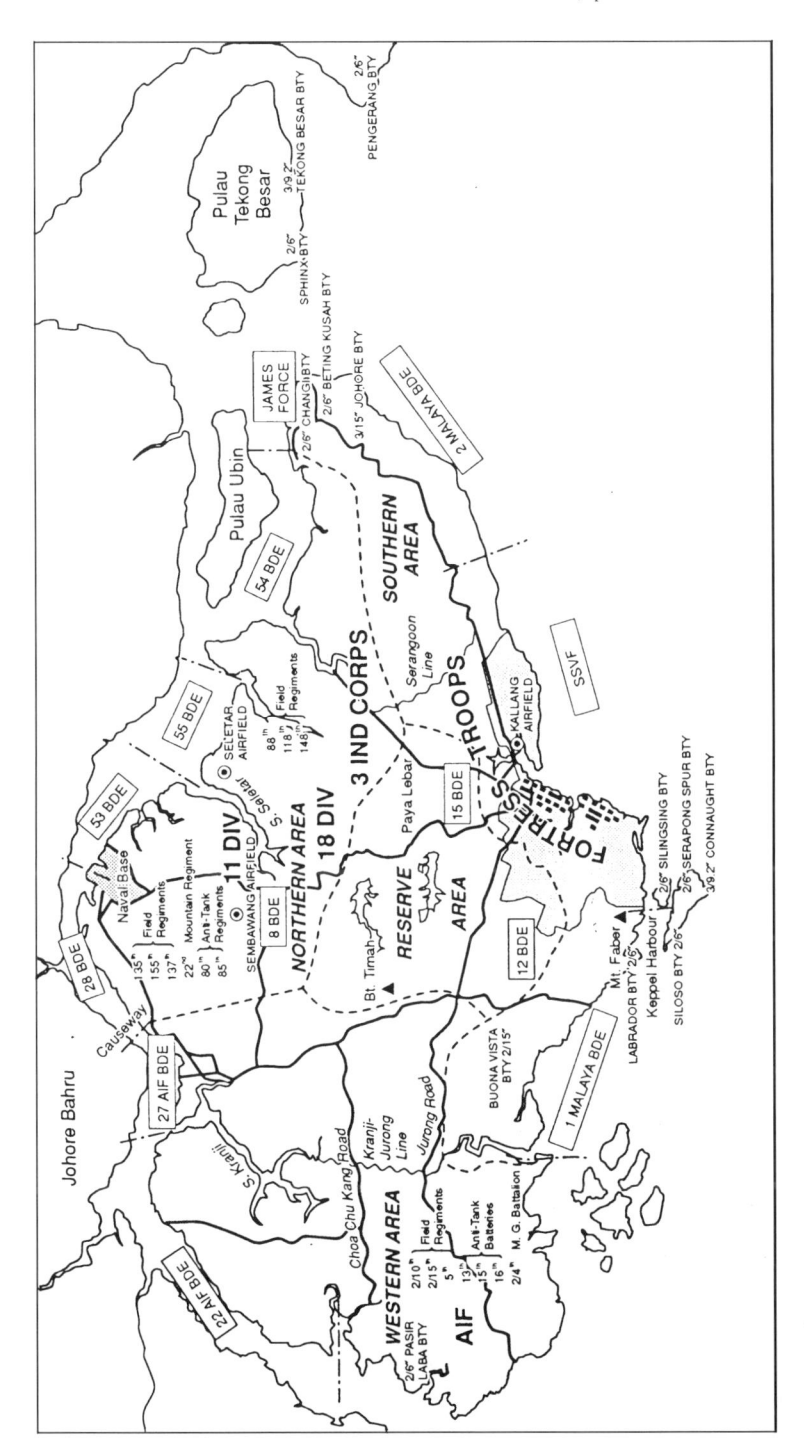

The Island Battle: Japanese Soldiers Remember ✦ 219

Deployment for the defence of Singapore, February 1942

Crossing the Straits in the Face of the Enemy

Following their successful campaign against numerically superior forces, Japanese war memoirs recall the elation and tension experienced by the soldiers as they dug into their positions at the southern tip of the Malayan peninsula. They felt proud. In 55 days, they covered 1,100 kilometres. They set a record by advancing on average 20 kilometres, fighting two battles, and repairing four or five bridges every day. In those 50 days of jungle fighting, soldiers lost on average 10 kilograms.[1]

The huge preparatory operation to cross the Straits was supposed to be completed by noon on 7 February 1942. This would give the troops four days to capture Singapore by *Kigensetsu*, 11 February, the birthday of the legendary first Emperor Jimmu and a national holiday. But by the 7th, only the artillery was in place and ready. All other troops needed one more day to complete their preparations. The General Staff were angry: orders were orders! Fortunately at this point, Lieutenant-General Yamashita stepped in decisively to allow one more day for battle preparations. This unusual generosity earned him tremendous admiration and gratitude from each of his divisional commanders. Everyone pledged in his heart to honour their leader by doing their very best in the coming battle.[2]

Sappers cut paths through the jungle, each leading to secretly prepared harbours along the Skudai River. The engineers, worried about the chance of boats running aground, fixed the embarkation points too far into the water. In addition, they miscalculated the timing of the tides. They had not taken into account the three hours it would take, from actual boarding time to departure time, between nine in the evening and midnight. The soldiers cursed these idiotic errors, as they made their way with difficulty towards their distant launches, trying to scale their sides and losing several boats that drifted out to sea. All the while, sappers were shouting out the vessel numbers for the various platoons to embark in, waving hands, calling the artillery and assigning them reserved gun emplacements on the folding boats. Overseeing the chaos, the eerie silhouettes of the engineers on the boats called out in leaden low voices, looking very business-like as they directed operations.[3]

Each captain had a schedule by which he had to reach the Straits. The tide was pulling back, making the river narrower, causing ships to bang against each other. It was time to leave. A signalman in the stern of the boat communicated with the others using signal flags. Ochi's boat left its moorings and picked up speed down the Skudai River into the Johore Straits. A hundred and fifty boats, moving together like a shoal of piranha, quickly reached the Skudai's wide mouth at the Straits and spread out, making way for the next craft pouring into the Straits behind them.[4] Crossing the Straits was their final hurdle. The tension experienced at this moment is captured in every account, and each soldier who wrote about it remembers it with awe. They would be as sitting ducks on the Straits. The burning question was: how far across the Straits would they get, before being shot at? In most cases, the writers recall the first shots coming at them when they were just a little more than half-way across, from about 400 metres' distance.

War memoirs then tell about the first fights on the beaches. The most difficult landing was experienced by the Imperial Guards, who had one position in the mangroves inundated with oil and set ablaze by the Australians:

> Tsuchikane had stumbled into another company's position. Quickly he began to move back in the direction he'd come from. Again a shell exploded near the soldiers he had just left.
>
> "Mother! Mother!"
> "Don't die! Don't die— you must not!"
> "Tenno heika banzai—Long live the Emperor!"
>
> Tsuchikane pulled himself together, carefully lifting his legs to join his unit. Close to him, fire lashed out over the burning mangrove. It spread quickly, feeding on oil poured into the Straits, gushing out onto the surface, and then shining on the water in a ghastly scene of Dante's inferno.
>
> "Mother! Mother!"
>
> The moaning voice could still be heard. It was a picture of hell— *Abikyokan*— Buddhism's worst of all hells. Stumbling along the edge of the beach, Tsuchikane's gun felt slippery in his hands. Fire in all directions threatened to engulf him. Where to go? It seemed impossible to advance or retreat!
>
> "We'll burn to death just standing here—let's attack!" Corporal Nemoto yelled to Tsuchikane.
>
> "If we're going to die, better in an attack," agreed Tsuchikane.
>
> Shouting out their battalion and platoon names, they advanced, hoping to be recognized.
>
> "Corporal Nemoto, Corporal Tsuchikane!"

One, then two comrades joined them.⁵

Machine-gunner Ochi Harumi from the 5th Division described their first contact with the Australian 2/20 AIF defence positions in the Sungei Buloh beach area:

> The Japanese tore into the enemy with blood-curdling sounds.
>
> *"Fix bayonets! Attack!"*
>
> No longer human at the hour of death, the Japanese darted after the enemy, goring anyone in their path with the bayonet. During the frenzied killing on the beach, the soldiers lost their spiritual balance.⁶ Like rabid dogs they chased after the enemy, their sense of self-preservation having turned them inside-out. Even platoon and company commanders, men who were supposed to be level-headed and calm, were carrying bloody swords, as they, too, were drawn into the mad dance of death. The Australian 2/20 sentry units were on the edge of annihilation.
>
> Ochi reckoned that the Australians could have put a stop to the killings with fire from a flank and a bit more *sang-froid*. It would have been a simple remedy—just one heavy machine-gun opening up suddenly from the side. Fire from the flank was the greatest danger to the direct assault tactics that Ochi's platoon was using. Without it, the chaotic killing became a one-on-one affair, direct assaults in which the invader proved the more desperate. For the defending Australians, it was kill or retreat. For the Japanese, it could only be kill or be killed.
>
> The Australian forces began to retreat with their Thompson guns. Ochi's unit pursued them about 100 metres into the jungle where in an opening the ridge sloped down into a valley. Below ran the enemies' silhouettes, south.⁷

Severing Wrists of Fallen Comrades in the Heat of Battle

One experience that regularly comes up in the Japanese war memoirs is the disposal of fallen comrades in the heat of battle. These are descriptions of the harrowing experience for the young men having to sever the wrist or finger of their fallen comrades and later to ossify them in a lull during the battle. Sergeant Arai from the 18th Division describes it thus:

> Arai jumped off the bow, and was about to call the wireless troop commander, when a cold hand stroked his ankle. Nine corpses floated in the water, head upward, in a line next to each other. A chill ran down Arai's spine. Were they shot while crossing, and then washed up, or after they had landed? But reflections be hanged! Quick! Cut off a wrist or a finger of each dead man. Chop, chop, chop. Into a box, there's no time to bury them. Just a quick prayer. Rest in peace. Then forward! He must fire the green "success" rocket: Regimental Command has landed—the sign for 18th Division General Mutaguchi Renya to embark on the third wave across the Straits. It was five past one in the morning of 9 February.[8]

During a lull, one would burn away the flesh and give the bones to one of the deceased's close comrades for him to take care of until the remains could be returned to his hometown in an urn. Imperial Guard Corporal Tsuchikane had this experience:

> The platoon commander ordered him to cut off dead Captain Matsumoto's wrist and lent him his company sword to do the job. It would not cut. Tsuchikane tried again and again and finally the bone snapped. They dropped the severed wrist into Matsumoto's mess tin and put it carefully away into the ordnance bag of Senior Soldier Otsuka who hailed from the same province.[9]

> After a further battle, they were able to rest in a bombed-out house. First they took from the mess tin the dead Captain's hand and began to grill it. *"Shuu, shuu,"* it sizzled, with lots of grease escaping from the hand. Strong smoke with a dreadful stench soon filled the room. Picking the bones from the charcoal, they transferred them to a British tobacco tin, which they passed to the safe keeping of their war buddies. They, in turn, put the bones in a white cloth and stored the package with great care in their service bag.

> The soldiers had promised each other that they would enter Singapore together, even if it were only their remains. They had fought together until today, they had eaten the same rice, dived

under the same bullets, and they felt a bond no different from that of brothers. Perhaps it was even stronger by knowledge of man's fleeting existence experienced each day over the past months.[10]

Seven Days of Battle

For seven days in February, Singapore was one gigantic chessboard on which "yellow" invaders challenged "white" defenders, inexorably pushing the British-led forces into a tight corner at Keppel Harbour, Hospital Hill, and finally also at Paya Lebar, in the eastern sector of Singapore Island where the Imperial Guards were turning on the pressure. After crossing the Straits, the Guards advanced quickly into the northeastern section of the Mandai ridge, just beyond the causeway, which was held by the Australian 27th Brigade. As Brigadier Maxwell lost his forward units, the 5th *Kobayashi* Regiment advanced its right wing on West Hill 145, and its centre and left wings on East Hill 60. After occupying Seletar airbase, Lieutenant-General Nishimura then ordered an advance towards 5th and 18th Divisions. These zigzag directions, however, caused the 13,000 Imperial Guard troops considerable confusion, as they were sent first east and then west in a southerly direction to sever the island's eastern outskirts from Singapore City.

Japanese observations about the enemy's fighting spirit are not always flattering. After securing the adjoining Race Course in their path, one 5th Division unit was looking for the Golf Course on their way to the MacRitchie Reservoir:

> Close-cropped luxuriant acreage spread before them. Was it a club house? Soldiers could be seen carrying things into a building and coming out empty-handed.
>
> *"Darn! It must be their provisions and fodder warehouse—let's take it!"*
>
> A dangerous undertaking, across 800 metres of golf green! The house was heavily guarded, with around 200 soldiers about and six armoured vehicles in the vicinity.[11] Ochi's side opened the attack, creating total confusion. "Forward!" the Commander shouted. Grimy in deep black soot, the Japanese whirlwind uttered its beastly war cry, the beautiful English lawn turning into a terrible killing field, with British and Australian soldiers fleeing in all directions, each for himself.

No, Ochi thought, the British and Australians were not inferior, but in the decisive moment, when faced with the only option, to show spirit in the defence of Singapore, many were unable to pull the trigger, and focused instead on escape. Amply rewarded, Ochi's object turned out to be the provisions and fodder storage, that General Percival had been so worried about.[12]

Percival himself was then close by at his Sime Road Headquarters. Disturbed by the sound of machine-gun fire, Percival sent out his aide-de-camp to investigate the situation. When Stonor of the Argylls reported back that a battle was going on at the end of the golf course, about a mile from where they were, the General decided it was time to join rear headquarters at Fort Canning in the downtown area.[13]

Eliminating Australian Positions and the Problem of Taking Prisoners

In the ferocious fighting during the initial stage of the invasion, it was often difficult to take prisoners. Imperial Guard Tsuchikane describes their first contact with the enemy after landing and marching inland in the Mandai area:

> Amid the platoon's murderous yells, Tsuchikane hurled himself forward, straight into the enemy position. Many of the Australian 27th Brigade were already turning their backs to him. Tsuchikane closed in on one, ran after him, pulled him to the ground, and with his bayonet pierced his opponent from the back of his shoulder out through the front. The enemy expired with a deathly yell, as Tsuchikane pulled out the blade, splattering his jacket with a crimson red.
>
> The Australian position had stood on a slight rise and the Aussies had put its height to good use by concentrating heavy flank fire from a fixed position down onto the approaching Japanese enemy. Many of the dead lay just beneath the rise. Having lost their minds, some of the defenders had simply been cowering in terror, trying to squat down and avoid hand-to-hand combat. They, too, were bayoneted and shot without mercy.
>
> The company captured a number of heavy machine-guns and 18 prisoners of war, several among whom were British, including a

red-bearded officer. The prisoners, however, were dangerous baggage. Taking them into the next battle would greatly hamper tactics. They would require several guards at a time when the attackers themselves had suffered 60 dead and wounded and the battle for Singapore was just beginning. Fortunately, an artillery unit in the rear area was willing to accept the 18 prisoners, to the great relief of the Imperial Guard company.[14]

Soldiers' Misgivings About their Generals' "Mistaken Strategy"

The Japanese hoped to conquer Singapore by 11 February, the birthday of their first Emperor Jimmu and a national holiday. On that day, however, they had only just taken the Bukit Timah feature. They hoped the fall of this strategic point, together with leaflets dropped on enemy troops urging them to surrender, would pressure the British into capitulation. However, the British did not give up then. It has been argued that Singapore might have fallen on time, had the Japanese General Staff employed a concentrated instead of an enveloping strategy.

The original orders from Twenty-Fifth Army Headquarters had been to attack Bukit Timah from the north and south. But during the battle, the two-pronged attack was abruptly changed to an attack from all sides. This caused confusion. The 18th Division's 55th Regiment, actually on stand-by as reserve, got carried away, and advanced as far as a three-way road junction to the south. There its commander wanted to dash down 5th Division's main trunk route of the Bukit Timah and Dunearn Roads, but was rebuked for straying into another division's sector. The 18th Division's soldiers were surprised to be halted in their successful forward-most engagement at a time when 5th Division had not yet appeared on the scene! All very competitive, everyone wanted to be first into Singapore. Why hand the finest morsel, the Grande Finale, to the 5th Division? It made no sense from a military strategic point of view. If they dashed ahead, Singapore would be theirs for *Kigensetsu*.[15]

Indeed, on the Allied side, both Tomforce and Massyforce failed to recapture Bukit Panjang and were doing badly at Bukit Timah. There was a strong fear that if the Japanese continued to advance at their current rate, they would be able to split the British defences wide open and occupy the city by the morning of 11 February.[16] Percival, who had been planning for a two-month siege, had already realized the danger of the Japanese reaching Singapore City on the third day after the landings. At this point, he decided to effect a close defence perimeter round the town itself. His perimeter would run from Kallang airfield to Paya Lebar airstrip, Woodleigh crossroads, Thomson Village, Adam

Road, Farrer Road, Tanglin Halt, and thence to the sea, west of Buona Vista village. This tactical move involved the withdrawal of even all the beach defences. Percival also went to see Governor Sir Shenton Thomas, to explain the dangerous situation on the Bukit Timah Road axis, upon which Thomas ordered the destruction of the Singapore Broadcasting Station and most of the currency notes held by the Treasury.[17]

After a Japanese staff conference that night which lasted from 0100 to 0400 hours, the entire 18th Division branched off west, away from the front, down Reformatory Road—today's Clementi Road—to the southwest coast of Singapore Island.[18] This certainly initiated the giant pincer, but at Arai's sergeant-level, it seemed strange to divert 18th Division away from the main assault line down Bukit Timah Road, which would now only be followed by 5th Division. It seemed to him that, this way, they would never be able to deal the British the decisive blow. Separating the two divisions would only delay the fall of Singapore. But it was not for him to have a strategic opinion, as he stomped along in the dark rubber forest behind his regimental commander.[19] As they advanced, they could hardly see anything ahead but fireflies. On his heels followed the adjutant whom Arai repeatedly had to help up over the tree trunks. Many soldiers slept even as they walked. By daybreak of 12 February, they came to open fields, along which they proceeded on the eastern edge of a rubber plantation.[20]

Atrocities Admitted

Japanese war memoirs of the Malaya campaign are not all devoid of information about atrocities committed by their own side and some must be given credit for their frank and balanced accounts. Indeed, it would be interesting to compare these war memoirs with British or Australian or American war memoirs, perhaps of another time, and any possible descriptions of acts of brutality contained in them. Ardent Imperial Guard Tsuchikane Tominosuke's book, *Road to Singapore*, shows his growing disillusionment with the war. And Sergeant Arai remembers a horrible incident at an early stage of his 18th Division's advance to form the pincer down Reformatory Road:

> A small overseer's hut appeared on their right side. Three young girls with short cut hair were pursuing their jobs, seemingly oblivious to the war. The scene reminded Arai of the Chinese girls back in Canton. The soldiers were much attracted, but silently looking on, they passed the tantalizing scene.[21] Presently they came under mortar attack, intensive 20-minute bombardments every 30 minutes.

How could the enemy know the line of their attack when they were covered by the rich jungle foliage?[22]

When the third attack ended, headquarters moved up with General Mutaguchi, enjoying the thrill of the advance, and five tanks moved in. Opening their turrets, the operators were looking around them casually when suddenly the attack continued. This time the order went out to catch the three girls they had passed earlier on, "*under suspicion of having betrayed our position.*" Master Sergeant Arai looked on from his concealed position, as the girls were brought forward, and each bound to a wooden pillar. They were about 20 years old, and stood there with lowered heads. Arai doubted that they were guilty of anything. It happened all the time. Tanks routinely moved into the combat zone and were attacked—and that did not mean that anyone had betrayed them. Arai could not stand the sight of these poor girls and returned into his trench. When the heavy attack continued, all soldiers and officers ducked back into their trenches.[23] But the three girls bound to the poles were left out in the open. When the shells began to fall, they went half crazy with fear. Shaking their dishevelled hair, they cried out loudly. When the attack was over, they were still alive. Regiment Commander Okubo, who could take it no longer, ordered a soldier: "*Stab them!*"

But there was no reason to kill them, Arai thought. To deflect the situation and keep the soldier from doing it, he yelled out to him, "*Wait! Don't stab them there, you'll only mess up the place!*" The soldier looked at their commander who, saying nothing, disappeared inside his trench. Relieved, the soldier left the girls alone and went away. With the mortar attack having ceased, everyone became busy, contacting their next troops and sorting out their next advance and Arai forgot all about the girls.[24]

Arai's 114th Regiment was on the right wing up to this stage. Now they would be the left wing. Only their sides changed, they were always in the front, never in reserve. By 0200 hours of the morning of 13 February, information reached them that Hill 200 was completely secured. Better catch a nap, or lack of sleep would hinder tomorrow's big operations.[25]

But Arai could not sleep. The three girls in their pitiful situation, bound to the pole, kept coming to his mind. He could not leave them like that. He must go and release them. He would tell the Regiment Commander that he had killed them at another place. Arai approached the three poles and could make out faintly in the dark the white of their blouses, about fifteen metres away. No one was around. Not even a sentry stood there. The three girls kept their chins sunk on their chests, motionless, their black hair dangling forward in the breeze. Were they asleep?

Arai snapped his fingers to give them a sign. They did not stir. He crept up from behind and shook the first girl from the side. There was no reaction. He loosened the rope round her body to set her free. Something cold and wet dripped on his finger. Was it blood? Instinctively he withdrew his finger. Someone had cruelly stabbed her below the breast. The two others must have suffered the same fate, Arai thought. Inside, he felt that a fiendish inhuman devil had come to attack them, one much worse than the enemy they were presently facing. Arai went back into his trench with an unbearable feeling. He closed his eyes, but was unable to get the three girls out of his mind. If ever Japan became a war theatre, they would be visited with exactly the same beastliness, violence begetting violence, one bad thing leading to something worse. Sleep would not come.[26]

The Taking of Gillman Barracks and the Humiliation of its Commander

Arai relates a minor brutality of his own, at the time of surrender. It happened at Gillman Barracks, which by 1700 hours on 15 February had become the furthest forward position of 114th Regiment:

> The British had finally become aware that the 114th Regiment was advancing fast on Gilman Heights and Keppel Harbour. Coming under heavy fire, the 1st Battalion struck forward at around 1000 hours to Hill 130. To the right, the 3rd Battalion suffered many dead and wounded. Company Commander Tanaka, severely wounded and heavily sedated, kept repeating, *"The war is over, the war is over,"* with eyes wide open. British fire was coming in hard, as Arai moved forward into the protection of a tree and a house wall.[27] He remained in that position for two or three hours.

From 1600 hours to 1800 hours, British artillery pounded the position and many shells fell behind the 114th Regiment HQ. Arai was about 50 metres ahead, moving from Hill 130 to Hill 136, about 1 kilometre distant. The path sloped away at first, then ran level, with some shelter from houses and trees. Wriggling forward, down the slope, he wormed towards Hill 136 in the evening shadows of the rubber plantation, always under never-ending artillery barrage. The shells were targeted at the entire length of the hills above the southern shore. They came crashing down around Hill 130 and the adjoining Hill 95, to the south. The 7th Company was trying to secure that hill, but seven died in the severe bombardment. Arai heard sounds behind him. Sergeants Nakagawa and Katayama came crawling up. *"Ito and Matsumoto from the 114th HQ are dead,"* Katayama said. How close the two young soldiers had come![28] Anger welled up in Arai as he cursed the British artillery. The British infantry appeared on the verge of surrendering, he thought, yet their artillery keeps pounding us. They should all be shot.

Then at six, the guns fell silent. All firing stopped. Just nothing—along the entire front! Arai, Nakagawa and Katayama looked at each other. Singapore without shelling was a novel experience, extraordinarily out of place. An empty ringing persisted in the ears.

"Now is the time to run!" the three decided, jumping up. Four or five comrades nearby joined in their rush forward. They covered the remaining 100 metres to the foot of Hill 136 in a mad dash. Then they scaled the final 50 metres up the steep slope to where on top of the hill stood a large two-storeyed concrete barracks, with the walls painted black. Above the entrance was a big Red Cross sign. Was the sign a camouflage to escape Japanese artillery bombing? But when they entered, they found to their surprise 60 pale faces staring at them out of pyjamas, from beds arranged tightly in a U-shape in the wide room. The barracks had indeed been turned into a hospital. Those who seemed asleep, with only their faces turned to the entrance were the severe casualties. Those who sat upright in their beds and those standing next to their beds all held up their hands high in surrender. Only a moment ago, Arai had entertained the idea of killing them all, even in surrender. But now, looking into the ashen faces of these wounded soldiers, the thought quickly faded.

"*Who is the man in charge?*" Arai wanted to ask, in the English he had learnt 10 years back in junior high school. But nothing came out.[29] He stepped outside, where he found his Regimental Commander and his adjutant just reaching the top of Hill 136. They seemed to be well-aware of the existence of the barracks on the hilltop.

"*Vice-Commander, inside the barracks are many wounded British soldiers, about fifty to sixty!*" Arai said.

"*Aah, so desuka, is that so!? Call Lieutenant Marumo!*" He was the translator attached to their unit for the Malaya campaign. Kakuhira also ordered that the supervisor of the hospital be summoned. At once a British officer appeared; he was around 50, in beret and short trousers, with stockings in low shoes. "*Ask him about the British military dispositions,*" Vice-Commander Kakuhira ordered Marumo.

The translator was not much of a military man. After graduating from university, Marumo had worked as an English teacher. He had been drafted into the rank of lieutenant more for his English skills than for his qualities as a soldier. He was excessively polite and the opposite of the British major whose tone and expression and stiff upper lip showed that the interrogation was going nowhere.

Irritated, the fretting Vice-Commander asked, "*What is he saying?*"

"*He says that he is the Medical Corps Major in charge of this hospital. He respects international law. From that stance he takes a neutral view of the whole situation and knows nothing about military matters.*"

Like hell he does, Arai thought to himself, barely able to control his rush of adrenaline. He was standing to the immediate left of the major, with the regimental commanders and sergeants all waiting and gazing at Marumo, nauseated by the weak interrogation and the major's recalcitrant mien.

Arai could take no more. "*Sit down!*" he barked, hitting the calmly standing major with all his force on the left cheek. The slap sent the British Empire reeling to the floor, where it sat itself down on its knee, took off its green beret, and sheepishly turned to Arai with reproach on its face.

Instantly, the act relieved all tension. All were surprised to see the usually mild-mannered Arai slap this senior officer. In all his army life, not once had he been seen to slap a soldier. Arai himself was astonished about his sudden action. Was it a reaction to all the shelling he'd endured over the past 10 hours and the great loss of dead and wounded suffered in the past final hours? It certainly was infectious. The blow put some bite into Marumo's cross-examination, which now went well.

According to the major, this was Gilman Barracks and housed around 1,000 patients. One party stayed behind to guard the British wounded, as the 114th Regiment occupied the adjoining Hills 312 and 345. Where on earth was the British infantry? It was unbelievable to simply leave behind 1000 wounded soldiers to their fate, thought Arai. What kind of people were these? It was the same as letting wounded die before one's eyes without helping. If they surrendered, they should have been frank about it and raised immediately a white flag. Abandoned by their own soldiers, the frightened eyes stirred neither pity nor sympathy in Arai.[30]

Running Out of Ammunition

A lot has been said about whether the British should have surrendered at that point, or whether they should rather have risked an all-out attack and house-to-house fight until the end, as Percival seems to have been prepared to do. Whichever way one chooses to look at the intriguing and sudden finale, the fact is that the Japanese were down to their last supplies of ammunition:

By 14 February, the machine-gunners of 5th Division's 11th Regiment had only four-and-a-half cases of ammunition left. The total of 90 magazines available in the few boxes left would dispense 2700 bullets in 270 seconds. That meant that only two minutes 15 seconds worth of bullets remained for each of their two heavy machine-guns.[31] At the latest their ammo would be gone early next morning. Machine-gunners without bullets—ha, what clowns they were! But there was no other way than to forge ahead. If only to see Singapore—even if only with one eye left! *Chikatan, chikatan, chikatan*, their steam engine pushed on.[32]

Not all was plain sailing for the Japanese attackers. At the eastern end of the MacRitchie reservoirs, British troops still had lots of fight in them—and plenty of ammunition. Ochi records how an entire company of his 11th Regiment was wiped out on Hospital Hill in the final hours before surrender.[33] This was in the area of Mount Pleasant Road, where the recently arrived British 18th Division was engaged in a last-ditch defence.

Surrender

Japanese war memoirs of this campaign usually devote a chapter or an important section to emotions experienced by the victors upon hearing the unexpected news that the enemy had surrendered. At the same time, they also show that confusion reigned. Why was the enemy surrendering? No one was surrendering on their front, so who and what had brought about the capitulation? These questions were accompanied with an intense feeling of inter-divisional competition and jealousy for not being into Singapore first. Arai's 18th Division in particular was tortured by envy of having lost out to the 5th Division:

> Later in the evening, Arai [still at Gillman Barracks] sensed a sudden commotion from the rear, moving up to their front. It seemed to be coming from the west coast, out of the valley, rising up the hills, like a tidal wave about to engulf them. The sound was also heard on Hills 130 and 136, and on other elevations, ever more clearly. The roar grew closer and louder. The source of the noise must be somewhere out there. One could not see their silhouettes, but the force of their voices was shattering.
>
> *"BANZAI! BANZAAI—BANZAAAI!!"*
>
> The soldiers all along the front were congratulating themselves on an astounding victory won at the last desperate minute. Mixed in with the *Banzais* was also the breathless shout: *"114th Regiment! The enemy has surrendered! Hold your attack!! Hold your attack!!! Stop the advance!!"*
>
> *"So the enemy did surrender...?!"* Often thought about, but hard to believe, it had become reality. So all had been worthwhile. None of them had died in vain. They were here to stay.

At the same time, the announcement wafting from afar stirred also jealousy. *"5th Division must have stolen a march on us ... " "Being on the main trunk road straight into the city, it was only natural ..." "It couldn't be helped...them getting into Singapore much before us ..."* It was a mixed bag of emotions that assailed 18th Division soldiers, not quite satisfied with the perfect news, even if they should be glad about the victory, but the surrender had not come from their part of the city. They so badly had wanted to be first. After all, the 114th Regiment had reached the furthest objective of the campaign, Keppel Harbour, in downtown Singapore. Surely the surrender should have been declared in their section.

About 100 metres from their hilltop, they saw Private Kanda run up, shouting out the orders received from Divisional Headquarters. Arai called down, *"Kanda, we understand! We are up here!"* He looked at his watch. It was 20 minutes past eight in the evening. The sun had already set. In 20 minutes, it would be dark.[34]

At 2030 hours, Vice-Commander Kakuhira confirmed Kanda's message to "cease fire," and ordered each unit to secure their battle zone and wait for the next orders. In the meantime, they had to take care of the wounded and bury the dead. Arai gave his rice portion to a wounded comrade. At 2230 hours, Commander Okubo issued Order No. 70 from Gilman Barracks. It was the final order of the campaign:

1. The enemy has surrendered. We extend condolences to the fallen British Commonwealth soldiers.
2. The Regiment will retain its present position overnight.
3. Each unit will gather its forces and disarm the enemy according to orders. One detachment will inspect the wounded enemy assembled in Gillman Hospital.
4. I remain on Hill 136.[35]

With midnight the occasion, Commander Okubo mustered officers and soldiers for a minute of silent prayer for the deceased British soldiers, saluted the Regimental Flag with deep respect, bowed low in the direction of the Imperial Palace, addressed his thanks to the entire Regiment, and led three rounds of *Banzais*. For the first time in combat, Arai did not try to hold back his tears. It had been a savage war. Too many older and younger mates had died. Slowly the soldiers settled down, each one into his own memories, letting one scene pass after the other, with a heavy chest.[36]

Japanese victory parade, Fullerton Square, Singapore, 17 February 1942

Reminiscences

One thing that struck this author is the amount of regret existing in the memories of many Japanese war veterans he interviewed and whose diaries he used. It is somewhat out of line with the stereotype of Japan not apologizing or being insensitive to the damage done during the Asia-Pacific war. When we talk to those who had actually fought the war, we often get a different picture. Private Miyake Genjiro of the 5th Division, who had to carry out the actual executions in the Overseas Chinese massacres at the end of the Malayan campaign, remembers only too well. And as he planes his wood, as an old carpenter today in Shikoku, he mutters, "I don't want to talk as a human being. Why? Because of shame. Our shame. It's too difficult to talk about. But I can testify to it in my own person."[37] He does this in a remarkable video entitled "Aggression on the Malayan Peninsula: The War They Did Not Teach Us About."[38]

Former *Kempei-tai* Lieutenant Onishi Satoru, who held the fate of 10,000 Chinese in his hands at the screening centre at Jalan Besar, hurts today when he sees the four obelisks of the Singapore War Memorial:

> [They look to me like]…a spiked tower of one hundred and twenty metres that looms high in a plaza overlooking the city as a reminder of Japan's biggest mistake at the beginning of the Occupation. In this manner, the purge of the Overseas Chinese in Shonan will remain in the people's mind until the erosion of this tower which will take a long time. As a person who was deeply involved, I feel as if stabbed by a knife, aware of my responsibility towards the victims, to whom I offer my sincere and deep condolences. I am not trying to justify or to excuse ourselves. The purge was a cruel act committed by the Japanese Army. It constitutes truly shameful behaviour, and remains a most disgraceful act in the Great Eastern War."[39]

Those not involved in the purge feel less apologetic, but are not without remorse. When asked how he remembers the fall of Singapore today, 18th Division frontline Sergeant Arai has reworked his past by saying:

> When I look back, now that I have reached eighty and don't know how many years I've got left—when I come to think about death, I think I might have been better off to die along with those people who fell, one after the other, around me in Singapore. One has to die anyway. Is it not better to die at the time that one is required to die? That's what I think now. They died in a natural way, so when one could have died then, why not then?[40]

Old frontline machine-gunner Ochi feels that:

> Japan was doing too well at the beginning of the war. The attack on Pearl Harbour, the conquest of Singapore, the sea battle successes off Malaya, the occupation of one place after the other in Indonesia, and so on, each fed on the other and led to Japanese self-pride and conceit. Drunk as they were on their sole object of winning the war, generals were aiming at glory, their juniors at a rise in career, the people at a net profit out of the war, each seeking, with characteristic impatience and a quick temper, their own "net profit." Yet, after their tiny victories, to get proud and arrogant so quickly and to give free rein to self-interest and even public black markets, was truly deplorable. If such Japanese had controlled and ruled Asia, it would have become a miserable and pitiful place, indeed.
>
> The Japanese had not yet evolved into a constitutional people. So there was really no reason to beat the United States or Great Britain, who were already constitutional peoples. The biggest reason for Japan's defeat was her backwardness. It was good that Japan was defeated. Japan can now completely reform and remodel itself and its cultural standards. It's the young that must do this. Only the young can complete and achieve this.[41]

In Memoriam: Professor Henry Philip Frei

After delivering his paper at our conference on the fall of Singapore in mid-February 2002, Professor Henry Frei returned to Japan, fell ill and was hospitalized almost immediately. He died only a few weeks later, leaving behind his devoted wife Kyo and their teenage son Francis. Henry Frei was born and schooled in Switzerland. Early on he wondered whether he should go into hotel management, as so many of his contemporaries had done, but in the end he chose a career in academia and those who knew him as a devoted teacher, avid researcher and a kind, amusing colleague are confident that he made the correct decision. Henry was a consummate linguist—fluent as so many continental Europeans are in several languages. To the conventional list of English, French, and German, Henry added both Chinese and Japanese—his fluency in the latter becoming quite apparent the longer he remained in his beloved Japan. After completing his undergraduate education at the University of Berne in Switzerland, he spent a year working in the Western Australian bush before taking up postgraduate studies at the Institute of International Relations at Sophia University where he was awarded his doctorate. He remained for 15 years in the Japanese tertiary sector, culminating in his teaching history in Japanese at both Sophia and Waco universities in Tokyo. He eventually left Japan to join the fledgling Japanese Studies Department at the National University of Singapore. Japan remained in his blood, however, and it was no real surprise when he returned there after his stint of teaching history in Singapore—this time as a research professor at Tsukuba University. He subsequently moved across town to join the Tsukuba Women's University and take on more teaching and administrative duties.

Much as Henry loved teaching Japanese History, he was perhaps even more partial to devilling around in the archives, conducting interviews with ageing members of the Imperial Japanese Army and writing articles on Japanese foreign and defence policy both before and during the Second World War. He saw his book, Japan's Southward Advance and Australia: From the Sixteenth Century to World War II, as merely a launching pad for other work on Japanese military experiences in the Malayan and Pacific campaigns. His essay in this collection is just such an example. Had he lived he would have undoubtedly contributed far more to our knowledge of the motivational forces and personal feelings of the ordinary Japanese soldier in battle.

Henry Frei was a really genuine individual and a class act in a profession that boasts too much schadenfreude, and hypocrisy. It simply cannot afford to lose warm, talented, humane individuals like Henry. It was a privilege to know him and count him as a true friend. On behalf of the editors and contributors, his friends and colleagues,

Malcolm H. Murfett

NOTES—
1. O. Harumi, *Maree senki* (Malaya War Diary), Tokyo, 1973, 242, 256.
2. Ibid., 269–70; interviews, 6 May 1996, 15 October 2001.
3. Ibid., 276–77.
4. Ibid., 278–80.
5. T. Tominosuke, *Shingaporu e no michi: aru Konoe hei no kiroku* (The Road to Singapore: Diary of an Imperial Guard Soldier), Tokyo, 1977, Vol. 1, 182–83.
6. O. Harumi, *Maree senki*, 287–88.
7. Ibid., 289–90.
8. A. Mitsuo, *Shingaporu senki* (Singapore War Diary, Tokyo, 1984), 61–63; interview, Kokura, Kyushu, 10 October 1993.
9. T. Tominosuke, *Shingaporu e no michi*, 198; interview, 22 October 2001.
10. Ibid., 210–12.
11. O. Harumi, *Maree senki*, 312–13.
12. Ibid., 314–15.

13 A. E. Percival, *The War in Malaya*, London, 1949, 278.
14 T. Tominosuke, *Shingaporu e no michi*, 203–05.
15 A. Mitsuo, *Shingaporu senki*, 101, 121, 132.
16 See S. W. Kirby, *Singapore: The Chain of Disaster*, London, 1971, 240.
17 S. W. Kirby, *The War Against Japan: Volume 1: The Loss of Singapore*, London, 1957, 373, 399.
18 A. Mitsuo, *Shingaporu senki*, 119, 149.
19 Ibid., 118–19.
20 Ibid., 120.
21 Ibid., 149.
22 Ibid., 152.
23 Ibid., 153.
24 Ibid., 153–54.
25 Ibid., 157.
26 Ibid., 157–58.
27 Ibid., 181–82.
28 Ibid., 183.
29 Ibid., 184.
30 Ibid., 185–86.
31 O. Harumi, *Maree senki*, 331.
32 Ibid., 338.
33 Ibid., 344–59.
34 A. Mitsuo, *Shingaporu senki*, 187–88 and interview, 10 October 1993.
35 Ibid., 192–93.
36 Ibid., 194.
37 M. Genjiro, Video production by Eizo Bunka Kyokai, with commentary, *Shinryaku— Maree hanto: Oshierarenakatta senso* (Aggression on the Malayan Peninsula: The War They Did Not Teach Us About), Tokyo, May 1992, 110 mins., 65.
38 Ibid.
39 O. Satoru, *Hiroku: Shonan Kakyo shukusei jiken* (Secret document: The Purge of Overseas Chinese in Shonan), Tokyo, 1977, 132.
40 A. Mitsuo, interview, Kokura, Kyushu, 10 October 1993.
41 O. Harumi, *Maree senki*, 378.

CHAPTER 12

General Percival and the Fall of Singapore

by Clifford Kinvig

"It is damaging to be associated, however distantly, with a disaster," wrote Duff Cooper in the aftermath of the fall of Singapore as he prepared his material for the inevitable inquest.[1] Lieutenant-General Arthur Percival was not merely associated with the disaster; he seemed to some commentators to bear a large responsibility for it. As GOC Malaya, he led its land forces to their rapid and spectacular defeat by the Japanese and surrendered the vaunted "fortress" of Singapore after only a week's assault in a capitulation unparalleled in British military history. The shock of the defeat was all the greater since it stood in such stark contrast to the public confidence and apparent complacency about the security of Singapore which emanated not only from the local military high command but also from the authorities in London.[2] As the only senior commander to remain in post from the start of the Japanese offensive to its bitter conclusion, Percival appeared to bear a particular responsibility for its outcome. Furthermore, whilst the stunning defeat of the air and naval forces in Malaya seemed sufficiently explained by their qualitative and quantitative inferiority to the Japanese, so far as the land forces were concerned all that seemed to be remembered of them was that they were numerically greater than Yamashita's army.[3] In a brief and guarded evaluation of the débacle during a secret speech to Parliament, Churchill noted that he had been told there was a lack of firm leadership in the fight for Malaya. Much evidence seemed to point to the generalship of the GOC in explanation of the rapid defeat.[4]

Prior to his assumption of command on 16 May 1941, less than seven months before the Japanese offensive opened, Percival had an unusual military career. Its first phase of virtual non-stop operations began when, at the age of almost 27, he volunteered on the first day of the Great War. It lasted until 1922, by which time the officer who had never crossed the portals of Sandhurst had commanded everything from a platoon to a brigade, was highly decorated and already known to Churchill. The second phase, a small part of the folklore background to the fall of Singapore, is a period in which Percival had an unusual four postings at staff colleges and five in staff appointments, in three of which he worked for the future Chief of the Imperial General Staff (CIGS), General Dill; hence the shorthand description "brilliant staff officer and *protégé* of Dill." But it also included his time as Chief of Staff in Malaya 1936–37, at the conclusion of which he produced a prescient appreciation of a possible Japanese offensive. There followed three brief appointments as a major-general, two in command of divisions.[5] What is more significant for his generalship in Malaya than Percival's years as a staff officer and lack of recent operational command in war, is the fact that he was moving from the command of a British division at home, not to the command of a corps, the normal next step, but directly to the command of an army. This was an independent, multi-national, polyglot army at that, in steadily worsening military circumstances, pursuing a wildly inappropriate strategy and in a distant and largely neglected theatre of war. It was a more substantial and demanding elevation in one bound than any other of Churchill's wartime generals ever experienced. In these circumstances lies much of the explanation for his performance and perhaps for his general preference for prudence over risk.

The reputation as the eternal staff officer was reinforced by Percival's appearance and his personal manner. He was tall, angular, raw-boned, somewhat stooped and had protruding front teeth. His manner was low-key and he was a poor public speaker with the suspicion of a lisp. Percival's appearance certainly provided the press, Allied and Japanese, with the opportunity to create some of the most iconic images of the campaign. Long before historians had an opportunity to offer a researched evaluation, Percival was condemned by photography. His lack of a positive presence was of some but, it is suggested, only limited significance for the exercise of his role. In any event it was a personal manner which Churchill and the CIGS knew well and which he could hardly change.[6] Nevertheless, it became part of the Percival folklore. He was, however, unquestionably brave, remarkably fit and active and, by general agreement, very bright, determined and totally unflappable.

Percival operated routinely through the staff of his headquarters and in personal dealings with the other senior figures on the Malayan scene. It was a set of personalities and command circumstances which presented the GOC with considerable difficulties; only with Air Vice-Marshal Pulford and Major-General Keith Simmons were his relations harmonious, positive and fruitful. In the short space of the 70-day campaign, the GOC had three different Cs-in-C, Brooke-

"Condemned by photography:"
Percival arrives in Singapore, May 1941

Popham for the critical first three weeks, Pownall for a few days and Wavell for the remainder.[7] Although Percival got on well with Brooke-Popham, this first chief must carry a major share of responsibility for the disastrous opening of the land campaign and he and his staff the onus for much of the complacency and overconfidence with which the prospect of war in Malaya was gilded in 1941.[8] Pownall's move with Wavell to Java, when the latter became the first Allied Supreme Commander, inevitably put a fresh set of local responsibilities on Percival's shoulders. With Wavell himself, Percival's relations appear to have been formal, distant and soon tense. At the outset, Wavell's underestimation of the Japanese was as great as his overestimate of the capabilities of Percival's troops and the command abilities of Australian Major-General H. Gordon Bennett. At times, Wavell behaved towards his commander in Malaya with what one can perhaps best describe with one of Wavell's own phrases, "the privileged irascibility of the senior officer." His interference with the command structure and dispositions in north Johore was almost wholly deleterious and his contribution to the overall defence quite minimal, as several of the local senior officers confirmed.[9] Sir Shenton Thomas, the Governor and High Commissioner, was a great drag on Percival's military effectiveness and examples of his indecision, obstructiveness, general bureaucratic approach and lack of a sense of urgency abound. Thomas' cavalier approach to security issues before the Japanese offensive began was quite breathtaking. Yet it was Percival who tended to take the blame for not keeping the Governor, the premier colonial servant, up to the mark and he who bore the bulk of the additional workload that was created. Thomas did, however, honourably recognize his duty to remain in post to the bitter end.[10]

Crucial for the conduct of the campaign itself were Percival's relations with the commanders of his mobile formations, Lieutenant-General Sir Lewis Heath commanding III Indian Corps and Gordon Bennett the small Australian Imperial

Force (AIF) Malaya. The appointment of Heath and Percival to their respective positions by Delhi and London created one of the great military mismatches of the war. Expecting Heath, the knighted hero of the Keren, the first British victor of the war, to serve under a younger and junior general without recent operational experience and with none at all of the Indian Army was itself a considerable strain on their relationship. It was intensified by the very different personalities, military background and family circumstances of the two generals and, crucially, by their contrasting ideas of how the campaign should be fought.[11] Percival's relations with Bennett were similarly difficult. Bennett's ambitiousness, his irascibility, his inability to cooperate with fellow commanders made him a particularly difficult and unsuitable subordinate. Percival was to find Bennett's operational technique "very much out of date."[12]

The effectiveness of generals is significantly determined by the performance of their staff. It is from them that they get virtually all their advice and through them that their command functions are routinely exercised. Percival's staff was small—little larger than Dobbie had for the island of Malta—inexperienced, overburdened, in some cases untrained and, given that Malaya was widely regarded as a military backwater, of indifferent quality. War Office policy dictated that vacancies were to be filled locally. In consequence, as Percival wrote later of his staff, "Most of them were just regimental officers brought in for the occasion." Some had been promoted by two ranks to fill gaps in the establishment.[13] Because of problems with rates of pay and allowances, the Indian and Australian Armies were little represented in the headquarters: an understandable cause of friction. All these deficiencies shifted more work onto the shoulders of Percival himself and crucially determined the quality of the advice he was given and his knowledge of what was going on. Much of the criticism which the HQ attracted, and some which was directed at Percival himself, is explained by these factors.[14]

In the short period before the Japanese attack, Percival achieved a great deal. The bitter inter-service differences of the previous regime of Lieutenant-General Bond and Air Vice-Marshal Babington were replaced under Percival and Pulford by the closest professional regard and operational coordination.[15] They established a common operational HQ at Sime Road, a joint intelligence centre and a centralized air defence system of fighters and guns. S. W. Kirby, in some respects Percival's most substantial critic, records that with his arrival "a new spirit entered every sphere of activity, including training" in Malaya Command. A series of sound and valuable directives on training were issued. None at all had existed until December 1940.[16] Yet two particular aspects of the GOC's preparations during the brief months he had before war came have attracted critical comment—the relatively low priority he seemed to attach to training in jungle warfare and to the building of defence works.

The latter charge originated with Brigadier Simson, Percival's Chief Engineer, who made proposals to the GOC in mid-October 1941 for the construction of a comprehensive system of defence works along the length of Malaya's north-south communications, in Johore and on Singapore's northern coastline. Percival rejected these proposals for sound practical reasons: the need for War Office policy and financial approval, the shortage of labour and of the cash to hire it. This is all quite apart from the divergence from the agreed defence plan which the proposal represented. He had already given engineering priority to defence works at airfields, on beaches, at Jitra and elsewhere, and to the building of camps in Malaya as his garrison expanded.[17] However, Percival did agree to Simson summarizing the War Office instructions on anti-tank measures, bundles of which, by a serious oversight by Percival's staff, lay unopened in headquarters until discovered by Simson. The GOC agreed with the summary and authorized Simson to deliver copies personally down to brigade level and to brief commanders and staff appropriately. This prewar authority also specifically encompassed the construction under Simson's arrangements of some 3,500 concrete cylinders, enough for 350 anti-tank blocks for use by the mobile formations, with more already available in Johore. This was a major constituent of Simson's original proposal.[18]

As to preparations for operating in jungle conditions, training notes were issued by Malaya Command and a small personal booklet, *Tactical Notes on Malaya*, was written and issued to units. The training directives were all approved by Percival personally and clearly dealt with Japanese methods of infiltration; but many factors militated against successful training for this aspect of the campaign. Percival had to give a higher priority to basic individual and sub-unit training and the training of junior leaders since each of the Indian Army battalions lost on average 240 experienced officers, NCOs and specialists in India's emergency expansion programme, receiving raw recruits in their stead. Junior leaders were the very people on whom responsibility would fall in close country operations. This could also be combined more readily with the preparation of defences which, in lieu of civilian labour for which the War Office would not pay the going rate, had often to be undertaken by the troops themselves. Nevertheless Percival specified "that wherever possible, training should take place in 'bush conditions'." A further complication to all training was the piecemeal arrival of reinforcements. When Percival took command, only seven of the 15 brigades that took the field against the Japanese were present in Malaya; four of these were recently expanded Indian ones. European scales of transport and equipment were a further impediment to a genuine cross-country capability for the reinforcements. Few of these factors were susceptible to reversal by the GOC Malaya in the space of six months since many had cost implications beyond his control. Little actual jungle fighting took place in the Malayan campaign though the Japanese utilized close country more readily and skilfully than their opponents.[19]

Military intelligence was one area in which Percival was at a signal disadvantage. Although the local Japanese population was relatively small, fewer than 6,000,[20] these people were in charge of 187 major enterprises representing over one-third of Japanese assets outside the Japanese Empire and occupied China and these did not include the many Japanese-run small-time photographic businesses, barbers' shops, brothels and the like serving the general community, including many military units. With their strong national loyalty and racial and cultural homogeneity, these people represented a unique resource for the Japanese military planners. Aided by a few significant British traitors, a limited local fifth-column, and one outstanding intelligence coup,[21] the Japanese knowledge of British military strength, deployment and intentions seems to have been comprehensive.[22] While much has been revealed in recent years about Allied anti-Japanese intelligence successes, particularly in the run-up to the outbreak of the war, none of it has led the present author to doubt Professor Hinsley's conclusion that "there is practically no record of how and to what extent intelligence influenced the individual decisions of the operational commands" in the Far East. Nor does it alter his own view that, once the opening assault on Malaya began, the lack of aircraft and the progressive breakdown of the intelligence system based in Singapore meant that Percival was operating largely "blind" regarding Japanese strengths, tactical intentions and some of their important military capabilities. Percival himself did not regard Far East Combined Bureau, the main Allied intelligence organization, particularly highly. How much of this criticism is more properly attributable to the overriding intelligence assumptions and filtering made by the senior staff of Far East Command, and perhaps of his own headquarters, is unclear. The senior Army member of Far East Combined Bureau certainly believed that the complacent prejudices of the senior staff of Far East Command were causing the Cs-in-C to live in a fool's paradise. Shenton Thomas noted that Percival "never joined in [the] optimistic forecasts" which emanated from the senior military figures in Malaya. What is certain is that as the campaign developed, the GOC generally overestimated the number of Japanese divisions ranged against him and was in constant fear of additional assaults on Malaya's east coast and elsewhere.[23]

In December 1941, Percival's army faced the prospect of Japanese attack with the rough equivalent of 12 brigades. Of these, only two could be considered fully trained, five of his Indian brigades had been "milked" to form new divisions and one of his Malaya brigades was only just forming its second battalion. Much of the field artillery was still arriving only weeks before the Japanese struck. Overall, there was a shortage of several thousand rifles in the Command. Peacetime accounting, as determined by the Treasury, continued until three days after the Japanese landed. The Chiefs of Staff, who charged the Air Force with the primary defence of the naval base, gave Percival the subordinate tasks of defending the naval and air bases, internal security and dealing with "any enemy land forces which might succeed in gaining a footing despite the action of the Air Force." His directive from the C-in-C confirmed this.[24]

It was even stated by the Chiefs of Staff, barely credibly in the light of subsequent events, that once RAF Far East was brought up to full strength, the Army garrison could be reduced. The need to defend the airfields of northern Malaya, none of which was sited with any consideration for its territorial defence, in turn committed Percival to the defensive position of Jitra, the only site available that offered reasonable protection to the northwestern group of airfields. His other dispositions in Malaya were similarly dictated by airfield location, however badly sited these were for defensive purposes. Percival's brigades, supported by some Indian State battalions of very doubtful quality, were consequently scattered about the country, remote from each other and often from their superior HQs. Wireless communication in Malaya was erratic and much reliance was placed on the civilian telephone system; for lack of resources, the military had no direct lines of their own.

Percival would have been aware of the low priority which his Command was allotted in British grand strategy, but probably not quite how low this became after Dill lost his battle with Churchill over the relative priorities of the Middle Eastern and Far Eastern theatres, or how much lower still after Churchill's decision to send reinforcements to the Soviet Union, which forced both Eden and Dill to the point of resignation.[25] Should a Japanese invasion be impending, Brooke-Popham had proposed, and the Chiefs of Staff accepted, a plan for an advance into southern Thailand to their likely landing places in the Singora area, where there were also valuable airfields. The added attraction of such an advance for Percival was the opportunity it presented to catch any invasion force at its most vulnerable, as it debouched from the sea and before it could deploy any armour. He agreed with the feasibility of the C-in-C's plan, providing it consisted only of an operation to take Singora and the Ledge position on the Kroh road to Patani rather than the latter town itself, that he had the necessary advance warning, and given the Far East Command assurance that the Royal Air Force, *at its existing strength* [author's italics], could inflict 40 per cent losses on any Japanese invasion force.[26] Perhaps he shared Brooke-Popham's view that the Japanese in China had never been up against any real opposition when landing from the sea and had never had to tackle opposing fighters when on bombing missions. This advance into Thailand became known as Operation *Matador* and its planning was the subject of a special study by III Indian Corps. Since *Matador* and a defensive battle at Jitra were alternatives, 11th Indian Division, the formation given the task of northern defence, had to be prepared for either. In the circumstances of the time, with Air Force strength due to rise as time went on and no certainty of the imminence of a Japanese attack, *Matador* seemed a reasonable gamble. S. W. Kirby[27] has suggested an alternative strategy for the defence of Malaya and others have

The Malay Peninsula, 1938

accepted at least part of his reasoning, but aside from the benefit of hindsight his plan betrays, it simply was not a strategy available to Percival given his directive from the Chiefs of Staff and his subordination to Brooke-Popham.

In the event, *Matador* was not authorized by Brooke-Popham and its alternative, the defence of the line at Jitra, turned out to be a disastrous reverse for Percival's army and the most significant land action of the campaign in Malaya. The three brigades of 11th Indian Division were roundly defeated by what was little more than a probing attack by the Japanese advance guard, with 6th Indian Brigade reduced to half and 15th Indian Brigade to a quarter of its original strength. According to one of Percival's staff, the division's "losses in arms and equipment were almost fantastic." Although 11th Indian Division had to continue in the line for a further four weeks, it never regained its balance or had its morale fully restored.[28] Almost as disastrous for Army morale and certainly for Percival's ability to conduct a successful campaign were the destruction of Admiral Phillips' Force Z and the irreparable losses suffered by the Royal Air Force in Malaya, in the days before Jitra. The Japanese now had superiority in the air and on the seas around Malaya that gave Yamashita's army a flexibility Percival's was unable to contest.

Percival must shoulder some responsibility for this opening disaster since he accepted the practicability of *Matador* and gave 11th Indian Division the alterative tasks that complicated planning for the divisional commander. Furthermore, in resisting the request for a withdrawal from Jitra when it was first made, he was responsible for some of the confusion of the night withdrawal when he finally sanctioned it. However, it seems quite reasonable for the GOC to have expected a three-brigade division, in a partly prepared position, to resist the attack of two Japanese battalions supported by a few tanks and guns for longer than 15 hours. In fact, the critical responsibilities for the opening disasters of the land campaign lay with commanders above and below Percival. Heath later blamed him for "the appalling failure to come to a timely decision as to the cancellation of *Matador*" which so hamstrung the division between its two objectives. Yet *Matador's* cancellation was the decision of the C-in-C, not Percival. He expected the operation to be launched on 6 December or not at all; he told Brooke-Popham on the 7th that it was no longer feasible. Twice during the morning of 8 December, he asked for permission to despatch Krohcol, the force to block the Patani road, but GHQ would not sanction it and still spoke of *Matador* being a possibility. GHQ quite failed to realize that the advance to the Ledge position was vital to the operation of the whole northwestern defence irrespective of the fate of the larger plan.[29] Heath too was culpable for giving Major-General Murray-Lyon both the difficult task of commanding the three brigades of 11th Indian Division and the separate but vital Ledge operation over 50 miles away. He was tardy and lax in not ensuring that Krohcol was at full strength and ready to make for the Ledge at the earliest moment. Heath also erred in accepting the opinion of junior officers concerning the viability of the Grik road which further by-passed his main defences and in not going forward to see the overtaxed 11th Indian Division commander until the campaign was a week old.[30]

This opening disaster and Percival's refusal to countenance a similar early withdrawal of Brigadier Key's 8th Indian Brigade from Kota Bahru to Kuala Lipis produced the first major disagreements and a souring of relations between the two generals which grew worse as the withdrawal continued. It also began to expose the fundamental strategic disagreement between them. Heath pressed for a major withdrawal of 11th Indian Division south to the Perak River, and then, after the fresh disaster at Gurun, for his whole Corps to be concentrated far to the south in Johore in a defensive position on the line of the main north-south communications. For the GOC, this was the beginning of what he perceived as Heath's "withdrawal complex" according to which he declared, "Unless I issued definite orders as to how long such and such a position was to be held, I should find that it had been evacuated prematurely." This developing mistrust risked situations arising where Percival might reserve to himself withdrawal decisions that should normally be taken by the commander on the spot. There is some evidence from III Indian Corps engineers that units did withdraw over-hastily when obstacles had been created by the sappers which the infantry then left uncovered by fire, allowing Japanese engineers to do their repair work quickly and unmolested.[31]

By contrast, Percival's aim was to hold the Japanese as far north as possible for as long as possible so that the naval base might remain secure, reinforcements might have time to arrive unmolested by the opposing air forces and the raw materials of Malaya, rubber and tin, might continue to be backloaded and exported. This in turn required the airfields in central Malaya, both east and west, to be denied to the Japanese for as long as possible and for air resources to be husbanded for convoy protection and general reconnaissance rather than direct support of the Army. It was a strategy endorsed by the high command in Singapore and subsequently by the Chiefs of Staff. Percival reasoned that he had no option but to retain 9th Indian Division east of the central range for the protection of Kuantan airfield, and the Australians further south in Johore since he feared that the east coast, especially the Mersing area, was a likely Japanese objective. If the Japanese occupied Kuantan unopposed, they would be able to bring their Air Force 150–200 miles nearer to Singapore and the sea lanes than their newly-acquired bases at Butterworth and Gong Kedah permitted. This was a perfectly rational strategy at the time it was first enunciated in mid-December, when the northern front seemed to have been stabilized to the degree that Percival risked a seaborne attack on Japanese communications and called for some offensive action by the small Perak flotilla. However, it came at the price of calling for Heath to fight delaying actions with an already reduced and shaken division against a still small but tank-armed Japanese force. Its danger lay in exposing Percival's dispersed forces to piecemeal mauling, so that when they could be united further south with his reinforcements for a decisive battle, they might be too debilitated for the task. But without such a strategy, the risk was that the reinforcements might never get through. Defences were to be organized in-depth along the main lines of the Japanese advance, taking, Percival directed, "special regard to tank obstacles and cover from the air" in selecting defensive locations, but avoiding "sitting in prepared positions and letting [the enemy] walk around us."

From Kuala Kangsar southwards, the Japanese no longer had the option of easily turning 11th Indian Division's defences on the landward side. There was consequently the prospect of a more protracted defence. Brigadier Simson later recorded that during a visit to III Indian Corps, he discussed with General Heath a plan to construct defence works at positions along Heath's line of withdrawal onto which his troops could fall back, culminating in more extensive works in Johore. Simson put this proposal to Percival, together with a repetition of his own for the construction of defences along Singapore's northern coastline, late on the night of 26 December. He claimed that despite protracted argument, Percival rejected both proposals, on no other grounds than that "rearward defences are bad for morale—for both troops and civilians."[32] This supposed sentence of Percival's later became a mantra for his critics, though it is difficult to believe that his justification was not more lengthy and complex.

Percival's judgement has to be seen in context. At the time of this meeting, 11th Indian Division had only just crossed the Perak River; it was still 250 miles from Johore and 350 from Singapore itself. It had yet to mount a defence of the very strong position at Kampar where Percival hoped to make a protracted stand. With morale already fragile after the early disasters to all three services, what message would have been sent to troops and civilians alike if the engineer resources of the operational divisions, already heavily engaged and reduced by casualties as the record makes clear, were now invested in preparing defensive positions so far south of them and even on the island itself?[33] In fact, he by no means rejected the proposal entirely, as Simson implies. Within days of their meeting, he ordered north one of the fortress companies of engineers to help the Australians prepare defences in Johore, and also initiated a more limited scheme for 11th Indian Division than the one his Chief Engineer proposed, but restricted to the construction of anti-tank defences, without diverting the uniformed engineers and indeed without Simson's involvement.[34] It seems that Percival saw that the only practicable scheme was one which relied more on civilian assistance than on his already overtaxed corps and divisional sappers whose operational priorities Simson seemed to be attempting to determine.[35] This was, nevertheless, a snub to Simson to whom Percival, normally the most mild-mannered of men, seemed to have developed some antipathy after the late-night harangue.[36]

As for the proposal to construct defences on the north shore of Singapore itself, these would have done nothing to protect the operation of the naval base which was bound to be menaced by artillery fire and aircraft bombing if the mainland were lost. Their only role would have been that of denying the base and the island itself to the Japanese. Matters had yet to reach the point at which this would have a higher priority than the range of denial and demolition tasks— including some which were technically an Air Force responsibility—to which Percival's engineers were fully committed. All available engineer units and materials from the south were already being sent north in an endeavour to help hold the Japanese in Perak and subsequently in Johore. As Kirby confirms, "Any attempt to build fortifications on the northern side of the island would have been futile before the 8th January" when the force fell back to Johore. Nevertheless, preliminary defence work on the island had been in progress since early December.[37]

After the engagements at Kampar and Telok Anson, Percival planned a phased withdrawal down the west coast, communications timed to ensure that the airfields at Kuala Lumpur and Port Swettenham were not surrendered until his expected reinforcements arrived. However, the attempt at a defensive stand in the Trolak area proved not only unavailing but the second major disaster of the land campaign. The battle of Slim River, as the Trolak engagement became known, was a rout which effectively destroyed 11th Indian Division as a fighting force. The defeat of this formation, it can be said with hindsight, gravely imperilled the chances of a prolonged defence when Percival, augmented by reinforcements, decided to make a firm stand further south in Malaya. It also induced Wavell to impulsive and unwise intervention. The question is whether, at the time, Percival should have anticipated that there was a disaster in the making and taken a gamble with his forces on the east coast to strengthen those in the west. The troops of 11th Indian Division were indeed very tired, but the newly-promoted Major-General Paris and Brigadier Stewart, both with long experience in Malaya, were now in charge in the Trolak sector. The opportunity was taken for the position to be fully reconnoitred, anti-tank obstacles, mines and artillery deployed, and the position defended in-depth. There was at least a reasonable prospect of a successful delaying action there. However, basic mistakes by these local commanders in deploying units, guns and defences played an important part in the débacle.[38] So did the speed and resourcefulness of the Japanese commanders and their engineers, whilst the attacks of their Air Force denied sleep to the weary defenders and impeded their preparations. In his postwar comments, Heath, who would have preferred the able Brigadier Key as the new commander of 11th Indian Division, blamed Percival for agreeing to Stewart's dispositions, in particular the outpost line which he placed forward of the main position at Trolak. In fact, the outpost battalion initially fought well, forcing the Japanese infantry commander to await the arrival of his tanks before he pressed on and giving warning of the tanks' arrival.[39]

If Percival had allowed Heath to concentrate his whole Corps west of the central range, either deployed in-depth with 11th Indian Division or with 9th Indian Division used for a counter-attack as Heath proposed, it is quite possible the disaster of the Slim River battle might have been averted or its consequences mitigated. But Percival's concern was that most of the east coast of Malaya "might have been made for an invading force to land upon." In particular, if 22nd Indian Brigade had given up the defence of Kuantan early—the air forces first abandoned it on 10 December—there is no knowing how the availability of its airfield might have affected the development of overall Japanese strategy for, with clear air superiority and command of the local seas, Yamashita always had the initiative. In the event, the brigade was withdrawn on 3 January after a hard action with the advancing Japanese. Percival wanted it to hold the airfield until 13 January so that 53rd Brigade might arrive safely from India, but the increasingly critical situation in the west meant that he could not risk its destruction at Kuantan. Nevertheless, it was partly doubts about his degree of air superiority, which the earlier possession of Kuantan would certainly have enhanced, that later deterred Count Terauchi, the Commander of Southern Army, from landing the remaining two regiments of the 18th Division at Endau. Instead, they had to make the time-consuming journey from Singora, 400 miles to the north, and in vehicles borrowed from the other divisions, before they could make an impression on the campaign. An early substantial landing at Endau, with air cover from Kuantan, might have considerably altered the complexion of the campaign. Throughout their offensive, the Japanese showed an admirable keenness to exploit airfields at the earliest opportunity.[40] Furthermore, the defence in the west was already being complicated by the Japanese amphibious hooks along the coast that threatened to bypass the main defended localities. Nevertheless, it was British tactical errors and Japanese resolution, opportunism and close air support, rather than any shortage of manpower among the defenders, that undid the three brigades at Slim River. They were opposed, after all, only by a motorized infantry battalion and a tank regiment.

Prior to the Slim River defeat and the withdrawal of 9th Indian Division from east of the central range, Percival had already conferred with his formation commanders about the next phase of the campaign. He decided not to fight for the three small states of Selangor, Negri Sembilan and Malacca where the good road communications would have presented a decisive advantage to the tank-armed Japanese. Instead, he determined on a major last-ditch defence of the mainland of Malaya in north Johore where he planned that Muar–Segamat–Mersing would form the main line of resistance. Bennett, who had little regard for the fighting qualities of Heath and his Indian Corps, suggested that his Australian division should now change places with III Indian Corps and take over the main western defence. Although Bennett had long been studying the problem of defending Johore, Percival rejected his proposal as too complicated administratively, preferring to divide Johore vertically with Heath commanding western Johore with the still-unbroken 9th Indian Division, the reduced and exhausted 11th and reinforcements soon to arrive from India, leaving Bennett to defend the east with his 8th Australian Division. This plan allowed each force to deploy in-depth and fall back, if necessary, on its own communications. Percival had already begun backloading the huge quantities of stores and reserves at Kuala Lumpur, having ordered Heath to deny the airfield there and at Port Swettenham until 14 January. These timings and arrangements were thrown entirely awry by the speed and completeness of the Slim River defeat and the arrival of Percival's new C-in-C, General Wavell, on his first visit.[41] Wavell went forward to see Heath and the defeated commanders in 11th Indian Division and then, with only a day's acquaintance with the local situation and without any discussion with the GOC Malaya, peremptorily issued his own plans for the defence of Johore.[42]

The fight for Johore began a decisive phase in the battle for Malaya and Singapore, one which held the prospect of an end to the demoralizing withdrawals. Percival's forces were at last concentrated, the threat to the east coast, while in no way diminished, was at least now reduced to a single predictable area with which communications were good. Furthermore, land and air reinforcements, for whose safe arrival so much had been sacrificed and from which so much was expected, were now in play. In place of the advice and encouragement Percival would have welcomed from Wavell in such a situation, few actions could have been better calculated to diminish his authority and complicate what turned out to be a difficult tactical situation than Wavell's arbitrary decision to divide the north Johore battlefield not vertically but horizontally and to put Bennett in command of Westforce on the basis of the briefest acquaintance. The Australian and his small divisional headquarters soon found themselves trying to manage the operations of four brigades, one from his own division which now joined Westforce and three others with which he and his staff were entirely unfamiliar, disposed over such an area that communications, and therefore command, were very difficult. Heath and his headquarters were relegated to the rear area in south Johore and command of the battered 11th Indian Division—now, at Heath's request, commanded by Major-General Key—in the west and 22nd Australian Brigade on the east coast. Percival's published accounts record this intervention by Wavell without comment, but clearly it produced not only faulty dispositions and command arrangements which he soon had to change, but also a great deal of additional work for the army commander. "I am convinced that the formation of Westforce was a bad error," Kirby later declared to Percival, "things would have been much better if your plan...had been followed."[43] Because of yet another amphibious hook by the Japanese behind the Westforce line, Heath was soon involved in active operations again. With Bennett's forces spread widely and with the two commanders not on good terms, Percival found it necessary to coordinate their activities himself. "Had this not been done, we would have lost the Segamat Force as well as the Muar Force," he wrote later. His failing faith in Bennett as a commander was surely a further reason for his close control.[44]

Percival's command of the Johore operations is open to several challenges. The first is that he ignored Wavell's instruction that the soon-expected 53rd Brigade should replace the Australian brigade covering Mersing as soon as possible. This would have allowed the Australian division to fight as a single unit in the west and 9th Indian Division to be employed in the rear of the Westforce position. Percival maintained that he had no "record or recollection" of any such instruction, though it had always been his intention to reunite the Australian brigades when a suitable replacement became available, but "the swift march of events on the west coast eventually made this [transfer] impossible." The need for speed dictated the despatch of 53rd Brigade direct rather than its move to Mersing to release the Australians. Neither he nor Wavell wished to take too great a risk with the Mersing area.

The second major criticism is that Percival left the decision for two subsequent withdrawals until too late: the first, which effectively sealed the fate of 45th Indian Brigade south of Muar; the second which saw 15th Indian Brigade similarly cut off and scattered south of Batu Pahat.[45] Percival attempted to hold onto the Muar position, despite the Japanese success in breaking through 45th Indian Brigade's extended positions, because he did not want to force an early withdrawal of the remainder of Westforce and mindful of Wavell's injunction that "the battle is to be fought out in Johore without thought of retreat." Having reinforced Westforce and its rear with more than four battalions there seemed a good prospect of the position being held. Only later did Percival discover that the best part of the Imperial Guards Division was committed to the attack in the coastal area, while the failures in communication and the tactical difficulties of 53rd Brigade were not factors he could reasonably have anticipated. As to the Batu Pahat position, both Percival and Heath regarded its retention as vital. Its loss would have uncovered the lateral road to the east coast and with it the rest of Percival's line, besides an airfield within 60 miles of Singapore and the line of observer posts that gave the minimum warning to Singapore of air attack. For these reasons, Brigadier Challen's repeated requests to withdraw were turned down. Finally, when on 25 January, Percival did agree the brigadier might pull back, the coast road behind him had been cut and the relieving brigade was unable to get through despite repeated attempts.

That these were misjudgements by Percival should not obscure the fact that a fighting withdrawal is the most difficult operation of war in which movement timings are critical but difficult to judge. Moreover, if the Johore positions fell, a retreat to Singapore was inevitable, and Percival was operating under Wavell's specific instructions to hold the line there. Indeed, the C-in-C later applauded the extended resistance on the west coast front. During the Johore fighting, Percival was operating under the most intense pressure. Motoring daily to the battle zone after early morning discussions and instructions for his staff in Singapore, conferring with his commanders and attempting to coordinate their operations, visiting some of the formations and then completing the 160-mile round trip to Singapore for further meetings with staff, discussions with the civil authorities and then, an additional chore which the new command situation enjoined, drafting personal reports to Wavell—all this proved a great burden. The strain of the 18-hour day, which was seldom lightened by successes on the battlefield, was immense. It is not surprising that this period did not see Percival at his most incisive or that amid the complex and confused fighting, misunderstandings should have occurred.

The defeats in Johore and the withdrawal of the army to Singapore, rather than the surrender of the island itself, represented the final failure of the "Singapore strategy." The naval base, soon defenceless against Yamashita's guns and vulnerable to air attack from all the Japanese air bases on the mainland, no longer had any positive value to the Allied cause. Percival was faced with the quite different task of denying its use to the enemy's warships and tying down Yamashita's divisions for as long a siege as possible. Whilst the public at large, many of the troops in Malaya and notably Prime Minister Churchill, might have considered Singapore a self-contained fortress and its close defence a natural objective, Percival, Wavell, the Chiefs of Staff and indeed the Japanese, all knew that it was not. The naval base's only satisfactory northern defences had lain in mainland Malaya. Major-General Kennedy, the Director of Military Operations in the War Office, later recorded "Our view, however, was that the 'last ditch' would have to be on the mainland in Johore, and not on Singapore Island. The island had never been considered defensible from close attack." Wavell's report from India was later to note that in earlier planning "the provision of elaborate defences all round Singapore Island could only be regarded as insurance against an unlikely and hazardous enterprise." Heath's judgement was that a full denial scheme for the island would have required "three years intensive labour and expenditure exceeding the cost of a battleship." Churchill's memorable surprise at the situation, "The possibility of Singapore having no landward defences no more entered my mind than that of a battleship being launched without a bottom," was no doubt what drew from Percival the private postwar comment, "I am afraid the Prime Minister's writings display his complete ignorance of the way the Singapore defences were developed and of the defensive principles which governed them."[46] But defence of the island itself was now the aim. Those in a position to know, including the current and the previous CIGS, did not believe it would be held for very long. Kennedy expressed the view of the War Office *cognoscenti* when he wrote, "We regarded it as almost certain, once the Japanese were established in Northern Malaya, that Singapore was doomed."[47]

On 23 December, following a staff study, Percival ordered Fortress Commander Keith Simmons to arrange a reconnaissance of the north shore of Singapore to select appropriate defensive positions. Early in January, his despatch records, he gave orders for the construction of the northern defences "at once as an urgent measure." Falk has noted that this sounds slightly implausible, coming so soon after his rejection of Simson's proposal; but events had moved on, even over this short period. At the conference on 5 January to plan the defence of north Johore, Percival also issued instructions to Simmons to pay particular attention to the defence of the island's west coast, so his concern was evident at this stage. Percival's claim seems no more improbable than Wavell's in his own despatch that on 9 January he was shocked to see that no northern defences existed and immediately ordered their construction, for two weeks later he was writing guardedly to Percival that "Your preparations [of defences] must, of course, be kept entirely secret," so conscious was he of the need to fight out the battle in Johore without the troops being "allowed to look over their shoulders" to Singapore. If preparations were to be kept entirely secret, Percival later commented, not very much could actually be done on the ground. It seems that Wavell's reservation as to morale was one which Percival shared. There may be an element of hindsight in the wording of both despatches.[48]

By the time both commanders acted on the matter of the north coast defences, the means to develop them rapidly were dwindling fast. As the bombing intensified in January, it became more difficult to engage and retain civilian labour for any projects, while engineers to supplement and supervise it were also in short supply, many having been sent north to the battle area. Percival had also agreed that labour priority should go to airfield repair and airstrip construction for the arriving *Hurricanes*. Against Percival's wishes, Brigadier Simson, long the advocate of Singapore defences, had been appointed Director General of Civil Defence and thereafter could devote only a fraction of his time to his military duties, most of which fell to his Deputy, Colonel Urquart, whose postwar report made it clear that Simson's new organization was able to supply him with less than a quarter of the labour he demanded. It seems that little progress was made until late January, when reinforcements from India and Australia were assigned to this work, with much undertaken later by the defending units themselves. Percival believed that the northern and western shores of the island were too intersected with creeks and mangroves for any recognized form of beach defence and ordered the plan to be based upon small defended localities covering all known approaches from the coast. Although much was achieved, the retreating troops from Malaya were nevertheless shocked to discover that the vaunted fortress of Singapore was nothing of the kind when they finally withdrew to it. Thus, backed by Churchill's expressions of surprise, another element in the legend of the fall of the island was created.[49]

Percival's force for the defence of the island was at least three times as large as the 30,000 men Yamashita had for his assault, but this "bayonet count" is grossly misleading. Yamashita's 30,000 were his combat troops; his 50,000[50] combat support and L of C troops stretched back along his invulnerable lines of communication into Indochina. All of Percival's support troops were now part of the Singapore garrison, although some were without, and others had never fired, their personal weapons. The figure also included a large number of non-combatant medical units.[51] A significant proportion consisted of the reinforcements—18th Division, 44th and 45th Indian Brigades, 3,000 individual Indian reinforcements and almost 2,000 Australian reinforcements—of whom much had been expected. They added greatly to Percival's numerical strength but, given their state of training, much less to his fighting effectiveness.[52]

The odds against a protracted defence were indeed overwhelming. The Japanese had complete air and naval supremacy and almost complete freedom of action. The morale of the Imperial Japanese Army was high after its repeated successes. It soon assembled in Johore the landing craft including, to the defenders' surprise, the tank landing craft, needed for the crossing. Two of Yamashita's three divisions had considerable experience of landing operations. In Percival's army, morale had been battered by the initial rapid defeat of the naval and air forces, by the continual withdrawals and by the absence, for most of the brief campaign, of any air support or any tanks. Most serious were the casualties among senior officers, especially battalion commanders and particularly those of Indian units, where loyalty and discipline had been under strain from Slim River onwards. There had already been significant desertions. Even among the Australians, who exhibited fine fighting qualities in the Johore battles, there was dissension among the senior officers and indiscipline in the ranks.[53] The eagerly-awaited *Hurricanes* were confidently expected to sweep the Japanese opposition from the skies, but they were many too few for the task, inferior in manoeuvrability to their opponents and their crews quite unaccustomed to local conditions.[54]

Percival's despatch and his book *The War in Malaya* both declare that he anticipated an attack in the northwest of the island, but it is clear that, at the time it came, he was expecting the assault on the northeast and concentrated his greatest strength there. He later confessed that these statements were incorrect and dictated by hindsight.[55] His final dispositions were also against the advice Wavell gave during his visit on 20 January, that 18th Division should be positioned in the area most likely to be attacked by the Japanese. Wavell considered that this would be the northwest, and that the Australian Division should be deployed in the next most dangerous sector, the northeast. But the C-in-C's opinion, like Percival's own at that stage, was no more than a preliminary judgement which neither commander was able to back with strong intelligence. "With no air reconnaissance and very little other intelligence, it was difficult to know which [area] would be selected," wrote Percival later. Both commanders' early views reckoned without the disasters that overtook the army in south Johore and forced the GOC to combine his weakened Indian divisions, which the 18th Division then supported on the east coast. Force of circumstance seemed to play as much a part as deliberate planning. "We were living so much from day to day at that time that one just had to make the best of what happened to be available," confessed Percival. Wavell later agreed with the final dispositions and confirmed his agreement in writing. The most valid criticism of Percival on this issue is not that he backed his own hunch rather than Wavell's, but that he should have clearly backed either without firm intelligence. If both fronts were equally liable to attack, as they plainly were, they should have been equally strongly defended.[56]

Percival was surely correct in believing the coast itself had to be strongly held and the Japanese prevented from landing in any strength and quickly counterattacked if they did get ashore. The close country of Singapore and the proximity of the supply depots to likely landing areas effectively made the choice for him. Yet for his ready counter-attack force, Percival had only the weak 12th Indian Brigade of his Command Reserve and Heath's Corps Reserve of the equally weak 15th Indian Brigade. The disparity in strength between the threatened fronts in Heath's Northern and Bennett's Western Area was considerable, with a similar imbalance within Western Area itself between the front of Taylor's 22nd Australian Brigade and Maxwell's 27th. The fear of additional attacks, especially from the Anambas Islands, where a Japanese convoy was concentrating, never seems to have left Percival, who mistrusted the intelligence warnings that the convoy was not destined for Singapore but Sumatra.[57] At times, he believed that Yamashita had as many as five divisions in reserve. He kept three brigades on the well-fortified south coast in case other assaults were directed there. Two of them were probably inadequately trained for mobile operations, but the third, 2nd Malaya Brigade, was a valuable force containing two regular British units, one a machine-gun battalion. It would have been an admirable addition to Bennett's front, perhaps taking the vital Kranji/Jurong sector and allowing the Australian brigades to concentrate further west. It is nevertheless the case that Wavell agreed with the dispositions along the south coast, even though the specific point of moving them to the north was raised with him by the Chiefs of Staff.[58]

When the Japanese made their assault in strength on the 22nd Australian Brigade's front, almost inevitably they were able to infiltrate between the company locations. Percival had to counter-attack this initial assault quickly; once it became a secure and expanded lodgement, the fate of his army was sealed whatever threats might develop elsewhere. But he allocated his reinforcements piecemeal and with the same prudence as had been so necessary on the mainland. First, his Command Reserve and then Heath's were put under Bennett's command; later he allocated the three-battalion "Tomforce"—all drawn from different brigades—to the fight in the west and followed this with two single battalions, and finally the three-battalion "Masseyforce." His failure to organize a larger, concerted counter-attack more quickly and his piecemeal employment of the largely fresh, if ill-prepared, units of 18th Division to support different localities drew subsequent criticism even from his own staff. A counter-attack was certainly required, but it is doubtful whether this unfortunate division would have been able to move and act with the necessary speed and resolution. *In extremis* as Percival now was, perhaps it should have been given the chance.[59] When the Japanese paused to regroup as the reinforced Westforce began to consolidate along the Jurong-Kranji "switch line," Percival issued his "secret and personal" instruction defining the final perimeter to which the army would retire should the Japanese eventually break through along the threatened Bukit Timah Road. This was a necessary instruction but its wording was insufficiently precise for the impulsive Bennett, who immediately passed it to his subordinate commanders with disastrous results.[60]

The crucial battle for Singapore was under the control of the least able and least reliable of Percival's divisional commanders. Bennett's headquarters was, as usual, far back from his brigades and since he seldom visited his subordinate commanders, he was increasingly out of touch. He ignored earlier instructions to develop the defences of the Jurong "switch line" and failed to send patrols across the Straits until the final night before the Japanese attack. By the morning of 11 February, Bennett had under his command not only his own two Australian brigades and the 44th Indian Brigade, but also three other brigade-sized groups, an independent battalion and two companies of the Chinese-manned Dalforce. It was not a force the Australian, out of touch with events at the front and increasingly incapable of cool decision-making, could properly manage. The counter-attack he was charged with organizing failed as the Japanese made their next moves. The Jurong "switch line" was uncovered prematurely, partly as a result of Bennett's dissemination of the final perimeter instruction. This precipitated the withdrawal of the army to its final perimeter after which surrender was inevitable and unlikely to be long delayed.

In blaming Bennett for much of the failure of Westforce, one is at the same time exposing Percival's most serious failing as a general—a lack of ruthlessness. There was sufficient evidence of Bennett's limitations as a commander for Percival to have considered his replacement before operations even began. General Sturdee, the Australian Chief of Staff, gave him the opportunity during his visit in autumn 1941, but Percival declined it. Other generals who have shared Percival's low-key personal manner have nevertheless had the required unsparing inner core of severity. Percival also found that "a serious handicap [was] imposed on the campaign by Heath's attitude" concerning the official strategy and by what Percival regarded as his withdrawal complex. If the GOC lost confidence in his Corps Commander to this extent, the only solution was to ask for his removal. This would have been a difficult issue in view of Heath's seniority, experience and ability, but it should have been faced. Percival would have had more confidence in Barstow as Commander of the Indian Corps, just as in Callaghan, Bennett's artillery commander, commanding the Australians. Brigadier Maxwell, whose actions were later instrumental in allowing the Imperial Guards Division to gain a firm footing on the island, should certainly have been sacked for dereliction. Percival chose to attempt to manage his difficult subordinates rather than have more compliant ones appointed. A similar lack of "steel" in Percival underlay the failure to follow through major orders and ensure they were obeyed to the letter. But he was accustomed to operating within a military culture and staff system of subordination, loyalty and obedience that plainly did not apply throughout his multi-national force.[61] Equally, his caution should have been left behind in Malaya; it had no place in Singapore once the Japanese were establishing their foothold.

It may be that a more dynamic commander than Percival, one with Wavell's recommended "streak of the impresario," could have done more to rally the troops for the final defence once they were confined to the island and the GOC was more visible to all. But soldiers' morale is sustained more effectively by the experience and expectation of victory and by confidence that they have the weapons to secure it, than by anything else.[62] Malaya Command had suffered almost two months of unrelieved defeat and withdrawal and there was little to suggest that a turnaround was in the offing, despite Percival's public announcement that help would assuredly come. The reinforcements proved unavailing, the *Hurricanes* failed to turn the scales of the air battle and there was no answer to the intensity of the Japanese bombing which was producing hundreds of casualties daily from January onwards among civilians alone.[63] The Royal Navy's evacuation of the naval base—without reference to Percival or their nearby formation—the security of which had provided the central rationale of the campaign, and the Royal Air Force's final quitting of its battered airfields, already suggested that the defence of the island was a lost cause; Percival's 1 February instruction on the operation of the scorched earth policy for the island merely confirmed it. It was one thing to surmount the practical difficulties of operating the denial policy whilst trying to fight a battle, quite another to counter its implications for morale when the army was holding its final defences, as Percival attempted to explain to the Chiefs of Staff. When he at last agreed to the firing of the military and civilian petrol and oil stocks for which Admiral Spooner had been pressing for days, it was clear that Singapore was doomed. Without much of the military wherewithal for continued resistance, with water and petrol about to run out, none of Percival's generals disputed his decision to surrender.[64]

Another GOC, still operating within the constraints of Percival's directives, might well have fought a different campaign. He, perhaps, might have avoided the confusion of late withdrawals, holding the Japanese longer at Trolak, saving the brigades lost at Muar and Batu Pahat and launching a more effective counterattack on the island itself, but he would not have saved Malaya and Singapore. For their loss, Kirby argues, "The blame must be placed squarely on the shoulders of successive British governments whose decisions from 1919 to 1941 built up a chain which inevitably led to disaster."[65] It is not a verdict many would dispute. Furthermore, Terauchi and Yamashita were quite capable of modifying their strategy to take account of the moves of their opponent, as they were ready to do if *Matador* had been operated, as they did at Endau and in their assault on the island itself and as no doubt they would have done if Kirby's "alternative strategy" or any of its variants had been attempted. They had the ideal combination of flexible military instruments to permit this. No alternative GOC, however capable, could have made good the absence of an air force and a navy, the dearth of tanks, the lack of training for his army or indeed the total unreality of the "Singapore strategy" which created the circumstances the Malayan campaign imposed upon Percival. "If we had had our best general out there it would have made no difference," wrote Ian Jacob, one of Churchill's inner circle, knowing how rapidly the Far East had been pushed from second place to fourth in British strategic priorities. Percival's performance in the brief campaign was far from perfect, but it is difficult to dissent from his own simple verdict, delivered in response to a Japanese reporter when he was a prisoner in Changi: "I lost because I never had a chance." It is perhaps carping to wish that he might have managed to do so a little more slowly.

Major-General Clifford Kinvig is a graduate of Durham and London Universities and was Director of Education in the British Army. He is the author of several publications on the war against Japan including Scapegoat: General Percival of Singapore, *and* River Kwai Railway. *He is presently researching a study of the British Intervention in Russia 1918–1920 and a further book on British involvement in the war with Japan.*

NOTES—

1. J. Charmley, *Duff Cooper*, London, 1986, 63. Churchill promised an inquiry once the war had ended but one was never held.
2. "No one gave me a hint before the invasion that we were in danger of defeat," wrote the Governor, Sir Shenton Thomas, after the war. Whilst battlefield realities quickly altered Malayan perceptions, they were slow to change those in London. When the Japanese campaign was half completed, Thomas complained that the BBC broadcasts were still "so complacent and misleading" they were jeered at by Singaporeans who were choosing instead "to listen to Tokyo." Rhodes House Library, Thomas Papers, Box 2 File 5; PRO, CO967/79, Thomas to Secretary of State for the Colonies, 26 January 1941.
3. This was something of an exaggerated perception the official histories tended to reinforce. Figures for the Japanese are still disputed. For more realistic assessments see S. Falk, *Seventy Days to Singapore*, London, 1975, 271; P. Elphick, *Pregnable Fortress*, London, 1995, 185–187 and A. Warren, *Singapore: Britain's Greatest Defeat*, Sydney, 2002, app. 2.
4. Churchill, 23 April 1942, recorded in C. Eade, *War Speeches of Winston Churchill*, Vol. 2, London, 1952, 242. This was the speech in which Churchill argued against an inquiry into the fall of Singapore, whilst giving his own brief and tendentious account of the disaster.
5. At the end of Percival's first tour in Malaya, the GOC General Dobbie wrote of his work being "of the highest order" and the improvement in the local defence organization "largely a result of his efforts." Confidential Report for 1937, MS (CR) P8785, Ministry of Defence, London. For the detail of Percival's career, see C. Kinvig, *Scapegoat: General Percival of Singapore*, London, 1996.
6. Dill had once written of him, "He has not altogether an impressive presence and one may therefore fail on first meeting to appreciate his sterling worth." Confidential Report for 1938.
7. Air Chief Marshal Sir Robert Brooke-Popham; Lt.-Gen. Sir Henry Pownall; General Sir Archibald Wavell. This embarrassingly rapid change of senior commanders was later cited as one of the reasons why the JPS in London recommended against having an official inquiry into the fall of Singapore: PRO, CAB119/208.
8. Examples are: Brooke-Popham's optimistic interpretation of the intelligence with which the FECB and London were supplying him; his Chief of Staff Maj.-Gen. Playfair's lecture on the impossibility of a Japanese invasion of Malaya during the northeast monsoon; the C-in-C's inexplicable conclusion to the same effect at the September Imperial Conference; the conviction of Brooke-Popham's chief planners of the superiority of the Allied air forces and their ability to seriously damage any Japanese invasion fleet. The staff of the C-in-C were also said to interfere overmuch in the affairs of Malaya Command. Ong C. C., *Matador*, 214–33; IWM, Grey Papers, Capt. Grey, Fall of Singapore etc.; PRO, CAB101/150, Percival to official historians; CAB101/149, Simson to official historians; LHCMA, Brooke-Popham Papers, V/8; IWM, Heath Papers, Heath Lecture on the Malayan Campaign; IWM, Maj.-Gen. Grimsdale, Thunder in the East, 12.

9   The senior staff officer of the 8th Australian Division, Col. Thyer, considered that Wavell's contribution to the campaign was "negligible"; Maj.-Gen. Key's view was that he "hardly uttered and was uninspiring." Wavell's exhortatory message of 10 February 1942 was bitterly resented. Quoted in J. Smyth, *Percival and the Tragedy of Singapore*, London, 1971, 263–64.
10 PRO, CAB101/150, Percival to official historians, 3 November 1954. Colonel Grimsdale of the FECB gives many examples of the Governor's laxity over security and notes that from spring 1941, FECB took the unusual step of ceasing to pass him sensitive material. Years earlier, Dobbie had had similar difficulties with Thomas. "That man [the Governor] will break my heart" was Percival's vivid recollection of Dobbie's exasperation in 1937.
11 Against Percival's four postings to staff colleges, Heath turned down the opportunity to attend even one. Percival had not married until forty and his family remained in England. Heath, a widower, had just remarried and his new young wife, soon pregnant, remained in the theatre with him throughout the campaign. PRO, CAB101/150, Percival to official historians, 9 January 1954.
12 Thyer to Smyth, 11 May 1970 quoted in J. Smyth, *Percival and the Tragedy of Singapore*, 255; PRO, CAB106/162, Thyer and Kappe Report on operations of 8th Australian Division in Malaya; CAB101/150, Percival to official historians, 9 January 1954. When Bennett produced his report on the campaign, the Governor General of Australia took the unusual step of getting the British High Commissioner to write to Attlee, cautioning him not to take much notice of it and remarking on Bennett's "doubtful reputation for reliability" and "unsavoury reputation as a Sydney businessman." PRO, WO141/98, Sir Ronald Cross to Attlee 23 March 1942 and December 1942.
13 All his general staff officers at lieutenant-colonel rank or above were promoted by at least one rank—one of them by two.
14 *Army List 1942*; *Operations of Malaya Command 8 December 1941–15 February 1942*, London Gazette Supplement 38215 dated 20 February 1948 (Percival's Despatch), Section V; A. E. Percival, *The War in Malaya*, London, 1949, 31–32; PRO, CAB101/150, Percival to official historians. One experienced Australian staff officer commented, "Malaya Command staff comprised some cream, and then it went straight to skimmed milk," CAB106/151.
15 According to Maj.-Gen. Playfair, Chief of Staff to Brooke-Popham, this dispute led to such "personal animosity and open abuse" that it became "a common topic among civilians." See Playfair, Some Personal Reflections on the Malayan Campaign, PRO, WO106/2620. A disappointingly thin memoir from a future official historian. Percival had been given "special instructions to smooth out difficulties which had arisen," CAB106/45; A. E. Percival, *The War in Malaya*, 31.
16 S. W. Kirby, *Singapore: The Chain of Disaster*, London, 1971, 95; IWM, Percival Papers, P49, Ashmore, Some Personal Observations of the Malayan Campaign 1940–42.
17 "To have gone for all that Simson wanted would, I am sure, have been impossible," concluded the official historian in 1954, "I do not feel that Percival is open to criticism on this matter." PRO, CAB101/149.

18   PRO, CAB101/149, official historians correspondence with Brig. Simson; I. Simson, *Singapore : Too Little, Too Late*, London, 1971, ch. 5; A. E. Percival, *The War in Malaya*, 183–84; Ashmore. Kirby's judgement of Simson's evidence concerning defence works resulted in only a brief mention in his official history, *The War Against Japan*, Vol. 1, London, 1957, 235. More extended coverage, based apparently on the same evidence, is in S. W. Kirby, *Singapore*, 116–18.

19   T. H. Wade, *Prisoner of the Japanese*, Kenthurst, NSW, 1994, ch. 5; A. E. Percival, *The War in Malaya*, ch. 5; IWM, Sound Records, Maj.-Gen. B. W. Key, 6170–06; Ashmore.

20   It was nevertheless significant in relation to the European civilian male population, which numbered only 9,000.

21   This was the *Automedon* affair, which put into Japanese hands an important Cabinet-level appreciation of Far Eastern military policy as at August 1940.

22   H. Kobayashi, "The Post-War Treatment of Overseas Japanese Nationals," in P. Towle et al., *Japanese Prisoners of War*, London, 2000, 165; P. Elphick, *Far Eastern File*, London, 1997, chs. 10, 11 and 17; M. Smith, *The Emperor's Codes*, London, 2001, 94, 101–02. Lieutenant-General Sugita, the senior intelligence officer on Yamashita's staff, claimed that the Japanese had been "not particularly well informed about Singapore" and "very poorly informed" about Johore State. Surely an intelligence officer's response which much Allied evidence seems to contradict: PRO, CAB106/180. P. Elphick, *Singapore*, chs. 4 and 7, *Far Eastern File*, especially chs. 14 and 17 and *Odd Man Out*, passim; A. E. Percival, *The War in Malaya*, ch. 6.

23   F. H. Hinsley, *British Intelligence in the Second World War*, Vol. 1, London, 1979, ix–x; J. Connell, *Wavell: Supreme Commander*, London, 1969, 60; Percival, *Despatch*, Section 8; Ashmore, 11; IWM, Maj.-Gen. Key, Sound Record 6170–06; Thomas' comments on Percival's *Despatch*, Rhodes House, Oxford, Thomas Papers; IWM, Heath Papers, Percival to Heath 14 May 1946. Captain G. N. Grey, RN, a member of the staff of GHQ Far East, cites Brooke-Popham and his Chief Planning Officer disregarding a particularly prescient intelligence forecast of the Japanese invasion and campaign plan produced by FECB as "alarmist and defeatist": IWM, Grey Papers; IWM, Grimsdale, 17. It is uncertain whether Percival ever read the detailed but equivocal *Japanese Army Memorandum* which is discussed in M. H. Murfett et al., *Between Two Oceans: A Military History of Singapore From First Settlement to Final British Withdrawal*, Singapore, 1999, 197.

24   Percival's *Despatch*, para. 24. The C-in-C's directive repeated these Army responsibilities while making it clear that the denial scheme for air bases was a RAF responsibility: PRO, WO172/1.

25   The first convoy of military supplies reached Archangel on 31 August. By 11 October, a total of three convoys had delivered several hundred *Hurricanes* and some tanks. HMSO, *Convoys to North Russia*; R. Woodman, *Arctic Convoys*, London, 1994. Churchill even proposed to offer the Russians the unfortunate 18th and the 50th Division for their southern front. A. Danchev and D. Todman (eds.), *War Diaries 1939–45: Alanbrooke*, Stanford, 2001, 206. Sir Archibald Southby's view, a mite optimistic perhaps, was that "one month's supply of the aircraft sent to Russia would

have saved Malaya," Hansard 378 HC Debates 61 quoted in L. Allen, *Singapore 1941–42*, London, 1977, 17.
26 When Percival submitted his draft despatch after the war, the Air Ministry contested his claim that the 40% destruction assurance had ever been given, though not "on strong enough ground to press the matter very forcibly." However, it continued to press and the percentage figure was removed from the final version and did not appear in Percival's book. Nevertheless, it has ample corroboration. Percival's *Despatch*, para. 47 and *The War in Malaya*, 65; LHCMA, Brooke-Popham Papers, V/8/40; IWM, Percival Papers, P/88, Percival to Professor Butler, 7 January 1962; PRO, CAB106/80, Heath to official historians; WO106/2620, Playfair reflections.
27 S. W. Kirby, *Singapore*, 113–16.
28 The division's losses at Jitra included 50 field guns, 50 heavy and light machine-guns and 210 trucks and armoured cars. See Ashmore. "We had to be grateful to General Percival," wrote Tsuji, "not only for provisions for the men, but also for cars and gasoline abandoned in abundance." Tsuji Masanobu, *Singapore: The Japanese Version*, Mayflower Dell edition, 113.
29 IWM, Heath Papers, LMH 7; PRO, CAB101/150, Percival to official historians; WO172/15.
30 Even when release was given, Krohcol was not concentrated at the border. Its second battalion had not arrived from Penang and its volunteer battery was not ready for action, although Percival had ordered the mobilization of the volunteers and the second degree of readiness for his entire force over a week earlier.
31 PRO, CAB101/150, Percival to official historians, 30 November 1953 and 9 January 1954; R. P. Pakenham-Walsh, *History of the Royal Engineers*, Vol. IX, Chatham, 1958, p. 143; E. C. W. Sandes, *The Indian Engineers 1939–47*, Kirhee (India), 1956, ch. 7.
32 I. Simson, *Singapore*, 62–63. Simson's account is the only one we have of this meeting, which apparently began at 2330 hours and lasted for two and a half hours. S. W. Kirby, *Singapore*, 168–69, includes a version of Simson's story. Both accounts were published after Percival's death. Kirby's earlier official history did not mention it. It is notable that Percival had earlier warned Kirby that if his official history were overcritical of himself or his subordinates, "I will ask for permission to express my own views on the actions and decisions of my superiors, my subordinates and other leading personalities more freely than I have done." PRO, CAB103/340, Percival to official historians. Simson's account of Percival's supposed attitude to fixed defences has been detailed in many subsequent histories and became one of the "case studies" in the imaginative piece of psychological speculation by N. F. Dixon, *On the Psychology of Military Incompetence*, New York, 1976.
33 That Simson intended to use all his available engineers is clear: "This was probably my last chance...to turn nearly 6,500 Commonwealth engineers (plus civilian labour) on to the construction of defence works." I. Simson, *Singapore*, 168.
34 Under Percival's scheme arranged with the Director of Public Works, State engineers rather than military ones were to form work groups and report to formation HQs. "Object is to prepare series of obstacles, especially anti-tank obstacles in great depth

on probable lines of enemy's advance," wrote Percival to Heath and Bennett on 29 December 1941: PRO, CAB 101/150; Percival's *Despatch*, paras 204–05 and 219. PRO, WO172/17, serial 1532.

35 Simson commanded very few engineers; the majority, about 18 companies, were controlled by the Commanders Royal Engineers (CRE) of the various formations. Heath confirmed that his engineers were "fully occupied." In fact two field companies of them had been required to fight as infantry as early as the battle of Jitra and other companies were frequently required to defend themselves when working on demolitions. Their casualties were heavy. R. P. Pakenham-Walsh, *History of the Royal Engineers*; I. Simson, *Singapore*, ch. 7; S. W. Kirby, *Singapore*, 168–69; E. C. W. Sandes, *The Indian Engineers 1939–47*; PRO, CAB106/80, Heath to official historians.

36 Further light is shed on the fixed defences issue in Simson's lengthy and repetitive postwar correspondence with General Kirby—himself an engineer—which Kirby concluded with the remark, "By overstating your case [you] have driven us to the conclusion that you cannot be accepted as an unprejudiced witness." PRO, CAB101/149.

37 LHCMA, Pownall Papers, Postwar note by Lt.-Col. Phillips (formerly GSO1 Ops Malaya Command) to General Pownall; PRO, CAB101/149, Kirby, office note July 1954; WO172/162; WO172/167.

38 At Trolak, Paris gave the forward position to the weariest brigade, the 12th Indian, allocated only a fraction of the anti-tank mines—40 out of 1,400 available—and a single troop of anti-tank guns to each of his forward brigades. The brigade commander, Stewart, failed to block the alternative tank approaches or to deploy two-thirds of his artillery support. S. W. Kirby, *Singapore*, 176–77. "Undue reliance was placed on the stopping power of a few concrete pillars, three anti-tank guns and the paltry minefields": PRO, CAB106/55, unpublished History of the 11th Indian Division, chs. 12–13.

39 S. W. Kirby, *Singapore*, 176–80; S. L. Falk, *Seventy Days to Singapore*, New York, 1975, 148–53; IWM, Heath Papers, Heath Commentary, LMH4.

40 S. W. Kirby, *Singapore*, 197. The force which finally landed at Endau included an airfield battalion sent to operate the Kluang and Kahang airfields as soon as they were captured.

41 In fact, Wavell visited Malaya the previous November as C-in-C India when his postvisit letter had contained the memorable sentence, "Personally I should be most doubtful if the Japs ever tried to make an attack on Malaya, and I am sure they will get it in the neck if they do!" LHCMA, Brooke-Popham Papers, V/5/5, Wavell to Brooke-Popham, 13 November 1941.

42 A. E. Percival, *The War in Malaya*, 207–10 and *Despatch*, paras. 290–93.

43 PRO, CAB101/150, official historians to Percival, 11 January 1954. In 1954, Percival was still tight-lipped about Wavell's intervention, writing, "I am not prepared to give an opinion as to whether it [Wavell's plan] was a good one or a bad one. I simply want to make it clear it was not mine," Percival to official historians, 3 January 1954; but six years later he was prepared to write, "Wavell did not know what he was talking about. I think I am right in saying that Wavell had

never been in the Far East before": IWM, Percival Papers, P/44, Percival to Professor Butler, 25 March 1960.
44 S. W. Kirby, *Singapore*, 184–86; S. L. Falk, *Seventy Days to Singapore*, 159–61; PRO, CAB101/150, Percival to official historians, 3 January 1954.
45 In fact, 15th Indian Brigade did not share the fate of 45th Indian Brigade; about 1,200 of its men eventually struggled back to the British lines and 2,000 were evacuated by sea.
46 J. Kennedy, *The Business of War*, London, 1957, 196; PRO, CAB106/80, Heath to official historians; W. S. Churchill, *The Second World War IV: The Hinge of Fate*, Boston, 1950, 49; IWM, Percival Papers, P/44, Percival to Frank Owen, March 1959.
47 J. Kennedy, *The Business of War*, 197; LHCMA, Ismay Papers, I/14/69, Jacob to Ismay 24 January 1959. The new CIGS General Sir Alan Brooke had been even more pessimistic, writing on 13 December that he doubted Malaya would hold out for a month. A. Danchev and D. Todman (eds.), *War Diaries 1939–45*, 211–29.
48 Wavell's *Despatch*, para. 21; PRO, CAB101/150, Percival to official historians, 30 December 1953.
49 PRO, WO172/15, Staff Appreciation, 22 December 1941; Percival's *Despatch*, Section XLV; Wavell's *Despatch*, 3–4; S. L. Falk, *Seventy Days to Singapore*, 201–12; PRO, CAB106/120, Percival to official historians, 21 September and 30 December 1953, 3 January 1954. A valuable chronology of the steps taken to prepare Singapore's defences is given in M. H. Murfett et al., *Between Two Oceans*, app. 2.
50 This is an estimate. Twenty-Fifth Army had a total of 66,753 combat support and LofC troops. A proportion of both categories would have been concerned with the Imperial Guards Division's Sumatra operation. Details from Twenty-Fifth Army staff notebook supplied to the author by National Institute for Defence Studies, Tokyo.
51 The Malaya Command medical establishment included seven military hospitals, 16 field ambulance units, three casualty clearance stations and numerous smaller medical units and personnel attached to units. The staff of the field ambulances alone amounted to almost 4,000 men.
52 None would have been allowed near the battlefront in the Middle East without further training and acclimatization. The despatch of 18th Division had a political rather than a military justification; that of the Indians and Australians was a serious blunder. There was a more suitable regular division available in India, whilst 16,000 unallocated Australians had been available in the reinforcement pool in the Middle East in December and 87,000 trained militiamen in Australia, from whom volunteers might have been sought. J. Smyth, 155–57; L. Wigmore, *The Japanese Thrust*, Canberra, 1957, 258 n.
53 Brigadier Maxwell commanding 27th Australian Brigade had no heart for the defence and had formed up before Percival to argue against it. Report of Lt.-Col. Phillips, PRO, WO106/2573C. For desertion and indiscipline generally, see the judgements in P. Elphick, *Singapore: The Pregnable Fortress*, especially ch. 13, M. H. Murfett et al., *Between Two Oceans*, app. 3, A. Warren, *Singapore*, ch. 16 and Ashmore.

54 PRO, CAB106/47, Maltby Despatch 1948; H. Probert, *The Forgotten Air Force*, London, 1995, 56.
55 Percival's postwar muddle over this issue is perhaps understandable. At a conference on 29 January 1942, he appears to have anticipated an attack in the west. Ashmore, 18.
56 PRO, CAB 101/150, Percival's correspondence with official historians, 30 December 1953 and 22 January 1954; S. L. Falk, *Seventy Days to Singapore*, 223–24.
57 It is noteworthy that the last official escape flotilla, which carried the other two service commanders Admiral Spooner and Air Vice-Marshal Pulford, appeared to sail directly into the path of the Sumatra invasion force, about which intelligence had warned.
58 S. W. Kirby, *Singapore*, 213–14 and 235; PRO, CAB101/150, official historians to Percival, 22 January 1954; WO 172/15.
59 Ashmore, 19a. Key supports the view that a divisional counter-attack by 18th Division would not have been possible: "I doubt if this could have been done in time—big distances were involved—units scattered and in many cases away from roads. I agree it looks right on paper, but I doubt if it was feasible." PRO, CAB101/165, Key to official historians.
60 Malaya Command Operation Instruction No. 40, App. K to Percival's *Despatch*. The wording of this order was no doubt the work of the lieutenant-colonel who signed it, but it should have been checked by Percival.
61 Key commented, "Whilst I did not consider Percival to be a dynamic leader of a lost cause, the issue would have been the same whatever general had been in command. Percival was straight as a die with a very good brain. And what a situation he had to face." J. Smyth, *Percival and the Tragedgy of Singapore*, 261. Percival believed that Heath had an "Indian Army complex" which limited his loyalty to the "Imperial Army of Malaya." Of cooperation with the Australians, he wrote that some of their senior officers "hardly seemed to speak the same military language." PRO, CAB101/150, Percival's confidential note to official historians, 8 January 1954.
62 This is supported by an interesting comment on Montgomery: "In those first few weeks when Montgomery arrived to talk to us, we regarded him as a funny little man in an Australian hat with a nasal voice who spoke in excruciating clichés which embarrassed rather than uplifted us. However, we were vastly encouraged by our new greatly improved weapons and that these were for the first time in plentiful supply. We could at last penetrate enemy tanks at an acceptable range." T. Bird (Rifle Brigade 1939–46), *The Times*, 27 September 2001.
63 According to Simson, citing his DGCD Report, civilian casualties were in the order of 2,000 per day, 400–500 of them deaths, during the final two weeks on the island. I. Simson, *Singapore*, 96. T. Kitching, Diary, January–February 1942, The Fall of Singapore, Royal Commonwealth Society Records, Cambridge University Library, 13AM XII/i, broadly supports these figures. Kitching was the Chief Surveyor of Singapore.
64 As the surrender was being discussed, Bennett apparently suggested a combined counter-attack to recapture Bukit Timah. "This remark came so late and was by then

so irrelevant, that I formed the impression at the time that it was not made as a serious contribution to the discussion but as something to quote afterwards," wrote Maj. Wild. IWM, Heath Papers, Notes on Capitulation of Singapore. For the surrender conferences and subsequent negotiations with the Japanese, see Percival Papers, P31, Record of the Fort Canning Conferences, Maj. C. Wild, and L. Allen, "The Surrender of Singapore: The Official Japanese Version," *Durham University Journal*, Vol. XXIX, No. 1, December 1967.

65   S. W. Kirby, *Singapore*, 256. This is his last word on the matter, but he is not entirely consistent, suggesting earlier (see note 27 and S. W. Kirby, *Singapore*, 255) an alternative strategy for the defence of Malaya that might have allowed sufficient time for Australian reinforcements to arrive from the Middle East. The present author believes that such a strategy would not have gained sufficient time and the reinforcements would, in any case, have been directed elsewhere.

CHAPTER 13

The Indian Army and the Fall of Singapore
by Alan Warren

When looking back at the loss of Singapore to the Japanese in 1942, it should be remembered that half of the troops comprising the British Empire's defending force were drawn from the Indian Army. During the Second World War, as had been the case from 1914 to 1918, the Indian Army was deployed overseas to support the British Empire's war effort. The Far East and Middle East were viewed by British war planners as India's outer bastions. Thus it seemed logical that Indian Army formations be committed to the Far East as part of an improvised scheme of imperial defence.

The 4th and 5th Indian Divisions were sent to the Middle East during 1939–40. Throughout the crisis period of 1940–41, with the United Kingdom under threat of invasion, the War Office was loath to send troops away from home. Yet the Chief of the Imperial General Staff, General Sir John Dill, was keen to build up the Far East's garrison with troops mainly from India and Australia.[1] After the fall of France, the Government of India had offered to raise an extra five divisions for overseas service. Of these, the 9th and 11th Indian Divisions were despatched to Malaya. In 1939, the Indian Army had been a little over 200,000 strong. But by the end of 1941, it expanded by means of voluntary recruitment to almost 900,000 officers and men, and would grow to over 1.8 million by the end of 1942.

The Indian Army on the eve of the Second World War was not a national or nationalist army. A sizeable minority of the army comprised British units attached to serve on garrison duty in the sub-continent. Most of the field artillery in India was served by British gunners. In addition, Gurkha troops from Nepal were another integral component of the army. The majority of the Indian Army's units originated from within the borders of today's India and Pakistan. Indian Army units had a complex social profile. In practice, the peacetime army was drawn from a very small minority of the population, and had strong ties to the Punjab province.

Indian races noted for their physique, martial self-image and political reliability, such as Dogras, Garhwalis, Mahrattas, Sikhs, Jats, Rajputs, Pathans and Punjabi Muslims, were heavily recruited. Carefully targeted recruiting in districts with strong associations with the British-Indian government made up for the fact that both Crown and Empire were hazy concepts. Soldiers, known as "sepoys," were often enlisted from the same families and villages as existing servicemen. Most Indian battalions comprised a mix of different races and religions, each organized into a separate company as a safeguard against mutiny. The Gurkhas were the principal exception to this arrangement. By the 1930s, mutiny was not a pressing issue for the commanders of the Indian Army, but as recently as 1915, half the 5th Light Infantry had run amok at Singapore. Almost 100 sepoys were killed or executed in the course of crushing the mutiny.

The senior half of an Indian battalion's officers were holders of a King's Commission, 12 to 16 at full strength. These officers came out to India from the British Royal Military College at Sandhurst. They were given pay bonuses for passing compulsory language exams, and gradually learnt a great deal about sepoys by living amongst them. At the close of the First World War, Indians began to receive commissions. But the "Indianization" of the officer corps was a very slow process between the world wars. By 1939, only one in seven officers serving with the Indian Army was an Indian, and these men were concentrated in particular units.

Two special types of officers, called *Jemadars* and *Subedars*, held a Viceroy's Commission and comprised the junior half of a unit's officers. VCOs were Indians promoted from the ranks, usually after at least ten years' service. They were the principal link between the Army's mostly British officers and the sepoys. One shortcoming of the VCO system was that, without the western education British and Indian officers took for granted, even the most talented VCO was to some extent isolated from his superiors by culture and language.

Prior to 1939, a single Indian battalion was attached to the peacetime garrison of Malaya. The first of a steady stream of Indian formations to arrive in Malaya was the 12th Indian Brigade, which disembarked late in 1939. By late 1941, a total of six brigades had arrived to complete the 9th and 11th Indian Divisions. Three of these brigades contained a British battalion, and with the exception of a mountain regiment, all field and anti-tank artillery was served by British personnel. The commanders and senior staffs of Indian formations were British. In Malaya, the segregation of races was more vigorously practiced than in India. Junior Indian officers who had expected to be treated like their British counterparts of the same rank were often offended to varying degrees. Nationalist unrest became evident in a couple of units, and certain Indian officers had to be sent home.

The III Indian Corps headquarters was set up to control the Indian divisions in Malaya. The Army officer sent to command III Indian Corps was Lieutenant-

General Sir Lewis Heath. Heath was senior to Lieutenant-General A. E. Percival, GOC Malaya Command, in date of rank, but Percival's subordinate in Malaya. This was because Percival had been appointed by London, and Heath by New Delhi. The two appointments were made independently of each other.

Lewis Heath was born in India in 1885, and educated at Wellington school. He joined the Indian Army in 1906, suffered a permanent injury to an arm and lost an eye in Mesopotamia during the First World War. Heath never attended the Staff College, but turned down a nomination to attend in order to command a corps of frontier irregulars.[2] He went on to command a brigade in Waziristan during one of the Northwest Frontier's frequent tribal revolts. After the outbreak of war, he led the 5th Indian Division in a victorious campaign against the Italians in Eritrea in 1940–41. Heath was one of the first Indian Army generals to win a corps command in an overseas theatre during the Second World War. A calm, cheerful and approachable man, Heath was also a handsome widower, and was joined in Malaya by his fiancee, a New Zealand nurse, whom he soon married.

According to Percival, Heath never showed any outward signs of resenting his position. The two men were on friendly but distant terms. It was quite usual for generals of the British and Indian Armies to work together in a unified command structure. A proportion of senior appointments in the Indian Army were always held by British Army officers. Percival's appointment as GOC Malaya was strongly influenced by the fact that he had previously served as a staff officer in the colony, but he had only limited experience of the Indian troops that formed his command's main field formation. Though Percival saw service in France, Flanders, North Russia, Ireland, West Africa, Malta and Malaya, he had never been posted to India.

The III Indian Corp's divisions were deployed to defend the northern and eastern land and sea frontiers of the Malayan peninsula. In northeast Malaya, the 11th Indian Division was camped near Jitra, from where it could either advance into Thailand towards Singora, as part of an operation named *Matador*, or take up defensive positions to shield nearby aerodromes. Throughout 1941, formations in Malaya were still in the process of having their equipment upgraded to a standard taken for granted in other theatres of war. An officer of a Punjabi regiment noted that his unit was forced to train with wooden anti-tank rifles and to maintain a supply of Molotov cocktails. Units arriving from India were particularly behind in terms of acquiring new equipment. Peasants who had grown up amid bullock carts had to become accustomed to lorries, Bren Gun carriers, mortars and radio sets. Matters were not helped by the inexperience of many officers and NCOs. Questions of anti-tank defence were particularly neglected, partly as a consequence of the lack of a British tank force in the colony that might have focused commanders' minds on that important issue.[3]

When war broke out between Japan and the Western powers, Malaya was rapidly invaded by General Yamashita Tomoyuki's Twenty-Fifth Army, comprising the 5th, 18th and Imperial Guards Divisions. Indian troops were involved in the fighting from the outset. Around 5,300 Japanese troops landed at Kota Bahru, on the northeast coast of Malaya, in the early hours of 8 December. The invaders' objectives were three aerodromes close inland. The initial wave of Japanese troops to land suffered severe losses and, for the only time in the campaign, the Royal Air Force inflicted heavy damage on Japanese shipping. The four Indian battalions of the 8th Indian Brigade, under the command of Brigadier B. W. Key, were handled in a sound fashion, prior to undertaking a planned withdrawal inland. Japanese-acknowledged losses on land and sea at Kota Bahru were 320 killed and 538 wounded; 8th Indian Brigade's losses were 68 killed, 360 wounded and 37 missing. There would not be many engagements in the whole subsequent campaign for which the death toll ran so heavily in the defenders' favour.[4]

Meanwhile, in northwest Malaya, the campaign opened disastrously for III Indian Corps. The 11th Indian Division, after the cancellation of operation *Matador*, hurriedly settled into their allotted positions near Jitra. The main Japanese invasion force destined for Malaya landed at the Thai ports of Singora and Patani. Japanese troops advancing from Patani by an inland route quickly bundled back the Indian detachment opposing them, and began to threaten the right flank of the Jitra line. The Japanese 5th Division's advance guard also made rapid progress southwards from Singora, under the watchful eye of Twenty-Fifth Army's Chief of Operations, Lieutenant-Colonel Tsuji Masanobu. Two Indian battalions were dispersed by tank attack north of Jitra on 11 December. Both the 1/14 Punjabis and 2/1 Gurkhas were unable to mount an effective anti-tank defence. The troops and their commanders were surprised that the Japanese could bring armour into action so quickly.

At Jitra, the 11th Indian Division's 6th and 15th Brigades held a long front, with the depleted 28th Brigade in reserve. During the night of 11/12 December, enterprising Japanese troops infiltrated the defenders' position using the cover of jungle and rubber plantation. The 15th Brigade's right-hand battalion, the 2/9 Jats, held a difficult 3000-yard front. The Jats' left-hand company position was overrun by morning and counter-attacks failed. As there was no strong divisional reserve available to seal off the penetration, Major-General D. M. Murray-Lyon asked Malaya Command for authorization to withdraw. After nightfall, Percival granted permission for a retreat and a disorderly night march followed. A number of units broke up in the darkness, and a cruel blow was dealt to the collective morale of the Division. The attacking Japanese force was the equivalent of just two battalions strong. The assault had been opportunistic and not the result of meticulous planning.

Over the next few days, hundreds of prisoners were rounded up wandering in the jungle. One of the prisoners was Captain Mohan Singh of the 1/14 Punjab. Mohan Singh met the exiled nationalist Pritam Singh and Major Fujiwara, the Japanese officer responsible for organizing subversive activities among Indians in Malaya. Fujiwara and Pritam Singh explained to the captured Indian officer the aims of the Indian Independence League, and avowed Japanese plans to liberate Asia from colonial rule. Mohan Singh was asked to join their organization and take charge of his fellow Indian prisoners. Mohan Singh quickly put his existing allegiances aside to seize the chance offered him.

In the rain and darkness of the night of 12/13 December, the 11th Indian Division's units headed southwards from Jitra as best they could. The Division's first aim was to get behind the Sungei Kedah. The trunk road's bridge over the Kedah was at Alor Star, and most of the force had to pass through this bottleneck. At the Alor Star bridge, stragglers and transport continued slowly to hobble or drive through after dawn of the following day. That morning, Murray-Lyon fainted from tiredness by the roadside. The General recovered quickly, and at 0930 hours he was near the Alor Star bridge with a party of senior officers. Onlookers watched as motorcycle despatch riders emerged from the town, on the north bank of the river, and roared across the bridge in front of a staff car and a couple of lorries. As the lead cyclist drew level with Murray-Lyon's party at the south end of the bridge, the cyclist grimaced and waved. Murray-Lyon gasped, "My God, that's a Jap!" The recklessness of the Japanese cyclists took the troops in the vicinity completely by surprise. The leading cyclist rode clear to safety as the General and his colleagues drew their revolvers, and with help from nearby troops, shot down the next two riders.[5]

Murray-Lyon immediately ordered the wide Victorian bridge, already prepared for demolition, to be blown for fear of another "tank blitz." What happened next is best told by Murray-Lyon:

> Now a most regrettable incident took place, but one which illustrates the state of the morale of some of the units of the Division at this stage. When the bridge went up, although there had been no firing except for a few revolver shots against the motor cyclists and one burst of LMG fire, the 1/8 Punjab, which was sitting down in a palm grove about 600 yards from the bridge, rose as one man and started to run down the road in panic. Two Companies of 2/16 Punjab did the same. (Both these units were greatly under strength by this stage.) It was only by getting into my car and getting ahead of them that I managed to stop them and turn them back. In the case of the 2/16 Punjab Companies I actually had to threaten some men with my pistol before they would stop.[6]

That a general was required to intervene personally in such a fashion did not bode well for the future of the division.

The south bank of the Sungei Kedah was held until the evening of 13 December. Indian, Gurkha and British troops then spent another exhausting night amid rain and traffic congestion, traversing 20 miles of road to Gurun, later described by Percival as one of the best natural defensive positions in Malaya. In an engagement at Gurun beginning on 14 December, the 11th Indian Division suffered another serious defeat at the hands of light Japanese forces. Its 6th Brigade was shattered by an overnight attack straight down the trunk road. Japanese tanks entered Gurun Village on the morning of 15 December. Murray-Lyon's troops began another retreat towards the Perak River. Penang Island was abandoned in the process. The 12th Indian Brigade was brought forward from Command Reserve to reinforce the Division, and sent to oppose a Japanese drive along an inland route running from Kroh towards Grik and the Perak River.

The land battles in northern Malaya took place whilst disaster was overtaking the Royal Navy and Royal Air Force in the Far East. The Japanese quickly established sea and air supremacy in the region, a supremacy they never relinquished for the rest of the campaign. To make matters worse, an Indian Army air liaison officer based in northern Malaya, Captain Patrick Heenan of the 3/16 Punjab, was later arrested and executed for espionage. Apparently Heenan spent part of a six-month furlough in Japan before the war and continued to mix with Japanese at Singapore in 1941. Heenan was in the habit of making clandestine trips into Thailand, and was caught in possession of a small, disguised radio transmitter. Heenan may have flirted with Japanese intelligence, but exaggerated estimates of his effectiveness have little basis.[7]

At his Singapore headquarters, General Percival was appalled at how quickly the 11th Indian Division had collapsed in northwest Malaya. However, Percival was just as concerned about the possibility of Japanese landings on the southeast coast of Malaya, or a *coup de main* on Singapore itself. In light of events in northern Malaya, Heath and Percival spoke on the telephone about future strategy. Heath told Percival:

> The 6/15th Brigade will not be of the slightest fighting value for a matter of many days. It is therefore for consideration for the whole Command to assist in this very delicate situation…It seems to need two forces—at least one fresh Australian Brigade—to be formed at once at Ipoh and for the 11th Division and 12th Brigade to go back to the Perak line. Perhaps it will be necessary to go back to the Slim [River].

Heath was clearly asking for reinforcements. But, despite the obvious extent of the 11th Indian Division's defeat in Kedah State, Percival did not agree with Heath's assessment of the situation. From Singapore, Percival told Heath:

> We don't want to dissipate forces from down here. I think the right course is to try if you can to get back behind the Perak line at least for the first step. This is my feeling, and also for the Slim River line to be reconnoitred.[8]

Percival was loath to transfer the 8th Australian Division northwards for fear of leaving southern Malaya and Singapore denuded of troops in the face of the threat of new Japanese landings in Johore. Forty-one Japanese transports carrying the second flight of Yamashita's Twenty-Fifth Army had arrived at Singora and Patani on 16 December, but Percival could not predict the destination of the next convoy. As he later explained:

> Until the Japanese had definitely shown their hand there was always the possibility that the threat against Thailand and northern Malaya was intended to draw off our forces to that area with a view to facilitating seaborne operations against Johore.[9]

Yet Percival did not want to withdraw from northern Malaya too rapidly for fear that the Japanese Air Force would obtain bases from which they might attack reinforcement convoys bound for Singapore.

By 23 December, the 11th Indian Division retreated behind the Perak, the broadest river in Malaya. But the Perak was not a very useful barrier as it ran largely north to south. Nonetheless the retirement behind the river provided a good opportunity to dismiss Murray-Lyon. There was no denying the fact that Murray-Lyon's period of command was an unmitigated disaster. Despite the shortcomings in prewar defence preparations in northern Malaya, errors in operational command played a major role in the Division's defeat. The comparative skill of Brigadier Key's handling of the fighting on the east coast highlighted that point. The finding of a replacement for Murray-Lyon became another field of disagreement for Percival and Heath. Heath wanted to put an Indian Army officer in command of the division. As Key had been the outstanding brigadier in the campaign to date, Key was Heath's nominee. But Percival decided to make the 12th Indian Brigade's Brigadier A. C. M. Paris, a British service officer, the Division's new commander.

By late December, the Japanese 5th Division and a newly arrived regiment of the Imperial Guards Division were ready to advance across the Perak River. The 11th Indian Division next made a stand at Kampar, 20 miles south of Ipoh.

On 1–2 January 1942, the 15th Indian Brigade performed well. However, Japanese landings on the coast threatened to bypass Kampar and the division began another retreat further into central Malaya. As the 11th Indian Division retreated down the west coast of Malaya, the 9th Indian Division fought a relatively separate battle in eastern Malaya. Key's 8th Brigade withdrew down the railway from Kota Bahru, whilst on the east coast, Brigadier G. W. A. Painter's 22nd Indian Brigade held Kuantan Town and aerodrome. General Percival wanted to retain Kuantan for as long as possible in order to prevent the aerodrome falling into Japanese hands. Yet despite the fact that Japanese troops were advancing down the east coast from Kota Bahru, Painter was keen to keep his seaward defences fully manned. Heath had to intervene to order Major-General A. E. Barstow, the 9th Indian Division's commander, to direct Painter to redeploy his troops to face north. But at the end of December, Japanese troops attacked the brigade as it was redeploying. By the time the aerodrome was abandoned on the night of 3/4 January, the brigade had suffered heavy losses. Lieutenant-Colonel A. E. Cumming of the 2/12 Frontier Force Regiment won the Victoria Cross for his work with the rearguard as the brigade retreated inland. The III Indian Corps' grip on central Malaya was beginning to slip.

At a senior commanders' conference convened by Percival on 5 January, it was decided to evacuate Kuala Lumpur, and form a new defence line at the northern border of Johore State. Percival ordered Heath to deny the Japanese the aerodromes of Kuala Lumpur and Port Swettenham until at least 14 January in order to help shield the arrival of a reinforcement convoy expected at Singapore about that date. Percival urged Heath to delay the Japanese and to accept casualties up to a reasonable limit.[10]

North of Kuala Lumpur, the 11th Indian Division made its next stand at Slim River. A 40-mile stretch of swampy jungle effectively covered the coastal flank of the Slim River sector, though there was a danger that coastal landings by the Japanese further south might cut off the division. The wily Yamashita, never one to miss an opportunity, was planning just such an operation, but Heath managed to assemble an ad hoc force, including the 15th Indian Brigade, to contain Japanese troops advancing up river along the Sungei Selangor's north bank in the early days of January 1942.

The 12th Indian Brigade, now 11th Indian Division's leading formation, dug positions at Trolak, north of Slim River. Slim River was an excellent anti-tank obstacle, but the trunk road and railway crossed the river five miles apart. North of Slim River at Trolak, the road and railway ran close together to form a single corridor. Here the brigade, very tired after three weeks continually in action, built and wired new posts, subject to frequent aerial strafing and bombing. Behind the 12th Brigade, the 28th Indian Brigade bivouacked near Slim River. General Paris' divisional headquarters was located 10 miles to the rear of Slim. Oddly, both the 28th Brigade's supporting field artillery regiment and the bulk of the divisional anti-tank regiment were also resting in bivouac well to the rear of Slim River. In theory, the 12th Indian Brigade's new position was not difficult to defend. The Brigade's three battalions were deployed in a line down the trunk road, one behind the other, first the 4/19 Hyderabads, followed by the 5/2 Punjabis and 2nd Argylls. The Punjabis manned the Brigade's principal defence line. The Hyderabads were only meant to fight a delaying action in front of them.[11] But there was no natural tank obstacle in the Punjabis' area. To make matters worse, Brigadier I. M. Stewart ordered the roadway kept undamaged so that Bren Gun carriers and armoured cars could work with the Hyderabads further forward. Paris and Stewart both felt that artillery had only a limited role to play in the dense country north of Trolak.

Rapidly advancing Japanese troops made contact with the 12th Indian Brigade by the afternoon of 5 January. There was skirmishing over the next two days. The 12th Brigade was due to withdraw behind the 28th Indian Brigade on the night of 7/8 January. Late on 6 January, an Asian refugee came into British lines with information. He was brought to 12th Brigade's headquarters for questioning. The man claimed he had seen a column of "iron land-ships" at Sungkai, eight miles north of Trolak. He also said the bridge at Sungkai had been repaired. Stewart concluded that the vehicles were only lorries.[12]

On 7 January, an extraordinary battle took place. In the early hours of the morning, a Japanese tank regiment, with only limited infantry support, advanced down the jungle and rubber-lined trunk road. The 4/19 Hyderabads, with just a single anti-tank gun in their area, were swiftly bundled aside by the tanks. The onward rush of the armoured column, a column that contained the better part of 30 light and medium tanks, was brought to a halt at 0430 hours when it ran into a small minefield in a cutting in front of the Punjabis' posts. Half a dozen tanks were put out of action in a stiff fight lasting two hours, but by dawn the Punjabis had been overrun. Communications had broken down so badly that news of the battle's progress was still to reach units further south. The Argylls were soon routed near Trolak village and the bridge over Trolak stream was captured intact before sappers could demolish it. An artillery battery supporting the 12th Indian Brigade near Trolak retreated south of Slim River.

Worse was to come for the division. Pursuant to an order received earlier that morning, the 5/14 Punjabis were marching up from their bivouac to a position south of Trolak. At 0730 hours, they were marching alongside a cemetery when they were surprised by 15 tanks and some lorried infantry. The battalion was scattered by the tanks, which drove on to penetrate the position of Gurkha units of the 28th Indian Brigade further down the road. It was later claimed, perhaps apocryphally, that the first news 28th Brigade's headquarters had of the tanks' approach was when the brigade-major saw tanks behind his shoulder in the reflection of his shaving mirror.[13]

To the rear of the 28th Indian Brigade's main position, the 2/1 Gurkhas were marching eastwards, away from the battle, in the direction of Cluny estate and Slim River road bridge. The road was narrow, twisting, and lined by dense rubber and jungle. The marching column was under the immediate command of Major W. J. Winkfield. The battalion was moving in open file on either side of the road. Winkfield felt a sense of unease amongst the troops behind him, and the noise of the battle seemed to be getting closer:

> The next thing I knew was a gun and machine-gun blazing in my ear, a bullet grazed my leg, and I dived into the ditch as a tank bore down on me. It had passed through half of my battalion without my realizing anything was amiss.

About a dozen tanks stopped for 10 minutes to fire into the rubber plantations bordering the road. Winkfield emerged from cover to find that his battalion had "vanished."[14] The tanks rolled on. The two remaining batteries of the 137th Field Regiment were parked nearby in Cluny Estate. The marauding tanks chanced upon the gunners whilst they were breakfasting, and paused to shoot them up with cannon and machine-gun fire. A few guns and some vehicles were hit, and the tanks drove off. In the absence of the regiment's commanding officer and headquarters, the battery commanders present at Cluny Estate assumed the day was lost. The officers gathered enough men together to spike the guns. The unit then dispersed into the jungle.

At 0840 hours, the first party of Japanese tanks reached the Slim River road bridge, which was captured intact from a party of sappers and anti-aircraft gunners. A dozen tanks trundled southwards until they ran into the 155th Field Regiment two miles down the road, driving up to join troops north of the river. The artillery column rapidly brought guns into action to knock out the leading tank. A hastily-arranged defence was able to stop the tanks making any further progress. As the 9th Gurkha Rifles' regimental historian sagely commented, "The single gun which stopped the Japanese tanks after a rush of 19 miles might have accomplished as much in the first hundred yards of the onset."[15] It had taken Japanese tanks only six hours to wreak havoc throughout the 11th Indian Division's two northernmost brigades. During the night, the survivors retreated southwards towards Tanjong Malim.

The British-Indian defenders of Malaya seemed to have learnt nothing since the opening of the campaign. Brigadier Stewart of the 12th Indian Brigade later said, with refreshing candour:

> I am rightly criticized for the location of Brigade Headquarters and for not using the Field Artillery in an anti-tank role...It is no excuse, but I had never taken part in an exercise embodying a coordinated anti-tank defence or this type of attack.[16]

But Stewart could hardly be blamed for the fact that the 24 guns of his supporting field regiment did not fire a single shot at the tanks over open sights. Sappers at Trolak and Slim River had failed to blow mined bridges at short notice. After a month in action without relief, the officers and men of the 11th Indian Division were both physically and mentally fatigued.

The 11th Indian Division sustained over 4,000 casualties at Slim. When the remnants of its 12th and 28th Brigades assembled on 8 January, they presented a sorry sight. Seven infantry battalions now comprised fewer than 1,200 officers and men.[17] But the battle at Slim was more than just another defeat. The destruction of the Division undermined the whole defence of Malaya. If the British were to fight a successful battle in Johore, with the aid of newly arrived reinforcements, a battle-ready 11th Indian Division was a prerequisite. Percival paid a heavy price for refusing to swap the exhausted Division with fresh troops sitting idle at Singapore and Johore. He had not monitored the 11th Indian Division's situation very closely and had only occasionally visited the formation since the outbreak of war.

Yet the 11th Indian Division's ordeal was by no means over. It was ordered to cover the evacuation of Kuala Lumpur until the night of 10/11 January. Several units in the 15th and 28th Indian Brigades were broken up in another round of failed battles. When the fighting reached Johore, the remnants of the exhausted Division passed into reserve. At Heath's request, Paris was demoted back to the command of the 12th Indian Brigade. Key of the 8th Indian Brigade, Heath's original nominee to replace Murray-Lyon, was belatedly made the Division's new commander.

Troops of the 8th Australian Division played the most prominent role of any Empire contingent in the Johore phase of the campaign. Astride the trunk road, the 9th Indian Division supported the 27th Australian Brigade in a series of battles against the Japanese 5th Division. But the newly arrived 45th Indian Brigade, positioned along the line of the Muar River, bore the brunt of the fresh Imperial Guards Division's thrust. The 45th Brigade had only sailed from India late in 1941. The troops thought they were heading for Iraq and a further long spell of training. Newer officers still lacked fluency in Indian languages, and the men were far from fully proficient at basic musketry. For instance, the 7/6 Rajputana Rifles had only 170 men with more than a year's service, and over 600 with less than a year.[18] Behind the twisting Muar River, the 7/6 Rajputana Rifles held nine miles of front stretching inland from the coast. The 4/9 Jats prolonged the line for another 15 miles, and the 5/18 Garhwal Rifles were in reserve near brigade headquarters at Bakri. The Australians' Major-General H. Gordon Bennett, the local commander in northwest Johore, expressly told Brigadier H. C. Duncan to position two companies from each of his two forward battalions on the north bank of the Muar River. The Brigade's units were thus ridiculously dispersed. When on 15 January, the Imperial Guards advanced boldly southwards towards Muar River, they rapidly infiltrated and routed the scattered companies. By late on 16 January, the Rajputana Rifles were reduced to two officers and 120 men.[19] Even the best-trained and acclimatized troops would have been overwhelmed in circumstances so hopeless for an effective defence.

Two Australian battalions were sent by Bennett to Bakri, to shore up the Muar front. But by its end, the battle cost the shattered 45th Indian Brigade, its commander, all three battalion commanders, and the outright majority of British officers with all three battalions.[20] According to the Jat Regiment's history, the commanding officer of its 4th Battalion was killed when his head was severed by a sword as he attempted to peer over a mud bank.[21] An Australian battalion commander said of the Brigade, after he encountered it at Bakri:

> I saw Indian troops in action in the German East Africa campaign [during] the 1914–18 war and have the highest regard for their fighting qualities, and have no doubt in my mind that the 45th Brigade had the same fighting material, but, in common with my officers, I felt extremely disturbed that it was necessary to have had to employ such immature and partly-trained troops. Most of the troops were I should say about 17 years old and had adolescent fluff on their cheeks.[22]

The remnants of the 45th Brigade took part in the Australians' battles on the road from Bakri to Parit Sulong from 18 to 22 January. The Brigade that emerged out of the jungle from Parit Sulong was too weak to be reformed and vanished from Percival's order of battle.

In the final withdrawal to Singapore Island, in the last days of January, further setbacks befell Indian troops. The 9th Indian Division was retreating southwards down the railway. Due to muddled command decisions, Brigadier Painter's 22nd Indian Brigade was cut off north of Layang Layang village during the night of 27/28 January. The following morning, Major-General Barstow was killed venturing forward with two companions into the gap that had opened between the brigades of his Division. The troops of the 22nd Brigade were laid low by exhaustion after becoming lost in the jungle. Another three battalions were destroyed in this dismal episode that was typical of so much that had happened in Malaya over the previous several weeks.

At Singapore, the besieged garrison hurriedly prepared for a Japanese assault under mounting air attack. Belatedly-arriving reinforcements raised the garrison to nearly 100,000 men, roughly half of whom were Indians. The 44th Indian Brigade and 7,000 Indian replacements were among the last batches of reinforcements. The 44th Brigade was a sister formation of the ill-fated 45th Brigade, and had also been scheduled to sail for the Middle East for a long period of much-needed training before it was despatched to Malaya.[23] The replacements packed off to Singapore, many without rifles, had been plucked straight from training depots.

The Indian battalion at Singapore in best condition was the 2/17 Dogras, but they had been banished to Pulau Tekong Besar, an island five miles from Singapore at the eastern end of the Johore Strait. Every other III Indian Corps unit had taken a battering on the mainland. A number of battalions were amalgamated to form stronger units, and then made up to strength with reinforcements. The 2/10 Baluch, 2/2 Gurkhas, 4/19 Hyderabad and 1/8 Punjab were the only Indian battalions from the mainland to retain their original form, and were dangerously top heavy with recruits. The 11th Indian Division absorbed the 9th to form a complete formation. Percival disposed the 8th Australian Division to defend the northwest coast of Singapore. The 11th Indian and 18th British Divisions defended the northeast coast. Other Indian and Malayan formations were in reserve or along the south coast. When the Japanese assault came against the northwest corner of the island on the night of 8/9 February, the 22nd Australian Brigade was bundled inland.

On the morning of 9 February, Percival ordered forward the 12th Indian Brigade from Malaya Command reserve. However, the Brigade had barely begun to recover from the pummelling it received at Slim River. It had been placed in reserve precisely as it was the formation least fit to defend a coastal sector. The 5/2 Punjab were still not ready for combat and had not rejoined the Brigade. The Hyderabads and the Argylls comprised less than 900 officers and men. The Brigade did not have a supporting artillery regiment. On the afternoon of 9 February, the 15th Indian Brigade was also released from a reserve role, and sent to the west of Singapore Island to help build a new defence line in the gap between the headwaters of the Kranji and Jurong Rivers. The shattered 22nd Australian Brigade and 12th and 44th Indian Brigades completed the force in the gap.

On the evening of 9/10 February, the Imperial Guards attacked the 27th Australian Brigade near the causeway. The Australian commander withdrew his men during the night, exposing the flank of the 11th Indian Division. Still, the following morning, the Division, under General Key's sound leadership, maintained much of its position thanks to a counter-attack by the 8th Indian Brigade, though the Garhwal Rifles composite battalion was broken up in the process. The situation for the defenders worsened over the next couple of days.

Plans to develop a counter-attack against the Japanese bridgehead were half-hearted as Percival was still worried about possible landings on other parts of the island, despite the fact that all three divisions of Twenty-Fifth Army were already committed to battle. Both the 12th and 15th Indian Brigades were smashed when the Japanese launched their main attack to seize Bukit Timah and the vital central sector of Singapore Island.

When a final perimeter was formed around Singapore town, the 11th Indian Division and 44th Indian Brigade held their sectors in a satisfactory manner, but they were never in the path of the main Japanese thrust. Two battalions of the 11th Division, the 1/8 Punjab and 2/10 Baluch, collapsed with mass surrenders under little pressure. The 2/10 Baluch were infiltrated and harangued by either INA or Japanese troops and persuaded to surrender. Irrespective of what exactly happened, the battalion's leadership cadre had been too weak and tired to withstand subversion.[24] Two Indian Commissioned Officers with the missing companies of the unit later became senior INA leaders, though the Baluchis as a whole had one of the lower rates of INA membership. Indian troops were not obviously involved in the riots that took place at Singapore's docks and other rear areas as defeat drew near. Observers remarked that, in general, Indian stragglers were bewildered and docile rather than belligerent.

Senior commanders met at Fort Canning during the afternoon of 13 February. Heath told the conference that he felt the situation was hopeless and Bennett agreed. The Japanese had come 500 miles down the Malayan peninsula and were now only three miles from Singapore River. Percival countered that he was not authorized to capitulate, and added, "I have my honour to consider and there is also the question of what posterity will think of us if we surrender this large army and valuable fortress." According to Percival, Heath then replied, "You need not bother about your honour. You lost that a long time ago up in the north."[25] Percival did not think the time was right to capitulate, and the defending garrison was ordered to hang on for another two days. Nonetheless, given the disasters that befell British forces in Malaya, relations between Percival and Heath, the two senior Army officers in the colony, had remained relatively civil for much of the campaign. But Heath's patience must have been sorely tested watching Percival make one mistake after another.

After the capitulation on 15 February, Indian prisoners were separated from their European officers, though not from their Indian officers and Viceroy's Commissioned Officers. On 17 February, whilst European troops marched to Changi, the great majority of the 45,000 Indian prisoners taken at Singapore were assembled at Farrer Park. Under the direction of Major Fujiwara, a Japanese intelligence officer, Captain Mohan Singh, Fujiwara's chief Indian collaborator, harangued the troops about working with the Japanese for the cause of Indian nationalism.

There were numerous Indian officers senior to Mohan Singh among the POWs taken at Singapore. Of almost 1,000 Indian Army officers captured in Malaya, the majority were British, but around a quarter were Indian, including numerous medical officers. The most senior officer was Lieutenant-Colonel Naranjan Singh Gill, who had been on the staff of the 11th Indian Division. Gill assumed command of an Indian Prisoner of War Headquarters. But he soon fell reluctantly into line with Fujiwara's and Mohan Singh's plans to raise a new force from captured personnel. Early in May, recruiting for an "Indian National Army" began in earnest.

Some Indian officers believed the Japanese claim that they had come to free Asia from European colonialism. After the war, though, few officers claimed that nationalist fervour was their sole reason for joining the INA. Captain P. K. Sahgal stated:

> After protracted discussions, the only solution that we could think of for our country's problems was the formation of a strong and well-disciplined armed body which should fight for the liberation of India from the existing alien rule, [which] should be able and ready to provide protection to their countrymen against any possible molestation by the Japanese, and to resist any attempt by the latter to establish themselves as rulers of the country in place of the British.[26]

Given the scale of British defeat in Malaya, there was a possibility that the Japanese might soon be in India.

Grievances amongst Indian officers about pay and racial discrimination came to the surface in captivity, as did opportunistic desires to avoid internment and gain promotion in the new army. Some officers doubted the integrity of the Japanese, and the ability of Mohan Singh to represent their interests, but joined rather than remain uninvolved. In the INA, VCOs became junior officers and this was an incentive for them to join. Postwar intelligence estimates concluded that 50% of Indian officers and 25% of VCOs joined the INA in 1942.[27]

The actions of Indian officers were an important influence on their men and disillusioned sepoys joined the INA by the thousands. Other Indian ranks had experienced defeat and been badly let down by their British leaders. Sepoys were told that the days of the British were over. They had no means of knowing if that was true. There was also strong pressure on Indian sub-units to stay together in a time of great uncertainty. The fact that the INA controlled most POW camps made it hard for the men in those camps to remain aloof, and was at times a decisive consideration. Sepoys were vulnerable to mostly subtle forms of coercion and persuasion. One senior Indian officer simply told a paraded battalion they could either dig latrines for the Japanese or become soldiers again.[28]

Those Indians who stayed out of the INA did so for a host of reasons. Some Indian officers were highly anglicized and sympathetic to the British viewpoint. Others had a long family tradition of service to the Indian Army, or believed that joining the INA was a genuine act of desertion. There was some suspicion of the motives of those jockeying for posts in the new army. A few officers and VCOs managed to escape to India from Malaya in 1942–43. Others escaped to India from Burma having joined the INA expressly for that purpose.

At Singapore and on the mainland, 55,000 Indian personnel were taken prisoner. Approximately 20,000 enlisted in the INA soon after its creation, and another 20,000 joined between June and August 1942, leaving only 15,000 who did not join.[29] Recruitment rates varied greatly between units. Among the infantry, British intelligence officers later singled out the Gurkhas, 7/6 Rajputana Rifles, 2/10 Baluchis, and Jind, Mysore, Bahawalpur and Hyderabad States Force battalions as having low enlistment rates, whereas the 17 Dogras, 18 Garhwalis, 4/19 Hyderabads, Kapurthala State Force, 9th Jats, and 14th and 16th Punjabis had high rates of enlistment. It must be noted, though, that in January 1943 many men from the Dogras and 14th and 16th Punjabis left the INA. A total of 16,000 men were formed into an INA division. Mohan Singh wanted to raise a larger force but 16,000 was the ceiling set by the Japanese. The surplus volunteers remained as POWs.[30]

When British Indian Army officers at Changi camp heard of the INA, they had mixed reactions. Heath felt that self-interest and ignorance were the main reasons for heavy enlistment. Some British officers were furious at the perfidy of their Indian officer colleagues and subordinates. Others were more understanding, and guiltily self-aware they had badly let down those Indians under their command. Armed INA Sikhs helped guard European prisoners at Changi, and took delight in requiring the white men to salute and perform other subservient tasks. Early in September 1942, an Indian firing squad executed two British and two Australian soldiers who attempted to escape. Among the squad's members was a captain of the Kapurthala State Force.[31]

As 1942 drew to a close, relations between the INA's leaders and the Japanese became strained. In December, both Mohan Singh and Gill were arrested by the Japanese. The INA collapsed briefly but in January 1943, a new administrative committee was formed. About 4,000 of the INA's 16,000 men left the force at this time. The arrival of Subhash Chandra Bose in Singapore, early in 1943, gave the stagnant INA a new lease of life. Bose was a veteran Indian nationalist politician. In 1941, he fled to Germany via Afghanistan and the Soviet Union. In Germany, Bose found Nazism attractive. He helped to raise a force for the Germans among Indian POWs held in Europe. Bose travelled to Japan by submarine in the early months of 1943. His nationalism was genuine and he had an inspiring and charismatic personality. A provisional Government of Free India was set up at Singapore later in the year. A rejuvenated INA enlisted another 10,000 POWs. By 1945, 18,000 Indian civilians in Southeast Asia had also enlisted. The 20–25,000 Indian Army personnel in the INA from 1943 onwards was fewer than in 1942, but a substantial body of men nonetheless.

With Bose's blessing, part of the INA was sent to Burma, and took part in a number of dismally unsuccessful operations in 1944–45. In the 1944 Imphal battles, the 1st INA Division sent 6,000 men to the front, of whom 400 were killed, 1,500 died of disease or exposure, 800 surrendered, and 715 deserted or went missing. Only 2,600 returned.[32] The 2nd INA Division was captured on the road to Rangoon early in 1945. A third INA division was still forming in Malaya. The military impact of the INA was negligible and the fighting spirit of its men often abysmal. The advancing Indian Army did not take kindly to the INA in Burma. In general, sepoys who fought and won hard campaigns against the Japanese had little time for those who had chosen to consort with the enemy.

Of the many thousands of Indian POWs who did not join the INA, or left in the early months of its existence, thousands were sent abroad to labour for the Japanese across the Pacific theatre. Many of these Indian POWs died by the time the war ended. Death rates were very high in some locations and at Wae Wae, on the north coast of New Guinea, starving Japanese guards resorted to cannibalizing their prisoners.[33] Without doubt, the death rate among those POWs who were not in the INA from 1943–45 was substantially higher than for those who were in it.[34] At the war's end, British officials determined that of 55,000 Indian POWs taken in Malaya, the INA enrolled 22,000 in their ranks from 1943 to 1945, whilst 15,000 POWs were shipped to the Southwest Pacific, and another 18,000 POWs were camped elsewhere in Malaya and the East Indies.[35]

Once the war was over, the British could not treat captured INA personnel as rebels in the strictest sense of the word, given the rapidly changing constitutional situation in India. By the close of 1945, Indian self-government was not far off. Bose was killed in an air crash in August 1945. In so far as Indian troops taken at Singapore came from within the heart of the Indian Army's traditional recruiting grounds, many ex-INA men had relatives in the Indian Army. One INA officer had a brother who won the Victoria Cross. During the war, INA agents landed in India for clandestine work were executed upon capture; but, for political and paternalistic reasons, British authorities in India had to take a soft line towards INA men after the war. Unless a specific crime was provable, INA prisoners were released and sent home. According to one set of figures, of 23,268 captured INA ex-POW personnel, after classification by investigating officers, only 3,880 were declared to be "white," meaning they had joined the INA either in order to desert or to infiltrate the organization.

These men were able to remain in the Indian Army. A further 6,177 were classified as "black," the hard core of the INA, and 13,211 were "greys." "Greys" were discharged and the "blacks" dismissed from the Army.[36]

In November and December 1945, a very public court martial of three Indian officers was held at the Red Fort in Delhi. The three officers were Captain Shah Nawaz Khan and Lieutenant G. S. Dhillon of the 1/14 Punjabis, and Captain P. K. Sahgal of the 2/10 Baluchis. All three officers were convicted of waging war against the King, and Shah Nawaz Khan was also convicted on a charge of abetment to murder. Sentences of transportation for life were remitted and the three men were cashiered. Yet the Indian political class defended the men on trial as patriots. The Red Fort trial was a public relations disaster for British officialdom. Other less public trials took place in 1946.[37] After India's independence from British rule in 1947, ex-INA officers were offered reinstatement in the Indian Army, but only at the rank they held at the time of the fall of Singapore. Few men took advantage of this offer, and ex-INA men were not welcomed by officers who had taken part in successful World War campaigns. Those Indian officers who had remained loyal in captivity carried on with their careers after the war, and several became senior generals prior to retirement.

When the campaign is looked at in review, from the British perspective, Indian troops have been heavily criticized in light of the mass desertions to the INA. Yet in the few profitable encounters for III Indian Corps formations in northern and central Malaya, such as at Kota Bahru and Kampar, Indians were as well-represented as British and Gurkha troops. Likewise, in Johore the underprepared 45th Indian Brigade fought no better or worse than the novice 53rd British Brigade. From 1942 to 1945, Indian Army formations performed creditably in North Africa, Italy and Burma. After a disastrous opening campaign in Burma, a retrained Indian Army won great victories against Japanese forces in 1944–45. The Allied army due to re-invade Malaya on 9 September 1945 was drawn from India. In an overall sense, the Second World War was a "successful" war for the Indian Army. But the political loyalty of a colonial force can never be entirely taken for granted. British political status in India in the 1940s was under threat in quite unique circumstances. This left the U.K.'s hired Indian military forces decidedly vulnerable to subversion in captivity.[38]

Alan Warren received his PhD in military history from Monash University in Melbourne, Australia where he is currently Lecturer in History. He is the author of Waziristan, the Faqr of Ipi and the Indian Army, *and of* Singapore: Britain's Greatest Defeat, *the most recent detailed study of the Malayan campaign and the fall of Singapore in World War II.*

NOTES—

1. W. S. Churchill, *The Second World War*, Vol. III, London, 1950, 379, 505–07, 577–78, 580–81.
2. A. Brett-James, *Ball of Fire: The Fifth Indian Division in the Second World War*, Aldershot, 1951, 16.
3. J. Ross and W. L. Hailes, *War Services of the 9th Jat Regiment*, ii, *1937–48*, London, 1965, 206.
4. Tsuji Masanobu, *Singapore: The Japanese Version*, Singapore, 1960, 96; Public Record Office (PRO), WO172/39, 9th Indian Division, 14 December 1941.
5. PRO, CAB106/54, Col. A. M. L. Harrison, History of 11th Indian Division, 40 and 46; A. E. Percival, *The War in Malaya*, London, 1949, 140.
6. India Office Library, London, (IOR) IOR/L/WS/1/952 - WS 16063, Maj.-Gen. David Murray-Lyon, *11th Indian Division: Short Summary of Events, 7–24 December 1941*, 4.
7. P. Elphick, *Singapore: The Pregnable Fortress*, London, 1995, 74–75 and 227; P. Elphick and M. Smith, *Odd Man Out: The Story of the Singapore Traitor*, London, 1993, 72–75.
8. PRO, WO172/18, Malaya Command, appendix V 8, 17 December 1941.
9. Imperial War Museum (IWM), Percival Papers, P 43, Comments by Percival on report by Air Vice-Marshal P. C. Maltby, 23 May 1947.
10. A. E. Percival, *The War in Malaya*, 208.
11. PRO, CAB 106/55, Harrison, 11th Indian Division, Malaya, 75; CAB101/156, Brig. I. M. Stewart, Comment on the Official History.
12. National Army Museum, Archives, London (NAM), 6509–14, Lt.-Col. C. C. Deakin, The Malayan Campaign, 1941–42, 5/2nd Punjab, 63–65.
13. IWM, Percival Papers, P 75, Lt.-Col. F. R.N. Cobley, Malaya Command, Typescript Report on Malayan Campaign, 1942–43, 153.
14. C. Mackenzie, *Eastern Epic*, London, 1951, 327; E. V. R. Bellers, *The 1st King George V's Own Gurkha Rifles: The Malaun Regiment*, ii, *1920–47*, Aldershot, 1956, 117.
15. G. R. Stevens, *The 9th Gurkha Rifles*, ii, *1937–47*, 1953, 170.
16. PRO, CAB101/156, Stewart, Comment on the Official History.
17. Tsuji Masanobu, *Singapore*, 175.
18. NAM, 7709–62, Maj. S. A. Watt, 7/6 Rajputana Rifles, The 7th Battalion in Malaya, 1942.
19. Ibid., 9–10.
20. Australian War Memorial (AWM), AWM 67, 11/6, 45th Indian Brigade.
21. J. Ross and W. L. Hailes, *War Services of the 9th Jat Regiment*, ii, 42.
22. NAM, 7709–62, Col. J. L. Jones Papers, Lt.-Col. C. G. W. Anderson, 27 and 29 May 1947.
23. NAM, 7309–2, account of Brig. G. C. Ballantine, 44th Indian Infantry Brigade, 2.
24. PRO, CAB106/58, Harrison, History of the 11th Indian Division, 29–31; W. S. Thatcher (ed.), *History of the 10th Baluch Regiment in the Second World War*, Abbottabad, 1980, 162.

25 IWM, Percival Papers, P31, Proceedings of the Conference Held at HQ Malaya Command Fort Canning at 1400 hours Friday 13 February 1942.
26 K. K. Ghosh, *The Indian National Army*, Meerut, 1969, 71–72.
27 IWM, 88/33/1, Lt.-Col. E. L. Sawyer, The Growth of the Indian National Army and the General Conditions of Indian POWs in Singapore from 1942 to 1945.
28 H. Toye, *The Springing Tiger: Subhash Chandra Bose*, Bombay, 1959, vii.
29 G. H. Corr, *The War of the Springing Tiger*, London, 1975, 116.
30 IOR, IOR/L/WS/2/45, Lt.-Col. G. D. Anderson, OC Combined Services Detailed Interrogation Centre, A Brief Chronological and Factual Account of the Indian National Army, 16 May 1942; K. K. Ghosh, *The Indian National Army*, 91.
31 IWM, 88/33/1, Sawyer, The Growth of the INA.
32 A. J. Barker, *The March on Delhi*, London, 1963; S. L. Menezes, *Fidelity and Honour*, New Delhi, 1993, 386–97.
33 W. E. H. Condon, *The Frontier Force Regiment*, Aldershot, 1962.
34 B. Farwell, *Armies of the Raj*, London, 1989, 339.
35 IOR, IOR/L/WS/1/1711.
36 B. Farwell, *Armies of the Raj*, 339.
37 K. K. Ghosh, *The Indian National Army*, 202.
38 In 1957, S. W. Kirby gave a total casualty figure for the Malayan campaign of 138,708, of which 67,340 were Indians. S. W. Kirby, *The War Against Japan*, i, London, 1957. This figure is certainly too high. In Volume 5 of *The War Against Japan*, London, 1969, 542, those figures were revised down to 130,246 and 60,427 respectively. F. A. E. Crew's *The Army Medical History*, ii, London, 1957, estimated Indian Army casualties in Malaya as 340 killed, 807 wounded, 4,909 missing and 57,682 POWs, a total of 62,931 assuming the wounded were either among the POWs or evacuated. Most of the missing men were very likely dead.

CHAPTER 14

"The men who did the fighting are now all busy writing": Australian Post-Mortems on Defeat in Malaya and Singapore, 1942–45

by Peter Stanley

Among the doggerel circulating in Changi early in 1942 was a satirical verse ending with:

> Third Corps do not confess,
> That they got us in the mess,
> But blames the whole disaster on Command;
> While the men who did the fighting,
> Are now all busy writing,
> And "sack the bloody lot" is their demand. [1]

As well as evoking the recrimination permeating discussion of the fall of Singapore, this verse emphasizes that written analyses of the campaign began in Changi within days of the surrender, by those who suffered the direct consequences of the defeat. These men's writing, however, has formed a surprisingly small part of the historical literature on the campaign. Sixty years since the fall of Singapore became a subject of historical debate, it is useful to look back at the first of those who wrote about it, the men of Malaya Command who became captives of the Japanese. By consulting sources from the period of captivity, the author hoped to evade the recrimination that has dominated the published literature. In considering their interpretations, it was clear that partisanship became apparent even as the guns of Singapore fell silent. Exposure to the records inevitably altered the focus of this research. It became largely a study of Lieutenant-Colonel Charles Kappe's *The Campaign in Malaya* in which a survey of the contemporary sources formed the context for a detailed study of this, the first history of the campaign.

This paper concentrates on the Australian evidence, and not merely as an advertisement for the collection of the Australian War Memorial. Rather, it is to serve as a reminder that hitherto the Malayan campaign has been considered overwhelmingly from British sources and from published sources. Other evidence, particularly from Japanese and Australian sources, has been too little used, and relatively few interpretations have been based adequately on primary evidence.[2] Despite the major part played by Australian troops in the campaign, very few authors have taken the trouble to consult the large body of primary material held in Australia. This paper, then, demonstrates the contribution Australian evidence—overlooked or under-used for 60 years—might make to understandings of the episode.

"Why did we lose Malaya?": Prisoners of War Seek Answers

With other British Empire troops on Singapore Island on 16 February 1942, Captain Herbert Geldard felt a "deep humiliation" at becoming a prisoner of war. The Australian liaison officer at Malaya Command headquarters, he immediately asked, "Why did we lose Malaya?" Geldard began analyzing possible explanations in his diary.[3] Many other men, with even greater reason to feel bewildered and confused, asked the same question and sought individuals or agencies on which to fix blame. "Men blamed officers," Geldard recalled of the early weeks in Changi, "junior officers blamed senior officers and junior formations blamed senior formations."[4]

Like Herbert Geldard, other officers reflected with a commendable professional objectivity on the Japanese achievement. Lieutenant-Colonel Leon Stahle, the 8th Australian Division's head of ordnance services, described the crossing of the Straits of Johore as "one of the world's great military feats." Yamashita's staff "planned perfectly [and] the men and officers crossed bravely and skilfully." As "a soldier and sportsman," and a member of the Australian Imperial Force in the Great War, Stahle conceded that "they are comparable with even our old AIF."[5] Other prisoners, however, understandably could maintain no such detachment. Reflection could easily become recrimination. Major Kennedy Burnside, a bacteriologist busy combating dysentery and malaria in Changi, recorded in his diary the Division's "disorganization, inefficiency, and incompetence." He regarded it as "a thorough and complete disgrace…one long tangle of bungling and inefficiency and outright stupidity."[6] Burnside lived alongside the divisional staff officers in Changi, and his judgement reflects gossip shared in their overcrowded quarters. It is notable, however, how contemporary sources generally do not reflect preoccupations evident in the later Australian historical literature, such as British culpability.

The most widely circulated and probably most persistent analyses of the campaign appeared in doggerel which men wrote and recited in the early months in Changi. Poems and verses can be found in notebooks and papers, especially those of other ranks, commenting bitterly on what had gone wrong and who was responsible. The notebook of Private A. R. Walton, for example, includes verses not only celebrating the campaign's few successes and mourning those who had died, but also pithily proposing explanations for the defeat.

> But when the sky is full of planes/ And every one a Jap
> It's then you wonder was it a dream/ For in the paper that you read
> Air Support will soon arrive/ As production goes ahead.[7]

Likewise, Staff Sergeant Robinson's notebook records verses, possibly by several authors, such as "Lies":

> They told us help was coming and in telling it they lied.
> We faced the foe together and many a soldier died.[8]

Their bitterness is evident in verses such as "The Army that was Betrayed":

> In the army that never was beaten, but the army that was betrayed,

or "Defeat," which blamed the loss on "complacency and smugness, plus inefficiency too."

Perhaps the ultimate in doggerel was the 65,000-word mock-epic poem, *Slaves of the Samurai*, written by Colonel Wilfrid Kent Hughes, the 8th Division's Chief Administrative Officer. In August 1942, Hughes was among the senior officers' party sent to Formosa and later to Japan and Manchuria. He wrote the poem in tiny script on scraps of paper hidden in a foot-powder tin. Published in 1946, it was one of the first narratives to describe captivity under the Japanese, albeit—because it described the experience of senior officers—one of the most benign. Beginning with the grand themes of Man and the Universe, it narrated the clash of empires in Asia and described the campaign, the surrender and life in a succession of camps. Hughes reflected on the defeat though, as a partisan of Major-General H. Gordon Bennett, he avoided the attribution of blame, especially since he shared captivity with Percival. Kent Hughes' judgment on the defeat was succinct but vague:

> ...perhaps a more important sphere
> Had claimed priority in men and gear.
> The troops on outpost had to pay the price
> Of wasted years of selfish avarice.[9]

Though increasingly oppressed by the physical and psychological burdens of captivity, Australian prisoners never forgot the brief but bloody month of fighting in January and February 1942. Units collated casualty statistics, searched for the bodies or graves of men killed in the fighting, built memorials and recalled the anniversaries of their actions. Indeed, the recollection of their successes bolstered a self-esteem eroded by a demeaning captivity. In January 1945, for example, Lieutenant-Colonel S. A. F. Pond sent to Brigadier Frederick Galleghan a letter expressing the regards of "all members of the 2/29 Bn" in memory of the 2/30's "baptism of fire in the engagement at Gemencheh." This, Pond wrote, "is still fresh in the minds of all."[10] Particularly early in captivity, men posed many questions and floated theories to explain the disaster they had been a part of.

Clearly many prisoners discussed the campaign in the long dark evenings in Changi. "Have to come to the conclusion," Sergeant Alec Hodgson confided to his diary after talking to men of several units, "that whole generalship broke down and there was never any serious attempt made to stop [the] Japs."[11] Other men made lists of reasons for the defeat. Staff Sergeant Arthur Robinson made a list of 35 reasons, including "Fifth Column," "Little air support," "Jealousy among officers," "Slackness during...training," "Wanting to know 'why'," "Too much personal gear" and (inevitably) "16" [sic] guns unable to fire inland."[12]

"Reasons for Our Defeat": Senior Officers in Captivity

While defeated commanders' experience as prisoners was physically less of an ordeal, captivity threw into close proximity men whose relations were often uneasy. The embarrassments of defeat made proximity uncomfortable. Major-General B.W. Key, who had commanded the 11th Indian Division, explained to the British official historian that his "natural inclination was to avoid any acrimonious discussions as to what had taken place."[13] In the case of Australian commanders and staff, the campaign added to grudges and feuds already productive of disasters during the fighting. The 8th Division's staff had been an unhappy one, largely because of Bennett's abrasive personality and paranoia over his staff's 'whispering' against him.[14] He had clashed with his senior staff officers—particularly the chief of staff, Lieutenant-Colonel Jim Thyer—and his brigadiers, among whom there was also a "prolonged antagonism."[15] Bennett's unauthorized escape from Singapore fuelled bad feeling. Thyer described to Lionel Wigmore how he and Wilfrid Kent

Hughes—a supporter of Bennett—"made a pact...never to mention Bennett." Though sharing an enforced and close captivity in Singapore, Formosa, Japan and Manchuria, the two never again alluded to their former commander.[16] Enforced company also bred confessions. Brigadier Arthur Blackburn VC, whose force had been captured in Java, recorded that an Australian brigadier in Singapore—and there were only two—told him that "I knew it was hopeless so I drew my men back from the beaches and let the Japanese through."[17]

Other officers, however, used the opportunity to write memoirs or formal narratives or analyses of the campaign, justifying their own part and criticizing with varying degrees of frankness and vigour the judgements and decisions of others. These included several Australian brigadiers and colonels, who seemed to have written in the six months before the departure of senior officers for Formosa and the formation of working parties sent from Singapore later in 1942. Harold Taylor, for instance, whose 22nd Brigade bore the brunt of the assault on the island, and gave more ground than any other, used the restoration of his formation's war diary to make an astringent attack on Bennett. He described Bennett as "a bitterly disappointed man who had seen his egotistical dreams fade away" amid ignorance, vanity and ambition.[18]

Lieutenant-Colonel Frederick Galleghan, who took over command of Australian prisoners in August 1942, completed a detailed typed manuscript on Japanese Army notepaper. He criticized Percival's dispositions on the island: "By trying to defend the whole coastline of the Island, General Percival was strong nowhere."[19] Galleghan advocated a different plan, conceding the northwest coast, holding a strong Kranji-Jurong line and using the 18th Division as a mobile reserve to counter-attack. Like other soldiers, Galleghan pondered the "Reasons for Our Defeat." Like others, his list was a long one. It included poor British leadership, training, the loss of command of the air and sea, and superior Japanese arms, intelligence and communications.[20] Galleghan concluded that while "the ultimate result of the campaign could not have been averted" a more skilful withdrawal in Malaya and more protracted defence in Singapore might have made a difference. Galleghan's battalion performed well in Malaya, especially at Gemas and Gemencheh. Secure in his unit's reputation, he could afford to be magnanimous.

"What we wanted to know": Dialogue with the Japanese

Because Changi was administered internally by the prisoners' own officers, very few of these documents fell into Japanese hands. However, the diary of David James, a British Japanese-speaking officer well-known to the Japanese, was stolen in July 1942. Translated and distributed to Japanese officers, they congratulated him on his summary of the campaign in Malaya.[21] The exchange worked both ways. Prisoners gathered evidence of what happened in the campaign not only from British and Australian sources, but also, at times bizarrely, from Japanese. Working parties clearing battle sites collated evidence of comparative casualties from the numbers of corpses they buried. In August, for example, a party returned from lifting mines at Mersing, on Johore's east coast. Their Japanese guards, who had fought in the battle for the island, wanted to know why the defenders' artillery did not fire at the landing barges crossing the Straits of Johore. "The only answer to that question," an Australian replied, "was that was what we wanted to know."[22]

The dialogue between victors and vanquished at times seemed surreal. About April, Brigadier Duncan Maxwell accompanied a wiring party from his brigade which was extending the apron wire to enclose more ground for gardens. As he stood watching his men, a car pulled up and a Japanese officer invited him in and engaged him in conversation, in French, the only language they shared. The Japanese officer—who had been an attaché in Paris—turned out to be Maxwell's "opposite number" in the fight for the causeway. The Japanese officer questioned Maxwell eagerly. He asked why Maxwell's batteries had shelled the Johore Bahru railway station when he knew that the Japanese were not able to use the trains. "I tried to put myself in your shoes," Maxwell explained. The absence of trains made the station useful cover for a battalion; accordingly Maxwell shelled it. "But that is what I thought and did," his admiring adversary replied. Emboldened by comradely exchange, Maxwell essayed a question of his own: How many "sampans" did the Australian artillery sink on the night of the crossing? The Japanese officer asked for Maxwell's estimate: 28. "Actually you sank 30." He added that the result was *"beaucoup de tués et beaucoup de blesses"* (many dead and many wounded).[23] Encounters with their captors did not always end as amicably, but the prisoners' curiosity about the Japanese would be evident in the formal records of the campaign completed in Changi.

"After a battle": The AIF War Diaries in Changi

For the first several months in Changi only "priority questions" dominated the attention of the captive commanders. Early in March, with the pressing matters of discipline, food, water, clothing, accommodation, power and above all hygiene and hospitals increasingly coming under control, AIF headquarters turned to a formal analysis of the campaign.[24] This would be based on the war diaries, many of which had been destroyed or negligently kept during the fighting. Lieutenant-Colonel Charles "Gus" Kappe was chosen to collect and if necessary reconstitute them. Kappe is central to the understanding of the wartime history of the campaign and deserves a proper introduction.[25]

Charles "Gus" Kappe was a professional soldier, a graduate of the Staff College at Quetta. He entered the Royal Military College, Duntroon at the age of 17 at the very end of the Great War, served in a variety of regimental and staff appointments and was posted to 8th Division Headquarters in 1940, becoming its Chief Signals Officer in July 1941. In the battle for Singapore, he organized and led an improvised force of signallers, known as the "Snake Gully Rifles." Though nominated as a technical specialist to be evacuated from Singapore, he and a party of 48 signallers missed their boat in the confusion of the docks.[26] Along with 15,000 other Australians, including his younger brother Alan, Kappe became a prisoner in Singapore.[27] Kappe was not greatly liked. When discipline slipped in the aftermath of the surrender, even his signallers expressed their disdain. Keith Wilson recalled that when the troops were filmed by the Japanese, Kappe told them to laugh and himself "guffawed in the most ridiculous fashion." Soon after, on the march into Changi, Kappe—"a bit of a blusterer"—reprimanded men for marching sloppily. A man told Kappe to "piss off" and when Kappe pointed out that he was wearing pips—badges of rank—the man told him to "shove them up your arse."[28] Out of a job after the surrender, he may have been seeking just such a challenge as the war diaries presented him in March 1942.

Unlike medical or engineer officers in Changi, Kappe had no obvious responsibility. Jim Thyer therefore asked him to compile the AIF war diaries. Thyer himself, conscious of Bennett's antagonism, carefully refrained from the task, wary that the veracity of the reconstituted diaries might later be challenged—as it was in the military and judicial inquiries held into Bennett's escape. The AIF Headquarters war diary records how this collation began from March. Frederick Galleghan observed how "it is easy to write a diary up after a battle" but at first Kappe had to chivvy officers to complete diaries and obtain maps.[29] "Still trying to re-write the Division War Diary," Captain Adrian Curlewis wrote unenthusiastically in May.[30] He hunted out company commanders who could write narratives rectifying the ignorance of battalion headquarters staff. Reconciling inconsistencies, Kappe described how he "cross-examined...most thoroughly" not only officers but "even other ranks directly connected with the event."[31] By early June, though some units were still dilatory, Kappe had gathered enough to prepare the first of a series of lectures that turned him into the Malayan campaign's first but also its most obscure historian.

"So we can know something": Lectures in Changi

Kappe's collation of the AIF's war diaries, Thyer recalled, "stimulated his interest in the campaign."[32] It led to the first of Kappe's lectures, "The Campaign in Malaya," on 30 June, presented as part of the brief flowering of educational endeavour known as the Changi University. Among talks on history, literature, travel and music, Thyer also lectured on "Leadership," reminding AIF officers of their responsibilities in captivity.[33] By this time, responding to the questions voiced by men of all ranks, several senior officers began to give lectures on the campaign. Lieutenant-General Sir Lewis Heath, who had commanded III Indian Corps, led the way, delivering frank and informative lectures. Copies of various versions of his lectures continued to circulate after he left Changi in August 1942. The commanding officer of the 5/2 Punjab Regiment, Lieutenant-Colonel Cecil Deakin, for example, spoke on "The Story of Slim River," answering many implicit questions about why the Indian formations gave way to the Japanese in Malaya.[34] Likewise, a Royal Air Force Group Captain lectured on the air forces in the campaign. Seeking to convince sceptical soldiers that their strictures were mistaken, he would have been gratified to learn that Lieutenant Lindsay Orr noted in his diary after a lecture that the Air Force "did a good job in Malaya."[35]

As well as presenting descriptions of the campaign, helping men to make sense of weeks they had experienced as chaotic or of actions of which they knew nothing, many of the lectures made a special effort to understand the victorious enemy. Senior officers sought to discern reasons for their success in Japanese military culture as well as in weapons and tactics. Heath, for example, praised the Japanese "spirit of self-sacrifice" and their ability to live off the country. Taylor attributed their tactical success to their "greater mobility and physical condition," riding on bicycles and carrying guns on their backs. Referring to the amount of motor transport in Commonwealth units, he considered that "we immobilized ourselves by having too much mobility."[36]

Gus Kappe was evidently a good speaker. "Splendid lecture by Kappe," Curlewis noted.[37] Based on his continuing questioning of men and officers, Kappe revised his lectures, with the help of officers and men eager to know what went wrong and why. Alan Rogers, a medical captain, typed out a further version, "so we can know something of this confused campaign if only I can get them home."[38] Kappe lectured with several intentions. As a senior officer who had experienced at first hand the consequences of allowing morale and discipline to slip, he sought to encourage pride in the Command's achievements in spite of the ultimate defeat. He tried, for example, "to dispel the idea that the gunners [had] let the infantry down."[39] After a lecture in December 1942, one of his audience recorded that "on the mainland the AIF did a good job [—] equal to the 1st AIF."[40] The lectures were not simply ways of killing time, either for Kappe or his audiences. They gave listeners the knowledge and explanations they craved, and which they doubtless passed on and discussed with those who had not attended. Men puzzled by errors or failures in battle could be satisfied with Kappe's accounts. In recording "some of the reasons for our defeat" Lieutenant Gilbert Hamilton, for example, noted how the failure to fire at the attacking Japanese in Singapore was because "our Heads thought there was going to be a siege and limited our guns to 12 rounds per day."[41]

Kappe's lectures gave his audiences opportunities to pose fresh questions. Alan Rogers, for example, did not simply type lectures for Kappe. Like many men, he was eager to know what went wrong, and took the opportunity to interpolate questions into Kappe's drafts. When Kappe blandly recorded that "permission was given to come back to Mandai"—one of the many unexplained or unauthorized withdrawals made by Australian units in Singapore—Rogers added, "Why?" When Kappe admitted a "lack of knowledge of decisions made at Bennett's headquarters," Rogers challenged, "*For what reason?*"[42] Kappe likewise sought out men who could help him refine his account and fill gaps in the records. His manuscript was based not only on careful scrutiny of Australian and—evidently—British formation and unit war diaries, but also on testimony collected from what Thyer described as "hundreds of persons ranging from private to Lieutenant-General."[43] In Changi, he told John Treloar, men "came to him to tell him where he was right or to add to his knowledge."[44] Thyer recalled how he "interrogated officers of the A[rgyll] & S[utherland] H[ighlanders] at some length."[45] He also drew on available Japanese officers, such as Lieutenant-Colonel Kamamura Saturo, who allowed him to resolve questions about the artillery support for the crossing of the Straits of Johore.[46] In this way, Kappe's history turned into a sort of debate between the historian and his readers. Writing for men with such a strong interest in the interpretations he reached, and who simultaneously were his "sources," placed him in a unique position among the historians of this or any other campaign. By early 1943, after a year of reading, talking and writing, Kappe was evidently committed to producing a history of the Malayan campaign.

"Lessons from the Malayan campaign": The Syndicates' Reports

The collation of the war diaries coincided with an optimistic but brief expression of the military spirit in Changi. In July, with Galleghan slated to succeed Major-General Callaghan, headquarters officers proposed that the AIF in Changi should be organized into units which could become combatants in the event of an Allied landing on Singapore.[47] Expressed circumspectly, for obvious reasons, the AIF diary referred to a policy including the force's "organization...for possible employment in a number of capacities."[48] The sceptical Ken Burnside recorded that Galleghan "believes that we will fight soon and that we must...get some training done in the meantime. I think he's an optimist."[49] Following the departure of senior officers on 16 August and the "Selarang Barrack Square Incident" early in September, in accordance with his vision to prepare the AIF for combat,

Galleghan reorganized his force. Gus Kappe was to command a composite 22/27 Brigade Group while Lieutenant-Colonel W. D. Jeater commanded a "base group" of service and support units. Preparing officers to lead the force in battle in the event of an Allied landing led Galleghan to institute refresher courses in military skills. He called in textbooks and encouraged officers to read them, held junior and senior officers courses and had syndicates of officers consider and report on the lessons of the Malayan campaign.[50]

At Kappe's orders, 16 "syndicates" of officers from the 22/27 Brigade Group convened during October.[51] Under a formal "directing staff" they were asked to consider the campaign and comment on the strengths and weaknesses of British Empire and Japanese forces. The syndicates comprised groups of infantry company and platoon commanders, but also of machine-gunners, mortar and Bren carrier platoon officers, field and anti-tank gunners, signallers and transport officers. Burnside, of course, was correct. Besides sharpening officers in danger of becoming idle, it achieved nothing. The course's legacy was to constitute the main official Australian post-mortem on the campaign. Much of the substance of the reports concerned the minutiae of equipment or method. The carrier platoon syndicate, for example, recommended, among other things, that "the drivers and gunners seats…be adjustable to comfortably seat *any* sized man."[52] The field artillery gunners specified that in future all vehicles should be equipped with metal channels, picks, shovels and axes and a towing rope.

Galleghan and Kappe revised and summarized the syndicates' reports. Though suggesting many changes to weapons, equipment and methods, they essentially confirmed the value of existing British Empire doctrine: "Read your [military text] books," Galleghan urged.[53] Given the remote likelihood of any relief arriving, Galleghan's syndicates look like yet another attempt to keep bored officers interested. There is more than a whiff of fantasy about the directing staff's assumptions, who asked the participants to suppose that the force they were analyzing would be "armed and equipped as we were prior to capitulation," but that it would also enjoy "air superiority and [that] tanks will be available." Still, the exercise has an enduring value in that it discloses deeper considerations.

Two of the subjects on which the syndicates did not offer putative lessons were, not surprisingly perhaps, the strategic situation which led to Malaya being chronically unprepared for attack, or the decisions of Australian or British commanders in the campaign. Since the campaign was obviously not lost because of the lack of sand-channels or adjustable seats, the reports might be thought to be useless. Though avoiding the questions which have interested most historians of the campaign, however, the syndicates' reports nevertheless disclose an awareness of other, deeper explanations for the defeat. Though avoiding questions of strategic and command responsibility, many reports strayed beyond the technical. Most syndicates commented on the contrast between British Empire and

Japanese troops. Since their capture, in their diaries, prisoners had had occasional opportunities to observe their captors and many reflected on what they observed. The syndicates' papers also developed the themes evident from the lectures delivered in Changi, seeing in the qualities of their adversaries an explanation for their success. They drew attention to the folly of the racial stereotypes so prevalent before February 1942. Kappe noted that "statements such as 'The Japanese don't fight at night' [and] 'One Australian is equal to 10 Japanese' proved to be absolute eyewash."[54] Though aware of Japanese weaknesses—their lack of initiative and dislike for hand-to-hand fighting—the syndicates' members repeatedly stressed the contrast between the two sides. A syndicate of company commanders, for instance, compared the veteran Japanese with novice Australians. They saw how the Japanese "spirit of discipline lies in each man," "a readiness to die for his cause" and "a remarkable aptitude for living off the land." In their own force, they saw "discipline poor," "many men too old" and "training inadequate." This was more than an acceptance of the reality of defeat. It signified a careful reflection on the more fundamental reasons for defeat.

Within a few months, most of the officers who drafted reports had left Changi, most with their men on working parties bound for Burma and Thailand. With them went Gus Kappe, and with him his growing manuscript history of the Malayan campaign. The manuscript played an ambiguous role in one of the great tragedies to afflict Australian prisoners of war.

"I had to look after myself": Kappe and F Force

In April 1943, Kappe was given command of the Australian component of "F" Force, among the most unfortunate of the prisoner-of-war working parties to leave Changi. Like "H" Force, Kappe's group was inadvertently never transferred from the Imperial Japanese Army's prisoner-of-war administration in Malaya to its counterpart in Thailand. Sent to the most remote sections of the Burma-Thailand railway during the monsoon, it suffered heavy casualties from starvation, overwork, brutality and conditions such as dysentery, beri-beri, malaria, tropical ulcers and cholera. F Force's ordeal in the railway camps of Songkurai, Neike and Taimonta is comparable to those of other prisoners at Ambon, Hainan, Palembang and Sandakan. Of the force's 7,000 members—3,600 British and 3,400 Australian—over 2,000 British and 1,068 Australian prisoners died on the railway.

Kappe's diary of the force's travails constitutes a meticulous record both of its ordeal and of the fates of its members, including emphatic protests to the Japanese complaining of brutality and neglect.[55] The detailed 50,000-word report that he and Captain Adrian Curlewis completed in May 1944 constitutes a sustained indictment of the Japanese and a testament to the prisoners' endurance in the face of indifference and brutality.[56] The contemporary records of F Force's members, however, suggest Kappe's severe shortcomings as a commander. Many despised him: some still do. Don Wall, a member of the force and a passionate chronicler of the experience of prisoners of war on the railway and in Borneo, wrote in *Heroes of F Force* of the admiration for the work of its medical officers and orderlies. Wall and many others particularly singled out a medical officer, Major Bruce Hunt—whom Kappe recommended for a decoration—for his heroic struggle against disease and the Japanese. By contrast, he describes Kappe as "inefficient and incompetent."[57]

Some of the criticisms are unjustified. Don Wall criticized Kappe for believing Japanese undertakings that the force was destined for rest camps. This is unfair. Galleghan was told that the force would be going to a "pleasant hilly place" with ample facilities for recreation, which is why 30% of the original force was unfit or sick before its members left.[58] Wall also believed that in order to leave first to secure the best barracks for his men, Kappe cancelled inoculations that would have saved men's lives in wretched jungle camps on the railway.[59] AIF medical records in Changi, however, disclose that inoculations were planned weeks before the force's departure, but that the second cholera and plague inoculations, scheduled for 21–22 April, could not be administered because the Japanese advanced the force's departure by several days.[60] Even so, it is clear that Kappe failed.

Joan Beaumont and Hank Nelson have discussed the demands of leadership in captivity, showing how discipline depended upon the establishment of informal rather than formal authority. Some senior officers could not meet the terrible challenge they confronted.[61] Unlike more forceful commanders in similar circumstances, such as "Weary" Dunlop or "Black Jack" Galleghan, Kappe lacked the gift to impose his will on his men or on the Japanese. When, in May, Kappe warned his men against the impossibility of escaping from Taimonta, he was probably seen to "bluster" as he had on the way into Changi. Lieutenant Ron Eaton, the 2/30's intelligence officer, for example, dismissed another address by Kappe as "general blah excuses for Senior Officers."[62] Even the history of the divisional signallers praised men who succeeded in escaping the day after his warning. His own unit's history implicitly portrayed him as a dupe of the Japanese.[63] Lloyd Cahill, who accompanied him as a medical officer, recalled that the men "had him wiped"—had dismissed him as ineffective.[64] Kappe described being beaten or humiliated while standing up to the Japanese.[65] The dominant perception among his men, however, was that he was weak. Some former prisoners of war even referred to him as "Kappe-san" or "Kappeama"— the Japanese suffixes implying his compliance.[66] Other men who knew him on the railway feel sympathy for a man exposed as unequal to the demands of leadership in captivity.[67] It is ironic that among the lectures he listened to in

Changi was one by Jim Thyer, who reminded his audience that "rank confers privileges, but it also imposes responsibilities."[68]

It is tempting to suggest that as a signals officer, Kappe was constitutionally comfortable with recording and transmitting rather than with commanding. His diary of F Force's ordeal is a full record but it does not reveal Kappe to have taken charge: He was remote, if not entirely ineffective. The evidence that he did not resist Japanese demands that sick men work or try to secure improved rations, accommodation or medical care comes mainly from the diary of Ron Eaton. In August, he described Kappe as "completely 'Jap Happy'…non-active and not accepting any responsibility for camp."[69] Wall described him as "cloistered…with other senior officers at the Songkurai camp in a hut on a hill, remote from the squalor and misery of the men's huts below them."[70] Here he kept his records and, it was rumoured, continued to write his history of the campaign.

It might seem incredible that Kappe should bring the manuscript with him to Thailand. Like all of F Force, however, Kappe had been told that it was destined to occupy comfortable camps. The force packed large amounts of equipment, including band instruments, most of which was dumped during the nightmare three-week 300-kilometre march through jungle and monsoon rain to the camps in northern Thailand. The manuscript was fortunate to survive. At least once the box in which it was carried was ransacked by Thais, and the maps accompanying it left Kappe exposed to charges that he planned to escape. A Royal Signals officer, Eric Lomax, was tortured and imprisoned in Outram Road gaol for being found with a map on the railway.[71] The manuscript was distributed among up to 20 prisoners, concealed in bags, boots and tool boxes.[72] On the way back from Thailand, Adrian Curlewis wrapped the manuscript in sacking and packed it with tools in one of two trunks labelled "Ordnance Stores."[73]

These boxes played a climactic role in the final drama of F Force and Kappe's manuscript. Kappe left Thailand with the first group of the force's fit survivors. They travelled by train to Bangkok and on 10 December embarked on an old tramp steamer bound for Singapore. Here his men's resentment came to a head. While Kappe was called away, his men broke into his trunks. Sergeant Keith Meakin, one of Kappe's signallers, described how the men found tinned herrings and Virginia cigarettes. They ate the fish, which they believed Kappe had retained from Red Cross stores and in any case should have given to their sick comrades still lying in attap huts at Songkurai. Later, Kappe rounded on them. "There are many versions of what he was reported to have said," Meakin wrote, but the most common account had Kappe taking off his shirt and offering to fight the culprits as his men booed and jeered and walked away. Later, he apologized, explaining to his signallers, "I had to look after myself to tell the story."[74]

"A British official history": Kappe's Manuscript

On their return from Thailand, Kappe and Curlewis wrote a long and detailed report on F Force's sufferings. However remote he had been, Kappe evidently understood enough of his men's ordeal to write movingly and in detail of the horror of long hours of labour on starvation rations at the urging of engineers and guards indifferent to the prisoners' plight. Though hardly mentioning Kappe in a long account of F Force—itself a telling judgement—Bill Sweeting drew on his report in his chapters of the official history. Indeed, one of the most moving passages in Sweeting's generally restrained account, describing the working routine on the railway, quoted Kappe's report verbatim.[75]

Once back in Changi, and after completing a detailed report on F Force's ordeal, Kappe devoted himself to his manuscript. He later estimated that he spent three to four hours a day or 25 hours a week for the duration.[76] He modelled his manuscript on one of the two examples immediately available to him. He could have attempted a history like Charles Bean's volumes of the Australian official history of the Australian Imperial Force in the Great War, with its focus on the experiences of the individual soldier in the frontline. As a regular soldier, lacking the vision and "span" that made Bean the writer he was, Kappe was unlikely to have followed this course.[77] As a staff officer, concerned with determining what had occurred in the campaign and more particularly what went wrong, Kappe adopted the alternative, an analysis based on the staff history, for which James Edmonds' British official history provided the model. He described his manuscript to John Treloar as "a British official history, not the kind written by Dr Bean."[78] He generally avoided mentioning personalities besides unit or formation commanders and favoured the passive voice: "Careful investigation has failed to reveal who was really responsible for the plan which permitted 27th Brigade to fall back."

But in revising the manuscript, Charles Kappe developed the instincts of a historian. He seized on key episodes, selected evidence and shaped it to form not only a technical analysis but an account answering important questions. An idea of its contribution may be gained from considering how Kappe treated the contentious days following the Japanese landing on Singapore Island on 8–9 February, when the Japanese 5th and 18th Divisions drove back the 22nd Australian Brigade from the swampy, mangrove-fringed shore of the Straits of Johore.[79] Kappe acknowledged the "bitter controversy" which continued "for weeks after the capitulation" between the infantry and the gunners of the 2/15 Field Regiment over the support the artillery did or did not provide that night. Kappe traced the multitude of individual actions over a long front and the contribution made by the batteries of the 2/15. He concluded that the claim against the gunners could not be substantiated. Though he rarely cited particular sources, he did use

Japanese casualty figures—half of which were inflicted on the night of the landing—to contest the insinuation that the 22nd Brigade "did not fight to its utmost." Kappe used the evidence in the war diaries, from fellow prisoners of war and from the Japanese, to construct a convincing narrative.

Despite the handicap of producing an official operational analysis, Kappe's writing is often vivid, departing from the impersonal prose of the military report. He had an eye for the striking phrase, quoting Taylor's prediction on the afternoon of 8 February, "Soon the leaves will begin to fall." In describing the Japanese fire landing amid the forward positions of the 22nd Brigade on the night of 8–9 February, he likens "the roar of the barrage" to "the terrific rumble of a tropical thunderstorm." In conveying the effects of the bombardment, he described "the face of a hill…so severely 'strafed' that by evening it resembled a ploughed field." He recalled telling detail, of how rubber trees inches-thick were cut through by intense machine-gun fire. Kappe's *The Malayan Campaign* needs to be combed through to compare it with Australian, British and Japanese sources, but it is worth the effort.

The manuscript, typed on odd sheets of paper—including the backs of Naval Message forms found in so many Changi collections—and heavily revised, came back to Australia late in 1945. Thyer based his official "Report of Operations" on the 8th Australian Division's part in the Malaya and Singapore campaign on it (and also Galleghan's narrative).[80] Thyer acknowledged Kappe's narrative as the basis of his report but added "opinion and criticism… in numerous places." Chapter VI, "Reasons for Rapid Defeat," frankly discussed the "delicate question" of "conflict in Command."[81] Thyer was at last able to settle an animosity which began in late 1941, imposed intolerable and costly strain during the fighting and rankled during long years of imprisonment. He described Bennett as incapable of accepting the orders of higher commanders or of winning the loyal cooperation of his subordinates. He based his estimate not only on his own experience but also on conversations with Percival, Heath and Key in captivity. Thyer also frankly acknowledged the losses to stragglers and deserters in the final days of the Singapore battle. Perhaps because he frankly admitted the animosities that pervaded the Division's commanders and staff, and alluded to the consequent effects on the Division's performance, Thyer's report was repudiated by Lieutenant-General Sydney Rowell, Chief of the General Staff 1950–54.[82] Though the report was used by both the British and Australian official historians, the 8th Division—alone of the Australian formations in the Second World War—had no official report.

The Malayan Campaign came to the attention of the Australian official historian, Gavin Long, through John Treloar, the head of the Military History Section, in October 1945. Long knew that the volumes of his history were years from completion. As a historian vitally interested in disseminating a variety of views, he encouraged Kappe to publish it: "The more that is published by men in the services the better," he wrote.[83] It soon became clear that the politics of the Australian Army would preclude early publication, and the story of Kappe's manuscript became a sad tale of disappointment.

His first disappointment was in failing to be appointed official historian for what became the volume *The Japanese Thrust*. Kappe had made clear to John Treloar—and through him Gavin Long—that he felt he knew more of the campaign than any other person.[84] He wanted to help produce the official history and even to be considered for the job. Long had not yet selected an author to cover the Malaya-Singapore campaign. Kappe was soon perturbed to learn the task had gone to Tom Mitchell—an 8th Division officer wounded in the campaign. Understandably outraged, Kappe considered Mitchell's "only qualification is that he has had a Varsity education."[85] Contrary to Kappe's implication, Mitchell was no mere dabbler, but was obliged to give up the task because he was "forbidden from holding two offices of profit under the Crown." Treloar suggested that "a volume impinging upon politics...might place a permanent officer in a difficult position."[86] Indeed, as a member of the unharmonious divisional staff and as a senior officer known to have failed on the railway, it was inconceivable that Kappe would have been nominated to write the history of such a sensitive campaign. Mitchell, however, failed to begin much less complete the research and by early 1948, Lionel Wigmore, a journalist like Long, was appointed. Kappe expressed his regret at again missing out but nevertheless offered to assist Wigmore and sent his manuscript to the Australian War Memorial for Wigmore to consult. It remained in the Memorial's strong room for the best part of a decade: *The Malayan Campaign* never appeared as a book.

"Some hard words": The Manuscript's Fate

Kappe was awarded an OBE in 1949, for "high courage, resource and leadership" in the campaign; no mention was made of his services in Thailand.[87] He was, however, disappointed in publishing the manuscript as a book. Though he claimed copyright over it, the Army regarded it as an official document and asserted its authority.[88] As a regular soldier who soon returned to duty, in 1946 going to Japan with the occupation force, he accepted the decision that he could not publish his account before Percival published his official despatch in the *London Gazette*, which appeared in February 1948. In the meantime, he was revising portions of the manuscript which Vernon Sturdee, the Chief of the General Staff 1946–50, considered "a little severe."[89] Wigmore, embarrassed perhaps at being given the job, offered to help Kappe cut the 200,000-word manuscript by half to make it publishable, but the offer came to nothing.

In the end, even after Percival's despatch appeared, Kappe was refused permission to publish while still a serving soldier. Not only would his work arouse controversy, it would do so at a time of particular sensitivity. Until 1948, the Australian Army had been a largely citizen force with a small regular "Staff Corps." Citizen and Staff Corps officers competed for appointments and commands in a contest in a vicious war of influence and innuendo. The tensions within Bennett's headquarters partly drew their venom from these long-standing divisions. In the aftermath of the Great War, regular officers were denied jobs and promotions. After 1945, they were determined that a regular Army was needed both to meet Australia's different strategic situation but also to ensure the humiliation and disappointments of the interwar years would not be repeated. Accordingly, the dominance of the citizen force was challenged by the creation of an Army in which regulars would become dominant. For Sturdee, publication of Kappe's work at a time when citizen officers were especially wary or angry was an unnecessary risk. Sturdee told Wigmore that Kappe had been refused permission to publish because it might "revive permanent forces versus citizen forces controversy." Kappe's offer to "soft pedal" Bennett was insufficient to sway Sturdee.[90] In any case, as a regular—indeed the commander of the first regular infantry brigade from 1951 to 1954—Kappe had a direct interest in the successful transition to the new Australian Army.

Through the early 1950s, Lionel Wigmore referred to Kappe's manuscript in writing his account of the campaign. He also arranged to send a copy to S. W. Kirby who was writing the British volume of the official history, *The Loss of Singapore*. Though acknowledging Kappe's work in the introduction to his volume, Kirby privately wrote to Wigmore patronizingly, "You realize, of course, that there are a great many inaccuracies in the story ... many of the comments are ill-formed."[91] In the light of the sensitivity of the story, it is quite possible that Kirby described as wrong what he disagreed with and found ill-formed what he found uncomfortable. Kappe began to suspect that his work was neither to be published nor used as more than a quarry for the official historians.[92]

Within weeks of retiring, in December 1954, Kappe published his history. It appeared in shortened instalments in the Sydney *Daily Telegraph* and the Melbourne *Sun* in February 1955.[93] This ephemeral form would have reached many former members of the 8th Division and "answers questions we've been asking for years," but it can hardly have satisfied an author who hoped to write an official history. Instead, Kappe remained out of the mainstream of writing on the campaign. Due to an oversight, the proofs of *The Japanese Thrust* were sent to him without a request to comment. By the time the error was rectified, it was too late to incorporate his suggestions into the final text. Kappe obstinately declined to take the initiative to comment unasked. Wigmore's volume, Kappe judged, "completely glossed over...errors and failings." He described *The Japanese Thrust* as "pitiful," a view not shared by reviewers of the volume in Australia and the U.K.[94] However, with Wigmore's history published, Kappe accepted that he would never see his work become a book. He allowed the sealed copy which had been held in the Memorial's strong room to be released and resigned himself to obscurity.

Increasingly afflicted by failing sight in retirement, Charles Kappe died of a heart attack in Brisbane in 1967. An obituary maintained that he had been "a relentless fighter for the welfare of his men" in captivity, and that his history had been "used as the basis of the official war history."[95] Neither claim was justifiable.

Consulted only to be rejected by Kirby, and treated with what he regarded as disdain by Wigmore, Kappe's work was otherwise disregarded. It does not appear in the bibliographies of any of the major re-evaluations of the Malaya-Singapore campaign, even the several extensively based on Australian records.[96] While reconstructing the 8th Australian Division's war diary, Adrian Curlewis foresaw that "some hard words will appear when the whole story is written."[97] Hard words made the whole story less likely to be told. It is perhaps fortunate that Kappe's manuscript survived at all. Kent Hughes discovered that at least one prisoner-of-war diary sent to Army Headquarters "was destroyed because it contained criticisms."[98] It was apparent that the experience of fruitlessly revising *The Malayan Campaign*, while seeing others' histories appear, made Kappe a more mature historian than he had begun. He moved from a chronicler and recorder of facts to a writer beginning to select and explain and even argue. At the same time, the pressure exerted upon Long and his colleagues pushed them in the opposite direction. Long replied to Kappe's criticism by conceding the impossibility of reaching an honest judgement while key protagonists were alive and prepared to sue. As a result, "most of us…working on this war history are tending more and more to set out the facts…and to superimpose relatively little of our own comment."[99] The difficulty of Wigmore's task should not be underestimated—he had as the responsible minister Wilfrid Kent Hughes, Bennett's supporter, who at various times expressed the desire to bring influence to bear upon the project. Still, it is apparent that Long and Wigmore spoke with discretion rather than with risky candour—on questions such as the proportion of Australian deserters abroad in Singapore in mid-February—rather than stand up to it; like Kappe on the railway, perhaps.

Kappe's *The Malayan Campaign* was not the only book on the campaign begun in captivity. The history of the 2/30 Battalion, begun "within a month of the fall of Singapore," was so far advanced that when published in 1949, its title page bore the name of Lance Corporal Cliff Bayliss, who died of cholera at Songkurai in Thailand as a member of F Force in May 1943.[100] Kappe's history, however, was the first complete history of the campaign. It was written by a participant, using records he largely assembled personally, revised and corrected after extensive interviews with many other participants.

Many of his informants later died as prisoners of war, in jungle camps in Burma and Thailand, in Borneo and Japan and at sea, being transported across Japan's wartime empire. For their sake, if none other, whatever its shortcomings, it deserves better than the obscurity to which it has been unknowingly consigned.

The history of Gus Kappe's *The Malaya Campaign* is a sad tale. In a sense, it is the tragic story of the story of a tragedy. Kappe's deficiencies as a leader in captivity, though lamentable, are not relevant to his pioneering historical research, which adds detail and elaboration to the existing knowledge of the campaign. His manuscript deserves to be better known and brought to the attention of those who can best appreciate the contribution it can still make to our understanding of the events in Malaya and Singapore 60 years ago.[101]

Dr. Peter Stanley is Principal Historian at the Australian War Memorial, Australia's national war museum and a centre for research. He has worked on many exhibitions in the Memorial, including the recent Second World War gallery. He has published widely on Australian and British imperial military history. In 2002, he will publish three books: Whyalla at War *(a study of the impact of the Second World War on an industrial town),* For Fear of Pain: British Surgery 1790–1870 *and (with Mark Johnston)* Alamein: The Australian Story.

NOTES—

1. L. Wigmore, *The Japanese Thrust*, Canberra, 1957, 511n.
2. Major works on the Malaya-Singapore campaign have been based entirely on published sources. Except for the official histories—which did not cite references—the only major works to use primary evidence have been A. B. Lodge's excellent study *The Fall of General Gordon Bennett*, Sydney, 1986; P. Elphick, *Singapore: The Pregnable Fortress*, London, 1995; Brian Farrell's chapters in M. H. Murfett et al., *Between Two Oceans: A Military History of Singapore From First Settlement to Final British Withdrawal*, 1999; and A. Warren's *Singapore 1942: Britain's Greatest Defeat*, Sydney, 2002. Though dealing in detail with Australian desertions in the battle for Singapore, Elphick used few Australian sources, and those only because they had been copied for the British official historians.
3. AWM PR91/194, Diary of Captain Herbert Geldard, AIF, Malaya Command, entry, 16 February 1942.
4. Ibid., 76. The passage was incorporated in A. J. Sweeting's section on prisoners of war in the Australian official history, *The Japanese Thrust*, 511.
5. AWM PR89/59, Papers of Lt.-Col. Leon Stahle, 8th Division Signals, AIF, diary, 19 February 1942.
6. AWM 3 DRL 7665, Diary of Maj. Kennedy Burnside, Mobile Bacteriological Laboratory, AIF, entry, 1 June 1942.

7   The Battle of Johore, in AWM PR83/3, Notebook of Pte. A. R. Walton, 27 Brigade Petrol Company, AIF.
8   AWM PR00472, Papers of S/Sgt. Arthur Robinson, 8th Division Signals, AIF, notebook, n.d.
9   K. Hughes, *Slaves of the Samurai*, Melbourne, 1946, 33.
10 AWM 3 DRL 2313, Papers of Brig. Frederick Galleghan, 8th Division, AIF, Lt.-Col. S. A. F. Pond to Galleghan, 15 January 1945. Galleghan's papers include letters from other units in Changi.
11 AWM PR91/141, Diary of Sgt. Alec Hodgson, 2/6th Field Park Company, AIF, entry, 2 March 1942.
12 AWM PR00472, Papers of Sgt. Arthur Robinson, notebook.
13 AWM 73, item 7, Official War Historian working notes, correspondence and source material (Kirby tour), Maj.-Gen. B. W. Key to S. W. Kirby, 27 September 1952.
14 A. B. Lodge, *The Fall of General Gordon Bennett*, 65–67.
15 Thyer's introduction to AWM 54, 553/5/23, Part 1, Operations of 8th Australian Division in Malaya 1942, describes the antagonism between himself and Bennett, Bennett and Taylor, himself and Taylor and Taylor and Callaghan.
16 AWM 93, 50/2/23/480, Correspondence with Col. J. H. Thyer, Thyer to Wigmore, 30 March 1952.
17 AWM 67, item 3/36, Arthur Blackburn; quoted in A. Warren, *Singapore 1942*, 332–33, n. 40.
18 AWM PR85/42, Papers of Brig. Harold Taylor, 22nd Australian Infantry Brigade, AIF.
19 AWM 3 DRL 2313 Papers of Brig. Frederick Galleghan, Campaign narrative, 39.
20 Ibid., 65–68.
21 D. James, *The Rise and Fall of the Japanese Empire*, London, 1951, 245.
22 AWM 3 DRL 7665, Diary of Maj. Kennedy Burnside, entry, 18 August 1942.
23 AWM 73, item 7, Brig. D. S. Maxwell to Gavin Long, December 1952.
24 AWM 52, 1/5/19, War diary, Headquarters AIF Malaya, February 1942–February 1943, Notes of Conferences March–May 1942.
25 Kappe signed his signature as Kappé. In typed and printed documents, however, the difficulties of adding the accent reconciled him to its absence. His name was pronounced Kappe, not Kappé, and I have accordingly not used the accent.
26 AWM 52, 7/16/8, War diary, 8th Division Signals, February 1942.
27 Private Alan Kappe, also of 8th Division Signals, survived the Burma-Thailand railway, in a different force to his older brother.
28 K. Wilson, *You'll Never Get Off the Island: Prisoner of War, Changi, Singapore, February 1942–August 1945*, Sydney, 1989, 6–7.
29 AWM 73, item 51, Lionel Wigmore, interview notes, interview with Maj.-Gen. F. Galleghan, Canberra, 1 February 1950.
30 Entry, 27, 28 May 1942, P. Poole, *Of Love and War: The Letters and Diaries of Captain Adrian Curlewis and His Family 1939–1945*, Sydney, 1982, 132.
31 AWM 93, 50/2/23/116, Records of...Lt.-Col. Kappe, 8th Division, Kappe to Wigmore, 16 April 1952.

32 AWM 93, 50/2/23/480, Correspondence with Col. J. H. Thyer, James Thyer, [critique of] *The Japanese Thrust*.
33 [Typescript pending donation], Leadership, lecture by Col. J. H. Thyer, 18 June 1942.
34 The Story of Slim River, in AWM PR85/145, Papers of Capt. Alan Rogers, 3 Advanced Depot Medical Stores, AIF. The folder also contains an anonymous lecture, The Story of Muar.
35 AWM PR89/77, Diary of Lt. Lindsay Orr, 8th Division AASC, AIF Diary, 10 August 1942.
36 Transcripts of lectures by Heath and Taylor in AWM MSS793, Papers of Lt. Gilbert Hamilton, AASC, AIF.
37 Entry, 9 June 1942, P. Poole, *Of Love and War*, 133.
38 AWM PR85/145, Papers of Capt. Alan Rogers, entry, 3 February 1943.
39 AWM 93, 50/2/23/116, Kappe to Wigmore, 16 April 1952.
40 AWM PR89/77, Diary of Lt. Lindsay Orr, entry, 18 December 1942.
41 AWM MSS793, Papers of Lt. Gilbert Hamilton, notes from lectures in Changi Prison camp.
42 AWM PR85/145, Papers of Capt. Alan Rogers, draft of Kappe's lecture, The Malayan Campaign. The draft is annotated to make clear that the questions are Rogers'.
43 AWM 93, 50/2/23/480, Correspondence with Col. J. H. Thyer, James Thyer, [critique of] *The Japanese Thrust*.
44 AWM 93, 50/2/23/116, Record of telephone conversation between John Treloar and Kappe, 25 January 1946.
45 AWM 93, 50/2/23/480, Thyer's answers to Questionnaire No. 2, April 1952.
46 AWM 93, 50/2/23/116, Kappe to Wigmore, 16 April 1952.
47 S. F. Arneil, *Black Jack: The Life and Times of Brigadier Sir Frederick Galleghan*, Melbourne, 1983, 116.
48 AWM 52, 1/5/19, War diary, Headquarters AIF Malaya, February 1942–February 1943, Notes of First Conference of Area Commanders & HQ Staff, 30 July 1942.
49 AWM 3 DRL 7665, Diary of Maj. Kennedy Burnside, Mobile Bacteriological Laboratory, AIF, entry, 6 August 1942.
50 I am grateful to Mr. Bart Ziino, one of the Memorial's 1997 Summer Vacation Scholars, who drew my attention to these reports in his unpublished research paper, "'A Bad Show': The Fall of Singapore and its Controversies."
51 AWM 52, 1/5/17, Notes and Reports on Malayan Campaign Officers Training, 6 October 1942.
52 AWM 52, 1/5/17, The Carrier Platoon in Malaya.
53 AWM 52, 1/5/17, Notes on lessons from AIF ops in Malaya.
54 AWM 52, 1/5/17, Kappe, Notes on Operations in Malaya.
55 3 DRL 2695, Diary of Lt.-Col. C. H. Kappe, 8th Division, AIF.
56 AWM 54, 554/11/4, Part 4, Report by Brig. F. J. Galleghan on prisoner-of-war camps in Singapore, Appendix I, The History of F Force [by Kappe and Curlewis]. Reports by British officers and by British and Australian medical officers in other parts of AWM 54, 554/11/4 document the force's ordeal in great detail.
57 D. Wall, *Heroes of F Force*, Sydney, 1993, 2.

58 AWM 54, 554/11/4, Part 4, Report on Conditions of Prisoners of War in Thailand, May to December 1943.
59 D. Wall, *Heroes of F Force*, vi–vii.
60 F Force medical tests, various minutes dated April 1943, AWM 54, 481/8/25, part of medical returns and correspondence handed to medical historian.
61 J. Beaumont, *Gull Force: Survival and Leadership in Captivity 1941–1945*, Sydney, 1988, 95; H. Nelson, *POW: Australians Under Nippon*, Sydney, 1985, 59–62.
62 Entry, 11 July 1943, D. Wall, *Heroes of F Force*, 60.
63 J. W. Jacobs and R. J. Bridgland, *Through: The Story of Signals 8th Australian Division and Signals AIF Malaya*, Sydney, 1949, 231–32.
64 Telephone conversation with Dr. Lloyd Cahill, 23 January 2002.
65 [C. H. Kappe] "The Story of the F Force," in *Mufti*, March 1953, 16; April 1953, 24.
66 Conversation with Prof. Hank Nelson, who interviewed members of F Force; J. Burfitt, *Against All Odds: The History of the 2/18 Battalion, A.I.F.*, Sydney, 1991, 150.
67 Telephone conversation with Dr. Lloyd Cahill, 23 January 2002.
68 [Pending donation], Lecture by Col. J. H. Thyer, 18 June 1942, 8.
69 Entry, 6 August 1943, D. Wall, *Heroes of F Force*, 72.
70 D. Wall, *Heroes of F Force*, 79.
71 E. Lomax, *The Railway Man*, London, 1996.
72 [Box accompanying] C. H. Kappe, "What Happened to Turn Singapore into a Colossal British Defeat," *Daily Telegraph* (Sydney), 6 February 1955, 12.
73 G. Mant, "The Way I See It," *Sunday Sun* and *Guardian*, Sydney, 23 November 1947; AWM Registry files 419/54/1, Historical Records – General Account of Malayan Campaign compiled by Lt.-Col. C. H. Kappe.
74 D. Wall, *Heroes of F Force*, 126. Hank Nelson's interview with Erwin Heckendorf (Keith Murdoch Sound Archives of Australia in the 1939–1945 War, AWM, S763) confirms the gist of Meakin's account, as does Lloyd Cahill's recollection.
75 L. Wigmore, *The Japanese Thrust*, 578.
76 Record of telephone conversation between John Treloar and Kappe, 25 January 1946; AWM 93, 50/2/23/116, Kappe to Wigmore, 16 April 1952.
77 A. J. Sweeting, who worked closely with Long and Wigmore on the Australian Second World War official history and who wrote the chapters on "Prisoners of the Japanese" observed of Kappe, "To write a history such as Bean's required rare qualities of character and temperament which Kappe seems markedly to have lacked."
78 Record of telephone conversation between John Treloar and Kappe, 25 January 1946, AWM 93, 50/2/23/116.
79 AWM MS 1393, C. H. Kappe, The Malayan Campaign, chapter XXI.
80 AWM 54, 553/5/23, Operations of 8th Australian Division in Malaya 1942. Parts 1 and 2 of this item differ only in various clippings and correspondence attached to it.
81 Ibid., 191–93.
82 A. M. Koch, OIC Military History Section, to Director, Australian War Memorial, 10 October 1953, [correspondence attached to] AWM 54, 553/5/23, Part 1.
83 AWM 93, 50/2/23/116, Gavin Long to John Treloar, 8 October 1945.

84 AWM 93, 50/2/23/116, Record of telephone conversation between John Treloar and Kappe, 25 January 1946.
85 AWM Registry files 419/54/1, Kappe to Treloar, 31 January 1947.
86 AWM Registry files 419/54/1, Treloar to Kappe, 6 February 1947.
87 AWM 192, Index card, Col. C. H. Kappe, OBE.
88 AWM Registry files 419/54/1, Kappe to Treloar, 16 December 1946.
89 AWM 93, 50/2/23/116, Treloar to Long, 24 March 1948.
90 AWM 73, item 71, Notebooks of Lionel Wigmore, notes of an interview with Sturdee, 11 May 1948.
91 AWM 93, 50/2/23/116, Kirby to Wigmore, 29 May 1953.
92 Although Kirby appears to have been sent a copy of Kappe's original manuscript, he seems not to have incorporated it into the official papers of his official history project held by the Cabinet Office and deposited in the Public Record Office. The only Kappe material held in the PRO is CAB106/162, a copy of the Thyer/Kappe "official" 8th Division report.
93 Though he claimed to have made only "minor amendments," it is clear the articles were heavily condensed to about 30,000 words from his original 200,000-word manuscript, and had probably been ghosted by a journalist familiar with the papers' tabloid style.
94 AWM Registry files 419/54/1, Kappe to J. McGrath, Director, Australian War Memorial, 18 February 1958. A. J. Sweeting quite rightly describes Kappe's reaction as "the comments of a disgruntled, prejudiced and embittered man."
95 *Courier Mail* (Brisbane), 24 October 1967, National Library of Australia biographical file.
96 That is, A. B. Lodge, *The Fall of General Gordon Bennett*; J. Uhr, *Against the Sun: The AIF in Malaya, 1941–42*, Sydney, 1998; and A. Warren, *Singapore 1942*.
97 Entry, 1–13 May 1942, P. Poole, *Of Love and War*, 130.
98 AWM Registry files 419/54/1, Report of conversation [by OIC Military History Section] with Col. Kent Hughes, 28 March 1948.
99 AWM 93, 50/2/23/116, Long to Kappe, 17 September 1957.
100 A. W. Penfold et al., *Galleghan's Greyhounds: The Story of the 2/30th Australian Infantry Battalion*, Sydney, 1949, np.
101 I am especially grateful to those who have helped me. They include both members of Charles Kappe's extended family and former members of F Force—Dr. Lloyd Cahill, Mr. Keith Meakin and Mr. Don Wall. As will be apparent, they hold very different views of Kappe's conduct while in command of F Force. I have largely accepted the evidence of the former prisoners who knew Kappe. Difficult though it may be to accept, the balance of evidence overwhelmingly confirms their view. I appreciate the difficulty the Kappe family faces in accepting an interpretation that must be unwelcome to them. Facing a similar challenge of loyalty was Mr. A. J. Sweeting, who made invaluable criticisms on an earlier draft of this paper. I am also grateful for the assistance of my colleagues in the Memorial's Research Centre and Military History Section, and to Mr. Roger Lee of the Australian Army History Unit, which generously met the costs of my participation in this conference.

CHAPTER 15

The Fall of Singapore Revisited

by Sandy Hunter

It falls to me to bring this amazing conference to a close and attempt to draw together the threads of the very intensive deliberations that have occupied our attention for the last two days. But let me begin by offering some words of thanks. First, we are all deeply indebted to the contributors whose papers have shown a great scholarly quality, depth of analysis and objectivity that have done great justice to the Malayan campaign, its origins and its consequences. May I offer them our thanks and say how much I look forward to the publication of the proceedings of this conference that will set the seal on a notable commemoration of the sad events of 1942. And then, I believe that you would want me to express our gratitude to the National University of Singapore and, especially, to Professor Tan Tai Yong and his staff who have been behind the success of the last three days. And finally, may I thank you, the audience, for your interest and attention. We have participated together in an event of international stature.

Let me turn now to what is not so much a summing up as my amateur reflections on what we have heard and on the context of the Malayan campaign and the fall of Singapore. It would plainly be hard to do justice in detail, to the very thoughtfully researched contributions that it has been our privilege to hear at this conference. We have enjoyed a veritable kaleidoscope of impressions and analysis. Let me therefore confine myself to offering some of my own observations, largely on the immediate circumstances of the campaign itself, as we draw the event to a close.

We have sought to shed light—ideally new light—on these near-seismic events of 60 years ago that fundamentally changed the face of this region. Our distinguished contributors have done so with rigour and objectivity. To my great satisfaction, they have offered explanations for Japanese success and British failure rather than dwelling on the allocation of blame. They have drawn lessons and conclusions from a complex and possibly over-debated tragedy which, in truth, should probably reflect credit only on some of the fighting men of all parties. Yet it is a tragedy that has profound lessons for military men of all ages. There are lessons, too, for their political masters whose instincts are often to pursue policies that would seem to offer defence on the cheap and to over-commit their forces. As in the case of the fall of Singapore, there will always be political leaders ready to shelter their own reputations behind military failure, and to avoid their fair share of public opprobrium.

Perhaps I may be forgiven for suggesting a few very gentle health warnings that amateur historians like me should attempt constantly to keep in mind! By its very nature, a disaster of the proportions of the fall of Singapore exposes us all to the dangers of retrospection. To a less distinguished audience I would have used the more everyday and overworked word "hindsight," with all its connotations of wisdom after the event. In one sense, my warning may be argued to strike at the very heart of all historical analysis but I do believe there are dangers in undisciplined hindsight when exercised by people like me, with a vested interest in the reputation of the military establishment. Whatever our origins, it behoves all of us, of later generations, to form and articulate our judgements with care, with grace and with humility. Added to these dangers, I believe, must be the propensity of present generations to make judgements on the basis of today's standards and attitudes, rather than by reference to contemporary behaviour. Even the most resistant of my generation and others have been profoundly influenced—often imperceptibly—by the prejudices and diktats of today's political correctness and by the received wisdom that the military are by definition, either fools or knaves. That may well be so, but that is a conclusion best reached objectively, case by case!

Other obstacles hinder our attempts to get at the truth of the Malayan campaign and the fall of Singapore. Many of the early postwar writings were, quite understandably, coloured by the horrors of the years of occupation and captivity that followed the capitulation. They were often informed by understandable anger and an urgent wish to assign blame. Many of the accounts written by key players at every level may now be seen to be marked by an almost predictable lack of objectivity and by the disingenuousness of authors seeking to get their retaliation in first! Some are anodyne; others bitter and even vindictive. Yet few fail to play some part in the jigsaw of historical analysis.

To do justice to those whose conduct of affairs we have studied over the last two days, we must ourselves avoid falling into the trap of viewing the principal characters in this tragedy as the cartoon or caricature figures they have often become in the mind of posterity. It is instructive to remember that in the propaganda of the day, such stereotypes abounded. The buck-toothed and myopic

Japanese; the chinless, ineffectual Englishman abroad; or the strapping and totally discipline-averse Digger—all these and others may inevitably have coloured our outlook and these sub-conscious images must be stripped away from our attempts at objective judgement. It should never be forgotten that propaganda was a powerful tool used aggressively by both parties, neither of whom was innocent of the use of racial stereotypes as a weapon in the conflict. The reality is that the people and institutions of 1942 were markedly different in attitude and outlook from those of the year 2002. The world of 1942 was one in which mass travel had not yet loosened the bonds of insularity that then characterized most of its people. These were the days before we had coined words like "multiculturalism."

Other words, now rightly regarded as racist and unacceptable, were in common use. Just how consciously deliberate and evil such attitudes were in their day is a moot point. What is unarguable is that this was the context and environment of the day. Later suggestions of racist influences in, for example, the interpretation—or misinterpretation—of intelligence may indeed be correct— but probably only up to a point. In this regard, many of us will have found John Ferris' analysis[1] compelling in its identification of a set of factors, entirely more subtle and complex than crude racism. In a similar way, later generations have become accustomed to explaining away gaps in source material in terms of "cover-ups," to use the phrase so beloved of today's journalists. Conspiracy is more exciting and attention-grabbing than incompetence, yet we must be aware that, even today, the world probably harbours more incompetents than conspirators. In 1941, the politico-military establishment of the British Empire was characterized by conscious centralized control at the highest strategic level and often by near-tactical meddling by those holding the reins. Yet the communication chains between governments and commands were tortuous and often ambiguous. The imperial defence Ministries in London—Admiralty, War Office and Air Ministry—formed together a ponderous bureaucracy, despite the immediacy of the exercise of power at the hand of Winston Churchill—not always with the enthusiastic support of the Chiefs of Staff. As an aside, it is instructive to recall that it would be another 40 years before a moderately effective, integrated U.K. Defence Ministry would exist in Whitehall. In 1941, the necessary involvement of other governments did nothing to simplify matters.

In 1941, rigid inter-service demarcation, a product of interwar struggles, ensured that cooperation between the services in the field was more a matter of chance and local goodwill than of confident expectation. These characteristics were to be seen to a greater or lesser degree in every theatre and at every level. They had certainly been very evident in the run up to war in the Malayan theatre of operations. Here, the breakdown of communication between the GOC and his Air Force counterpart is well documented. Perhaps more destructive, the power and often unhelpful influence of the Civil Authority, vested in the Governor Sir

Shenton Thomas, was mirrored by obstructive attitudes in civil government and in the population towards military preparations for war. There is strong evidence to suggest that the impending battle was regarded by too many as an unwelcome distraction from the real business and priority of commercial and social life.

Against that backdrop, the inadequacies of the arrangements for command and control of inadequate and fragmented in-theatre forces are stark in hindsight. The appointment of an elderly and out-of-touch Commander-in-Chief may be viewed as a half-hearted attempt to paper over the cracks of a fissiparous and potentially dysfunctional military establishment. That he had no staff to speak of and no authority over a key component of his forces merely exacerbated the situation. It is worth noting in passing that it would take another 20 years for a truly unified command to be created over the Commonwealth forces in Singapore and Malaysia. In 1941, the individual services—elsewhere as in Malaya—were set in their ways, protective of their territory and woefully ill-coordinated.

Perhaps, unfairly, we may conclude that many of the services' stereotypes rang true in the Singapore of May 1941, when Lieutenant-General Percival arrived as the new GOC Malaya. The Royal Navy—not under Brooke-Popham's command—maintained its habitual aloofness and apparent willingness to answer only to the King and to the immortal memory of Horatio Nelson. The Army seemed to many to display an unhealthy doctrinal rigidity and, at the same time, an unwarranted self-confidence. It reeked of tribal, if not racial self-satisfaction. And the bloody-minded persona of the Royal Air Force was the product of bitter inter-service battles for survival in the 1920s and '30s. This inadequacy was compounded by the exaggerated claims of airpower theorists whose dreams would certainly not be realized in the battles for the Malayan Peninsula and Singapore Island.

The world situation in 1941 produced resource issues that dictated the priorities decided on responsibly at the time but later rather glossed over by Winston Churchill and the home government. In 1941, in what became known as the Battle of the Atlantic, German U-boats appeared to be heading for victory, with drastic consequences for the Atlantic lifeline. In the desert, Rommel's star was in the ascendant and there, too, many of the deficiencies of British leadership, equipment and training later to be seen in the Far East were all too evident. By mid-year, Hitler's forces having struck at the Soviet Union, the need to be seen to satisfy Stalin's demands for equipment would increasingly divert aircraft and tanks from other theatres. Additionally, the perceived requirements of home defence would continue to deny other theatres reinforcement by well-trained and equipped units and formations. In reality, these latter were all in short supply, yet were what Brian Farrell so cogently describes as the key to any significant reinforcement,[2] had it been logistically possible. In any case, a realistic "flash to bang" time for such reinforcement would have required action in early 1941 at the latest. The

Percival, far right, en route to surrender negotiations, Singapore, 15 February 1942

Soviet dimension post-*Barbarossa* simply compounded the problem of priorities. Most of all, this was a time when achieving and sustaining agreement that the war policy of the Allies was "Germany first" made it quite unthinkable to appear to take the eye off that ball.

One further area of resource deficit had undoubtedly affected Far East Command in the prewar years and certainly was evident in the critical months as the Japanese invasion approached. The Command's Headquarters—at all levels—enjoyed neither sufficient numbers nor quality of what we now describe as human resources. Brooke-Popham, as we have heard, certainly did not have a staff adequate to his responsibilities and, for example, the modest calibre of many members of the fragmented intelligence community was all too clear. It is probably not unfair to conclude that the Far East was never likely to have been regarded as of premier league status and that it had as low a priority for high quality commanders and staff as it had for first-rate equipment.

It was in these circumstances that Percival spent his early months as GOC Malaya and prepared for what, like it or not, would be a "come as you are party." He and his Commander-in-Chief had been dealt an exceedingly weak hand and we have been reminded repeatedly over the last two days just how poorly that hand was played in the event. That said, most now agree that a better playing of the hand would have had only a marginal effect on the outcome of the campaign.

It is 60 years since Singapore fell in what must have been recognized as a campaign that owed at least as much to the ineptitude of the long-term development, resourcing and direction of Empire defence policy as to the undeniable brilliance of the Japanese attack. In that time, much has been written that is critical of these self-evident failures and blame has been freely apportioned, sometimes unfairly and often in angry terms. Through it all, few have sought to question the spirit of most of those who fought and survived the horrors of captivity. Many of these themes have been thoroughly explored during the last two days and we may now enjoy a deeper understanding of the origins and outcome of the fall and, not least, their all-important American ingredients.

There is little more to be added after two packed days. Let me end, therefore, by offering you two quotations that to me sum up the nature and origins of the disaster that befell the British Empire in the days between 8 December 1941 and 15 February 1942. They are from two very different personalities, each of whom played a notable part in the campaign and its aftermath. The first is from Lieutenant-General Percival, whose essential dignity and magnanimity in the face of sustained and sometimes unfair criticism are to be found in these words. In preparing for this conference, I corresponded with his son, Brigadier James Percival, who drew my attention to these words of his father's, written in 1949:

> A great many of the causes which contributed to our defeat in Malaya had a common origin, namely the lack of readiness of the British Commonwealth for war. Our shortage in fighting ships and in modern aircraft, our lack of tanks, the inexperience of many of our leaders and the lack of training of most of our troops can all be attributed to a failure to prepare for war at the proper time. In 1941, when the crisis came in the Far East, it was too late to put things right. Then we were engaged in a life-and-death struggle in the West, and war material which might have saved Singapore was sent to Russia and the Middle East. The choice was made and Singapore had to suffer.
>
> [And here I emphasize words that Brigadier Percival suggested I should stress:]
>
> *In my opinion, this decision, however painful and regrettable, was inevitable and right.*

And finally, some words from a distinguished Australian officer who, many would say rightly, has had a much better press than the general who will forever be associated with "Britain's greatest defeat." Sir Edward Dunlop—"Weary" Dunlop of honoured memory—wrote in 1951:

> Inadequate planning and allocation of resources led to the vaunted 'impregnable fortress' of Singapore proving instead to be a 'naked island.' The disastrous loss of the *Prince of Wales* and the *Repulse* and the paucity and poor quality of Allied aircraft, made possible swift landings by the Japanese to the north of Singapore. The Japanese flair for infiltration, which allowed them to by-pass fixed defences on the major lines of communication, necessitated endless, exhausting withdrawals by the Allies. Yet neither the Allies' failure in defence planning nor their ineptitude in the conduct of the campaign dimmed the valour of their forces, who fought at such a sad disadvantage.

With these words, ladies and gentlemen, I hope you will agree that we may regard our task as complete.

Air Vice-Marshal Sandy Hunter is a graduate of the Arts and Law faculties of Aberdeen University in Scotland. His military career included service in Singapore as a reconnaissance pilot at Tengah during the Indonesian Confrontasi. In later appointments, he served in Moscow, in Germany commanding an Army support squadron, and in Cyprus as Joint Force Commander. He was Director of Public Relations for the Royal Air Force and Commandant of the RAF Staff College. He is a graduate of the Royal College of Defence Studies and takes a keen interest in military history.

Notes—
1   Published as essay number five in this volume.
2   Published as essay number eight in this volume.

Appendix

Conference Program and Paper Abstracts

SIXTY YEARS ON–
THE FALL OF SINGAPORE REVISITED

A Conference to Commemorate the 60th Anniversary of this Major Event of the Second World War

---

15–17 FEBRUARY 2002
UNIVERSITY CULTURAL CENTRE
NATIONAL UNIVERSITY OF SINGAPORE

ORGANIZED BY
Department of History
National University of Singapore

SPONSORED BY
The Tan Foundation
The Lee Foundation
Singapore History Consultants
University Cultural Centre, NUS
and
The National University of Singapore

15 February 2002

Registration and Reception
University Cultural Centre
and
Department of History

0900
Depart for Changi POW Chapel and Museum

0930 – 1100
Visit Changi POW Chapel and Museum

1100 – 1230
Visit Kranji Commonwealth War Cemetery

1230 – 1330
LUNCH

1330 – 1700
Field trip, tour of Singapore battlefield sites
(Lim Chu Kang, Sarimbun, Bukit Timah, Labrador Park)

16 February 2002

0830 – 0900
Registration and Reception
University Cultural Centre

0900 – 1100

Opening Remarks and Welcome Address
Prof Shih Choon Fong
President & Vice-Chancellor, National University of Singapore

Assoc Prof Lily Kong
Dean, Faculty of Arts & Social Sciences (NUS)

Malcolm H. Murfett (Singapore)
The Singapore Naval Base and Strategy: Overview and Historiography

Peter Dennis (Australia)
Australia and the Singapore Strategy, Before the War

1100 – 1115
TEA/COFFEE BREAK

Christopher M. Bell (USA) **The Royal Navy and the Singapore Strategy**	Keith Neilson (Canada) **British-Soviet Relations and the Approach of War with Japan**
Greg Kennedy (UK) **British-American Relations and Maritime Preparations for Pacific War 1933–41**	Martin Thomas (UK) **The Fall of Singapore, the Vichy State, and the French Empire in Asia**

1245 – 1400
LUNCH

John Ferris (Canada) **British Perceptions of Japanese Airpower 1921–1941**	Kent Fedorowich (Canada) **Evacuation Policies in Hong Kong and Malaya/Singapore, 1941–42**
Henry A. Probert (UK) **Airpower and the Malaya/Singapore Campaign**	Raymond Callahan (USA) **The Worst Disaster? Churchill and Singapore**

1530 – 1545
TEA/COFFEE BREAK

Brian P. Farrell (Singapore)
1941: An Overview

17 February 2002

0830 – 0900
Registration and Reception
University Cultural Centre

1100 – 1115

Akashi Yoji (Japan)	Ishizu Tomoyuki (Japan)
Yamashita and his Command of the 25th Army	**Colonel Tsuji and the Conduct of the Malaya/Singapore Campaign**
	Sibylla Jane Flower (UK)
	Capture and Interrogation of Allied POWs During the Malaya/Singapore Campaign

1030 – 1100
TEA/COFFEE BREAK

Henry P. Frei (Japan)	Alan Warren (Australia)
The Japanese Conquest of Singapore Island	**The Indian Army and the Malaya/Singapore Campaign**
Chua Li Shan, Ng Chuin Song, and Xie Lihui (Nanyang and Anderson Junior Colleges, Singapore)	Clifford Kinvig (UK)
Singaporean Participation in the Defence of Singapore	**Percival, his Army, and the Malaya/Singapore Campaign**

1230 – 1330
LUNCH

John Moremon (Australia)
Logistics and the Malayan Campaign

Peter Elphick (UK)
The Cover-Ups: Dirty Laundry of the Malayan Campaign

Peter Stanley (Australia)
Explaining Defeat: Australian Officers' Post-Mortems on the Battle for Singapore, Changi 1942

1530 – 1545
TEA/COFFEE BREAK

1545 – 1630

Sandy Hunter (UK)
The Fall of Singapore Revisited

Students register for the conference, 16 February 2002

Prof. Shih Choon Fong, President & Vice-Chancellor, NUS, views Total Defence Day exhibit, 16 February 2002

Conference Program and Paper Abstracts ✦ 327

Ms. Kelly Lau, seated left, and volunteers, 17 February 2002

The editors and volunteer assistants, 17 February 2002

Mr. Lewis Altman, British WWII veteran, raising an issue, 16 February 2002

Xie Lihui presenting part of a paper on Singaporeans in the defence of Singapore, 17 February 2002

Conference Program and Paper Abstracts ✦ **329**

Final session, Theatre, University Cultural Centre, 17 February 2002

Descriptions of Sessions & Abstracts/Summaries of Papers—

SIXTY YEARS ON– THE FALL OF SINGAPORE REVISITED

A Conference to Commemorate the 60th Anniversary of this Major Event of the Second World War

Organized by

Department of History
National University of Singapore
16-17 February 2002
University Cultural Centre
National University of Singapore

Session 1, The Singapore Strategy—

This opening session is devoted to the interwar controversy over the construction of a naval base at Singapore and the infamous "Singapore strategy" by which the British Royal Navy was to use the base in time of war. This is one of the most enduring controversies in the long history of the defence of the British Empire, let alone regarding Singapore. There are two presentations in this session.

Malcolm H. Murfett	*The Singapore Naval Base and Strategy: Overview and Historiography*

This paper revisits a number of issues that simply refuse to die away even sixty years after the fall of Singapore. It aims to question the very premises upon which this naval strategy was formed and begins by examining the decisions reached on such crucial matters as the location and resources of the naval base, the lack of a sufficient defensive perimeter in Johor, and the ramifications of the Washington Conference on defence planning in the Far East, together with the increasingly suspect set of assumptions that went along with it. It also considers the role the Royal Navy was expected to perform in the Far East once it arrived in the region and probes to see whether or not these operational plans stood the faintest chance of success or if they were based largely on wishful thinking and a marked lack of realism. It will also address other aspects of projected British-American naval cooperation in these years and the abject failure of the Eden plan in particular, before going on to deal with the Backhouse-Drax "flying squadron" alternative to the "main fleet" concept and queries whether either strategy could actually work in the volatile circumstances of the time. In the end, of course, the Admiralty was not able to send a balanced fleet to the East when it needed to and even chose the wrong man to command it when it eventually sent a truncated "flying squadron" to Singapore in the closing weeks of 1941. In conclusion, the paper ends by re-examining the oldest controversy related to this entire military disaster, namely, the belief held in many quarters in Southeast Asia and throughout the Australasian Dominions that in not sending the main fleet to Singapore at its time of greatest need, the British selfishly managed to betray all those who relied upon them for their security.

Peter Dennis	*Australia and the Singapore Strategy, Before the War*

The fall of Singapore, along with the Gallipoli debacle, ranks as one of the defining moments in Australian military history. The Australian literature on each campaign overwhelmingly attributes the failure to British incompetence at various levels, while largely exculpating Australian involvement. Indeed, Gallipoli has come to be seen as a triumph of Australian values, the birthplace of the enduring "Anzac legend." The fall of Singapore, however, has never been seen other than as an unmitigated disaster, not least because it led to the imprisonment of thousands of Australian soldiers in conditions that have also become part of our national memory. As with most popular "understandings" of historical events, that pertaining to the fall of Singapore has elements of truth. The "Singapore strategy" was based on a willingness to wish away unpalatable possibilities, and when those possibilities became reality, to persist in a wilful readiness to deny that reality. However, when Prime Minister John Curtin protested to Winston Churchill that a British failure to reinforce Singapore at any cost to the war effort elsewhere would be regarded as an 'inexcusable betrayal', the charge was poorly based, though understandable in the critical days of late 1941 and early 1942. When similar accusations were made by another Labour Prime Minister, Paul Keating, on the occasion of the 50th anniversary of the fall of Singapore, they merely demonstrated how little the popular understanding had evolved, and how ready Australian politicians were to score political points.

This paper examines internal Australian opposition to the "Singapore strategy," opposition that came almost exclusively from within the ranks of the Australian Army. Throughout the 1920s and 1930s various senior officers in the Australian Army voiced growing concerns about the viability of the "Singapore strategy," and argued that the heavy emphasis in Australian defence expenditure on the Navy, at the expense of the Army (and, although they naturally did not emphasize this, the Royal Australian Air Force), dangerously unbalanced Australia's military capability and left the country exposed to attacks that could not be prevented by a reliance on the base at Singapore to protect against all eventualities in the region. These reservations were increasingly publicly aired, and came to a head in 1937 when a senior officer, Colonel H.D. Wynter, was removed from his position as Director of Military Training and demoted for his public criticisms of government policy and expenditure priorities. Thereafter criticism was muted and confined to internal service circles. Wynter's demise marked the triumph in Australia of the uncritical acceptance of the "Singapore strategy," underscored by what one historian has called a sense of complacency. Yet whether the failure of the "Singapore strategy" can be seen as a wider failure of the concept of imperial defence, as some critics would insist, is debatable. When Curtin made his famous appeal to the United States in December 1941, he was placing Australia firmly in the American imperial camp—where our current political leaders seem most comfortable.

Session 2, Naval Problems Before World War II—

It was obvious after the First World War that any future clash between Japan and the leading Western powers would revolve around control of the seas. That made naval forces central to the strategic and diplomatic calculations of those Western powers, especially the United States and the United Kingdom. There are two papers in this session devoted to examining these naval questions.

Christopher M. Bell *The Royal Navy and the Singapore Strategy*

It is now widely accepted that Britain's "Singapore strategy" was inherently unrealistic and unworkable from its conception. The Royal Navy has been condemned for adopting a rigid and inflexible strategy for a conflict with Japan, and for stubbornly clinging to this strategy until the outbreak of war in 1941, when it ultimately resulted in the disastrous loss of Force Z. However, the "Singapore strategy" that historians have attacked is often no more than a caricature of the Navy's plans for protecting Britain's Far Eastern interests. This paper, while not denying that naval leaders of the interwar period made serious mistakes, will argue that most of the criticisms that have been levelled against the Navy are either overstated or unfounded. It will show that the Royal Navy was not oblivious to the difficulties of a "two-hemisphere war;" that its preparations were more flexible than has previously been recognized; that a wide range of contingency plans were actually developed to deal with the Japanese threat; and that the disasters of 1941 were largely unconnected with the shortcomings of the Navy's interwar planning. The Royal Navy attempted to deal with the Japanese threat in a realistic and forthright manner: The greatest problem it faced in 1941 was not an obsolete and impracticable strategy, but insufficient resources for a global struggle against three major powers.

Greg Kennedy *British-American Relations & Maritime Preparations for Pacific War 1933–41*

Anglo-American strategic relations in the interwar years were centred largely around the issue of containing Japanese aggression in the Far East. Part of that ongoing interaction was the question of how far Britain could depend on the United States becoming involved in the defence of the status quo in that region. Tied into that question, stemming from the Washington Conference System and the Four and Nine Power Treaties, was the issue of basing and the ability of the Americans to actually project maritime forces into the region. British planning and diplomatic actions in the interwar years attempted to assure the American strategic planners that Singapore was a viable alternative to the Philippines, if that basing establishment was lost due to Philippine independence. As well, the development of Pearl Harbour and the continued maintenance of American facilities in the Philippines were of interest to the British, in that the more effort that was dedicated to the establishment of a real American capability in that theatre, then less emphasis was put on the British need of preparing to go it alone in any conflict with Japan. Thus, the question to be addressed is, if there was a marked improvement in confidence in the Americans to act in a coordinated fashion with the British against a Japanese attack, was there a logical decreased demand on Singapore to be a British Fleet base? These factors were of particular concern after the outbreak of war in Europe in 1939. This paper will look at what Britain's strategic defence planners thought the American factor in the Pacific was, in case of a war with Japan, and what impact that had on how Singapore was developed, as well as the "Singapore strategy" in general.

Session 3, International Relations Before the War

The outbreak of two separate Great Power wars in Europe in 1939 and Asia in 1937 forced all the Great Powers to reconsider their foreign and defence policies. The dramatic turn of the war in Europe in favour of the Axis powers in 1940 made that reconsideration even more urgent for everyone. Much depended on how diplomacy could be used to respond to changing circumstances, for better or worse. There are two papers in this session devoted to that dimension.

Keith Neilson *British-Soviet Relations and the Approach of War with Japan*

While much ink has been spilled in discussions of the "Singapore strategy," much less has been written about British diplomatic efforts to defend their position in the Far East. This is unfortunate, as it tends to obscure the reality of actual British policy in the Far East. As London had insufficient military force available to defend both the Far East and Europe simultaneously, the British Foreign Office pursued a delicate balancing act. Since the other Western nations involved in the Far East—primarily the Soviet Union, the United States, France and the Netherlands—were themselves either unwilling or unable to take a lead in curbing Japanese expansion on the Asian mainland, the Foreign Office was forced to attempt to convince the Japanese that an informal "alliance" or community of interest existed among these powers and that an attack on one of them would be considered an attack on all of them.

The focus of this paper will be on a particular case: British-Soviet relations as they pertain to the Far East.

This was a particularly difficult affair. Not only was there the tendency for both London and Moscow to attempt to get the other to bell the Japanese cat, but also, on the British side, there were divided opinions about how (and whether) to effect such an arrangement. The Treasury, for example, felt that the Foreign Office's policy was incorrect; instead, people like Sir Warren Fisher, the Permanent Secretary at the Treasury, preferred to improve relations with Japan, at the expense of any British-Soviet arrangement. Such a policy was also pushed by the Admiralty, which wished to reduce its naval commitments in the Far East. And there were ideological considerations. Many in the Cabinet did not wish to treat with the Soviet Union, feeling that its actions through the Comintern made it a thoroughly unacceptable partner, even in the kind of "virtual alliance" that the Foreign Office advocated. This was a factor even within the Foreign Office, where opinions varied as to the correct line of policy.

Martin Thomas   *The Fall of Singapore, the Vichy State, and the French Empire in Asia*

The paper will analyze the reactions of the Vichy state and its loyalist colonial régime in Indochina to the mounting threat of a Japanese descent on Malaya in 1940–41 and, ultimately, to the fall of Singapore itself. The paper contends that Pétainist France retained an abiding interest in the preservation of British Malaya even as British-Vichy relations shifted towards open imperial confrontation during the course of 1941. The fate of French colonial authority in Vietnam, and the parallels between the French experience of Japanese incursion and eventual occupation and the British collapse in Singapore, will also be examined. The singular French colonial expedient of unstable co-existence with Japanese occupation forces, itself pivotal to the Japanese land advance through Southeast Asia, will be discussed and the underlying community of colonial interest with Britain brought out. Finally, reactions in Vichy and Saigon to the fall of Singapore will be considered in light of the ramifications of the British imperial collapse on the future of the French Empire in Asia. This will involve some assessment of Vichy French perceptions of Vietnamese nationalist calculations regarding the downfall of European colonial authority across Southeast Asia. In sum, the paper will test common assumptions about the supposedly monolithic nature of Vichy collaboration, the complicity of the French colonial authorities in Japan's southward advance and Pétainist opposition to British imperial rule.

Session 4, Airpower and the Defence of Malaya and Singapore—

It was obvious from the First World War on that anyone fighting a major war would need to be strong in the air if they wanted to be victorious. Everyone paid attention to developing their airpower. When the course of events forced the British to turn to the Air Force instead of the Navy, to take the lead in defending their Far East colonies, this only accentuated the importance of airpower. The two papers of this session discuss how well the British and the Japanese prepared themselves in the air for modern war, and what impact airpower had on the campaign.

John Ferris *British Perceptions of Japanese Airpower 1921–1941*

The paper will trace the evolution of official and unofficial British perceptions of Japanese airpower through the interwar years. It will avoid the trite conclusion that British observers misunderstood everything they saw and that these errors stemmed simply and solely from racism—after all, the official British view of the quality of the Imperial Japanese Army between 1919–41 was very favourable. Instead, this paper will argue that the roots of the problem were both intellectual, in the sense of British ideas about the nature of Japanese national character and of the characteristics needed to be a pilot, and observational—the result of ample access to Japanese military aviation and aircraft industry between 1920–32, when in fact their quality was poor; followed by an inability to gather information after 1932, because of Japanese security procedures, at precisely the time when the quality of Japanese aircraft, its industry and of the naval air service, began a dramatic rise. Under these circumstances, British analysts simply assumed that nothing had changed, and went on believing that the Japanese were as poor as they had been in the 1920s, precisely at the time that the Japanese entered the ranks of first-rank airpowers. This paper will explain clearly the nature of these British perceptions and their influence on defence policy between 1939–41, particularly in leading decision-makers to overestimate the ease of the air defence of Malaya and of an air offensive against Japan, and to spend more time in thinking about attack than defence.

Henry Probert *Airpower and the Malaya/Singapore Campaign*

There is no denying the fact that the British-led air forces, officially relied on to carry the burden of defending Malaya and Singapore, failed to accomplish any of the missions necessary to that task. The Japanese invasion force was not savaged, let alone destroyed, at sea. The capital ship force was not protected from the air. The fighter force lost air supremacy over the battlefield almost immediately. The bomber force failed to stop the Japanese build-up of airpower. Reinforcing fighters failed to regain air supremacy from the enemy. There is also no doubt that this weakness in the air was a decisive factor in the outcome of the campaign. But the causes of this weakness have little to do with the air and ground crew who fought the campaign, and can only be fairly determined by establishing the factors that hampered preparations for defence before the outbreak of war in the region. By examining the question of airpower in the Far East as a factor in British grand strategy before December 1941, and the problems Far East Command then faced upon the outbreak of war, this paper will argue that the roots of defeat in the air over Malaya and Singapore lie earlier and elsewhere.

Session 5, Questions of National Policy—

The dramatic turn for the worse in the war in Europe in summer 1940 made the British situation in Asia very perilous indeed. This brought up questions of great importance for national war policy, ranging from specific considerations such as how best to protect the subjects of a multi-racial empire without provoking any panic or recriminations, to the broadest questions of grand strategy and the central direction of the war. The two papers in this session examine these dilemmas of national policy during the uneasy months the British Empire was at war in Europe but not yet in Asia.

Kent Fedorowich *Evacuation Policies in Hong Kong and Malaya 1941–42*

Until recently, the trials and tribulations of European civilians interned by the Japanese in the Asia-Pacific region between 1941–45 have received little attention from scholars. Despite the publication of a number of personal accounts from former internees between the late 1940s and early 1960s, academics have been preoccupied with the larger geo-political, strategic and military issues that unfolded in the Far East during the Pacific War. However, the resurgence in prisoner-of-war studies has prompted renewed interest in the parallel plight of civilian internees. Public interest has also been sparked by the vociferous campaign undertaken by former Allied POWs and internees seeking an official apology (and financial compensation) from the Japanese government for the horrendous treatment many received during captivity. Revelations over enforced prostitution of mostly Korean 'comfort' women, but some European females as well— dramatically sensationalized by Hollywood in the star-studded movie *Paradise Road*—have kept civilian internment in the public eye. Finally, the release of war crimes files and other official records in a number of Western democracies has, in turn, inspired a younger generation of scholars interested in oral history, colonial elites and war and memory to re-examine this hitherto forgotten episode of human endurance.

A number of questions remain unanswered however. Why, for example, were so many civilians captured? Were there not contingency plans for the evacuation of European civilians from British Far Eastern colonies? And what plans, if any, had been made for important members of the Asian population to flee Japanese aggression? The purpose of this paper is to examine these and other questions. Using a comparative framework, the paper analyzes the relative success of the Hong Kong government in getting as many of its European civilians out of the exposed colony with the ad hoc and last minute policies of the Singapore government. One of the more interesting facets is the tension that existed between the civilian and military authorities over the formulation and execution of these policies; and the recriminations which were unleashed during the secret wartime post-mortems (especially over Singapore between the former C-in-C Far East, Air Chief Marshal Sir Robert Brooke-Popham and Governor Shenton Thomas).

Raymond Callahan   *The Worst Disaster? Churchill and Singapore*

He never set foot in Singapore but Winston Churchill is an inescapable presence in the history of its fall, not only because he was Prime Minister in 1941–42 but also because he shaped the story of the British war effort for a generation after the postwar publication of his still quite influential memoirs. Any reconsideration of his role in the fall of Singapore, therefore, has to address two questions: his influence as a wartime policymaker—in many ways *the* policymaker as far as Singapore was concerned—and the power of his postwar prose. This paper will examine those two questions by looking at the following points: At what point in his long career was Churchill really influential in shaping the defence of Singapore? As Prime Minister, could he, within the framework of his strategic priorities, have done better to provide for the Far East? Was he candid with his Commonwealth partners in Australia? And once battle was joined, did he help or hinder the campaign? As for postwar prose, on what basis did Churchill construct his account of the loss of Singapore? And why was it so influential? This paper will argue that, given the complexity of the problem to be solved, Churchill did not do anything as Prime Minister about which it can fairly be said caused Singapore to be lost when it might otherwise have been held—but his postwar explanation, while not untrue, did subtly deflect much of the responsibility in a particular direction.

Closing Session, 16 February 2002: Where we stand so far—

The first day of conference sessions is devoted mainly to prewar problems. The second day of sessions focuses more directly on the campaign itself. The papers also vary in focus from examining global events to studying developments on Singapore Island. At this midpoint in the sessions, we need to pause to examine the connections between these different perspectives, to pull them together. One summary paper is devoted to prodding this general discussion.

Brian P. Farrell *1941: An Overview*

Most papers on the first day of the conference are devoted to developments leading up to the outbreak of war between Japan and the Western powers, whereas those on the second day focus mainly on the Malayan campaign and the battle of Singapore itself. The focus of the conference will therefore oscillate between appraising processes dating back two decades, to detailed examinations of several days; and, from another angle, range from analyzing events on a global scale, to close study of the fighting on the island itself. This paper will provide, at the midpoint of the conference, an overview that brings together the long-term perspective, the broad global perspective, and the immediate situation. The paper is a synthesis and summary of arguments and issues drawn out by others, in order to generate a discussion that will tie the different presentations together. The paper will argue that by examining global developments, and comparing how all the major powers responded to them, it can be concluded that the apparent vulnerability of Malaya and Singapore in 1941 was as much of an illusion as the strategy by which the British thought they could be defended in the first place.

Session 6, The Imperial Japanese Army and the Malayan Campaign—

The only way to understand any military campaign is to look at the story from "both sides of the hill." Over the years, more attention has been devoted to the defence of Singapore in English language studies, which might be natural but is not sufficient. We need to hear not just about how the defenders lost Singapore, but how the attackers conquered it. There is one paper in this session devoted to that dimension of the campaign.

Akashi Yoji   *Yamashita and his Command of the 25th Army*

On 15 February 1942, Lieutenant-General Arthur Percival, commander of the British-led forces defending Singapore, surrendered to Lieutenant-General Yamashita Tomoyuki, commanding the Twenty-Fifth Army of the Imperial Japanese Army. Yamashita was given 100 days to take Singapore. His conquest of the British fortress in 70 days was the most brilliant campaign in modern military history. Military historians are unanimous that Yamashita outgeneraled Percival who was no match in every respect in generalship. Yamashita was one of the best known Japanese generals and was a tragic figure, because the more he became prominent in Army politics and as a war hero, the more some in Army circles were jealous of his widespread popularity, jealousy that kept him from Tokyo most of the wartime years. Then in October 1944, he became the commanding general of the Fourteenth Area Army, charged to defend the Philippines in a hopeless campaign. After the war, he was tried as a war criminal and sentenced to death by hanging in a "legitimate lynch" military court in Manila, and executed in February 1946. Apart from the discussion of Yamashita's generalship in the Malayan campaign, this paper explores his military career in the 1930s during which he became a central figure in Army politics. His role in it had much bearing upon his career for the remainder of his Army life and upon his relations with the Emperor and General Tojo Hideki. The paper also describes the human side of Yamashita's personality that left him with the legend of being a tragic figure among Japanese generals.

Session 7, Controversies Surrounding the Japanese in the Malayan Campaign—

Wherever it went in the Second World War, the Imperial Japanese Army left behind an enduring trail of controversy regarding how it conducted itself in battle and afterwards. Malaya and Singapore were no exceptions. There are two papers in this session dedicated to examining some of these controversies, including the conduct of operations, the treatment of prisoners of war, and the treatment of civilians.

Ishizu Tomoyuki Colonel Tsuji and the Conduct of the Malaya/Singapore Campaign

If anyone deserves the title Organizer of Victory in the Malaya/Singapore campaign of 1941–42, it must be Colonel Masanobu Tsuji of the Imperial Japanese Army. First as director of a planning staff organized in January 1941 to map out the conquest of Malaya, then as Director of Operations at 25th Army Headquarters, Tsuji had his hand on the tiller from start to finish. But Tsuji was also a controversial figure, disagreeing heatedly with Yamashita on several issues during the campaign, seen by some as a plant for a hostile faction in Japanese Army politics, and blamed by others for more sinister events after the British surrender. By focusing on the role of Tsuji in the campaign, drawing on his diary among other sources, this paper will assess the influence of personalities on its conduct and outcome. It will argue, among other things, that Japanese success was due not so much to alleged well-prepared and executed operations on their part but rather to confusion in Allied military strategy for the Far East theatre.

Sibylla Jane Flower   **Capture and Interrogation of Allied POWs During the Malaya/Singapore Campaign**

This paper will examine the capture and subsequent treatment of Allied prisoners of war during the Malayan campaign. The Japanese had not anticipated the surrender of prisoners in such numbers and for this reason the invasion forces included few officers who were equipped with the necessary language skills and powers of interrogation. Thus three of the first POWs to be captured—a British Army officer and two aircrew—were sent to Saigon and interrogated by the *Kempei-tai* under torture. Imperial Japanese Army orders stipulated that prisoners captured in the field were to be sent to unit headquarters for interrogation. Thus a feature of the campaign is the widely differing treatment accorded to captives by individual Japanese officers. Certainly not all the POWs whose lives were spared by the Japanese in Malaya were likely candidates to yield information; it is thus instructive to analyze the circumstances of the capture of the POWs in the two principal jails on the mainland, that at Taiping where nearly 400 were held, and Pudu in Kuala Lumpur where the POWs numbered initially over 800. There is enough evidence to illustrate both acts of mercy by the Japanese and savage reprisals sometimes to avenge the death of a commanding officer or of a comrade. Discussions on the course of the Malayan campaign between Allied officers and their Japanese counterparts during the first months of the captivity when the POWs were in the hands of fighting troops yielded information which helps to account for some of the worst atrocities. Finally, consideration will be given to the question of hostage-taking by the Japanese, particularly in the confined space of Singapore Island immediately before the surrender.

Session 8, The Battle for Singapore Island—

The final fight in the campaign was the week-long battle for Singapore Island itself, in February 1942. Questions about this fight persist. Was it a futile anticlimax, or a dramatic showdown that might have gone the other way? And why did it end so quickly, or was that a foregone conclusion? Two papers in this session are devoted to analyzing these questions about the final battle of the Malaya/Singapore campaign, fought on this island and indeed in part on the site of this very campus.

Henry P. Frei — The Japanese Conquest of Singapore Island

Few campaigns have been more covered, explained, and rectified than the Malayan campaign. We know about the traumatic fall of Singapore above all from the British and Australian sides, the Chinese, Indian, and Malay sides. What strikes one as odd in the fascinating Western-oriented literature is the paucity of detail on the *Japanese* soldiers in the field—the *raison d'être* of the campaign and fall—who remain a largely faceless mass bicycling their way down to Singapore. It is timely to review the fall of Singapore from the Japanese side, and focus on the psychology and motivation of the Japanese infantryman who created that momentous event in modern world history. This paper offers excerpts from Japanese war memoirs followed up with interviews with five soldiers of the 5th, 18th, and Imperial Guards Divisions, and with Lieutenant Onishi Satoru from the Military Police. The scenes from the island battle are part of a longer manuscript completed with the aim to show both the heroism and cowardice, the humanity and barbarity of the Japanese soldier, as he fought his way down the Malayan peninsula towards the conquest of Singapore. The main part introduces details and topics from the last four chapters ("Crossing the Straits in the Face of the Enemy," "On to Bukit Timah!", Victory, Dissipation), focusing on the final fight for the island. The final part deals with the reminiscences of the soldiers: What meaning did the conquest have then, and how do they look back on it all today?

Chua Li Shan, Ng Chuin Song, and Xie Lihui — Singaporean Participation in the Defence of Singapore

This paper will examine how and why Singaporeans themselves participated in the defence of their island, and the various consequences their actions produced. Drawing on a range of primary and secondary sources, including oral histories, it will analyze both the battle of Singapore and the grim experience of occupation, as seen by Singaporean eyes. Topics to be discussed include the activities and experience of the hastily organized irregular formation known as *Dalforce*, and the resistance struggle against Japanese occupation that involved various different groups. The paper will argue that British reluctance to draw on Singaporeans to help in their own defence was unfounded and costly, that the contribution Singaporean fighters made to the defence deserves more recognition than it has received, and that the burden of carrying on the struggle against the occupier after Singapore surrendered was borne almost entirely by these fighters.

Session 9, The Defending Army and the Malaya/Singapore Campaign—

The ground force that found itself saddled with the main burden of defending Malaya and Singapore when war finally came was Malaya Command, a hastily reinforced and heterogeneous imperial army. A British general commanded troops from the U.K., Australia, India, New Zealand, Malaya and Singapore, some of whom arrived literally at the last stage. The performance of Malaya Command has always been at the very heart of the lasting controversies over why Singapore was lost so rapidly and easily. There are two papers in this session that discuss these issues.

Alan Warren   *The Indian Army and the Malaya/Singapore Campaign*

About half the troops comprising the British Empire's army in Malaya were drawn from the Indian Army. India was, after the United Kingdom, the most vital part of the British Empire. India's abundant manpower was ideally situated for service in both the Middle East and Far East theatres, both of which were important to Britain's attempt to forge a viable global presence. In the context of 1940–41, with the U.K. under threat of invasion from the German Army in France, the Indian Army became increasingly valuable as a source of troops that might be quickly deployed to other fronts. The British were not able to send either a fleet or an army from the United Kingdom to the Far East, but plenty of Indians and other imperial troops were available. In Malaya, there was already a sizeable Indian community working in the rubber industry. The Indian Army of the interwar period was not a national or nationalist army in the contemporary Western sense. However, within its ranks there was a sense of region, district and community. At the outbreak of war, the Indian Army was a little over 200,000 strong, but by the end of 1941 it had expanded by means of voluntary recruitment to almost 900,000 officers and men. And expanding any army in a hurry presents problems. During 1940–41, the 9th and 11th Indian Divisions were despatched to Malaya to form the III Indian Corps under the command of Lieutenant-General Sir Lewis Heath, who was the second most senior Army officer in the colony. This paper will review the Indian contribution to the campaign. Indian troops in Malaya have been heavily criticized in light of the mass desertions to the Indian National Army. Yet in the few profitable encounters for III Corps formations in northern and central Malaya, such as at Kota Bahru and Kampar, Indians were just as well represented as British or Gurkha troops. Likewise in Johore, disaster befell Australian and British formations more or less as swiftly as Indian units. Certainly a number of British Indian Army brigade and divisional commanders made some very poor decisions that contributed to the speed of Singapore's fall. Yet there is often not enough information available with which accurately to assess the losses of those Indian battalions most heavily engaged. This paper will argue that the Indian Army was among the scapegoats singled out for an unreasonable share of the blame for the loss of Singapore.

Clifford Kinvig   *Percival, his Army, and the Malaya/Singapore Campaign*

This paper examines the performance of General Percival as GOC Malaya Command from 16 May 1941 to 15 February 1942 and assesses his contribution to the outcome of the Malayan campaign. It considers the local defence arrangements he made during the period before the outbreak of war, the nature of his staff machine, his relations with the principal military and civilian figures in the local scene, the strategy he adopted for the campaign and his direction of the land forces throughout it. The paper evaluates the strategic and military situation within which Percival took his major command decisions and considers the principal criticisms which have been made of his generalship. The following will be examined in particular: operational relations with senior commanders; opening strategy *Matador*/Jitra; withdrawal policy (Percival vs Heath); tactical differences with Heath; the role of fixed defences (Percival vs Simson); the policy for the defence of the East Coast; Slim River disaster; denial policy; the defence of north Johore; Singapore's northern defences; dispositions for and defence of the Island itself.

Session 10, Different Dimensions of the Malayan Campaign—

Any military campaign involving hundreds of thousands of people is an immensely complicated human activity with a wide variety of different aspects. The focus tends always to be on operations, on the fighting, and that is no surprise. But there is more to war than fighting. Without supplies, no one can fight. And any fight inevitably generates controversies, over things that someone tried to cover up, or arguments about why events turned out the way they did. These aspects of a campaign are all related to fighting, but should not be swept up in the story by it. The three papers of this session are intended to prevent us from doing just that.

John Moremon *Logistics and the Malayan Campaign*

It is often suggested that the major difference between the opposing forces in the Malayan campaign was that the Japanese were "lightly equipped" whereas British, Indian and Australian troops were "overburdened." The Japanese use of bicycles to maintain momentum illustrates this point, however this key difference in equipment and tactics has tended to obscure the fact that movement and maintenance of forces in Malaya was otherwise fairly conventional. Both sides made extensive use of the railways and roads and, particularly in the case of the Japanese, sea transport to deploy and maintain forces in the field. The shocking string of defeats suffered by the British Empire forces has also promoted an idea that every facet of the defensive effort, including supply, broke down; however this was not necessarily the case as neither side suffered a total breakdown of supply. This paper explores Japanese and British Empire operational logistics in the campaign to show how the Japanese were able to continue pressing against the retreating forces for 70 days and also, equally as important, how the British Empire forces were able to maintain the string of attempted stands and delaying actions.

Peter Elphick *The Cover-Ups: Dirty Laundry of the Malayan Campaign*

Military victories have parents galore, but defeats are orphans, deprived waifs of no acknowledged paternity. Singapore, the worst defeat in British military history, was the most deprived orphan of all, with no one in London, Canberra, Delhi or Singapore willing to take much responsibility for it. The defeat resulted in a whole series of cover-ups, some of them extant to this day. These cover-ups included outright closing of some official records, "weeding" others by removing pages or sections, excising issues from postwar official histories, and even closing ranks in a conspiracy of silence by many veterans of the campaign. This paper will explore some of these cover-ups, discussing what the problem was, how and why it was concealed, and how the author penetrated into the story. Cover-ups include issues involving espionage and the Indian Army, defence measures, and even Prime Minister Churchill himself.

Peter Stanley   *Explaining Defeat: Australian Officers' Post-Mortems on the Battle for Singapore, Changi 1942*

"The men that did the fighting are now all busy writing ...":
(post-mortems in Changi, 1942)

From 15 February 1942, the soldiers of the 8th Australian Division went into captivity at Changi as part of a defeated army. Despite the heroic tragedy of Gallipoli, this was an unprecedented experience for Australian soldiers. Australian troops entered the Malayan campaign only in mid-January, but they played a major part in the battle for Singapore Island. The two Australian brigades suffered severely in the fighting, losing 1,789 killed and 1,300 wounded in a month of intense fighting in Malaya and Singapore. They had been defeated by an enemy they regarded as inferior, culturally, militarily and, as they would have said, racially. In the early months of captivity, before the various "forces" were sent to Borneo and to the Burma-Thailand railway, Australian officers in Changi began to ponder what had happened in the fighting in Malaya and on Singapore Island. "Syndicates" met, trying to establish what had happened, what had gone wrong, and who had been responsible for the defeat. The papers produced in the course of these deliberations were preserved in the Division's war diary, now held in the Australian War Memorial. These post-mortems provide a first-hand but by no means simple interpretation of the campaign. They were produced by protagonists, in exculpation as well as reflection. They reflect what Australian officers thought at the time rather than in the retrospect of decades, but also leave many meaningful silences. Fingers are pointed, nods are made, punches are pulled; much is left unsaid. The Australian post-mortems are interesting because they begin the process of reflection, analysis and recrimination over the lost battle for Singapore which has continued between the British Commonwealth protagonists for sixty years.

Final Session, 17 February 2002: The Fall of Singapore Revisited—

Air Vice-Marshal (Retired) A.F.C. Hunter, British Royal Air Force, lived through and helped make one period of Singapore's military history within the British orbit, as a young bomber pilot stationed at Tengah airbase during the *Confrontasi* with Indonesia, in the 1960s. Maintaining his ties with Singapore while rising through the ranks, Sandy Hunter closed out a distinguished service career, including a term as Commandant of the RAF Staff College, and devoted more time to a life-long interest in military history. Two years ago, Sandy suggested that the enduring public interest and scholarly activity in many countries regarding the Malayan campaign and the fall of Singapore made a reconsideration of those events worthwhile, and what better time than the 60th anniversary, what better place than the National University of Singapore. We took him up on it. And to respect the old tradition of the price of volunteering, to him now falls the task of summarizing and commenting on the arguments, analyses and theses presented by the papers read at this conference he first envisaged. His summary will inspire one final general discussion on the questions we have been considering here this weekend.

Index

A
Adam Road 226
Admiralty, the 3, 12, 14-18, 47, 48, 52, 54, 56-59, 78, 96, 315
   and Imperial Defence 4-5, 47, 50, 58, 79, 123-24
   and naval base 47, 50
   and Japan 48, 52, 96, 98-99, 157
   and USA 15, 48, 57-58
   and defence of Malaya / Singapore 47, 50, 58, 79
   and "Singapore Strategy" 5, 47, 50, 58, 79
Air Ministry (British) 96-98, 315
Aitken, J. 138, 141
Alor Star 192, 215, 274
American-British-Dutch-Australian Command (ABDA) 164-65
Anglo-Japanese Alliance 4, 9, 47, 157
Annam 77, 81
Anschluss 15
Anti-Comintern Pact 15
Asaeda Shigeharu 199, 213
Attlee government ii, iii, 167, 168
Australia, and the fall of Singapore i, 39
   and defence of Malaya / Singapore 30-36, 162
   and evacuation of (European) civilians from Hong Kong / Malaya / Singapore 124-25, 127-28, 130, 140
   and Imperial Defence iv, 29-37, 39, 162-63
   and naval base 30, 34, 36
   and Singapore Strategy 20-22, 30-37, 39, 162-63
   and United Kingdom 20, 22, 44, 50, 58, 162-63
   and USA 39
   defence policy 29-39
   political controversies 32-39
   post-mortems, fall of Singapore ii-iii, 20, 167, 296, 300
Australian Army, the 30-39, 243
   Or Australian Imperial Force (AIF) Formations & Units
   6th Australian Division 163
   7th Australian Division 163
   8th Australian Division vii, 195, 253, 276, 280, 282
   9th Australian Division 163
   22nd Australian Brigade 253-54, 282
   27th Australian Brigade 280, 282
   11th Mixed Brigade 38

B
Backhouse, Roger 15-16
Baguio 201
Baldwin, Stanley 34, 157
Barbarossa, operation 175, 177, 180-81, 188, 316
Barstow, A.E. 260, 277, 281
Battle of the Atlantic 160, 316
Batu Pahat 254, 261
Bennett, Gordon
   and 8th Australian Division 195, 242
   and battle for Johore 253-54, 281
   and battle for Singapore 259
   recriminations, fall of Singapore 292-94
   relations with Heath 252-53
   relations with Percival 254, 259
Blenheims 211-12

"Blue Water" school of thought and British grand strategy 32, 69, 75
Bisseker, F.D. 137, 139, 141
Bombay 140
Bonnet, Georges 78-80
Borneo 82, 85
Bren Gun carriers 272, 278
British Army
   and defence of Malaya / Singapore 5, 7, 11, 69, 76, 116, 166
   and grand strategy 7, 69
   and Imperial Defence 30, 69, 76, 166
   Formations and Units
      18th Division 139, 163, 167, 233
      Royal Engineers 73
      Krohcol 248
      Massy force 226, 259
      Tom force 226, 259
      West Force 254, 259
British Commonwealth 9, 11, 20, 22, 128, 140
British Government
   and defence of Malaya 3-5, 7, 17, 18, 42-44, 49, 60, 68, 69, 73, 75, 77-78, 82, 114-17, 125, 159, 160, 173, 176
   and defence of Singapore 3-5, 7, 11, 15-17, 42-44, 47, 49, 50, 52, 54-62, 68-69, 73-78, 82, 85-88, 114, 125, 159-61, 173, 176, 180-81
   and Dominions 4, 20-21, 29, 34-36, 42, 44, 50, 58, 130-31, 140, 156, 158
   and Dutch East Indies 7, 138, 140
   and France iv, 68-71, 75, 78-79, 82-88, 95, 125
   and Germany 157, 159-60, 174-75, 177, 179
   and home defence 158-61, 166, 168, 176-79, 316
   and Imperial Defence 3-5, 14-16, 21, 29-36, 42-44, 47-52, 54-62, 68-69, 73-78, 82, 85-88, 114-17, 123-24, 133, 157-61, 173-74, 176-78, 180-81, 316, 318
   and India 158, 162
   and Japan 42, 45, 47-49, 51-52, 54, 56, 61, 68, 79, 85, 99, 113-17, 125, 157-60, 163-65, 176, 178, 180
   and "Singapore Strategy" iv, 3-5, 15-16, 21-22, 30-36, 42-44, 47, 49-52, 54-62, 68-69, 73-78, 157-59, 161, 176
   and USA iv, 12-14, 22, 42-45, 47-62, 156-60, 163-65, 175-78
   Empire World War II 173-81
British Intelligence (on Japan) 103-17
British Isles 16
Brooke, Alan 161
Brooke-Popham, Robert 106, 115, 133, 161-62, 165, 316, 318
   post-mortems, fall of Singapore 123, 143
   and evacuation issue, Hong Kong 129
   and operation Matador 191, 246, 248
   relations with Percival 242
Bruce, Stanley 30
Bruche, Julius 32, 34, 36-38
Buffalos (Brewster) 20, 114-15
Bukit Panjang 196, 226
Bukit Timah 185, 196-97, 226-27, 259, 283
Buona Vista 227
Burma 81, 140, 163-64, 167, 189, 194, 199, 216, 285-87
   Internment Camps 308
Burma Campaign 210
"Bicycle Blitzkreig" 192

C
Callaghan, C.A. 260
Camranh Bay 77-78, 81, 84
Canada 130
Canberra 21

Castex, Raoul 74, 78
Ceylon 81, 131, 140
Chamberlain, Neville 47, 158, 162
Changi Internment Camp 208, 211-12, 215, 283, 285, 290-96
Chappell, R.W. 107, 109-10, 115
Chatfield 16
Chiang Kai Shek 80-81
Chiefs of Staff (British)
  and imperial defence 9
  and Singapore strategy 11, 16
China i, 44, 47, 112, 115, 123, 125, 140, 167
  Sino-Japanese War / and Japanese aggression 12-13, 49, 54, 73, 76, 77, 79-81, 83, 103, 110, 174, 198
Churchill, Winston
  and Americans 157-160, 163-65, 167
  and Australians 156, 159, 162-65, 167
  and British grand strategy 158-60, 163, 164, 168, 177
  and defence of Singapore / Malaya 159-61, 164
  and Dominions 156, 158
  and fall of Singapore i, ii, v, 3, 156, 160, 165-68
  and Imperial Defence 158-60, 162-66, 168, 315
  and naval base 9, 161
  and "Singapore Strategy" 22, 159, 161-62
  as Chancellor of Exchequer 9, 157
  as First Lord of the Admiralty 156
  as Minister of Defence 156
  as PM i, 132, 156, 159, 161-62, 177, 185
CIGS 241, 255
Civil Aviation Department (British) 96
Civilians
  Chinese 127-29, 136, 138, 140, 143, 144
  Eurasian 127-29, 140

European 122-29, 131-36, 138, 142, 144
Indian 136, 138, 140, 142
Malay 138
Co-prosperity Sphere 87
Colonial Office 128-31, 137-38, 140, 144
"Comfort" women 122
Committee of Imperial Defence 3, 5, 7, 34, 47, 48, 54, 75, 123, 165
Commonwealth forces, Singapore and Malaysia 316
Cooper, Duff 132-39, 162, 240
Craigie, Robert 56, 57
Curlewis, Adrian 302-03, 307
Curtin, John 20, 22, 36, 162-63, 167

D
Daladier, Eduard 73-74, 77, 79-81
Darlan, Francois 74, 78-79, 82, 84, 87-88
Darwin 17
de Gaulle, Charles 84
Deakin, F.W. 165
Decoux, Jean 68-69, 82-87
Delhi 140
Denmark 21
Dill, John 125, 161-63, 241, 246, 270
Dobbie, William 7, 243
Drax, R.P. Ernie-Earle 15-17
Dreyer, Frederic 50
Dunearn Road 226
Dunlop, Edward 301, 309

E
Eden, Anthony 13-14, 125, 246
Endau 252, 261
Europe 44, 56-60, 76, 87, 113, 160, 173, 179
Evacuation Representation Committee (ERC) 129, 130

F

Far East Combined Bureau (FECB) in Singapore 107, 115, 245
Far East Command 114-16, 176, 245, 246
Farrer Park 283
Farrer Road 227
Fiji 128, 129
Five Power Naval Limitation Treaty 9
Ford Factory 185, 197, 202
Foreign Office (British) 45-48, 52, 54, 56, 59, 81, 95, 104, 125, 126, 129, 143, 209
Fort Canning 225, 283
Fort McKinley (Manila) 128
France
    and Germany 68-69, 72, 74, 81-82, 86
    and Imperial Defence 68-85, 87-88, 174
    and Italy 71, 74, 82
    and relations with Japan 68-69, 79-81, 83-84, 86-87
    and Singapore Strategy 21, 68-74, 76-79, 82, 85, 88
    British – French Alliance / Co-operation 73, 78-79, 81-84, 87-88
French Africa 72-75, 85, 87
French Intelligence (on British Imperial Security & defence of Singapore) 70-77, 83- 88
French Intelligence (on the Japanese) 77, 79, 82-86
    Indochina colonies 17, 68, 69-73, 75-77, 80-82, 84-85, 87-88
    Interests in the Mediterranean 70, 74, 78-79, 87
    Vichy France 68, 69, 79, 80, 83-87
Fujiwara Iwaichi 209, 274, 283

G

Galleghan, Frederick 294, 301
    and Syndicates' report 298-300
Gemas 193, 202
Gamelin 67, 75, 78
GC & CS 98-99
Genju shobun 199
Germany 86, 102, 285
    and France 68-69, 72, 74, 81-82, 174
    and Japan 188
    and operation Barbarossa 175, 177, 179-81, 188
    and the United Kingdom 16, 21, 59, 107, 158, 160, 174-75, 177, 179-80
    and the United States 57, 59, 174-75, 181
    turn to extremism 1930s 54, 157, 174

Ghormley, R.L. 58-59
GHQ 248
Gilman Barracks 229-34
Gilman Heights 229
Gneisenau, the
Grasett, A.E. 123, 125
Great Depression 12, 32
"Green Scheme" for Naval Base 7, 8
Grew, Joseph 48-49, 53
Guam 11, 46, 53, 60
Gulf of Siam 17, 78
Gurun 249, 275

H

Hainan 78, 80-81, 190
Halifax, Lord 58, 125, 126
Hall, George 127, 129, 131
Hampton, T.C. 58-60
Hankey, Maurice 34-39
Hankow 110, 113
Hanoi 68-71, 78, 80-83, 85, 88
Hart, Thomas 17
Hayashi Tadahiko 199, 213

Heath, Lewis
   And III Indian Corps 134-35, 242, 249-50, 252, 271-72, 297
   And battle at Slim River 252-53
   And battle for Johore 253-54
   And defence of Singapore 255, 252-59
   And Malayan Campaign 248-54, 275-77, 280
   and operation Matador 248
   on the INA 285
   relations with Percival 243, 248, 260, 272, 283
Heenan, Patrick vii, 275
Hitler, Adolf 175, 180-81, 188-89, 316
HMS Cumberland 77
HMS Dorsetshire 77
HMS Eagle 98
HMS Hermes 77
HMS Indomitable 17
HMS Kent 50
HMS Prince of Wales 3, 17, 20, 84, 86, 97, 113, 163, 191, 319
HMS Renown 97
HMS Repulse 3, 17, 20, 84, 86, 97, 113, 163, 191, 319
Hoare, Samuel 45
Hong Kong v, 4, 12, 50, 52, 70, 78, 81, 86, 209-10, 216
   defence of Hong Kong 82, 103, 110, 115, 123-26
   Evacuation of Chinese and Eurasian communities 127-29
Hong Kong government & Evacuation of civilians (European) 123-32, 144
Hornbeck, Stanley 49, 55, 56
Hosho (Japanses aircraft carrier) 99, 100
Hospital Hill 224, 233
Hull, Cordell 44, 49, 55
Hurricanes 114, 256, 257, 260

I
Imperial Conference 21, 30
Imperial Japanese Army (IJA), the 101, 106-08, 110, 181, 185, 211, 257
   and conquest of Singapore 185, 196-97
   and occupation of Singapore / Malaya 198-99, 203
   and war atrocities Singapore 199
IJA Air Force (IJAAF), the 95, 107-10, 112-13, 115
IJA Formations and Units
   25th Army vi, 132, 190-99, 210, 218
   3rd Air Group 195
   5th Division 189-92, 194-97, 224, 226-27, 232-34, 273, 276, 280
   8th Division 191
   18th Division 189-97, 203, 224, 226-27, 233-34, 252, 273
   56th Division 189
   Engineer Corps 192
   Imperial Guards Division 189-92, 194, 196, 221, 224, 226, 254, 260, 273, 276, 280-82
   and assault on Singapore 194-97, 226, 286
   and Malayan Campaign 185, 190-194, 273, 276
   Southern Army 86, 87, 195
Imperial Japanese Navy (IJN), the 14-16, 94, 95, 100-01, 104, 181
   22nd Naval Air Flotilla 84
   and Sempill Mission 96-100, 102
   "Flying Squadron" 100
   threat to British empire, pre World War II 9, 11-16, 43, 96
Imperial Japanese Navy Air Force (IJNAF), the 94, 97, 98, 100-01, 108-09, 110, 112-13, 115, 166
India
   and Imperial defence 270-71
   and defence of Malaya / Singapore i

Government of 140, 270
nationalism 209, 274, 283, 284
Indian Army, the 106, 243, 244, 270-71
   and battle of Singapore 281-83
   and defence of Malaya 270-81
   and Imperial defence 270-72, 287
   and Malayan Campaign vi-vii, 273-81, 287
   Gurkhas 270-71
   Reinforcements for Malaya Singapore 257, 281-82
Indian Army Formations and Units
   III Indian Corps 134, 242, 246, 249, 250, 252, 271-73, 277, 282, 287
   2nd Argylls 278
   9th Gurkha Rifles 136, 279
   6th Indian Brigade (11th Indian Division) 273, 275
   8th Indian Brigade 273, 277, 282
   12th Indian Brigade 271, 275-80, 282-83
   15th Indian Brigade 273, 277, 280, 282-83
   22nd Indian Brigade 277, 281
   28th Indian Brigade 273, 277-80
   44th Indian Brigade 282-83
   45th Indian Brigade 280-82, 287
   4th Indian Division 270
   5th Indian Division 270, 272
   9th Indian Division 249, 252-54, 270-71, 277, 280-82
   11th Indian Division 191, 246, 248-53, 270-77, 279-80, 282-83
   1/14 Punjab 273-74
   1/8 Punjab 274, 282-83
   2/10 Baluch 282-83, 285
   2/17 Dogras 282
   2/12 Frontier Force Regiment 277
   5/18 Garhwal Rifles 280, 282
   2/1 Gurkhas 273, 279
   2/2 Gurkhas 282
   4/19 Hyderabads 278, 282, 285
   2/9 Jats 273
   4/9 Jats 280
   2/16 Punjab Companies 274
   3/16 Punjab 275
   5/2 Punjabis 278, 282
   5/14 Punjabis 278
   7/6 Rajputana Rifles 280-81, 285
   137th Field Regiment 279
   155th Field Regiment 279
Indian Independence League 274
Indian National Army (INA) 209, 215-16, 283-87, vii
Indian Prisoner of War Headquarters 284
Ingersoll, Ralph 14, 15, 58
International Politics interwar period 173-75
Ismay, Hastings 161, 165
Italy 57
   and France 71, 74, 82
   and Japan 95, 188
   and the United Kingdom 15, 21, 59, 95, 107, 158, 177
   and United States 59
   turn to expansionism 1930s 54, 157

J
Jalan Besar 236
Japan 173-175, 180, 181, 189
   ambitions in Asia / Far East Interwar period 12-13, 48-54, 56-59, 61, 68, 73-78, 81, 85, 103, 157
   and British Empire 50, 52, 54, 59-61, 68, 76, 78, 85, 87, 157, 159, 175, 188-89
   and China 73, 76, 77, 79-81, 83, 85, 103, 110, 112, 115, 125, 174, 181, 188, 198
   and conquest of Singapore i, v, 85-86, 185, 196, 197
   and French Indo China 73-74, 76, 78-79, 81, 83-85, 87
   and Indian POWs 209, 215

and Malayan Campaign 18, 85, 87,
    185, 189, 190-94
and USA 13, 14, 47, 50-53, 57-60,
    68, 102, 173, 175, 181, 188-89
Interrogation of POWs 210-13
treatment of POW vi, 122, 143,
    198-99, 209-16, 300-01
Japanese POW Administration, Malaya
    215, 300
Japanese Soldiers
  and battle of Singapore 218, 220,
      224-27, 229-30, 232-33
  and fall of Singapore 233-34
  and fallen comrades 222-24
  and Malayan Campaign 218, 220-21
  and war atrocities 227-29, 236
  Arai Mitsuo (Sergeant), 18th Division
      218, 223, 227, 228-34, 236
  assault on Australian positions 225
  inter-divisional rivalry 226, 233, 234
  Ochi Harumi (Machine-gunner), 5th
      Division 218, 220, 222, 224-25,
      237
  Onishi Satoru (Liutenant), military
      police 218, 236
  Miyake Genjiro (Private), 5th Division
      218, 236
  Tsuchikane Tominosuke (Corporal),
      Imperial Guards Division 218,
      221, 223, 225, 227
Jellicoe, John 4
Jitra 191, 209, 244, 246, 248, 272-74
Johore 72, 139, 164, 192-94, 244,
    249-55, 276, 281, 287
Jones, Stanley 135
Joint Intelligence Committee (JIC) 111,
    114-15
Joint Overseas and Home Defence
    Sub-Committee 123
Jurong 258-59

K
Kallang (airfield) 226
Kampar 192, 193, 202, 250-51, 276, 277,
    287
Kappe, Charles vii, 291
  and compilation of AIF (Australian
      Imperial Force) war diaries
      295-304
  and F Force (POW working party)
      300-03
  and lectures, aftermath of
      post-Malayan Campaign of
      Malayan Campaign? 297-98
  and Syndicates' reports 298-99
  and The Malayan Campaign
      manuscript 304-08
Kasimagaura 97-98
Keating, Paul 39
Kedah 276
Kelly, Denis 165,166
Kempei-tai 199, 212-13, 236
Keppel Harbour 224, 229, 234
Key, B.W. 249, 251, 253, 273, 276, 280,
    282, 293
Kirby, S.W. 243, 246, 251, 253, 261,
    306-07
Kirimomi Sakusen 191, 193, 196
Kodoha faction 186-87, 200, 204
Kota Bahru 18, 185, 190-91, 203, 211,
    249, 273, 277, 287
Kranji 196, 258-59
Kuala Kangsar 191-92, 250
Kuala Lumpur 133, 192-93, 212-16, 251,
    253, 277, 280
Kuantan 18, 20, 85, 249, 252, 277

L
Lavarack, John 32-36, 38-39
Layton, Geoffrey 138, 143
League of Nations 30, 52, 173-74
Leahy, William D. 58, 59
Ledge Operation 246, 248

Learmouth Power Committee 5

M
MacArthur, Douglas 202
MacDonald, Ramsay 51
MacRitchie Reservoir 224, 233
Malacca 252
Malaya Command 244, 260, 273, 290-91
Malayan Civil Service 134, 141
Malayan Police Force 142
Malayan Special Branch 142
Malayan Survey Department 142
Manchukuo 189, 198, 200-01
Manchuria 124
Mandai 196, 224, 225
Manila 12, 84, 127, 201
Marsh, Edward 165
Matador, operation 191, 246, 248, 261, 272-73
Maxwell, D.S. 260
Meigo Sakusan 69
Melbourne 32, 37
Menzies, Robert 21, 162-63
Mersing 249, 254
Midway 11
Military ethnocentrism / Ethnocentrism 105, 106-07, 112-13, 178
Military Intelligence Department (MID) 104
Mitsubishi 100-02
Mohan Singh 274, 283-85
Molotov cocktails 272
Mounbatten, Lord Louis 165
Muar 192, 193, 214, 254, 261, 281
Munich crisis 15, 44, 60
Murray-Lyon, D.M. 273-76

N
Nagato (seaplane carrier) 100
Nanshin-ron 8
Naranjan Singh Gill 284-85

Naval Base, Sembawang 18, 42-45, 50, 68
   and Imperial Defence 34, 42-44, 52, 54-55, 58-59, 73, 75
   King George VI dry dock 77
   selection and building of 5, 7-9, 50, 52, 54
Nazi-Soviet Pact 124
Negri Sembilan 252
Netherlands East Indies T, 17, 57, 75, 83, 138, 140, 189
Newcastle 32
New Zealand i, 20, 44, 50, 58, 156, 159, 162
Noble, Percy 81, 82
Northcote, Geoffrey 125, 126, 129-30
Norton, E.F. 129-30
Norway 21

P
Painter, G.W.A. 277, 281
Palliser, A. 18
Paris 68-69, 71, 75, 78, 82, 98, 174
Paris, A.C.M. 251, 276-80
Parkhill, Archdale 34, 36-39
Patani 18, 185, 191, 246, 248, 273, 276
Pax Britannica 4
Paya Lebar 224, 226
Pearce, Georje 27
Pearl Harbour 11, 17, 18, 43-47, 52, 57, 69, 84, 85, 99, 116, 163, 173, 175
Penang 72, 134-37, 139, 192, 203, 210, 215, 275
Perak 135-36, 191-92, 249-51, 275-76
Percival, Arthur 133, 135-36, 139, 141, 161, 164, 166, 191-93, 198, 201-02
   and battle of Singapore vii, 193, 225, 258-61
   and defence of Johore 253-56, 280
   and defence of Singapore 226-27, 255, 283, 318

and Malayan Campaign 248-53, 261, 275-77
and Military Intelligence 245, 258
and operation Matador 191, 248
and plans for defence of Singapore / Malaya 243-46, 250-53, 275-76
and surrender of Singapore 185, 196-97, 202, 240, 261
and troop morale 195, 250, 256-57, 260
as GOC Malaya 240-61, 272, 316, 318
defence preparations Malaya 243-44
defence preparations Singapore 195, 226-27, 243-44, 250-51, 256
held responsible for fall of Singapore vi, 240, 318-19
relations with Heath 242-43, 260, 272, 283
relations with Bennett 195, 242-43, 254, 259
elations with Wavell 243, 253-54
Petain, Henri 83-85, 87
Philippines 189, 198
and battle between Japanese forces and the Allies 188, 200-01
and evacuation of civilians from Hong Kong 124-27
and Independence 50, 52
and surrender of the Japanese 203
and United States 43, 46, 50-54, 59
as American naval base 43, 46, 51-54
Phillips, Tom 17-18, 20, 163
Port Swettenham 251, 253, 277
Post-mortems, fall of Singapore ii, iii, 123, 143, 166, 167, 255, 258
Pound, Dudley 3, 18
Pownall, Henry 162, 165-68, 242
Prisoners of War, Australian recriminations, fall of Singapore 290-94
post-mortems on defeat 296-00

treatment by Japanese 300-03, 308
Pritam Singh 274
Public Works Department (PWD) Malaya 132, 139, 141
Pudu Jail 214-15
Pulford, C.W.H. 241, 243
Punjab 270

R
Racism 69, 73, 79-80, 84, 95-96, 102-07, 111-13, 115, 127-28
Recriminations, fall of Singapore 143, 144, 166-68, 255, 290-94, 318
Red Fort Trial 287
"Red Scheme" for Naval Base 7-9
Reformatory Road (now Clementi Road) 227
Riau Islands 7
Richmond, Herbert 31-34. 37
Ridout, Dudley 7
Roosevelt, Franklin
and decisions to enter World War II 175, 181
and the British 13-15, 44, 51, 58
and naval bases, Pearl Harbour and Philippines 43, 53-54
and naval blockade against Japan 14
and the Philippines 53-54
relations with Churchill 159, 167, 177
Roux, Henri 74-75, 77
Royal Air Force (RAF), the 94-96, 100-02, 107-12, 114-16, 161
and air power 94, 103, 159
and defence Malaya / Singapore iv, v, 75, 94, 103-04, 114-16, 159, 245, 246, 248, 260
and grand strategy 95, 103, 114-15
and imperial defence 94, 103-04, 114, 159, 166
and Imperial Japanese Army Air Force (IJAAF) 107-10, 115

and Imperial Japanese Navy Air Force
    (IJNAF) 94, 96, 108, 115
and Japan v, 94-96, 103-04, 107-12,
    114-16
and Malayan Campaign 248
and naval base 103, 159, 245
and Singapore strategy 103
Royal Australian Air Force 31, 33, 35-37
Royal Australian Navy 31, 33, 35-37, 39
Royal Navy Air Service (RNAS) 96, 100,
    108
Royal Navy (RN), the 94, 96, 99, 100,
    106-07, 157-58, 316
  and airpower 75
  and Australia 31
  and defence Malaya / Singapore iv,
      15-18, 20, 43-44, 47, 56, 75-76, 94,
      260
  and Imperial Defence 4, 9, 12, 16,
      29, 43-44, 47, 50, 56-57, 61, 76,
      124, 157-58
  and Japan 9, 15, 43, 48, 94-96,
      99-100, 108
  and naval base 43-44
  and Singapore strategy 9, 12-13, 16,
      31, 43-44, 47, 56-57, 76, 157-58
  and USA 8, 12, 16, 43, 48, 51, 57-61
Royal Navy (RN) Formations
  and France 84
  Eastern Fleet 17
  Fleet Air Arm 97, 100, 108
  Force Z 3, 16, 18, 20, 84, 107, 248
Rutland, Frederick 98-99
Ryujo Maru 191

S
Saigon 70, 77, 81-84, 87, 190, 211
Savile, Leopold 7
Scharnhorst, the 86
Scullin, J.H. 32, 33
Seabridge G.W. 134, 137
Selangor 252

Seletar Airbase 224
Sempill, Master of 96-99, 104
Sempill Mission 96-100, 102, 104-05, 110
Sepoy Mutiny 1915 271
Seppuku 204
Shanghai 54, 77, 85, 110, 125
Shedden, Frederick 31-38
Shepherd, M.L. 35, 36
Sime Road 225, 243
Simon, John 48, 54
Simmons, Keith 241, 255
Simson, Ivan 139, 141-43, 244, 250, 256
Singora 18, 185, 191, 203, 211-213, 246,
    252, 272, 273, 276
Sino-Japanese War 77, 80, 109, 188
Skudai River 220
South Africa 131, 162
South China Sea 3, 18, 20, 78, 83-85
Southeast Asia Command 165
Soviet Union iv, 112, 114, 174
  and operation Barbarossa 175, 177,
      179, 181, 188, 316, 318
  and Japan (Manchukuo) 189,
      200-01
  and the United Kingdom 160, 179
  Nazi-Soviet Pact 124
Soviet Army 189, 200-01
Spain 15
Spitfires 113
Spooner 133, 140, 260
Spratley Islands 80
SS Duchess of Bedford 135
SS Empire Star 142
Stanhope, Lord 78
Stewart, I.M. 251, 278-80
Stimson, Henry 54
Straits of Johore 5, 17, 18, 85, 194, 195,
    220
Straits Times 134, 137
Subhas Chandra Bose 285-86
  and Government of Free India 286
Sudetenland 15

Sugita Ichiji 197, 213
Sumatra 194-95, 199
Sydney 4, 32

T
Taiping 192, 212, 215
Tanglin Halt 227
Telok Anson 251
Tengah 71-72, 196, 211
Thailand 18, 74, 75, 77, 82-84, 87, 115, 185, 190-91, 209, 211, 215, 246, 272, 276
   Burma railway 210, 215, 300
   Internment Camps 300-02, 308
Thomas, Shenton 84, 123, 128, 130, 133, 135-41, 143-44, 198, 245, 316
   and evacuation issue, Hong Kong and Malaya/Singapore 128, 130, 135-41, 144
   as Governor of the Straits Settlements 84, 123
   and Japanese offensive, Malaya & Singapore 191, 193, 227, 242
   post-mortem, fall of Singapore 143
   relations with Cooper 133, 136-39
Thomson Village 226
Thyer, Jim
   official report on 8th Australian Division 304
   relations with Bennett 293, 296, 302
Tienstin 113, 125
Tojo Hideki 186, 189-201
Tonkin 79, 81, 83
Toseiha faction 186, 187
Trolak / Slim River 251-53, 257, 261, 276-80
Truk 11
Truman, Harry 202
Tsuji Masanobu 215-16
   Chief of Operations, 25th Army 210, 273
   operations officer of the 25th Army vi, 192-94
   relations with Yamashita 192-93, 202
   treatment of Allied POWs 210, 213
   war atrocities, WWII 199

U
United States of America
   and evacuation of civilians from Hong Kong 130
   and Japan 12-14, 17, 18, 43-45, 47-53, 55-60, 68, 175
   and Singapore strategy 22, 42-44, 47, 55-62
   defence policy 43-62
   international relations 13-15, 42-62, 174-75, 177, 179, 181
   relations with UK 13-15, 42-45, 48-62, 156-57, 175
United States Navy 8, 11, 14, 43, 45-46, 48, 50-51, 57-60, 99-00, 160, 173
Upham, Frank Brooks 50
USS Panay 13, 14, 57

V
Vanisttart, Robert 45, 48
Vickers 95, 96, 100, 102

W
War Cabinet (British) 125, 133, 138
War Council, Singapore 133-39
War Ministry (Japanese) 186, 189, 198-200
War Office (WO), the 3, 5, 123, 125-26, 131, 138, 139, 166, 209, 243-44, 255, 315
Washington 163, 164
Washington Conference 5, 7, 9, 12, 30-31, 48
Washington Treaty System 9, 42, 46, 49, 51, 53, 61, 71

Wavell, Archibald 106, 114, 136, 164-68, 242, 251, 253-258, 260
White, Brudenell 31
Whitehall 13, 15, 18, 49, 96-97, 99, 103, 113-16, 143
Wood, C.C. 165
Woodleigh 226
Wynter, H.D. 36-39

Y

Yamashita, Tomoyuki vi, 132, 189, 201-04, 213, 220
   and assault on Singapore 194-97
   and conquest of Singapore 185, 196-97, 202
   and Malayan Campaign 189-94, 189, 203
   and occupation of Malaya / Singapore 198-99, 203
   and relations with the Emperor 187-88, 201, 204
   and war atrocities 199, 201
   as Commander of the 25th Army 185, 189-97, 202, 220
   Military career 186-88, 202, 204
   Relations with Tojo Hideki 186, 189-201
Yokosuka 100
Young, Mark 128, 130-31